Islam for the Politically Incorrect

ISLAM FOR THE
POLITICALLY
INCORRECT

by

Khaled Diab

GILGAMESH
PUBLISHING LTD

Dedication

In memory of the mother of my world

For the love of my life and for our little sonshine.

Islam for the Politically Incorrect

Published by Gilgamesh Publishing in 2017
Email: info@gilgamesh-publishing.co.uk
www.gilgamesh-publishing.co.uk

ISBN 978-1-908531-80-3

© Khaled Diab 2017

CIP Data: A catalogue for this book is
available from the British Library

ACKNOWLEDGEMENTS

This book has been enriched and enhanced by the many people who have taken the time to share their thoughts and opinions with me, either specifically for this book or for my previous writings on the subject. Many thanks to them. I am also grateful to the many people, both friends and strangers, from various backgrounds, attitudes and cultures who have shared their insights and opinions on the many thorny themes covered here. This has been at times enlightening and edifying; at others, troubling and terrifying.

I would like to thank the team at Gilgamesh for their role in making this project a reality: Max Scott, Henry Harding and Octavia Warren – as well as Lucy Lyon for putting me on to their scent.

Thanks are also due to the many friends who encouraged me to set out on this journey and egged me to keep on going, as well as all the friends and acquaintances on social media who took the time to provide their input and feedback on certain aspects of the project.

More specifically, I would like to express gratitude to those who took considerable time out of their busy schedules to read and comment on the various chapters, which helped me to improve and enrich the text. Thank you Holly Dagres, Max Rodenbeck, Faisal al-Yafai, Brian Whitaker, Kapil Komireddi, Margarida Santos Lopes, Paul Schemm, and Ayman ElKhatib.

Finally, I would like to thank my wife, Katleen, for being my muse and for having the patience and good humour to bear with the intensive labour involved in producing this book, during which writing got in the way of life and life got in the way of writing. Our son, Iskander, has also been supportive and curious, despite the fact that he would much rather that I had written a children's storybook, rather than a boring book for grown-ups.

CONTENTS

FOREWORD

Dear Donald Trump,
Dear bigots of the world,

You are a world authority on Christianity. I know because you said so yourself... and, what with the deluge of fake news and biased media, we must trust only you and your flood of tweets. I wonder what Pope Francis made of your claim that "nobody reads the Bible more than me"[1] when you met him at the Vatican? The pontiff has not pontificated on the subject, so we are likely never to know.

At the time, those haters at *Catholic Online* mocked you. Calling you a "presidential hopeless", they pilloried your religious claims, including your slip of the tongue in referencing Two Corinthians, rather than Second Corinthians.[2] Second, two, they are all the same number, right? *Catholic Online* predicted: "Americans will wake up and understand that Donald Trump is *not* the man he claims to be and cannot be trusted to follow through with any of his promises."[3] And how wrong they were... well, at least on the first count.

Not all Christians are so sceptical. Some even believe you to be the "Trump of God" foretold in 1 Thessalonians 4:16 and the "last trump" prophesied in 1 Corinthians 15:52 (that is First Corinthians, not One, but who's counting), both of which are sure signs of the second coming. Some spoil-sport experts on the Apocalypse claim that this only works in English, and in the King James Bible to be specific,

9

and that the original Greek refers to "trumpet".[4] Trump, trumpet – what's the difference, right?

As a sign of your humility – a trait you have always done your utmost to hide – you have admitted that your pontifical knowledge of Christianity does not extend to Islam. "Donald J Trump is calling for a total and complete shutdown of Muslims entering the United States," you said during your presidential campaign, referring to yourself humbly in the third person, "until our country's representatives can figure out what the hell is going on."[5]

The reason for this ignorance is simple and so obvious that Donald Trump has identified it without any prior knowledge of Islam or Muslims and has said it so many times that it barely merits repeating. The great enemy of the American people is political correctness. "We must stop being politically correct and get down to the business of security for our people," you said after a terrorist attack carried out by Muslim extremists. "If we don't get smart it will only get worse."[6]

And to ensure that it does not get worse, Donald Trump has been getting smart. Despite your early blanket condemnation of Islam and all Muslims, you have decided that some Muslims are actually fine, like the Saudis. "This is not a battle between different faiths, different sects, or different civilisations," you said, sounding remarkably like Obama, during your visit to Saudi Arabia, the first foreign country you visited as president. "This is a battle between barbaric criminals who seek to obliterate human life, and decent people of all religions who seek to protect it."[7] During your entire speech, you did not mention "radical Islamic terrorism" once, even though you chided Hillary Clinton for allegedly refusing to use the term, an accurate alternative fact which those pesky fact checkers contest.[8]

Why didn't you use it? Because you have discovered the truth. Crooked Clinton was lying, again. When she said that *radical Islamic terrorism* were not "magic words", she was obfuscating and dissimulating. Those words are possessed of a black magic so potent that he or she who utters them can unleash forces so devastating that they would make America quake again. Not being patriots, Obama and Clinton did not want you to know this secret. Luckily, you found out in the nick of time and averted an apocalypse.

But allow me to break the truth to you and shatter the post-truth, Mr President. You are being led astray, or are wandering off, as is your wont, in the wrong direction. Neither your former position regarding Islam nor your current position regarding Arab despots and dictators are right.

I know you will likely dismiss me as part of the politically correct, tree-hugging, climate change-believing, moral-relativist brigade. But rest assured, I abhor political correctness. I say what I mean and mean what I say. I describe what I see and see what I describe, without airbrushing out inconvenient truths or pasting in half-truths. I am not a partisan and owe no allegiance to anyone or anything, except my conscience. I find bigots who claim they are "politically incorrect" are more incorrect than anything else.

I am politically incorrect in the purest sense of the term. I don't mince my words to curry favour with any political current or in-group, or to scapegoat anyone, and call out bullshit where and when I encounter it. I find the worldviews of bigots of all stripes, whether non-Muslim or Muslim, objectionable, dubious and dangerous.

So, Mr Trump, if you really want to know "what the hell is going on," I invite you and all the other bigots out there to join me on a mind-expanding journey through Islam(s), an odyssey through time and space, passing through the main thoroughfares and back alleys of history, society, culture, politics, theology and, above all, people. Islam is not just scripture. It is far more than Muhammad and the Quran. It is the lived and diverse experiences of hundreds of millions of people, past, present and future. Allow me to introduce you to this human kaleidoscope.

Khaled Diab

Tunis, 2017

CHAPTER ONE

Introduction: A world of Islams

Whether Islamophobes or Islamophiles, conservatives and extremists agree on one thing: Islam is an easily identifiable, singular entity that possesses a clear and unique essence. Islam is evil, one side screams. No, Islam is benign, the other side retorts. Islam is enlightened. No, Islam is benighted. Islam is the religion of peace. No way, it is the religion of war. Islam only knows hatred. No, Islam is all about love.

However, what this essentialisation overlooks and distorts is that Islam cannot be separated and disentangled from its social, economic, political, cultural, geographical and historical contexts. There is no 'true Islam' – though some forms of Islam are truer than others. Even if Islam is about monotheism, the one God, it is not a single, coherent monolith. Despite what devout believers and staunch disbelievers would have you believe, Islam is not an immobile, static, unchanging edifice etched into a timeless, unshakeable mountainside. Islam is not and has never been one take-it-or-leave-it, all-or-nothing package.

The world is replete with many Islams, which differ, sometimes subtly, at other times fundamentally, across time and place. From the most pious to the most lapsed, Islam has always been 90% interpretation, with the other 10% open to interpretation. What we refer to as 'Islamic' differs from one person to the next, from one country to another, and from one period in history to the next.

In short, Islam is a very broad church – no religion that has survived and thrived for centuries can afford not to be. And I use the term church, here, consciously and intentionally. Despite harebrained claims that Muslims worship a different god to Christians and even to Jews, this is patently untrue. In fact, Islam is a clear extension and continuation of the Abrahamic tradition that preceded it, and the differences – in terms of theology, beliefs, attitudes and lifestyles – within each of these religions are as great, if not greater, than the differences between Islam, Christianity and Judaism. Some intellectuals and scholars, such as Egypt's Youssef Ziedan, argue that the three Abrahamic faiths are "one religion, sharing one essence," though, in his book on the subject, he bizarrely calls this single essence "Arab theology", even though it was not invented by Arabs or Arabic speakers.[1]

Why this book?

Islam has become one of the most explosive and controversial issues of our time. Much of the controversy revolves around profound misunderstandings and misapprehensions, whether borne of unintentional ignorance or wilful denial. These misconceptions, lies, half-truths and post-truths are incredibly dangerous in the volatile world we currently inhabit. With all the upheavals and conflicts currently plaguing the Middle East, one manifestation of which has been the growth in intolerant and violent Islamic extremism, and the rise in far-right (or alt-right if you prefer), anti-Muslim populism, demagoguery and bigotry in the West, With the upheavals and conflicts, ... the Middle East, it is all the more important to find a solid ground upon which to craft a useful argument about the topic of Islam.

In America and Europe, the notion is gaining ever more momentum that there is a grand global jihad which poses an existential threat to western civilisation and could destroy everything they hold dear. This jihad is not only being waged by the Islamic State (IS or ISIS), al-Qaeda, and other radical jihadist outfits, but also by refugees and migrants, not to mention the Muslim minority already in Europe and the United States. Likewise, in many Muslim-majority countries, the idea has gained massive traction that there is a crusade or a war against Islam in motion, and that the West (formerly known as Christendom) is out to wipe Islam off the face of the earth.

Neither of these essentially apocalyptic ideas is accurate or true, but they are immensely troubling and dangerous. They are troubling because they create warped and inaccurate perceptions of the tensions, conflicts and upheavals afflicting our societies, regions and the world, leading to misdiagnoses which result in the wrong policy medicine being prescribed and misguided actions being pursued. They are dangerous because, if they win enough converts to their cause or create enough fear and terror, those who believe in a cosmic clash, whether figuratively or literally, will hate outsiders and make the lives of minorities ever more precarious and vulnerable, and could lead us down the path to global conflict.

This book aims to provide a corrective and an antidote to these and other damaging misconceptions. Equally importantly, if not more so, it is about stories. It is about taking an exhilarating and fascinating journey through time and place, encountering the grand and the everyday, the magnificent and the mediocre, the monumental and the mundane, the human and the superhuman, the humane and the inhumane, the holy and the profane, the eccentric and the conventional, the outlandish and the common.

Islam for the Politically Incorrect is not chronological and does not present a conventional historical narrative, but employs something akin to the stream of consciousness approach used in fiction. But it is most certainly not a work of fiction. It is very much rooted in fact, and not of the alternative variety popularised by Donald Trump's counsellor Kellyanne Conway.[2] Unlike former White House spokesperson Sean Spicer and his boss,[3] I will never disagree with the facts, but I will express some disagreement with how facts are interpreted or omitted.

Instead, the book is divided into theme-based chapters. Each chapter explores an issue around which revolves controversy, confusion, widespread misconceptions and/or profound disagreement. Some themes are obvious and feature prominently in the public debate, such as the status of women, sex or the lack thereof, the theory that we are witnessing a clash of civilisations, and the significance of Muhammad and the meaning of his mission. But these I approach from an original perspective, mixing history, politics, society, anecdotes, as well as the personal testimonies of myself and others. Other themes are more obscure and shed light on the sheer diversity and pluralism of what we refer to as 'Islam'. These include the much-overlooked status of Muslim men, a brief history of Muslim drinkers and the status of alcohol throughout the history of Islam, as well as an exploration of perhaps the Muslim world's most forgotten and ignored minority, atheists.

In this book of well over 100,000 words, I have endeavoured to highlight the richness, diversity and nuance of Islam, including the good, the bad, the ugly and the beautiful. Despite my best efforts, there are undoubtedly important elements missing. This is inevitable, given the space available. In addition, I am only human and do not possess knowledge of everything. Moreover, despite my best efforts to be balanced, the text is coloured, to varying degrees, by my own perceptions, experiences and biases.

Confessions of faithlessness

As those familiar with me and my journalism and writing will know, I am a progressive, socially liberal, secular atheist – and, so, not a 'Muslim' in the typical sense of the word.

In the interest of full disclosure, and to give the reader insight into where I am coming from, allow me to describe here my path to abandoning religion. When it comes to finding religion, we hear of epiphanies, moments when someone suddenly wakes up and sees the light. I don't know if this is true, since I've never experienced a religious awakening. When it comes to losing your religion, it is more like, in my experience, a slow bleed or a debilitating terminal condition in which there can be periods of recovery but the end is not far off; it involves soul-searching and soul-destruction. It took me many years of doubt, the questioning of religion, as well as long stretches of ignoring it.

Even as a child, many aspects of religion bewildered or confused me. One of the greatest early mysteries of religion for me was how an accident of birth could determine so much – at least, for the vast majority of people. Growing up in London, the idea that my English friends and their families might have to suffer eternal damnation troubled me greatly, as it meant not only that people I loved and cared for seemed to be hell-bound, but so was the vast majority of humanity – such a waste of good people was just not right. My late mother, being a great believer in human dignity and also having a number of great English friends, was troubled by this question too, I could sense. She explained that Christians and Jews were "*ahl el-kitab*" ("People of the Book") and so would not be punished by God for not believing in Islam because they were ignorant of it or misinformed about it. Moreover, people who were not People of the Book and had not received the true message of Islam could not and would not be held responsible for not embracing it, she assured me.

This question has been debated by Muslims for centuries and opinions have varied greatly, with the more open-minded holding similar views to my mother, while zealots believe that only practising, believing Muslims will gain salvation at the end of time. One reported saying of the prophet, or *hadith,* quotes Muhammad as saying that to save the souls of Muslims, God would, "deliver to every Muslim a Jew or a Christian and say, 'That is your rescue from Hell-Fire.'"[4] That would imply that saintly Christians or Jews would be evicted from paradise to make way not only for saintly Muslims but also for Muslim sinners. Of course, Islam is not alone in this regard. Indeed, smaller religions can be much more extreme. Take Jehovah's Witnesses. Of all the untold billions of humans that have ever lived, Jehovah's Witnesses believe that only 144,000 people will make it into heaven – not a great way to sell a religion, if you ask me – though those who embrace Jesus will live forever in a world free of crime and sin.[5] Regardless of what the afterlife holds in store, this did not stop my mother going against the English norm of the time of shunning Jehovah's Witnesses and she invited in those knocking at our front door for a cup of tea and a chat. She even built up a years-long friendship with one Jehovah's Witness, a French woman living in London with her very large family.

Paradise itself was something that my young mind had difficulty conceiving of, and with the narrowing of imaginative capacity that accompanies age, it is becoming even harder to comprehend. The idea of heaven, of course, has its appeal and has tempted many a sceptic to embrace the faith eventually, often in old age. As a kid, I would close my eyes and try to get my head around the implications of perfection and eternal life. As an adult, I thank God that I do not believe in heaven and hope he will have the good grace to keep my lack of faith strong, as I do not wish to hang out for eternity with the fundamentalists, fanatics and zealots who have muscled their way to the front of the queue.

Even if God does eventually pardon most of us and offer paradise to everyone who has not sinned excessively, this raised another, related doubt. If God is all-powerful and all-seeing, why could he not have found a more effective way to inform his creations of what they had to do? In fact, given his immense powers and his omnipresence, which I was told was enough to know my every thought and action, God should have the ability to communicate directly with humans, without need for middlemen (and it is almost invariably men), whose messages never reach everyone and which seem inevitably to become distorted. Believers will tell you that this is the whole point, it is part of the test, to see whether you will believe. But why test people whom you intentionally made to be imperfect because you created them with imperfections, and then judge them on the basis of a message garbled and distorted in its communication, even though you know exactly what they are going to do before they do it?

The contradictions in God's apparent sense of justice have long miffed me. Why did he give so many good people such a hard time and grant so many bad people extravagant blessing in this world? If Islam was his final, perfect religion, why are so many Muslims living life as the wretched of the Earth? Why is faith in God and loyalty to him, like some godfather in the mafia, more important than somebody's moral fibre and the good they do to their fellow humans? Over the years, I heard so many Islamic scholars and preachers say that even a person who spends their entire life wronging and abusing others but shows genuine remorse and repents on their deathbed, God would forgive them and open the doorway to heaven. This is supposed to highlight God's infinite mercy, and perhaps it does. But it has a flipside. Someone who doubts or rejects God's existence but spends their entire life doing good, rather than espouse a few seconds of belief before they breathe their last, will most likely burn in hell. Like a dictator, God seems to value obedience over competence, to prefer blind acceptance to free inquiry.

My mother was always open to discussing my array of doubts and questions (though I was reluctant to express some), reassuring me that this is precisely what God wanted, that he did not want people to believe in him unquestioningly. Later, I discovered that even if God and his apostle, Muhammad, invite us to seek out the truth and knowledge, there is a catch: the conclusion you must reach (which is supposedly self-evident), is predetermined, and failure to find the 'correct' answer has dire consequences in the hereafter.

I was also never able to get my head around some of the things which constitute wrongs or sins. Take, for instance, the mixing of the sexes. If a man and woman are alone, the devil is their companion, or so many Muslims believe. But why should something so harmless be considered so sinful? Rather than demons whispering in my mind, being with a woman was more akin to angels singing and good genies dancing, I felt. Moreover, this gives Satan divine attributes, like omnipresence and omniscience – not only is he chilling with every single unmarried man and woman hanging out together in the world, he is also constantly whispering in the minds of every single believer, everywhere.

As I got older, the glaring contradictions contained within scripture and Islamic tradition, and religion in general, haunted me. Islam is supposed to be, for example, about all believers being equal in the eyes of God, yet some believers are far more equal than others, such as men. In addition, the fact that Islam, like other ancient religions, originally allowed slavery – even if it did encourage masters to set their slaves free[6] – troubled me. If we are all equal, why allow one of us to own another? The various justifications I have heard never alleviated my unease, or raised further doubts about other aspects of faith. One common explanation I have heard is that God could not force believers to change their way of life too radically or too rapidly, and by placing restrictions and regulations on slavery, he was paving the way to its abolition. The trouble with this theory is that it complicates a host of other issues. God had no qualms about imposing sudden change in other areas. Being a jealous God, he told the Arabs that they must not worship any other god but him. If God liked to guide his faithful gently and gradually towards the truth, why not phase out polytheism rather than outlaw it immediately?

Even if we accept that God or Muhammad truly intended to phase out slavery, not to mention concubinage and polygamy, as Muslim reformers argue, this leads to another intellectual impasse. This strongly suggests that Islam was a product of its time, while the mainstream Muslim view is that Islam is timeless and relevant for all ages. If it is, then why is it, like all ancient religions, showing its age so badly and ageing so gracelessly? Moreover, if Islam is a complete guide to life, as so many believe, why is it so full of gaps, not to mention contradictions, and why do we need the supplemental tool of the *hadith* which use Muhammad's sayings and actions as a model for our own and as one of the main tools for developing Islamic laws? Surely, God could have included everything we need in his holy book? To be fair, there is no Quranic basis for deriving Islamic practices or law from the *hadith*. In addition to the Quran describing itself repeatedly and in varied ways as complete and perfect, nowhere does it require Muslims to follow Muhammad, except in so far as he delivers the message. Even the verse many scholars use to justify the *hadith*, namely, "Whatever the Messenger has given you – take; and what he has forbidden you – refrain from," is used disingenuously, as it totally ignores the rest of the passage, which refers only to the distribution of war booty, which should not just go to the rich, but also to orphans and other needy.[7] In one of those bizarre twists of logic or pious paradoxes, Islam's most authoritative *hadith* collections contain *hadith* which forbid the collection and utilisation of *hadith*! "Do not take down anything from me, and he who took down anything from me except the Quran, he should efface it," Muhammad is reported to have commanded his followers.[8] These contradictions at the very foundations of the faith illustrate how one thing and its polar opposite can both be justified as 'Islamic'.

Moreover, why does God place us insignificant beings at the centre of his inconceivable universe? It is inconceivable that we are at the very top of all this creation – and if we are, then the universe must be a sadly substandard place. Beyond the metaphysical, an enormous difficulty I had with religion, and one that only grew with time, is that history in religion bears little to no resemblance to actual history as it occurred. Many of the stories told in the Quran, Bible or Torah did not occur or did not occur as recounted – and these 'alternative histories,' as we may wish to call them, are causing humanity a great deal of problems.

Science is another challenge for the would-be believer. Although modern Muslims pride themselves on the notion that their religion is a rational and scientific one, with an entire industry that has emerged to demonstrate how vague verses in the Quran supposedly presaged and predated modern discoveries, such attempts cannot escape the inevitable erosion that comes with the emergence of a devastating body of scientific facts that contradict what religion tells us. This is blatantly clear in the clearly dated Quranic conceptions of astronomy and the cosmos. Even if we consider that the notion of seven heavens is metaphorical, there are passages that appear to describe the Earth as being the centre of the cosmos, with the sun and moon orbiting it. Even more unscientifically, some stories in the Quran seem to describe a flat earth. In one story, the character Zul-Qarnain ("The Two-Horned", whom many Muslims believe to be Alexander the Great)[9] travelled west until "he reached the setting of the sun [where] he found it set in a spring of murky water."[10] In another part of the Quran, God supposedly informs us that "We have beautified the world's heaven with lamps, and We have made them missiles for the devils,"[11] as though the stars were not giant balls of flaming gas, some of which can envelope thousands of our own sun, but small decorative fairy lights or blazing fireballs that could be chucked at demons. This betrays a profound misunderstanding of the creation he is supposed to have created. Like with Genesis in the Torah or Old Testament, the Quranic creation myth is highly problematic from a scientific point of view. Not only was the universe supposedly created in six days (which some explain away as metaphor), the Earth was bizarrely created before the seven-layered outer space in which it is located: "It is He who created for you all of that which is on the Earth. Then He directed Himself to the heaven, and made them seven heavens."[12] God can also "roll up the heavens as a recorder rolleth up a written scroll"[13] or that God could "cause a piece of the sky to fall",[14] as if the sky were a ceiling or the canvas of a tent. Like with the earlier Jewish and Christian traditions, the Quranic account of the creation of humanity, namely the story of Adam and Eve and the idea that humans were shaped from clay[15] or dust,[16] is just as problematic scientifically as the creation of existence.

This discrepancy between modern science and religious science, and the cognitive dissonance it creates, is magnificently expressed in the dilemma facing practising Muslim astronauts. How do believers who reach the heavens, without the inconvenience of needing to die first, pray at the allotted times, how do they face Mecca and how do they determine when to start and end their fasts during Ramadan? To resolve the 21st-century challenges caused by an ancient belief system, a special conference was convened by the Malaysian National Space Agency to help its first astronaut navigate his faith while on the International Space Station.[17]

Many believers say that marvelling at the miracle of the universe can only confirm and strengthen one's faith – which they are entirely entitled to do. However, for me, the reality of the universe fundamentally shatters any possibility of faith in religion. If there is a god, (s)he set off the Big Bang and then took cover to view the handiwork of the magnificent laws set in motion to govern the universe. (S)he is not an interventionist micro-manager who, for some unfathomable reason, decided to place us, insignificant flecks on the back of an insignificant speck that we are, at the centre of their entire scheme. While I accept the possibility that a creator exists, mainly because we cannot prove it either way, I reject the truth of religion. As the sum of our knowledge expands exponentially, the threadbare nature of the 'truths' contained within religion become ever more exposed, until they become impossible to patch over, requiring an ever greater leap of faith to cross the widening abyss separating fact from faith. And at the end of the day, religion is about faith. It is about accepting what it calls truth without proof. And that ultimately and fundamentally lies at the core of why I reject Islam and other religions. That said, I do not begrudge or deny a person's right to accommodate or ignore all the evidence against religion by reading scripture in allegorical, metaphorical or even literal ways. Some extremely intelligent people whom I respect have done or do just that. However, by a similar token, believers too must accept my scepticism and disbelief.

As a young adult, I simply ignored religion as much as I could in a society, Egypt, where religion refuses to ignore you. I lived my life according to the mix of humanist and humane principles with which I was comfortable. If asked, I would describe myself as "non-practising", "lapsed" or "secular" – delaying the inevitable reckoning with myself. Sometimes I would get into philosophical, metaphysical or intellectual discussions with friends about religion. I recall wandering the darkened streets of Cairo with an Egyptian friend who was a declared atheist. Even though we... even though we agreed on most of the same points, I admitted to him that I was not quite ready to abandon the last vestiges of faith. Far more than peer pressure, I think it took me so long to admit that I was a non-believer because of my mother, I now realise in retrospect, after her passing.

Being highly intelligent, tuned into her children's varying mentalities and the long and sometimes heated debates we had about religion, my mother had figured out for herself that I had lost and abandoned my faith before I ever told her. My eventual declaration of faithlessness obviously hurt my mother, not for any worldly reason, but because she did not want to see her eldest son punished in the hereafter. However, she had raised us to be independent thinkers and doers, and to make up our own minds about everything, so she accepted my lack of belief and wished that the fact that I was, in her eyes, essentially a good person would lead to God pardoning me and offering me salvation. When my mother died in 2016, I wondered if this would lead me to a crisis of faithlessness, if the shock of losing the earthly giver of my life would propel me back to the heavenly creator of hers. But it did not. Not in the slightest. At my mother's wake, friends and family, with a Quranic reader reciting from the holy book in the background, tried to console me by telling me that, amongst other things, God must love mum because he took her during Ramadan, but that, sadly, gave me no comfort. The only comfort I was able to draw was that her pain and suffering had disappeared alongside her consciousness, that the hell of disease in which she had been plunged was finally over.

Despite the tolerance and acceptance of my conviction in my family, amongst my friends and generally from my readers, not every Muslim non-believer is willing or able to divulge their unbelief – and, in that regard, I count myself extremely fortunate.

Why the author?

My confessions of unbelief will raise the question in some people's minds as to why I should write this book and why I am qualified to write it. Certain conservative Muslims may claim that my rejection of religion disqualifies me from writing about it, or worse. But however much they dislike or reject it, religion can be and has always been written about from a secular perspective. More importantly, as long as the majority of Muslim societies regard Islam as something you are born into and not something you choose (unless you are a convert), then I am, at a certain level, as Muslim as the next person, and have every right to express my ideas and thoughts. Besides, it would be a poor world indeed if only people who belong to the 'in group' were allowed to write or speak about it. In a free world of free inquiry, anyone can write or speak about anything they want and they should be judged on their knowledge, the robustness of their arguments and the intelligence and lucidity of their thoughts, and even the aesthetics of style and articulation.

In addition, the fact that I was raised as a Muslim has instilled in me a profound respect for and deep awareness of that part of my heritage. Moreover, with a foot and other limbs in more than one world, having grown up, lived and worked in both the Middle East and Europe, I can provide a rich multicultural perspective on issues which affect Muslims and non-Muslims alike.

That said, a few disclaimers and provisos are in order. In this book, I have striven to give a platform to as many different types of voices as I can, to provide the reader with insight into the complex worlds we tend to describe with the single word of 'Islam'. However, unless otherwise stated, the interpretations and conclusions I reach are entirely my own. The people I quote or refer to in my book may strongly agree with some things I say, and may passionately and fundamentally disagree with others. They are in no way responsible for my interpretations and conclusions.

The reader should also be aware of a simple fact. For better or worse, I do not represent anyone other than myself. I do not, nor do I pretend to, speak on behalf of 1.6 billion 'Muslims'. Though my book provides lots of information to non-Muslims, I am not a 'native informant'. I do not advocate (neo-)imperialism and, being an opponent of oppression in all its forms, I do not and will not provide a moral fig leaf for any oppressors, whether they be foreign or native.

Nor do I speak on behalf of the West, with its billion or so inhabitants, depending on how you define it. I am also not a Muslim 'Uncle Tom' or 'coconut'. Any so-called western perspectives or values I possess are out of conviction and the fact that I have spent at least half my life living in Europe, which makes me western too, no matter how much my use of this description has riled white supremacists and neo-Nazis. My European identity is as much a part of who I am, as are my Muslim and Arab heritages.

In fact, I do not like such exclusionary labels. Although terms like Islamic, Christian, Arab, western, etc., do reflect reality at a certain level, they do not and cannot reflect reality in its entirety nor can they express the complexity of each of our identities. Furthermore, these labels are often used to advance and perpetuate vested interests, deepen divisions and stymie positive change.

With all this in mind, dear reader, please join me on this journey of discovery, in which we will explore what sets Islam apart but, most importantly, what makes it a part of the general story of humanity.

CHAPTER TWO

Muslim women: Femininity, feminism and fantasies

Despite having a taste for gold-gilded opulence that would be the envy of an Arab dictator, President Donald Trump cares about the plight of Muslim women and worries about their oppression at the hands of Muslim men.

And, naturally, Muslim women rejoiced at Trump's victory – well, at least a handful did. "I don't fear Donald Trump and I don't fear the policies that he's talking about. What I fear is the extremist interpretation of Islam that is spilling blood on the streets of our world," Asra Nomani, who describes herself as a Muslim reformer, told CNN following the controversy surrounding her OpEd about voting for Trump. "He is confronting the issue of ideology."[1]

And with his ban on all foreign Muslims entering America, Trump truly is confronting the issue of 'ideology' head on, since flesh-and-blood Muslims are clearly indistinguishable from their religion. As every right-thinking (with the emphasis on far-right or alt-right) person knows, all Muslims are to blame for the actions of radicals because 'moderate Muslims' exist only in the fantastical utopias of 'Leftistan.' "The terms 'extremist' and 'moderate' serve only to reinforce our collective delusions," wrote Rod Liddle, the controversial British journalist, while metaphorically slapping Brits out of the trance that was leading them to sleepwalk towards and drown in the ocean separating them from Islam. "Those two terms lose all meaning when applied to the fissiparous and splenetic tribes of Islam."[2]

With those "fissiparous and splenetic" hordes massing at the borders, no wonder Donald Trump ran to prevent these people from entering America and multiplying like bacteria (unless they come from countries which buy US weapons or sell us their oil). "When I'm elected, I will suspend immigration from areas of the world where there is a proven history of terrorism against the United States, Europe, or our allies," candidate Trump said following the massacre at the Pulse gay club in Orlando in June 2016. "Remember this, radical Islam is anti-woman, anti-gay, and anti-American," he added (as if he were describing the alt-right), noting that he was the true friend of women, not Hillary Clinton.[3]

As is well-documented, Donald "Grab Them by the Pussy" Trump is a great respecter of women, especially those with a "young and beautiful piece of ass."[4] That is why he firmly believes that "putting a wife to work is a very dangerous thing" and "when I come home and dinner's not ready, I go through the roof."[5] Donald Trump not only holds Muslim women in high regard, but before he even took office, he had rolled out policies to 'empower' them to shed their hijabs by provoking a huge spike in anti-Muslim hate crimes. The reality TV president's respect for Muslim women was also on full display when Trump went through the roof at the criticism of his politics of hatred and division delivered at the Democratic National Convention in 2016 by Khizr Khan, whose son, Captain Humayun Khan, was a decorated soldier killed in Iraq.

But instead of attacking his critic directly, the then Republican presidential candidate took aim at Khan's wife. "I'd like to hear his wife say something," he quipped.[6]

"If you look at his wife, she was standing there. She had nothing to say," Trump elaborated in a later interview. "She probably, maybe she wasn't allowed to have anything to say."[7]

In a moving article, Ghazala Khan, the silent wife in question, explained that her silence was not because she was some kind of downtrodden Muslim woman, but was down to grief. "It has been 12 years, but you know hearts of pain can never heal as long as we live," she wrote. "The place that emptied will always be empty."

"Donald Trump has children whom he loves. Does he really need to wonder why I did not speak?" Ghazala Khan asked.[8]

Offensive and insensitive as Trump's comments were, he was bringing nothing new to the table. Tapping into what seems to be his family's knack for borrowing, Trump was recycling one of the most common stereotypes about Islam in western Islamophobic circles: the notion that Muslim women are silent, weak, submissive, subservient creatures living under the thumb of their menfolk.

In fact, earlier in the Republican primaries, one of Trump's rivals made a remarkably similar point. "[Muslim] women must be subservient," insisted Ben Carson, the neurosurgeon who was out to prove, but failed, that running for president wasn't brain surgery. "And people following other religions must be killed," he added for good measure.[9]

I wonder if Carson would have the guts to tell Hend Wagih (Egypt's first female bodyguard) to her face that she is subservient to men.[10] I should warn him that she is a champion martial artist and a bodybuilder.

And this feminine silence and subservience apparently carries huge hazards. Former British prime minister David Cameron reportedly linked this "traditional submissiveness" to the radicalisation of young Muslims because, apparently, mothers are too afraid to speak out against radical imams.[11]

Hidden sexiness

It may come as a massive surprise to conservative Westerners that their ancestors did not view Muslim women as obedient, asexual and sexually repressed beings but rather as plucky, oversexed and promiscuous.

This is made abundantly clear in the fantasy of the harem, filled as it was, in the imaginations of orientalists, with erotic dancing girls and sensual temptresses. Classic European paintings of the harem almost invariably feature nude beauties, who are often naked even when socialising together as women, without a man in sight, as if the harem's dress code was birthday suits only. The subjects of these erotic fantasies were often pale-skinned, partly as a reflection of 19th-century European racial chauvinism and in a nod to the popularity of Circassian concubines in the Ottoman sultan's harem. For instance, an 1888 painting by Jean-Jules-Antoine is titled the *White Slave*.

Interestingly, this eroticising of the 'exotic' woman can be seen in the Arab fantasies about Western women. "We're loose, obsessed with sex, batter our men, are bad mothers, and can't cook," Katleen, my wife, who is from Belgium, once joked, summing up pithily some common Arab prejudices.

The eroticising of Muslim women could also be found in European literature. During his sojourn in Egypt, the accomplished 19th-century French novelist Gustave Flaubert formed the opinion that women there were veritable sexual automatons. "The oriental woman is no more than a machine:

she makes no distinction between one man and another," the French man of letters concluded.[12]

This generalisation of daring proportions, implicating not just every woman in Egypt but every female in the entire Orient (however far that stretched in Flaubert's mind), was made not on the strength of years of experience or research but based on a brief relationship the writer had with a famed Egyptian courtesan, or *alema*, named Kuchuk Hanem. In Arabic, *alema* means a scientist or learned woman. But in colloquial Arabic, it is a euphemism used to refer to a senior dancer, who can often double as a prostitute or run a brothel, rather like a Japanese *geisha*. This is in sharp contrast to an earlier letter he wrote to his schoolmate the poet and dramatist Louis Bouilhet, in which he sounded infatuated with Kuchuk Hanem's beauty and passion. Of course, it is entirely possible that Flaubert's statement was not actually a generalisation but was intended for a very specific purpose: to get him out of the doghouse. His letter was addressed to the poet Louise Colet, who was Flaubert's paramour and the only woman he truly ever loved, and Flaubert seemed to be reassuring her that his consorting with prostitutes was neither here nor there when it came to their intense love affair.

Two fantasies collide

In modern depictions of the Muslim woman the erotic fantasies of yesteryear combine with the submissive and subservient stereotype. This was given creative (and clichéd) expression in the 2004 short film *Submission*, written by the Dutch-Somali former politician and ex-Muslim Ayaan Hirsi Ali and the murdered director Theo Van Gogh, who was brutally shot and stabbed to death by an Islamist terrorist.[13]

The film plays on the centuries-old sexual fantasy of the harem but with a modern twist: instead of the traditional conception of the licentious, oversexed Muslim woman, it features the broken and obedient female that dominates modern-day perceptions of benighted Islam. The work features four characters, all played by the same actress, whose stories, told as monologues, reflect, in Hirsi-Ali's typically simplistic and reductionist way, various verses of the Quran which express men's superior status. While the characters speak, these Quranic verses are projected on to the characters' bodies, which are barely concealed under a transparent chiffon – for many Muslims, the provocative style of the film distracted severely from its message.

Of course, parts of the Quran, some *hadith* (i.e. the actions and sayings of the prophet Muhammad) and male Islamic scholars have long told women that they reside below men in the pecking order. This is clear, for example, in the Quranic verse granting daughters half the inheritance of sons[14] or the verse informing men that they have authority over women because they pay their way.[15] And conservative Muslim men do take the issue of obedience and subordination seriously. This is highlighted in, for instance, the female-run Obedient Wives' Club, an organisation with a few hundred members, mainly in South-east Asia, whose name leaves little to the imagination. The OWC, which has sparked controversy amongst feminists and modernists in Malaysia, Singapore and other countries, encourages the good *Muslimah* (i.e. female Muslim) to obey and submit to her husband, especially in the bedroom, and to behave "better than a first-class prostitute" to keep him from straying.[16] The group has even issued a "helpful" sex manual to help members fulfil their roles as "whores" in bed.[17]

In addition to the insulting premise upon which this group is founded, it also highlights how women can sometimes act as the gatekeepers and defenders of the patriarchy. This was driven home to me at a press conference I attended in Ramallah in which the only woman in the room, a self-described feminist, declared that women's rights were subordinate to national rights and there could be no freedom for Palestinian women without first freeing Palestine – though why the same did not apply to men, I do not know or understand. This process has been termed the "patriarchal bargain" by the Turkish scholar Deniz Kandiyoti, and is visible in all areas of the world where "classical patriarchy" is prevalent. "The cyclical fluctuations of their power position, combined with status considerations, result in their active collusion in the reproduction of their own subordination," Kandiyoti wrote in a landmark essay. "Even though these individual power tactics do little to alter the structurally unfavourable terms of the overall patriarchal script, women become experts in maximising their own life chances."[18]

A telling example involved a female parliamentarian in Egypt who stirred outrage and controversy when she proposed to strip women of the custody of their children if they remarried.[19] This can have even more extreme manifestations, such as when a matriarch, or senior woman in the family, takes it upon herself to act as the guardian of the junior women in her charge, going so far as to mutilate her own daughter or granddaughter or niece. This is what happens with female genital mutilation (FGM), often euphemistically referred to as 'circumcision', which is carried out by female members of the family or a female midwife (known as *daya*, in Arabic).[20] "Depending on the skill of the practitioner, what's left is a smooth opening to the vagina and vivid, often jagged, memories for many women," observes

Shereen El Feki in her award-winning book on sex in the Arab world.[21] In relating her own trauma as an innocent, unknowing child seized in the middle of the night by what she thought were burglars but turned out to be women out to clip her clitoris, the celebrated Egyptian feminist Nawal El Saadawi relates her shock when she discovers one of her assailants was her own mother. "I just wept, and called out to my mother for her help," the novelist and doctor recalled. "But the worst shock of all was when I looked around and found her standing by my side."[22]

Female Genital Mutilation relates directly to society's obsession with virginity. Although FGM predates Islam and is a cultural rather than Islamic tradition in the countries which practise it, many believe their faith demands it. Its purpose is generally supposed to be to tame a girl's libido to avoid the 'dishonour' of promiscuity. Whether excising the outer portions of the clitoris has the desired effect of robbing a girl of sexual desire depends on the individual woman, the trauma and shame she feels and how painful the wound left over by the operation is, but the few studies on the subject have suggested that around half of FGM victims report no sexual feelings.[23]

Like the chastity belts of yesteryear and the chastity (or abstinence) rings of today, FGM reflects an obsession with virginity that is not unique to Islam. It still persists in traditional societies in Asia and Africa, and indeed, in the 'Bible belts' of a number of western countries. Why female virginity is so coveted has long miffed me, even now long after fatherhood has become straightforward to ascertain. Experience is valued in everything, it would seem, except in the world of traditional courtship. The reasons for this are manifold. There are the practical issues related to proving paternity in a patriarchal order that predates DNA testing or the risks associated with unwanted pregnancies in a moral code set down before the advent of effective contraception. For many men, female virginity embodies the notion of possession, and when one possesses they would rather own something 'new' than someone 'used'. That is why the hymen is so important; it is regarded by patriarchy as the ribbon which secures a woman's chastity and keeps her sexuality under wraps.

One vital factor behind the fixation on virginity is control and honour. There is the traditional patriarchal instinct for men to control women's bodies. Paradoxically, it can also be a vestige of lack of control. "Whenever people become less in control of their lives, they seek to control those aspects that are left to them," psychiatrist and human rights activist Aida Seif el-Dawla once told me in the Cairo offices of the Nadeem Centre, the charity she co-founded, which provides support to victims of violence and torture, including prisoners and detainees who have suffered police brutality and women who have suffered domestic abuse. "If you can't control your income, the fate of your family or the politics of your country, then you will try to control what you can, i.e. the private sphere." In addition, when men feel emasculated by the state and the harsh circumstances of life, questions of their 'honour' being held together by the flimsy thread of the hymen loom large.

Although practised now by native despots, this social contract offering men dominion over women as long as they accept the ruler's dominion over them was appropriated from the former imperial and colonial practices of the Ottomans, British and French. "The foreign overlords ruled the public sphere, local men ruled the private sphere, and women got nothing," as journalist Max Fisher put it. "Colonial powers employed it in the Middle East, sub-Saharan Africa, and in South Asia, promoting misogynist ideas and misogynist [sic] men who might have otherwise stayed on the margins."[24]

This helps explain why when Tunisians and Egyptians brought down their respective dictators, we saw a highly polarised and explosive situation in which many women were emboldened to demand their rights, while many men, fearful of the corrosion of their actual or aspirational male privilege lashed out, often violently. This was vividly exemplified by the surge of sexual assaults and rapes against the women who dared to cross the line following the 25 January 2011 revolution.[25] A similar dynamic is taking place in America and some other Western countries where the growing success and visibility of women has unleashed a furious backlash by men who feel they have been unfairly left behind or lost their once unassailable position, as epitomised by the angry middle-aged white man stereotype.

The conservative Islamic desire for subservience and subordination finds perhaps its ultimate expression in ultra-conservative Saudi Arabia, where a trend has been observed of men taking their maids as second wives, which is not unlike the middle-aged Western men who hook up with 'mail-order' brides from Asia. "Men in these cases want to feel superior and they want an obedient wife, more like a slave," explained Fatima Al-Rifaei, a Saudi psychologist.[26]

Gender equality or equivalence?

Even in secular Turkey, the Islamist resurgence led by Recep Tayyip Erdoğan has devoted itself to rolling back the gains scored by Turkish women in recent decades. Although Turkish law guarantees gender equality, Erdoğan thinks this is nonsense. "You cannot make women and men equal," the Turkish president told an audience connected to a women's rights group, "this is against nature."

Though I don't speak Turkish, I would have liked to be in the audience just to gauge how the presumably staunch feminists listening were reacting to the lead balloon of Erdoğan's words.[27] The dismay. The barely stifled outrage. So what was Turkey's big brother willing to offer his sisters instead of equality? "Equivalence of worth". What did Erdoğan mean with this enigmatic expression? It sounds like it could be something from an economics textbook or perhaps, genius that he is, Turkey's neo-sultan was alluding to Einstein's equivalence of energy and mass, i.e. $E = mc^2$.

No, what Erdoğan was hinting at is, rather like the segregationist idea of 'separate but equal', that men and women should play different (read, traditional) roles and are "equivalent" by doing so. Islam, according to Erdoğan, exalts women as mothers. "I know there will be some who will be annoyed, but for me a woman is above all a mother," the Turkish president said in a later speech, this time to mark International Women's Day, during which women around the world strive for equality, not equivalence.[28] Erdoğan's stance has been a common one since Adam entered humanity's mythical pantheon, as Eve can testify. After all, in Genesis' creation myth Eve, despite being the one equipped with a womb, is born of Adam, marking her inferiority and subservience for eternity.[29] This can be detected in everything from the Saudi Girls' Council, which was launched without a single female in the room, or the infamous image of Donald Trump signing an anti-abortion executive order surrounded only by men.[30]

Even the secular, enlightened ideals of the American and French revolutions were once rooted in sexism. The US Declaration of Independence–which was drafted at a time when women had no vote and no role in formal politics–does not loudly declare that "all people are created equal" or even "all humans", but "all men", and that "governments are instituted among men."[31]

Traditional girl power

What simplistic, reductionist views of Muslim women overlook is that the status, role and position of women in traditional Islamic society has varied significantly over time and place. In addition, even though women were traditionally regarded as inferior to men, this does not mean they were weak or submissive, or regarded as such, as many in the West believe.

"I laugh when I hear these things," confesses Rula Jebreal, the prominent author, journalist and commentator, who is a Palestinian with Israeli and Italian citizenships. "People with simplistic views have to go and visit the reality I grew up in. I was raised with strong women all around me, whether family or neighbours. The women who ran my neighbourhood were fierce, incredible women."

On her paternal side, Jebreal's family are part of the African-Palestinian community of Jerusalem's old city. On a visit home, she took me once to meet her family and community and I got to meet some of the formidable women she mentions, including her straight-talking sister and a female cousin who ran the local chapter of the Marxist-Leninist Popular Front for the Liberation of Palestine (PFLP). I have written quite extensively about the pivotal role women have played in the Palestinian struggle, as well as almost every other Arab struggle for independence, with perhaps the greatest sacrifice being made by Algerian women during their country's long and bloody struggle for independence from France.

And Jebreal's experience is not unique. I was also raised by strong-willed, formidable women, foremost among them my mother, who gave me my first lessons in life about respecting women and treating them as equals. My maternal grandmother Asma' never received a formal education, never worked outside the home and never heard of women's lib – at least not until her eldest daughter, my mother, grew up and started talking about equality. Despite accepting that a woman's place was in the home, my *Setoo* (i.e. my Granny) was no weak and submissive woman. In fact, by all accounts, she was tough as nails and queen of her castle, and woe betide anyone who trespassed on her turf, be they human or animal. My gran raised birds on her roof and one of the few memories I have of her is spending happy, fascinating hours on the rooftop watching her tend and feed her feathered friends. One day, when my mother was young, mice infested the pigeon coop, threatening my grandmother's precious birds. Springing into action, Setoo took the knife with which she cleaned the cage floors and grabbed hold of each and every mouse and ended its poor life, counting the carnage. When she returned downstairs she triumphantly announced a death toll of 40 or so rodents.

On another occasion, a burglar had the audacity – and misfortune – to land on Setoo's roof. Sensing that her precious birds were again in mortal danger, she leapt into action without a second thought for her own safety, in point of fact, it was the hapless thief who was in danger. My grandmother grabbed a knife from the kitchen and a stick. Looking out of the window, she ordered the burglar to stay where he was because she was coming to teach him a lesson. By the time she got upstairs, the terrified man had leapt on to a neighbouring roof and scarpered.

Like me, Afrah Nasser, the Ethiopian-Yemeni activist and journalist who was selected as one of the 100 most influential Arabs under 40[32] and was one of the BBC's '100 women who changed the world', has fond memories of a feisty grandmother. "When I was a child in Ethiopia, my grandmother was a businesswoman, even though she was illiterate," recounts

41

Nasser. "When she entered a room, the men were terrified of her. Since I was a child, I realised that just because you're a woman, that doesn't mean you're weak or submissive."

Nasser's mother, who was no weak and submissive woman who accepted her lot, fought a bitter battle in the male-friendly Yemeni courts to leave her abusive, layabout husband, even if it meant hardship, suffering and social ostracisation for her and her daughters. "I owe [my success] to my mother," Nasser told me when she was named among the Arab world's top young movers and shakers. "[She] managed to fight an abusive husband, fight a patriarchal Yemeni society which did not accept her as a divorced woman, and struggled financially to feed her two daughters." This kind of selfless sacrifice in a man's world is reminiscent of Sisa Abu Daooh, a woman who dressed as a man for four decades in order to work and put food on the table for her children after her husband died. At the time in conservative Luxor, women working in menial labour was frowned upon and her family wanted her to remarry, a proposition she rejected. "I have decided to die in these clothes. I've got used to it. It's my whole life and I can't leave it now," she said, after being honoured as 'best mum' by the Egyptian president Abdel-Fattah al-Sisi.[33]

Dressing as men is a common cultural motif in patriarchal societies, as epitomised by the likes of Joan of Arc. It is also a common dramatic or comedy device in art, from the *1,001 Arabian Nights* to modern cinema. Inspired by his own daughter's experience sneaking into a football match, the controversial Iranian director Jafar Panahi's *Offside*[34] followed a group of fictional, football-obsessed young women as they cross-dressed to skirt the prohibition on women entering stadiums. After being caught by the police, one of the women memorably asks her captor: "Why is it we are allowed to go to the cinema with men but we are not allowed to come to the football stadium?" The Iranian film censor was not amused and the film was banned from being screened in Iran, though I heard Panahi say that it was a huge hit in the underground film scene there.

My own mother, after sacrificing her career and dreams of becoming a successful writer to help my father build his own and to take care of her children, struggled for years to shelter us against his sternness and harsh disciplinarianism, then to support and feed us after my father sent us back to Egypt and effectively abandoned us there.

That Muslim women play an active social and economic role outside the confines of their home is not a new idea or trend, though the magnitude and quality has changed. In fact, in generations gone by, it was elite women who were kept out of public view – partly in keeping with the Hellenic and Assyrian traditions of seclusion and exclusion of upper-class women which early Islamic civilisation took over, and the centuries-long influence of Greco-Roman gender attitudes on the region.[35] But in Egypt, for instance, women in the countryside and among the urban working classes always worked and had a public profile, partly for practical considerations and partly, perhaps, as a residual leftover from the impressive array of rights ancient Egyptian women, who were the legal equals of men, enjoyed, which seem to have been unparalleled anywhere in the world until the 20th century. "In most of their manners and customs, [Egyptians] exactly reverse the common practice of mankind. The women attend the markets and trade, while the men sit at home at the loom," wrote a clearly dismayed Herodotus, the famed ancient Greek historian who wrote extensively about Egypt (women in his native Greece enjoyed almost no rights).[36] Despite the advent of patriarchal Judaism,

Christianity and Islam, Egypt still retained some remnants of its ancient Egyptian girl power. "In Egypt, the women are generally under less restraint than in any other country of the Turkish empire," observed the ground-breaking orientalist Edward Lane in the 19th century. "It is not uncommon to see women of the lower orders flirting and jesting with men in public, and men laying their hands upon them very freely." However, Lane, though he came from the puritanical and conservative Victorian era, unintentionally chanced upon how the patriarchy is often internalised by women, especially those of the better-off social strata: "An Egyptian wife who is attached to her husband is apt to think, if he allow her unusual liberty, that he neglects her, and does not sufficiently love her."[37] Lane also highlighted the precariousness and vulnerability of the Egyptian woman's lot. Though it was extremely uncommon for Egyptian men to have more than one wife, many were serial monogamists – some even marrying a different woman each month – and made full use of the ease with which a Muslim man can end a marriage, which must have been shocking for a Christian man from a land where divorce had only just been permitted, on limited grounds, through the 1857 Matrimonial Causes Act. Equally shocking would have been the temporary wedlock, known as 'Pleasure Marriages' ('*Zawaj or Niqah el-Muta'a*').[38]

However, the fact that Islam has always allowed women to own and retain property gives the well-off considerable behind-the-scenes sway, as reflected in the sheer amount of wealth women in the conservative Arab Gulf own, which could be over half.[39] In fact, social and economic class also plays a significant role, with women of the upper classes usually of a higher status than men of lower classes. "In one of history's ironies, Muslim women of the ruling class were the most powerful and wealthy women in the world in the medieval and early modern period," writes Middle East historian and commentator Juan Cole, "even though many lived like reclusive millionaires in the inner apartments of their mansions."[40]

Harem fantasies and realities

Although plenty of sex did take place in polygamous harems, they were not the glorified brothels or fleshpots of feverish European imagination. Derived from the Arabic word for 'prohibited' or 'forbidden', the harem was ultimately the private sanctuary of the family where the women of the household could roam free, without being inhibited by dress and social codes. At Istanbul's spectacular Topkapi palace (now a museum), whence generations of sultans ran the Ottoman empire, curators are at pains to point out to foreign visitors that the harem was simply the sultan's private quarters, where he could rest and relax with his family.

The Ottoman harem had another, less-known function. It was the unofficial nerve centre of the empire, and the women who inhabited it held immense backroom influence; they were the hidden hand which ran the state. This was almost a continuation of the behind-the-scenes power Byzantine empresses held in Constantinople prior to the arrival of the Turks, a Byzantine practice which bewildered the male-dominated Abbasid court, leading them to depict Byzantine women as licentious and immoral, just as European orientalists would later depict Muslim women in the 19th century.[41] The *Valide Sultan*, the sultan's mother, was perched at the top of this pyramid, usually second only in influence and power over imperial affairs to her son. For a 130-year period during the 16th to 17th century, the power of the *Valide Sultan* and *Haseki*

Sultan (sultan's wife) – many of whom began life in the harem as non-Muslim slaves – exceeded that of the sultan himself, even if he remained nominally in charge. This was known as the Sultanate of Women.[42]

This may explain why Turkey's first lady is so enamoured of the harem. A day after her husband had reiterated his view that a woman was primarily a mother, Emine Erdoğan said, much to the consternation of many Turks, "The harem was a school for members of the Ottoman dynasty and an educational establishment for preparing women for life."[43] Many citizens of the former Ottoman Eempire do not take such a rosy view of the harem. Referring to the "feudal oppression and foreign domination" of the Ottomans, Nawal Saadawi, the godmother of Egyptian feminism, describes Arab women who were "condemned to toil, to hide behind the veil, to quiver in the prison of a harem fenced in by high walls".[44]

While it is important to set the record straight that the harem was not some kind of orgy palace, this kind of neo-Ottoman revisionism is highly problematic. While, as noted above, the women of the royal harem played prominent political roles, this was behind the scenes, through their sons or husbands, and often involved ugly intrigues. This is not what the modern empowerment of women is about nor does it bode well for equality – though, of course, Erdoğan only aspires to "equivalence".

The new Muslim woman

'Islamic feminism' must seem like something out of a bad dream for western conservatives, as it encompasses two of the groups they hate most in a single package: Muslims and feminists.

This was plain to see in the right-wing reaction to Palestinian-American activist Linda Sarsour, who calls herself "unapologetically Muslim-American"[45] and claims to be a "feminist because I am a Muslim,"[46] when she co-organised the anti-Trump Women's March in Washington immediately following his inauguration in January 2017. In addition to far-fetched accusations that Sarsour has links to terrorism, she was branded as being pro-Sharia and, hence, not a feminist.[47]

"That awkward moment when you realise the organizer of the #WomensMarch is pro Sharia Law, the very opposite of women's rights," a self-described Trump supporter wrote in a tweet that was retweeted over 20,000 times.[48] After having looked into Sarsour's positions, I, like some other progressive Arabs and Muslims, find some of Sarsour's feminist ideas illiberal and rather regressive, such as her efforts to play down the level of oppression Saudi women must endure.[49]

However, this is not the reason why her conservative and rightist critics, many of whom want to turn back the clock on women's rights, were up in arms; it is because Sarsour is an outspoken woman and a vocal Muslim who believes the words Muslim and American can be uttered in the same breath, and can hold hands with a hyphen. And to top it all off, she wears a headscarf.

Indeed, Sarsour's views of a woman's place are mild compared to some of the female superstars of the American right. Like the co-option of certain women as gatekeepers of the patriarchy in Islam discussed earlier, some of the most outspoken defenders of the traditional patriarchal order in the West are women, some with incredibly high profiles. Take ultra-right American pundit and author Ann Coulter. Not only does she, like conservative Muslim clerics, support depriving women of their hard-won right to vote,[50] she also disdains feminism, whose failings are "manifestly obvious", and whose proponents she claims, with stunning superficiality (and inaccuracy), are all ugly, while "all pretty girls are right-wingers".[51]

Some conservative pundits are convinced that feminists and Muslims are one and the same – a notion that has undoubtedly been strengthened by the prominence of Sarsour in the Women's March. Conservative commentator Pam Geller, a self-proclaimed 'anti-feminist', sums this up when she asserts that "leftopathic" feminism "clings to its dogma of multiculturalism, and embraces the leftist ideology *du jour*, which in our own day is Islam".[52]

Like the American right, conservative Muslims also believe that feminism and their religion are incompatible. "Although Islam and feminism are not completely without common ground, the values and principles of Islam and feminism are generally contrary," writes Muhammad Legenhausen of the Imam Khomeini Education and Research Institute, despite the fact that Iran has a large feminist movement. "However, the feminist view that patriarchy is equivalent to the oppression of women is not compatible with Islam."[53]

Quite a few outspoken Middle Eastern feminists are also convinced that Islamic feminism is a contradiction in terms. "Islamic feminism is a delusion, a misconception and an oxymoron," argues Joumana Haddad, the Lebanese poet, feminist and atheist who was ranked by Arab Business Magazine among the top 100 most powerful Arab women in 2016. But there is a key difference between Haddad, as well other principled feminists who hold this view, and conservative Christians: she believes all monotheistic religions are "inherently misogynic [sic] and against gender equality, however we cherry pick them."[54]

On a personal level, I am of a similar opinion to Haddad and other feminists who see gender equality and religion as intrinsically incompatible. However, I am more sympathetic towards those who hold on to their faith and aspire to reshape it into a (more) egalitarian and tolerant form. This is partly because the notion that a religion is a complete package which you must take or leave in its entirety goes against how religion is actually practised and lived. As with other religions, there are many Islams, depending on place, time and group. Whether liberal or ultra-conservative, selective interpretation is the rule, not the exception, especially in light of the enormous number of contradictions contained in scripture. Moreover, religion may shape people's attitudes but equally, people's attitudes shape religion.

Christianity's view of women has also historically been regressive (and remains so in many parts of the world), yet the West managed to set in motion a pretty successful feminist movement without needing to abandon its faith – in fact, earlier reformers tried to place their empowerment in a Christian shell. For example, the British suffragette movement to campaign for women's right to vote was "not primarily political; it was social, moral, psychological and profoundly religious," according to Helena Swanwick, who was a prominent suffragette in the early 20th century.[55]

Like the suffragettes, my late mother was "profoundly religious" but considered herself to be a dedicated feminist who believed fundamentally in the equality of men and women. My mother was convinced that Islam was an egalitarian religion and the reason for the imbalance between men and women was not the fault of Islam but of male scholars who have had the dominant role in interpreting the religion for centuries. She was fond of railing against this injustice. "They tell a woman what they believe her duties are but ignore how the Prophet used to do chores, mend his own clothes and help care for the children, so why do they say housework is women's work?" was one criticism she repeated over the years.[56]

Regardless of what one thinks of the term 'Islamic feminism', one thing is for certain, feminism has a long history in Muslim societies. During Islam's so-called golden age, there were female scientists, scholars, philosophers, philanthropists (one of whom, Fatima al-Fihri established the world's oldest, continuously operating university, in Fez, Morocco)[57] and even warriors. However, they were only a small minority in a man's world, and the vast majority of women were home-makers. The plight of women led some early Islamic reformers to advocate for greater women's rights and even equality. One Muslim proto-feminist was actually a man, the classical Islamic polymath Ibn Rushd (1126-1198), known as Averroes in the West (see chapter 3).

The 19th century saw the kernels of the modern feminist movement emerge. In Iran, for example, there was Fatimah Baraghani (1814-1872), who adopted the honorific Tahereh (The Pure), when she converted to the new faith of Babism, the precursor to Baha'ism. A gifted poet and theologian, she campaigned for female emancipation, outraging an assembly of men by removing her veil in their presence. "You can kill me as soon as you like, but you cannot stop the emancipation of women," she is reported to have said before her execution.[58] Towards the end of the 19th century in Egypt, women activists' critique of their male-dominated societies took on a sustained, systematic and loud form. Although Qasim Amin, a man, is remembered today as the father of Egyptian feminism, he had female precursors and contemporaries, most of whom have been forgotten. One was Aisha Taymur, an early Egyptian feminist poet of Ottoman Kurdish extraction who wrote about the difficulties she faced as a female writer and the changing situation and aspirations of women in Egypt, calls for equality, education and work. Her 1892 pamphlet *The Mirror of Contemplation* "represented what should be legitimately considered the first national debate on gender issues and concerns," wrote Mervat Hatem, a political science professor at Howard University.[59] Interestingly, Taymur had plenty of Ann Coulters and Pam Gellers of her time who, feeling their traditional status and prestige threatened, vilified and attacked Taymur, accusing her of neglecting her family and using her poetry as a means of having affairs.[60]

The 1890s also saw the emergence in Egypt of magazines written by women for women. The trailblazer her was *al-Fatat* (Young Woman), which ran from 1892 to 1894, and was published by a Christian Syrian immigrant, Hind Nawfal, daughter of two writers who had come to Egypt to escape Ottoman censorship. Less radical than Taymur, it sought simply to give women a voice, rather than agitate loudly for equality.[61] It contained literature and poetry by women, and articles about home economics, knitting, beauty tips and inspirational women, with the occasional more radical article.[62] It was like a 19th century *Cosmopolitan* or *Elle*, but without the photos.

Although she was not Egypt's first feminist by far, Huda Sha'rawi (1879-1947) is widely regarded to be the founding mother of modern Egyptian feminism, partly because she founded the Egyptian Feminist Union. In contrast to her contemporary, Malak Hifni Nassif (1886-1918), who sought to empower middle- and working-class women through educational and marriage reforms in a culturally sensitive manner, Sha'rawi mainly focused on the plight of fellow elite women seeking to shed their veils, to westernise and to take part in public life, including participate in the 1919 revolution.

The change over the ensuing decades was enormous and rapid. By the 1950s, Egyptian women had gained the right to universal education, including at the tertiary level, had gained the right to vote (which was a rather meaningless right in Nasser's one-party state) and gender equality had become an official principle of the state, enshrined in the constitution.[63] These changes enabled women from my mother's generation, even those of modest means, to go to school, gain a higher education and make in-roads into the workplace. The daughter of an illiterate mother and a primary-school educated father, both recent migrants to Cairo from the countryside, my mother was the first woman in her family to go to university and to hold down an office job. She was also an aspiring writer, as well as a socialist and feminist, who allowed herself the audacity to dream of a society in which men and women were equals.

By the 1960s, it must have appeared to progressive Egyptian women, and women in other reforming Muslim countries, that they were on an unstoppable express train to equality. But, in the case of Egypt, the 1967 defeat, a stagnant command economy, followed by disastrous economic liberalisation, and the embracing of the Islamist movement by President Anwar Sadat to try to neutralise his leftist and secular opponents all led to an enormous and sustained backlash against women's liberation from the conservative and Islamic right.

Whereas in the 1960s and 1970s Egyptian women in the cities dressed in the latest western fashions, including miniskirts and sleeveless dresses, today, the vast majority of Muslim women in Egypt wear the hijab. There has been a similar process of what you might refer to as 'hijabisation' across the Muslim world, including Palestine, where I lived for five years.

"We didn't wear the veil. We mixed with boys. The girls were educated," recounts Rula Jebreal of her youth in Jerusalem, in the 1980s and 1990s. Indeed, over the decade I spent travelling in and out of Palestine and Israel, I noticed a perceptible conservative trend in dress (also amongst Jews), with the proportion of women in hijabs rising constantly.

But is this a sign of renewed oppression or a different form of liberation? This is a vexing and complex question, and its answer may surprise you.

The fabric of piety

Rarely, if ever, has a piece of cloth created such controversy. For European and American conservatives, the hijab threatens to shred the fabric of society. For conservatives in Muslim countries, the Islamic headscarf stitches society together and, like with the hymen, the honour of the family and the community hangs by the flimsy threads of the hijab.

In Europe, the hijab is widely regarded as a symbol of oppression and barbarity and the woman who wears one is often considered to be a downtrodden victim. Afrah Nasser, who normally leaves her curly hair exposed, decided, as a social experiment, to put on a headscarf in Sweden, where she lives, and gauge the reactions she received. "I wore a scarf, in the Ethiopian style worn by my grandmother. I looked like I was wearing a hijab," the Ethiopian-Yemeni writer and feminist explained to me in an interview. "My experience was so different to going out with my curly hair... Just going to the shop to buy something was horrible. They made me feel like an idiot."

"No matter how educated a *muhajaba* is, they treat her like an idiot," Nasser added.

With the degree to which hijab and Muslim women have become interlinked in the Western imagination, some cannot get their heads around liberal Muslim women who dress differently. For example, Rula Jebreal recounted to me an incident when she first started working on Italian television and turned up in a figure-hugging white dress: "The producer asked me if I was a Muslim because of the way I dressed. He couldn't understand that this was the way I had always dressed. He thought it was the influence of Italy on me."

Nevertheless, being a secular, liberal Arab woman has not shielded Jebreal from the rising tide of Islamophobia, with the hijab just the noose with which the far right wants to figuratively hang Muslims. This was on naked display when peroxide blond Geert Wilders with the eccentric hair, the Dutch precursor of Donald Trump, bizarrely proposed what he called a "head rag tax". What, you may wonder, was the leader of the Party for Freedom (PVV) thinking... or smoking?

Claiming that the hijab polluted public space, Wilders claimed taxing this 'symbol of oppression' was merely the application of the 'polluter pays' principle.[64] "We will finally get some money back out of what has cost us so much," Wilders, who prefers a full ban on the hijab, insisted.[65]

What Wilders believes he is legally unable to do in the Netherlands, his French counterpart has openly proposed in her own country. In October 2016, Marine Le Pen, the head of the far-right Front National, pledged that, if elected, she would ban the hijab and other symbols of the Islamic faith from all public spaces (previously she has proposed the banning of prayers on the street, the foreign funding of mosques and the study of other cultures in French schools),[66] not just from public schools, where it has been prohibited for some years. Although Le Pen made it to the second round of the French presidential election in 2017, fortunately for multiculturalism in France, she was routed by Emmanuel Macron.[67]

But in order to translate this blatantly discriminatory policy into law, Le Pen felt compelled to fit her proposal into France's long secular tradition, known in French as *laïcité,* and dress it up as a ban on all religious symbols in public, a necessary sacrifice, she insisted, in her battle against 'Islamic extremism', by which she meant Muslims. "I know that every French person, including Jews, can understand that if we ask for this sacrifice from them [in the framework] of the battle against the advance of Islamic extremism, they will make this effort and understand it," Le Pen said in a radio interview,[68] echoing the arguments for the burkini ban given by some French mayors, who claimed that it is part of the 'salafisation' of French society, - a term which appears to denote the same alleged phenomenon as 'Islamisation' but more so.

This has caused concern and outrage in some Christian circles. "Please pray for France and its future. No Christian should be forced to hide their faith," a writer with Catholic Online beseeched, apparently untroubled about Muslims and Jews having to hide their faith.[69] While demanding sacrifices from Muslims and Jews, Le Pen offered fellow Catholics a special pass to a secret trap door in her plan. She explained that her proposal was to ban "conspicuous" symbols and opined that the "Catholic religion doesn't have conspicuous symbols."[70] It seems that Le Pen has never met a monk, a nun, a priest, or has never seen Christians wearing crosses so big they make them walk with a slight stoop. Or perhaps "conspicuous" to the FN leader is a synonym for non-Christian.

Of course, not everyone is as hypocritical and racist, or Islamophobic. Secular intellectuals in France have long been anti-clerical and suspicious of religion. After all, the French revolution was a backlash against the two ruling estates, the clergy and the nobility, and against how the church legitimised the rampant inequalities and injustices during the *Ancien Régime*. During revolutionary France's First Republic, the so-called Cult of Reason which did away with God, and effectively deified humanity, but was also not terribly rational gained significant, if short-lived, influence, transforming many churches in France into Temples of Reason. During his Reign of Terror, Robespierre abolished this new cult to replace it with a Deistic religion, the Cult of the Supreme Being.

This *laïcité*-versus-sisterhood dilemma represents a challenge for French feminists. It leaves some feminists in a bind, torn between the values they believe in and the manipulation of those values by envoys of hate. "On the one hand, I support the intransigent application of secularism," wrote feminist and academic Bronwyn Winter. "On the other hand, I distrust a hypocritical and racist state."[71] Despite the presence of well-meaning feminists in France, mainstream French feminists' rejection of the headscarf, which was reportedly banned from their meetings before it was banished from schools, and their aloof attitude towards Muslim women, which has helped legitimise identity politics and the 'clash of civilisations' narrative, has drawn criticism from fellow feminists. "If French feminists saw scarf-wearing Muslims as oppressed women," contends Christine Delphy, author of *Separate and Dominate: Feminism and Racism After the War on Terror*, "it should be a reason not to expel them from school or to curtail their movements, but to embrace them."[72]

In fact, many intellectuals and even feminists in the Arab and Muslim world regard the expressed Western intent to free Muslim women from the chains of their hijab, niqab and other Islamic garb as simply an excuse for neo-colonial meddling. This was nowhere more apparent than in the United States' catastrophic invasions of Afghanistan and Iraq. "The advance of freedom in the greater Middle East has given new rights and new hopes to women there," then-president George W Bush said, in another example of his misplaced triumphalism.[73]

Of course, the reality on the ground was and remains very different. For instance, in Iraq, the hijab and other forms of covering went from being regarded as a symbol of backward tradition, and later a sign of Islamist defiance of the regime, to become a tool in the hands of conservative extremists to redefine the role of women; and not for the better, as Bush had alluded. "The harassment of women on the streets, death threats against professional women, the enforcement of the hijab among female employees… are all integral to the construction of new concepts about women and gender relations," observed Nadje Sadig Al-Ali and Nicola Christine Pratt.[74]

Dressed to resist

This kind of misuse and abuse of feminism for geopolitical gain has empowered Islamic conservatives to sell the hijab as a form of cultural 'authenticity' and a way of resisting western hegemony, which is supposedly cut from a different cloth. But despite these efforts by Western and Muslim conservatives on both sides of the divide to appropriate the hijab, and by extension Muslim women, to dress up their own political agendas in a mask of *faux* 'liberation', the issue of headdress is not at all black and white, nor clear cut. Muslims themselves, especially women, are deeply divided over the hijab and what it symbolises. Two Somali-Canadian sisters, Asha and Roda Siad, sisters I met, embody this divergence. One decided to wear the hijab and the other remained bare-haired – yet both women are empowered, independent-minded, adventurous documentary filmmakers who focus on the refugee crisis.

For women who voluntarily choose to cover up, it is empowering. It is an act of defiance, a symbol of cultural and religious pride, and a political statement. For example, my sister, Ghada, is a firm believer in gender equality, yet she decided to don the hijab when she was about 18, as an external symbol of the deep faith she felt inside. It was not a decision she took lightly, even asking me my opinion beforehand, but she has not looked back since. Over the years, her hip hijab has accompanied her on her many battles against the patriarchy and sexism, which crescendoed in her joining other young people in their demands for full equality during the heady early phase of the Egyptian revolution in 2011.

In a way, the spread of the hijab is a kind of cultural equaliser, a form of democratisation. As touched on earlier, when feminism first emerged in Egypt, veiling was the preserve of the aristocracy, as a sign that a wealthy man could afford for his wife not to work or to go out in public, and if she did, then it would be concealed from the prying eyes of the plebs. This is why the early fixation of wealthy feminists on the issue of removing the veil did not find resonance with their working sisters. "[This] was unlikely to evoke much enthusiasm... [because] the working women in factories and fields had never known what it was to wear a veil," wrote Nawal El Saadawi.[75]

Today, for many women, the headscarf is a necessary evil to allow them to navigate the public sphere, to gain an education and to work, while satisfying their families' desire that they do so 'virtuously'. This is particularly the case for women earning a living for solely pragmatic motives, i.e. economic survival. "The response of many women who have to work for wages... may be an intensification of traditional modesty markers, such as veiling," describes Denis Kandiyoti.[76]

For some, the headscarf is a conscious reaction against what they regard as the over-sexualised objectification of women, which is a major factor in the West and more liberal Muslim countries. "From perfume and clothes ads to children's dolls and X Factor finals, you don't need to go far to see that the woman/sex combination is everywhere," reflected Nadiya Takolia, who is part of Cambridge University's Scriptural Reasoning project and its Interfaith programme. "Knowing that our interpretation of liberal culture embraces, if not encourages, uncovering, I decided to reject what society expected me to do, and cover up."[77]

This is not, in my view, a convincing, or consistent, argument. Yes, forcing women, either through direct coercion or peer pressure, to dress in revealing clothes for the pleasure of men or to market products sexualises and objectifies the female form. But so, in its own way, does the Islamic requirement to cover up. Telling women they must conceal their beauty when out in public, rather than desexualising women, effectively sexualises pretty much every part of the female body. This objectification of a woman's body is not only demeaning to women but highly insulting to men. When justifying the hijab, one popular line of argument is that women who bare their hair arouse the lust of men. Some feminists counter that if the sight of their bodies causes such uncontrollable sexual desire in men, then the impetus should be on men to cover their eyes. In fact, the notion that a man cannot control himself in the presence of a woman, no matter how scantily dressed she maybe, is highly insulting to the entire male sex – we are scarcely all Trump-like creatures who, uninvited, kiss and grope women we find attractive. A spoof advertisement for a wonder drug makes fun of this idea. "Piagra – the first pill for men designed to help you maintain your piety," the parody commercial professes. "Piagra also helps guard your uncontrollable male urges if you shake a woman's hand or see a woman without the headscarf."[78]

Women are obliged to dress in such attire as a sign of their 'modesty', while most Muslim families and societies – with the exception of places like Afghanistan under the Taliban and ISIS-controlled territory – impose no such limits on their menfolk. In fact, it is not uncommon to see a pumped-up hipster salafist dressed in a T-shirt so tight that it shows every contour of his six-pack, or a shirt unbuttoned to mid-torso, accompanied by a phantom woman in robes so baggy and flowing, with face masked from view, that you can barely make out she has a figure at all.

One side effect of this hyper-sexualisation of women's bodies is the sexual harassment[79] epidemic sweeping through some Muslim societies. [80] After decades of hearing from Islamists and conservative scholars that a woman who fails to dress conservatively is like a lollipop attracting flies, with posters showing as much, sexual harassers have internalised the message and, through their actions, implicitly tell women that not only every inch of your skin but also your very presence in the public sphere is a sexual provocation and anything that happens to you is your own fault. This view has become so mainstream that talk-show host and TV presenter Tamer Amin saw fit to blame a law student who was mobbed and molested by a large group of male students on campus for the way she was dressed. "These are the clothes of a belly-dancer, to put it politely," Amin claimed, overcoming his feigned decorum to say she was "dressed like a tart".[81] The dean of Cairo University initially echoed this sentiment when he criticised the student's "out-of-the-ordinary attire", with the interviewer, herself dressed in tight clothes, agreeing with him.[82]

But Amin and the dean do not get it. Not only are victims not to blame for their tormentors' actions, sexual harassment is actually largely not about sex and is more a tool of dominance and control, whether consciously or subconsciously. This helps explain why, in Egypt, sexual harassment reached epidemic proportions in the wake of the revolution, escalating to widespread physical violence.

During the revolution, two long-standing and polarised social trends collided in the public sphere: the growing empowerment of women clashed with the radicalised rearguard, whether religiously or socially conservative, defending the threatened male order. America is also undergoing a similar polarising process. In Egypt, Tahrir was a microcosm of this clash. In one incarnation of the life of the square, women stood shoulder to shoulder with men, both genders risking their lives and livelihoods in the cause of radical change, with many of the men on the square firm believers in gender equality. In another manifestation, Tahrir would become a gladiatorial arena in which women would be assaulted and even gang-raped by vicious, ferocious, out-of-control mobs, some allegedly sent by the state, others allegedly by Islamists, as if to tell them, 'How dare you come out and protest? How dare you rise above your station? How dare you dream of or demand equality?; How dare you dishonour men in this way?!'

For their part, women and their allies are fighting back and forcing society to wake up this pandemic. Numerous anti-harassment initiatives have been established in recent years, including HARASSmap, an app for reporting and mapping sexual harassment incidents, as well as providing outreach activities and self-defence classes for women.[83] Some have gone to extremely creative lengths to challenge the culture of harassment and to empower women to go out on in public unmolested. One such effort was Ballerinas of Cairo. The brainchild of photographer Mohamed Taher, the initiative encouraged Egyptian ballerinas to let themselves go and dance in the street rather than on stage. The result was a series of captivating, elegant and enchanting images.[84]

Body politics

At a certain level, the hijab also signals a form of male ownership over a woman's body, informing other men that this woman belongs to a good and honourable family and is off bounds to you. Many a father, husband or brother have been known to punish 'their' women for the affront to their 'honour' caused by the way they dress. This sense of ownership and honour can be collective and relate to women who bear no relation to the outraged, beyond sharing the same nationality. This was amply revealed in Egypt, when a young woman decided to protest the patriarchy by doing the polar opposite of covering up.

Buoyed and emboldened by the 2011 revolution in her country, Aliaa ElMahdy, an activist who later joined the controversial Femen movement, posted a naked image of herself (a black-and-white shot of her wearing nothing but stockings with the only colour a pair of red shoes and a red ribbon in her hair) on her blog to express her opposition to the growing influence of Islamists and to demand her full freedom of expression. "Put on trial the artists' models who posed nude for art schools until the early 70s, hide the art books and destroy the nude statues of antiquity... before you direct your humiliation and chauvinism and dare to try to deny me my freedom of expression," she wrote defiantly.[85] It would seem that the best way to outrage the patriarchal male order is to protest in the nude, judging by the insults, threatened legal action and even death threats[86] which the nude activist received for this and subsequent stunts.

In less permissive countries than Egypt, you don't even have to go that far. This was demonstrated in Saudi Arabia by the abuse, death threats and calls for her execution a young woman received when she dared to post a photo of herself standing on a Riyadh street with her hair uncovered and not wearing the traditional *abayah*.[87] This incident also highlights an important point; that hypocrisy is a two-way street when it comes to attitudes towards Muslim women's attire. Many conservative Muslims I have encountered will cry oppression and demand that the religious freedom of Muslims in Europe be respected every time any restrictions on the *hijab* are proposed or implemented. But when I mention the restrictions on women's attire in countries like Saudi Arabia, Iran or Afghanistan, they usually claim that the situation is different, that people must respect the local culture. When I suggest that, by the same token, Muslims in the West should then have to conform to local norms, the respondent often claims that, no, this is not the case because, in a stunning example of circular logic, religious tradition trumps secular norms.

Prevalent conservative attitudes to the *hijab* can be problematic for liberal Muslim women who do not see a contradiction between their faith and the way they dress. "A sizeable number of people from my religion look at people dressed like me and write us off as women who have lost their way and veered off the path of Islam," writes Thanaa El-Naggar, who professes to practising Islam in short shorts.[88]

Practising Islam in short shorts, miniskirts, or summer dresses was far less problematic in bygone decades, as noted earlier, in those secular Muslim societies that have been overtaken by a wave of religious conservatism. Back then

63

and until the Islamisation of Egyptian culture took off in earnest in the 1980s, the dominant pan-Arab socialist culture discouraged the headscarf. For example, there is a recording online of a speech given by former Egyptian president Gamal Abdel-Nasser in which he jokes about how the Supreme Guide of the Muslim Brotherhood had demanded that Nasser force Egyptian women to wear the hijab. "Sir, you have a daughter in medical school who doesn't wear a headscarf or anything," Nasser responded to the Guide. "If you aren't able to impose the scarf on one girl, your daughter, how do you expect me to go out and dress 10 million in headscarves?"[89]

However, long before France imposed its ban on the hijab in schools, Turkey and Tunisia, despite both countries being overwhelmingly Muslim, introduced their own headscarf bans in schools, universities and public buildings. As part of Tunisia's decades-old policies of promoting gender equality, in 1981, the government banned the hijab,[90] partly in a bid to curtail the growing influence of Islamist groups in society, schools and workplaces, a ban which has long been criticised by human rights activists.[91] When Islamist president Recep Tayyip Erdoğan reversed Turkey's decades-old prohibition on the headscarf because "headscarf-wearing women are full members of the republic, as well as those who do not wear it," many secular Kemalists were outraged.[92] In some other countries, such as Egypt, there exists or existed[93] a *de facto* ban on headscarfed women appearing on television.

That Muslim-majority countries would restrict or prohibit the hijab may strike the outsider as odd, but at a certain level it has its own logic, which is only partly related to the elusive quest for 'westernisation' in the late colonial and early post-colonial eras. The subsequent search for 'authenticity' actually led to the adoption of new innovations as constructed traditions in some countries. Although veiling was common in places, in numerous Muslim-majority countries, the hijab did not really exist until the later decades of the 20th century. In diverse, multicultural, multi-religious Indonesia, the most populous Muslim-majority country, the hijab, known locally as *jilbab* (the Arabic word for a kind of loose gown), did not make an appearance until recent years, partly as an element of the quest for an Islamic brand of modernity and partly as a reaction to the ban on head coverings during the repressive Suharto years.[94] Indonesian critics see it as a troubling import from conservative Arab countries.[95] As noted earlier, covering up in Egypt was something only elite women did. This helps explain why bare hair was uncontroversial and nobody was troubled by the hijab issue, except for the Muslim Brotherhood.

In previous generations, exposed hair expressed little to nothing about a woman's level of faith: a woman could be a believer or a sceptic, practise the five pillars of Islam or none, be sexually liberated or conservative.

When the Islamist counterculture first emerged in Egypt in the 1970s, its members consciously adopted holier-than-thou dress that set them apart from the rest of the population, including hijabs, khimars (like hijabs but worn loosely over the shoulder and chest, to obscure the breasts) and niqabs, in rising levels of conservatism. The headscarf was largely associated with religiosity – it was a political and cultural statement asserting piety, often telling the bystander or observer that secularism had failed and, conveying the Islamist slogans of the time, "Islam is the solution" and the "Quran is our constitution".

The cultural revolution the Islamist movements set in motion in Egypt is remarkable in how far it managed to influence social practice without the need for actual legislation.

When my mother and aunts were young, the vast majority of Egyptian women did not wear a headscarf. When I was at university in the first half of the 1990s, a largish minority of women in my college covered up. After uni, gradually more and more women I knew personally started to conceal their hair, with some extremely surprising candidates. Today, though no reliable statistics exist, an estimated 70-90% of Muslim women in Egypt don some kind of religious headdress, which has led to the odd situation that uncovered hair is associated in many people's minds with Christians. Even those last bastions of liberal dress that I had known as a student toppled one after the other. The first time I saw headscarved girls at Cairo's elitist American University or carrying canson tubes at the Faculty of Fine Arts, I, at first, could not believe my eyes.

Veiled liberation

But one must never just trust one's eyes. Beyond these superficial, outward signs, there has been a process in motion that I call 'secularism in a veil' which has seen society go from "thinly veiling [its] traditional Islamic character in modern western cultural clothes, to dressing up their internalised modernism and increasingly secular reality in a reassuring and personalised Islamic garb," as I argued in 2009.[96]

As a sign that clothes really can be only fabric-deep, today there is a far greater number of liberated Egyptian women than there were in the 1950s to the 1970s. Education for girls is taken for granted, especially by the middle and upper classes, with girls often outperforming boys.[97] Women have made in-roads into just about every career path, and scored significant successes, and much of this with their hair concealed. This was beautifully expressed in the photo of a match between the Egyptian and German beach volleyball teams, in which, on the left, a covered-up Egyptian and, on the right, a bikini-clad German leap for the ball with the net, like a metaphorical cultural barrier, standing in-between them. "Left: The subjugation of women according to orientalists. Right: The subjugation of women according to occidentalists," I joked at the time.[98] In fact, the trend of Muslim women competing professionally in headscarves has become so immense that Nike launched its very own Pro Hijab, which in turn unleashed a huge conservative backlash in America.[99]

Though the hijab started as a radical political and religious statement, as its influence spread, it morphed into more of a cultural symbol for millions of women, and each has made it her own. The mind-spinning display of hijab styles and the dazzling spectrum of colours stands in contrast to the drab, shapeless styles of the Islamist pioneers. The coiffed hair often peeking out from under the rim, the heavy make-up, the skin-tight clothing that many hijabis sport reveal that culture has trumped religion, that the headscarf has become a form of Islam Lite for many.

This is also apparent in how Egyptian hijabis are to be found in places where it was once undreamed off – smoking *shisha* (waterpipes) in coffee shops, attending concerts, dancing at discos and even sitting in bars with drinking friends. I have even seen headscarved women drink alcohol on a handful of occasions, although some upmarket bars and restaurants dissuade them from entering. The sexual purity once associated with the hijab is far less common now. As the peer and societal pressure to cover up has mounted, some sexually open women don the hijab but get on with their love lives. Quite a few see no contradiction between their sexuality and their faith. This is visible among the young women sitting in dark corners along the Nile embankment stealing kisses from their boyfriends or the iconic photo which stirred up both admiration and dismay of a young couple engrossed in a passionate kiss. The girl is dressed in a pink hijab; the curly-haired boy, in a hoodie. The couple stand in front of a graffitied, rusty doorway with ageing posters advertising academic books, which suggests the photo may have been taken outside one of the print or photocopying shops near a university.[100]

In addition to this gradual corrosion of the hijab's conservative connotations, a growing number of women in Egypt (and elsewhere in the Muslim world), some emboldened by the 2011 revolution, are removing their headscarves. For most, this is an incredibly difficult decision to make, whether because of personal soul-searching and/or peer and familial pressure. One young woman who did so was boycotted by her father and confined to her room. But he eventually relented. "My father now shares pictures of me on Facebook," she said.[101] One Jordanian activist I know who ditched her headscarf after 11 years, decided to do so for a number of ethical considerations and due to the veiled messages the hijab sends out. "Veiled women who wear the veil out of modesty are implying that women who don't are immodest," she reflects. "Covering up as a duty for women and only women, on the basis that women are a source of 'temptation' for men, denies women their sexuality." In addition to how the hijab deprives women of their sexuality, she also objects to the culture of shame of the female form which surrounds the veil. "A woman's body is just that, nothing about it is shameful."

While women in Jordan and Egypt have to battle social norms and prejudices, in Iran, they have to battle the state. Perhaps as a cultural and social backlash against forced, state-sponsored religiosity, there is quite a groundswell of popular opinion and resistance against the veil in Iran. One early form of defiance was women pulling back their headscarves far enough to show off the front of their hair. "I saw the *manteaus* get shorter and the headscarves inch back for every year that passed," recounts Iranian-American analyst and commentator Holly Dagres, who spent her sensitive teenage years in Iran, and is writing a memoir about her experience. "Some Iranian women didn't care if hair was showing or if their tight manteaus showed their figure and even their behinds."

Sick and tired of the long-standing restrictions on their personal freedom, a growing minority of Iranian women have escalated their rebellion. In one campaign, called My Stealthy Freedom,[102] women post photos of themselves out in public with their hair bared. Some women, like the examples mentioned earlier, go as far as to disguise themselves as men. "In order to avoid the morality police, I decided to cut my hair short and wear men's clothes so that I can freely walk in the streets in Iran," confessed one such woman.[103]

Iranian men have also been cross-dressing. This was part of a publicity stunt in which men donned the hijab in solidarity with their female compatriots, under the "#meninhijab" hashtag. "When I wore the hijab, even just for a short period, I felt I was not myself anymore," one of the men who took part confessed. "It means that women when they leave their house everyday have to leave their real identity back at home. It's a horrible feeling to have a double identity for a lifetime."[104]

Dagres, who had been used to wearing shorts and T-shirts as a Californian girl, experienced a similar reaction to these Iranian men. "I never got used to wearing the hijab, but accepted it as a way of life," she admits. "Some Iranian women kept their headscarves effortlessly on – even when they had crazy beehive hairstyles – while mine always managed to slide off the back of my head."

The underground sisterhood

The sustained conservative and Islamist onslaught against women and women's rights has set back the clock in many parts of the Muslim world, with the most dramatic, extreme example being the areas under ISIS control. Whereas once Syria and Iraq had been at the forefront of the progressive Arab women's movement, women living in the self-declared caliphate survive under horrendous, inhumane conditions.

In contrast, the so-called Arab Spring has empowered and emboldened Tunisian women and enabled progressives and liberals to regroup. A sign of this is how women make up a third of parliamentarians in Tunisia,[105] the highest proportion in the Arab world, and better than many Western countries, including the United States, where women comprise a fifth of Congress.[106]

A similar, if less immediately visible process has been at play in Egypt. On the one hand, feminists and activists are depressed by the boys' club running the country and the brutal conservative and Islamist backlash polarising society. "The secularists and the conservatives are two faces of the same coin when it comes to women. Most of the politicians in both currents objectify women," Marwa Rakha, a journalist and radio and TV host, told me soon after the revolution. "Patriarchal values, religion, and traditions are not as easy to topple. It was easier to break free from Mubarak's regime than to break away from decades of preaching."

While the Egyptian constitution may state that all Egyptians are created equal, it remains the case that middle-aged Muslim men are more equal than others. Although the military-led political class running the country is still very much of the old school, Egyptian society itself is undergoing a massive and profound social revolution, including in the status of women.

In fact, I feel this post-revolutionary conservative backlash is less a function of the patriarchy flexing its muscles and more a sign of a weakened traditional male order desperately trying to reassert its shaken and failing authority. Although this has succeeded to some extent, many women have refused to be cowed and admirably still continue to play prominent roles in Egypt's revolution, both for collective freedom and their own. To name just a few, take revolutionary sisters Mona and Sana Seif, who played prominent roles in the revolution and continue in their activism, despite intimidation, detention and even imprisonment. Then there is veteran human rights defender and psychologist Aida Seif el-Dawla, who has been resisting the regime for decades, has endured intimidation, the freezing of assets and orders to shut down her NGO, and continues defiantly to run the Nadeem centre, which treats and defends the victims of torture and domestic violence.[107] Iranian women have also been at the forefront, as showcased by the Nobel peace prize awarded in 2003 to Shirin Ebadi, the prominent lawyer and human rights activist. Less acclaimed but no less courageous is Nasrin Sotoudeh, the lawyer's lawyer who has defended Ebadi and other activists, often holds one-woman protests and has a revolving door to prison.[108]

Women's attitudes – and men's attitudes towards women – have also undergone a perceptible shift over the generations. Whereas my mother's generation may have dressed more liberally, traditional roles and ideals were deeply entrenched, making liberation often fabric-deep, except for a small feminist minority which had to swim against a very strong tide. My mother, for example, had to fight tooth and nail against her father and the community to acquire a higher education and to gain access to the workplace, as well as to delay getting married, even by a few years.

Higher education and work are now a natural fact of life for millions of Egyptian women and women across the Muslim world, and the average age of marriage is incomparably high compared with previous generations, both out of economic necessity and changing aspirations and lifestyles. To illustrate, nearly two-thirds of Egyptian women aged 20-24 were married by age 20 in 1970. By 1995, this proportion had dropped to 41%, and this trend is continuing apace. These figures also obscure the large urban-rural divide, where women in the countryside are far more likely to marry at a younger age. With variations, these trends have been region-wide. "Young people marry at a later age in the Middle East (31 years of age for men, 23 for women) than anywhere else in the globe except for China, and early marriage among young women has fallen more dramatically than anywhere else in the globe," one study found.[109]

Many young women are delaying marriage because they wish to pursue master's degrees or PhDs or build a career first, while some simply do not wish to marry. There have even been campaigns against the still-prevalent derogatory notion that single women are unwanted 'spinsters'. A growing, if still tiny, minority of single women are choosing to live alone. And not all of them are of the upper classes. One young woman I met was born and raised in a small, conservative village outside Fayoum. University enabled her to escape the stifling atmosphere of rural Egypt. Not only does she live in her own apartment in Cairo, she has worked in China and the Gulf.

Though pioneering Egyptian women lack the safety net of a progressive legal system which safeguards their rights against regressive traditions, they are not waiting for their rights to trickle down from on top and they are refusing the postponement of their liberation until the full-scale revolution comes, as has been the case in the past.

Even in the most conservative corners of the Muslim world, women are becoming more strident in their demands for greater rights. An example of this is the campaign to allow women to drive in Saudi Arabia. Women's rights have even entered Saudi pop culture, with a number of recent hits lashing out against the marginalisation of women. One recent song which went viral and has been viewed millions of times, *Hwages* (Concerns),[110] features women dressed in niqab, partly as a nod to Saudi's repressive public dress codes and partly to conceal their identities. But rather than being modest and withdrawn, the young women play basketball, hurtle down the street on rollerblades and dance energetically. To the backing of a catchy beat, they sing of how "men make us mentally ill" and "crazy".[111]

In neighbouring Yemen, where the cause of female emancipation has progressed somewhat further than in Saudi, feminists are also witnessing a perceptible shift. "Before the social media boom, when people saw how well my sister and I were doing, people would advise us not to shine too much so as not to ruin your chances of marriage," recalls Afrah Nasser. "Following the social media boom, I've discovered that half my family and community follow me and my relatives are pleased and proud of me... My mother now understands clearly that I'm a feminist." This has led to more frank and open discussions about women's rights, Nasser reflects.

This has some feeling optimistic for the longer-term future. "I see an awakening... I think the Arab Spring unleashed dreams that will be very hard to contain," concludes Rula Jebreal. "I don't how long this will take but I have no doubt we will reach equal rights."

CHAPTER THREE

Muslim men: Emancipating the average Mo

The thing, in the Western mind, about Muslim and Arab men is that we're explosive and fiery. We bring fireworks wherever we go (preferably of the undetectable sort). We're such adrenaline junkies that we're addicted to extreme pastimes (such as terrorism and jihad), and we regularly go to raves where we mindlessly rage against the machine (while loudly chanting *Allahu Akbar*).

Of course, it is not Muslim men's fault that they are so violent and misogynistic. It is all because of the hormones. You see, they are so sexually repressed, that it transforms them into a kind of biological weapon, a hormonal warhead targeted at the licentious infidel. That is why leading terrorism expert, Islamic scholar and psychoanalyst, Bill "Bull" Maher, who cunningly disguises himself as a TV comedian, came up with a deceptively simple and inexpensive solution to Islamic terrorism; he quite literally wants terrorists to get fucked. "If Muslim men could get laid more, we wouldn't have this problem," Maher proposed. "There's probably no suicide bomber [who] after he died, people said, 'You know, that guy, he blew everybody up, but boy – he got laid a lot.'"[1] Yes, indeed, one imagines all those rappers, bar owners and gangsters who 'repented', disowned their former lifestyles, and then joined ISIS or al-Qaeda, never got laid in their former lives.

Muslim men have also conquered popular culture in a big way, which is not surprising as we put the fanatic back into fan. We are the nightmare incarnate of the West's leading dream factory, Hollywood – we're the "reel bad Arabs", as Jack Shaheen, the author of a book by the same title, would put it.[2] With a handful of exceptions, such as the legendary Omar Sharif,[3] Hollywood Muslims tend to be typecast as one variety of villain or another. "Hollywood's reel-bad-Arab formula has remained unaltered: filmmakers paint Westerners as bright brave heroes and Arabs as dangerous, dumb baddies," writes Shaheen in his exhaustive study.[4] In Arnie's 1994 hit *True Lies*, for example, Shaheen, who cleverly punned that "reel Arabs are not real Arabs,"[5] complains that Fox studios hired the Humane Society to oversee the treatment of animals but no such consideration was offered to Arabs and Muslims.[6] Frustrated Arab and Muslim actors confirm this. "I've been sent nearing 30 scripts for which I've been asked to play terrorists on screen," complained Amrou Al-Kadhi, a young actor of Arab origin. What is he whining about, you may wonder, at least he is in demand, unlike so many other actors? "Use [your] ethnicity as a playing card," one casting agent told him, urging him to see the bright side of life. "White actors are fucked in this day and age."[7] Apparently heeding this agent's sterling advice, Iranian-American comic Maz Jobrani has established his own acting school for Middle Eastern actors, where he puts his charges through a gruelling training programme in how to hold a Kalashnikov, scream "Allahu Akbar", slap Western hostages and die painfully.[8]

Yes, Muslim male actors have it lucky compared with their white colleagues. After all, white men do not dominate

Hollywood. 'Lying, socialist perverts' and 'limousine liberals' – to use the terms deployed by Trump supporters[9] – do. White men rarely land leading roles and almost never win accolades for their roles, no matter how superb their acting skills – in fact, a mere nine out of 10 acting Oscars have gone to white stars.[10] This was on stark display at the 2017 Oscars, where *La La Land*, an epic Hollywood musical about that most vital of topics – Hollywood – lost the Best Picture award to *Moonlight*, an artsy-fartsy film about a young black /man as he discovers he is gay – which one swooning critic described as "more like a symphony or a poem than a mere movie".[11] Mahershala Ali, who was crowned best supporting actor, happens not only to be African-American but also a convert to Islam, which makes him the first Muslim actor to win an Oscar. "It was foregone," Tucker Carlson, Fox New's most liberal face, clairvoyantly predicted after the event. "You knew that Moonlight had to win because you knew what the film was about."[12]

Despite the cut-throat demands of careers in terrorism and jihadism, Muslim men must also make time in their busy schedules to terrorise Muslim women, (a full-time job in its own right) and to seduce and defile Western women with their wily, cunning, post-truth ways. In the 21st century, Muslim men no longer have to die to get their promised 72 *houris*, those dark-eyed seductresses whom supposedly await the martyr in paradise. Heaven has become a place right here on Earth; and it is located in Europe. "For the Muslim man, [Europe] is better than paradise," writes Rohini Desilva, the Sri Lankan author of *9/11, Stealth Jihad and Obama*. "He can have sex with as many women as he likes. But he has no financial responsibility for any of them, or for the children he sires."[13] And just like the maidens of paradise, European women are presumably there just for the picking. Muslim men possess "a truly brutal hatred of women that demands we are slaves and absolutely believes it has the right to rape women who don't submit," contends Anne-Marie Waters, the director of Sharia Watch UK.[14]

But why voluntarily open the gates of Europe to the lustful Muslim hordes to pillage the West and rape its women? It is a manifestation of elite masochism, self-hatred and a bent for self-destruction; hara-kiri without the honour, if you will. "The Western world is dominated by leaders who despise its history and its heritage and are determined to bring an end to its power," concludes Waters.

Dangerous men or dangerous generalisations?

This composite image of the quintessential Muslim man is extremely misleading. That is not to say that these stereotypes hold no truth. Like many successful mythologies, they contain elements of truth. They may even have some basis in fact, but in facts taken in isolation, stripped off their context and nuance, taking extremes as representative of the mainstream. That is not to suggest that these extremes do not exist. They most certainly do. ISIS *is* like the very worst of the worst of Hollywood stereotypes about the violent, untrustworthy, sexually repressed and perverted Muslim and Arab male have jumped out of the film reel and into real life.

But this is no excuse for making dangerous generalisations. It is like considering the Ku Klux Klan and other American white supremacists and mass shooters as representative of all white American males, using the minority to discount the majority as violent and trigger-happy radicals, even terrorists. To highlight the absurdity of such generalisations, *Slate* ran a piece in which it proposed a spoof executive order temporarily banning white American men from the United States because, statistically, they pose a greater threat to US security than Muslims.[15] It would also be like extrapolating the reported sexual harassment "epidemic" on British and American campuses (where under 8% of incidents are said to be reported)[16] to conclude that Anglo-Saxon male academics are, as a group, sexual predators. While most people rightly reject the preposterous notion that white men possess an 'innate' violence and depravity, little such caution exists when it comes to Muslim and Arab men.

Even some Muslim reformers can fall prey to similar blanket generalisations and the temptation to paint all Muslim men with the same brush. Borrowing the famous War on Terror strapline, Egyptian-American journalist and feminist Mona Eltahawy wrote a controversial piece for *Foreign Policy* entitled, "Why do they hate us?"

"Until the rage shifts from the oppressors in our presidential palaces to the oppressors on our streets and in our homes, our revolution has not even begun," Eltahawy wrote in the piece. "Name me an Arab country, and I'll recite a litany of abuses fuelled by a toxic mix of culture and religion."[17]

Although Eltahawy's essay is, sadly for Arab women, factually accurate, to borrow her own phrase, the essay does not move beyond a long litany of abuses, and does not make any attempt to depict the complexity of the situation or to highlight the grey areas. Largely missing from her analysis are the diverse shades of opinion and attitudes across the Arab world, and the very real gains made by Arab women in many countries, especially in the professional and educational spheres.

As a long-time admirer of Eltahawy's journalism and activism, I find it hard to fathom why liberal, empowered Arab and Muslim women who have challenged discrimination in every walk of life hardly featured in her article, even though she meets with them regularly and posts about them on her twitter feed. Her loaded 'why do they hate us' question also turns a blind eye to a highly inconvenient reality for advocates of gender equality like Eltahawy and myself: like traditionalists everywhere, many Arab and Muslim men and women do not regard traditional gender attitudes and roles to be a sign of hatred, but rather of love and respect.

In common with the anti-Muslim Western narrative and the conservative Islamic discourse, Eltahawy's essay completely ignores a certain variety of Arab and Muslim men; those who believe in women's rights, either because they were raised by feminists or came to be convinced of their cause, and have stood shoulder to shoulder with women in their quest for equality. In fact, it strikes me that just as women have become a political football in the culture war between a hegemonic West and a defensive Muslim world, so too have men, with the West demonising and the East glorifying the traditional Muslim man, while men who hold other convictions or live by different principles are airbrushed out of the picture or lost in the ideological stampede.

When men were Men

This editing out of the modern Muslim man occurs not just in Hollywood but also in its Arab equivalents. Where progressives have failed to capture the imagination of the masses, conservative myth-makers have worked tirelessly to idealise and idolise the vision of invincible, insurmountable Muslim manhood. With some brilliant exceptions, television dramas, known as *musalsalat* in Arabic, tend to be the Arab world's strongest bastion of traditionalism and overt, unsubtle moralising, particularly during the fasting and feasting month of Ramadan.

One hit series which took the Arab world by storm about a decade ago was the Syrian soap opera *Bab al-Hara* (*Neighbourhood Gate*), which was first aired in 2006 and is now into its ninth series.[18] Set in French-mandate Syria between the two world wars, it paints a sentimental and nostalgic picture of a society peopled by brave and gallant men and their dutiful and obedient womenfolk. Director Bassam al-Malla said he intended to create nostalgia for "a world with values, honour, gallantry… and the revolutionary spirit."[19]

"[*Bab al-Hara*] evokes a sense of nostalgia for earlier better times, where 'real' men defended their communities from invaders and crooks," writes Zeina Zaatari, a researcher on gender and sexuality in the Middle East at the University of California, in a paper on the topic. "In the show, a division of space between the domestic/women's world and the public/men's world is clearly articulated." Through *Bab al-Hara*'s characters and narrative line, "desirable masculinity is contrasted with images of negative masculinity". One example of this negative masculinity cited by Zaatari is the character of Abu Bakr, who is out of work and a wimp who receives beatings from his wife, even though she wishes he can be like the other men that he sits with at the coffee shop. *Bab al-Hara* and similar dramas "reinforce patriarchal structures and lack of women's choice and agency, reifying masculinity as public and femininity as private," concludes Zaatari.[20]

It is, of course, doubtful that a world like that lionised in *Bab al-Hara* existed. As pointed out in the previous chapter, though women were far more invisible than today, they had already made enormous strides in their emancipation by the time depicted in the series, with a vibrant feminist movement already in place in the Levant, Egypt and the Maghreb countries. Today, this mythology is even further from the reality lived by the millions viewing it. In addition to the undoubted insult to women this denial of their role represents, the gap between the Arab man, (the 'average Mo,' if you will), and the Arab myth of manhood is bound to breed feelings of inadequacy, because the chasm between fantasy and reality is a yawning one.

In my view, this kind of mythologising of the past is not a sign of the patriarchy's enduring strength but is actually a manifestation of its weakness and vulnerability. This gap between ideal and reality carries echoes of England in the 19th and the first half of the 20th century. In his book *The English*, Jeremy Paxman writes that British men were "uneasily aware of the injustice of denying women a full role in society". As if commenting on *Bab al-Hara*, he notes that, "The stronger the challenge [to the male order], the more vociferous the evangelism about how the family was the cornerstone of the safe and ordered society."[21]

With notable and striking exceptions, across much of the Arab and Muslim world, women have gained, like their sisters in the West, considerably more rights and power than their mothers and grandmothers. Whereas previously women were hardly seen and could barely be heard in the public sphere, they are now muscularly making their presence felt in almost every walk of life, from the professional to the political, which traditionalist men have found to be emasculating and threatening. This was epitomised in the Arab uprisings and revolutions, where female activists could not and would not be cowed by the intimidation and violence of the state nor that of Islamist groups, enduring not only tear gas and bullets, like their male comrades, but also sexual assault and even rape. Some, like the Kurdish Peshmerga women's brigade, which attracts ethnic Kurdish women even from Europe,[22] have even taken up arms against perhaps the most regressive and repressive form of patriarchy in the world today: ISIS. Reportedly, some do so to escape abusive relationships[23] in a society where, despite progress, female genital mutilation, honour crimes and domestic violence remain quite widespread.[24]

Despite the hype in the media about the brave female fighters of the Peshmerga, there is nothing new about Muslim women taking up arms against injustice, neither in the Kurdish context nor further afield. Algerian and Palestinian women have done so, for instance. But patriarchy has a very short memory when it comes to women's sacrifices and would much rather forget and airbrush them out, in case women have the audacity to claim a reward, as occurred during the 2011 revolution in Egypt. "The attitude towards women has not been impacted by the historic victory," Marwa Rakha, an Egyptian author, broadcaster and blogger told me a year after the revolution. "Men chanted slogans against them like, 'Men want to topple feminists' and 'Since when did women have a voice?' They [i.e. women]were asked to go home and obey God. They were let down by the average Egyptian man and woman alike."

In addition to the ire targeted at women, men who step out of their designated roles are also targeted – not to mention mocked mercilessly. In contrast to the idolised 'real men' of the past in *Bab al-Hara*, another hit Ramadan series distorted the contemporary reality by depicting the modern man as weak, indecisive and dominated by the women in his life. Yehia el-Fakharani, one of Egypt's most accomplished actors, abandoned his normal roles of the sophisticated lawyer, MP or professor, to play that of a 60-year-old mummy's boy in *Yetraba fi Ezzo* (*May He Be Raised in his Good Fortune* 2007). In the series (for which he received one of the largest payouts ever for a Ramadan drama), his character, Hamada Ezzo, is completely dependent on his mother for direction in every aspect of his life.[25] "This kind of negative character is one of the causes of our falling behind the technologically advanced nations… We see his type frequently in our midst as Egyptians and Arabs," the London-based Arabic daily, *al-Hayat*, quoted el-Fakharani as saying. The actor went on to express his belief that the coming generation had to be harder working and more conscientious to keep up with the times and not depend on past glories.[26] While it is hard to fault this sentiment, the choice of a man living under his mother's thumb as a parable for the times is telling. *Yetraba fi Ezzo* is an odd way to inspire the young generation. If that were truly the writer's aim, why not, instead of fixating on a nearly retired man's subservient relationship with his mother, challenge the rigid and stifling pecking order that keeps the young from reinventing society or the prejudices that keep the female half of the population from fulfilling their full potential?

After all, in real life, Yehia el-Fakhrani is quite an admirable picture of the modern man, a middle-aged sexual', which makes his pandering to this warped view all the more confounding. He is gentle, caring, considerate and tolerant, while the women in his life are intelligent and successful. His wife, for instance, wrote a critically acclaimed TV drama chronicling the reign of King Farouq.

As long as conservative circles continue successfully to control popular public perceptions, equating female emancipation with male emasculation and modern men as unauthentic and weak, the quest for true gender equality will stall. Although Arab TV dramas carried examples of modern, progressive men, particularly in the 1960s and 1970s, these tended to be quite westernised (in the days when secularism and westernisation had not yet become dirty words), and hence rather alien to your average Arab man on the street. Film has been a far better progressive medium, particularly on the more experimental edges, but this does not reach the same kind of mass audience as *musalsalat*, particularly the Ramadan variety, especially as traditionally more liberal Egyptian and Syrian productions try to cater to the wealthy (and conservative) Gulf markets.

Some exceptional *musalsalat* manage to straddle the line between cultural 'authenticity' and modernity. One example is the long-running *Youmiyat Wanis* (Wanis's Diary), which ran for eight seasons between 1994 and 2013. It presented a model of the modern Egyptian family that won wide admiration, although Salafists condemned it for what they called its "populist secularism," because no mention is ever made of God, the Quran or the pillars of Islam.[27] In it, the father, Wanis, is not the be-all and end-all of the family, but everyone has, by Egyptian TV standards, a voice, from his working wife to his children, both boys and girls, and everyone makes mistakes, including the father and mother.[28] The series had such a cult following that many younger Egyptians knew its star much better as 'Baba Wanis' than Mohamed Sobhy.

Where Arab *musalsalat* have failed, Turkish soaps, which have featured taboo topics such as gender relations, drinking, premarital sex and even rape, have taken up the slack when it comes to *homo egalitus*. One example is the Turkish daily soap opera *Noor* in which the handsome, sensitive Mohannad is not only romantic but is also supportive of his independent-minded and empowered wife, Noor. Originally titled *Gümüş,* the melodrama was a flop in its native Turkey but became one of the largest hits ever in the Arab world, not to mention Greece and the Balkans. This reportedly left traditional Arab husbands in a pickle, as their wives demanded they act (and even look) more like their screen idol, Mohannad. "Men feel threatened. It is the first time [Saudi] women have a role model for male beauty and passion and can compare him with their husbands," Fawzaya Abu Khalid, a Riyadh-based writer and women's activist, was quoted as saying.[29]

The not-so-new Muslim man

One vital and often overlooked aspect of this struggle to empower men to be different, which I have written about on numerous occasions, is the challenging and redefining of traditional rigid stereotypes of manhood and masculinity, which turn women's rights into a zero sum, binary game in which what women gain, men lose. In fact, efforts to forge the 'new Muslim woman' have partly been hampered by the failure to imagine and empower her complement, the 'new Muslim man'. While independence-seeking Muslim women often have clear and positive role models to aspire to in their quest for emancipation, the men in their lives are often left swimming against the current of popular perception.

The trouble with prevalent stereotypes, in the West and in Muslim societies, about what a Muslim man is, or should be, is that many Muslim men fail to recognise themselves in them. This has been a regular topic of frustration and bewilderment for my wife too. Although her Belgian family did not succumb to the popular image of the misogynistic Muslim man and welcomed me with warmth into their fold, not everyone is so enlightened, with no shortage of people who feel quite entitled to ask all sorts of bizarre questions about our relationship over the years. The fixation television has with featuring and interviewing highly conservative Muslim men has caused Katleen to express outrage. A documentary we once watched about Belgian women who had married Muslim men, for instance, did not include a single secular couple. "They are

85

not the only men who exist. Why can't they bring on more people like you or our friends?" Katleen asked. This has two unfortunate side effects. Firstly, it skews and warps the West's view of Muslim men, depriving mainstream Westerners of knowledge of the sheer diversity of Muslim men out there. Secondly, it robs Arab and Muslim men, especially those who resist female emancipation not out of any abstract objection to gender equality but out of peer pressure and fear of ridicule, of examples and role models.

On a personal level, I believe whole-heartedly in gender equality and practise it to the best of my ability. This is not because I am westernised but is directly related to my upbringing by an extremely strong woman, my egalitarian-minded mother. From as far back as I can remember, she raised her boys to regard women with respect and as equals, both in words and in deeds. Unlike in traditional households, where the daughters often play the role of servants to the father and sons, waiting on them hand and foot, mum divided the housework equitably between her offspring – everyone was responsible for maintaining their own space and communal tasks were split up between the members of the family.

In addition to my mother and sister, I have also been fortunate enough to have been surrounded throughout my life by strong, smart, capable women, which, from an early age, shattered the myth that women are somehow inferior or less able than men. My wife, for instance, has dedicated most of her career to NGO work, specialising for many years in combating the spread of landmines and cluster bombs and helping survivors, which has taken her to numerous conflict zones around the world. Today, she is one of the youngest senior staff members at the UN agency where she works and spent a number of years working in male-dominated, Islamist-controlled Gaza, where she stayed put during the seven-week war in 2014, and where she won the respect of even ultra-conservative men with whom she came into contact.

And I am no anomaly. Although the proportion of men who believe in and live gender equality in the Muslim world is perhaps smaller than in the West, we are hardly an insignificant minority. Women's liberation and empowerment was a central plank of secular liberation and post-colonial movements across the Muslim world, including pan-Arabists, communists and secular liberals, at least in words, if not often enough in deeds. For instance, the Marxist-Leninist Popular Front for the Liberation of Palestine (PFLP) saw the empowerment of women as a crucial prerequisite for national salvation and justice, though its late leader, George Habash, admitted that he and his comrades had not done enough to bring this about.[30]

Many secular men raised before the spread of Islamist conservatism actually take gender equality for granted, at least in principle. And there are some who implement it almost religiously. "I have two children, a boy and a girl, whom I treated equally, in terms of upbringing, pocket money, responsibilities, duties, schooling and self-respect," says Said El-Said, a retired Palestinian professional who has been based in Switzerland for some four decades. "I talked to both of them about sexual responsibility and gave each a box of condoms when I felt the time was right." Some are bound to attribute El-Said's attitudes to his long sojourn in Europe, but he insists that nothing could be further from the truth. "Thanks to my parents, specifically my father… I never accepted how women were treated in the Middle East," he explains.

And others of his generation, especially those raised in leftist households, have similar recollections. Suad Amiry, the prominent Palestinian architect-turned-author, recalled how her father treated all her siblings equally to the extent that he bucked even the most deep-rooted conventions. "He called himself Abu Arwa,[31] so many people didn't think we had a brother called Ayman," Amiry told me during a long coach journey through Wadi el-Nar, one of the most dangerous roads in the West Bank. "He named himself after his eldest daughter and not after the boy."

The iconic Kurdish fighter, Hero Ibrahim Ahmad, one of the first to join the Peshmerga, has similar recollections. "When I was born, my father threw a party in my honour. That was unheard of in my day," she said in an interview, noting that he "believed in the equality of women and men". True to his convictions, Ahmad's father, who was secretary-general of the Kurdish Democratic Party, took his wife and kids into the mountains with him from where he engaged in combat with the central authorities in Baghdad.[32]

With the surge in the popularity of Islamism in recent decades, men like this began to die out, at least in the public sphere, joined the Islamists, or went underground, keeping their enlightened convictions closer to their chests. However, in countries like Tunisia and Egypt, which underwent revolutions for equality, a new, assertive generation of progressive men is making a comeback, with the number of men who openly and publicly identify with the feminist cause and advocate for gender equality exploding.

Take David Esam, who was raised in a traditional household in the city of al-Minya, which lies in Middle Egypt, the entry point to ultra-conservative Upper Egypt. Although Christian, his and his family's views on women differed little to those of their Muslim neighbours or indeed, to certain Bible Belt Christians in the West. With the exception of how women dress, Christians and Muslims in Egypt differ little in their attitudes towards gender and gender roles, placing a similar emphasis on female chastity and virginity, with the social restrictions that accompany them. Sadly, Female Genital Mutilation is a common practice amongst Copts,[33] as it is amongst Muslims. One can find Christian men in Egypt and other Arab countries whose position on women would make a salafi sheikh nod in pride.

"At first, I didn't think that women had rights. I just viewed them as complements to a man's life," Esam confessed to me. A number of factors combined to set in motion a major shift in Esam's attitudes. One, was his sister, specifically, a quarrel they had over the restrictions his mother imposed on her freedom.[34] Another factor was the books he started reading, including the writings of Egypt's foremost living feminist Nawal al-Saadawi. But perhaps the most critical factor has been the friendships he has made since the Egyptian revolution, which triggered an earthquake in Esam's consciousness, providing him with new horizons and role models. "Encountering young women and men interested in the women's cause made me more self-aware and critical of my surroundings," observes Esam, noting that he is now active in promoting social and legal rights for women and volunteers in the movement combatting sexual harassment.

Male feminist pigs

Like many other men who support and stand in solidarity with women in their quest for equality and emancipation, I regard myself as a feminist, a description which I discovered was a hot potato to use as a man, when I waded into the debate on the subject some years ago,[35] opening me up to attacks by misogynists and some radical feminists.[36]

In fact, in a Muslim context, where too many laws and popular opinions are stacked against gender equality and many women defend the patriarchy, women's rights activists need all the male support (but obviously not leadership) they can find. Besides, building additional gender lines, rather than crossing them, can create unnecessary polarisation and animosity. "We cannot have a situation where only women struggle for women's equal rights, while men fight for men's rights," cautions Jamal Chadi, a prominent human rights activist in Morocco and the Arab world.[37] But regardless of the label used, Muslim men can play and have played important supporting roles in the struggle for gender equality, ever since the earliest days of the struggle. One fun and poignant example of this was the Iranian #meninhijab campaign which I mentioned in the previous chapter.

Male involvement was particularly central in medieval Islamic societies, where women tended to have a minor public profile and to hold few direct positions of official power. One early Islamic advocate for female emancipation was the 12th-century Andalusian polymath Ibn Rushd (known in Europe as Averroes). "The competence of women is unknown... since they are only taken for procreation and hence are placed at the service of their husbands," the enlightened philosopher railed against the male order that prevailed in the society of his time. "Since women in these cities are not prepared with respect to any of the human virtues, they frequently resemble plants."[38] Despite his prudishness about sex, Ibn Rushd believed men and women to be essentially equals and that women had the potential to excel in all the top fields of the time, as stateswomen, philosophers and even warriors. In his conception of a utopian Ideal City, which is a novel re-dreaming of Plato's Republic, Ibn Rushd declared that "the women in this city will practise the same activities as the men", including in wars and combat.[39]

"Ibn Rushd's enlightened ideas led to his progressive thoughts towards women, which made him revolutionary," wrote Nadia Harhash for the Ibn Rushd Fund.[40] But, sadly, Ibn Rushd's revolutionary notions about gender came at the wrong moment, at a time when Islamic Andalusia's "golden age" of tolerance and rationalism was coming to an end to be replaced by the religious puritanism, fundamentalism and literalism of the Almohads, who set fire to Ibn Rushd's works.

Even today, when Muslim women are in a much better position to speak for themselves and fight their own corner, men can be in a better position to explain to other men why gender equality is the principled thing to do and why it is important not just to women but also to men – it is not a win-lose game, but a win-win proposition. "We often educate women on their rights, but in the end these women are surrounded by men: fathers, sons, and husbands who don't support women in obtaining their rights," explains Sherif Gamal of the Centre for Egyptian Women's Legal Assistance. "So, it is important to get through to the men in order for them to understand that women must have their rights too. We try to engage in a dialogue with these men."[41]

Even some of the most conservative quarters of the Arab and Muslim world are experiencing their own version of a male awakening, albeit more cautiously and from a lower starting point. It is perhaps unsurprising in light of the severe restrictions on Saudi women, such as the repressive guardianship system,[42] that one of Saudi Arabia's most prominent advocates of women's rights is actually a man. In what was a watershed case for women's rights in the kingdom,[43] lawyer and human rights activist Waleed Abulkhair successfully secured the release of Samar Badawi, who had been imprisoned for disobeying her abusive father. Contrary to popular opinion and the 'reformist' image the Saudi royal family attempts to project abroad, Abulkhair holds the regime responsible for the poor status of women. "The political establishment is to blame for all these restrictions, but it blames society which it describes as 'unreformable,'" Abulkhair told me in 2014, shortly before his imprisonment. "But in reality, the establishment wants society to remain conservative and for men to continue to dominate women, thereby neutralising half of society, while making the other half easier to control." For this reason, Abulkhair sees women's rights as intimately, and holistically, connected to the wider struggle for human rights. "Everyone here is repressed and we don't want an equality of repression," he claims. "In my view, the Saudi woman's problem is not with men but with the system."

Abulkhair is convinced that if the Wahhabi establishment would take a neutral stance towards personal rights and leave people to decide for themselves, then women's rights would advance by leaps and bounds in Saudi Arabia, especially in the west of the country. "Where I live, in Hijaz, the majority believes in respecting women and upholding their rights, and this was more apparent before the spread of Wahhabism at the hands of the authorities."

Unsurprisingly, Abulkhair's human rights activism and advocacy work has not endeared him to conservatives nor the authorities and he has been rotting in jail since 2014 after a counter-terrorism court sentenced him to 15 years.[44]

Men about the house

Like women who challenge the patriarchal status quo, men who rock the male order too much face an uphill struggle. "There are many men in the gender rights movement in Egypt who want to see gender equality realised, and do it in the face of challenges, such as ridicule from their 'fellow man'," writes Ahmed Kadry, a lecturer in gender studies.[45]

Resistance does not only come from men but also from traditionalist women. David Esam's own experience reflects the challenge of dealing with the role of women as gatekeepers of the patriarchy. "My mother is happy with the love, care and attention in my relationship with my sister," he explains. "But she does not approve of some of my positions encouraging my sister to pursue her interests in work, travel and friendships at university."

But courageous Muslim men are not only supporting the struggle for women's rights, they are waging their own battle to redefine the restrictive, binary notions of masculinity which blight their lives. This discreet, grassroots revolution is not being televised nor capturing headlines but it is significant nonetheless. "Many men do not want to be perceived as domineering patriarchs; they do not view fatherhood as the be-all and end-all of masculinity; they value conjugal intimacy and privacy, sometimes at the expense of larger familial commitments; and they often adore their wives as friends and lovers," observes Marcia Claire Inhorn, a medical anthropologist who carried out a rare and extensive survey into Middle Eastern masculinity.[46]

Inhorn's study focuses on the shifting attitudes of Middle Eastern men towards male infertility, once an enormous taboo and cause of shame because it undermined the traditional notions of male potency, virility and vigour. Traditionally, infertility was a subject rarely broached, except in conspiratorial whispers and gossip. Over the years, I have seen Egyptian films and TV dramas which deal with the topic but usually by employing extreme melodrama, with infertility more often than not blamed on the woman, wrecking marriages and, when it struck men, as a cause of such shame that it could drive the protagonist out of his mind. The men featured in Inhorn's book paint a radically different picture. While experiencing the inevitable disappointment that they may never have children, they tend to resist the culture of shame associated with their condition, with many building happy and loving marriages, with the affection that may have gone to a child directed towards the spouse instead. Inhorn even posits that, contrary to mainstream Arab notions, that childlessness actually made some marriages happier.

Indeed, although neither of us was infertile, my own wife and I delayed having children for quite a number of years, because we were not psychologically ready, were not sure we wanted to contribute to the population explosion, and had plenty of other things we still wanted to do with our lives. This, I feel, has made our relationship deeper and stronger.

Although many Egyptian women, like Muslim women in numerous other countries, have made significant inroads into the public domain, including the professions, academia and government, one final bastion of the traditional patriarchy is the family and the home. A woman may be the boss at work, managing an entire department or ministry, but at home her husband is still widely regarded as the lord of his castle. But even this last stronghold is experiencing a huge onslaught by anti-patriarchal forces. This is partly a result of career women discovering that they have been dealt a rough hand, working long hours at the office, only to return home to their second job. It is also a product of shifting attitudes to masculinity, with more and more men rejecting the notion that housework is somehow beneath them or that raising children is a woman's mission. Even some high-flying Arab execs are giving up workaholism for their kids. This was dramatically demonstrated by Egyptian-American businessman Mohamed El-Erian, who quit his job managing a trillion-dollar investment fund when his disappointed daughter wrote out a list of all the milestones he had missed in her childhood. "I now alternate with my wife in waking up our daughter every morning, preparing her breakfast and driving her to school," he was quoted as saying. "I'm also around much more often to pick her up after school and take her to activities."[47]

In my own family, things have gone further. The demands of Katleen's work has led to a situation of relative role reversal. Although we started out with my earning a fair bit more than my wife, ever since I went completely freelance, with the uncertainty and fluctuations in fortune that involves, the pendulum has swung the other way and now Katleen has become the main breadwinner by a large margin. In terms of principle, this does not trouble me, though it took some adjusting, since I have been accustomed to being entirely self-sufficient in terms of earnings, even supporting my mother and siblings for a number of years after my parents divorced. The comparative flexibility of my work and the fact that until recently she spent the week in Gaza means that I have become the primary carer for our son – an arrangement supported by my late mother as it embodied the values she had raised us on.

Our current arrangement is still very much a minority situation in Europe and is extremely rare in the Arab and Muslim world. That said, it is becoming more common. When I lived in Jerusalem, a Tunisian friend and neighbour, Habib, also took care of his children while his wife brought home the bacon (or beef, seeing as he was a Muslim). Unlike me, Habib had given up his profession, as a violin maker, to follow his wife around the world. In addition to his domestic duties, he occupied his time in running the parents' association at the school his kids and my son went to and playing the violin with a local orchestra (he also gave my son violin lessons at school). Belying his secular Tunisian upbringing and experience, Habib believed Islam was in need of a radical overhaul to make it relevant and appropriate to 21st-century living, from the number of times a Muslim should be required to pray, to gender roles and the need to separate faith from public life.

Before that, during my sojourn in Switzerland, an Egyptian friend, Omar, had also decided to become a stay-at-home dad, albeit temporarily. After a period of forced separation from his wife who was working in Geneva, he decided to throw tradition to the wind and quit his job in Cairo to become a trailing spouse. In so doing, Omar found himself having to swim against the tide of cultural convention. "My family in general felt that it was important that the man take the lead and not vice versa," he told me. "My friends shared similar views." Although he was still the same man, Omar sensed that the people around him started viewing him differently. "What was interesting to see was the behavioural differences that I felt from some of my family (both negative and positive) as well as friends when they realised that I was out of a job and staying at home," he recounted.

"Being a stay-at-home dad was a first for me," he admits. "I enjoyed aspects of it like learning how to cook, reading more, reflecting more on life, thinking of doing my own business, staying with my kid more."

Although Omar ended up finding a job in Geneva, his time as a home-carer instilled in him a greater respect for the traditional role ascribed to women, and he still shares in the child-rearing and housework. "It made me appreciate the responsibilities that go with staying at home and that, to a great extent, is as equal if not more demanding than going to work," he maintained.

The examples of Muslim men who break the stereotypical mould of Islamic masculinity as conceived in the West and in Muslim countries require greater mainstream attention. In Europe and America, this would help counter the increasingly prevalent hostility towards Muslims perpetuated by toxic typecasting and malicious myth-making. In Muslim societies, it would help empower men dissatisfied with traditional ideas of manhood to pursue alternative lifestyles inspired by positive role models who redefine masculinity in a more flexible and egalitarian fashion.

CHAPTER FOUR

Sexy Islam

To say that Islam lacks sex appeal in the contemporary West would be an understatement of massive proportions. In the mainstream Western imagination, Islam is the unsexiest religion known to humanity. Its relationship with sex is the stuff of sweat-inducing nightmares, rather than wet dreams. Conservative pundits and media never tire of telling us about Islam's sexual deprivation, sexual repression coupled with licentiousness, perversion and rape culture.

The political consequences of Islam's twisted relationship with sex are dire. Muslims do not get involved with radical Islamism and engage in terrorism because they have a political axe to grind or because they have political grievances against domestic despots or Western hegemony. No, they do it because they are sexually repressed. This was poetically highlighted, in 2009, by a sexually frustrated wannabe terrorist, a young Nigerian Muslim who had concealed a bomb in his underpants. "The bomb wasn't the only thing burning in his pants," the *New York Post* informed its readers. "Internet postings from accused knicker-bomber Umar Farouk Abdulmutallab reveal him to be a sex-starved, lonely, depressed man who felt shame over his carnal urges."[1]

More sinisterly still, Muslim men are overcome with an uncontrollable, innate urge to rape, even when they are taught otherwise. "They come to countries, they rape women. They are having a very difficult time learning not to rape women – even if they're infidel whores and have short skirts," Ann Coulter, the first lady of ultra-conservative punditry, told *Fox News*,[2] despite her earlier claim that university students who say they have been raped are just "girls trying to get attention," because to be raped a woman has, in Coulter's system of justice, to be "hit on the head with a brick".[3] This is terribly confusing. Was Coulter implying that Muslim men in Europe, in addition to their irrepressible compulsion to rape were also compulsive bearers of bricks, which they must carry on their person at all times so as to be able to carry out their dastardly deeds? Or do rape and misogyny only exist... when they are committed by Muslims, non-whites and, of course, Democrats?

When it comes to sex and atrocity, there is a deeper pathology at play in the Muslim psyche. Islamic extremists do not hate the West because of what it has done to their Muslim brethren, but, in a form of pseudo-Freudianism, because of their twisted relationship with their mothers and their suppressed sexual desires towards their sisters in Islam. "In this dynamic of sexual repression and misogyny, love is reduced to violent domination which becomes directly intertwined with terrorism against societies that allow women freedom, especially sexual freedom," writes Jamie Glazov, the managing editor of the neo-conservative *FrontPage* magazine.[4] To be clear, the terrorists hate us not because of our bombs but because of our sex bombs.

Glazov goes on to reveal his remarkable mind-reading skills. Muslim men, it appears, have a one-track mind, but, unlike men elsewhere in the world, it does not lead where you might suspect it would. "The man must constantly keep

Allah in his thoughts during intercourse. At the moment of ejaculation, when the union of the lovers reaches its full potential, the male is supposed to pronounce praise to Allah," he informs us.[5] And if the naive observer finds a parallel between a Muslim exclaiming "Allahu Akbar" during intercourse with a Christian shrieking "Oh God" during orgasm, then they really have been fooled by leftist propaganda. There is no moral equivalence between our exclamations and theirs.

Sexual repression and its discontents

There is little doubt that sexual repression and its attendant deprivation and frustrations, not to mention patriarchal oppression, are serious issues in many Muslim societies, particularly amongst conservatives and traditionalists. This is accentuated by the fact that millions of Muslims are getting married later and later in life, as they spend longer in education, work on building a career first or struggle to cope with the rising material requirements of marriage in a time of growing austerity. This has serious consequences for the individual and society, but not in the way portrayed by anti-Muslim bigots, who exploit sex, as they exploit gender relations, to advance their political agenda, not to construct a deep understanding of the issues at stake but to depict Islam as a uniquely benighted religion.

For instance, the notion that Muslims think of God while copulating is just bizarre. I know the god of monotheism is supposed to be omnipresent but Muslims tend to keep him out of their bedrooms, as thinking about God, scripture and religious duty while in the throes of passion is bound to be a turn-off and a damper to the believer's ardour in bed. Another thing which mystifies and miffs me is the contention that Muslims hate sex because they find it shameful.

Obviously, the lovers on the quieter stretch of beach near where I live in Tunis – an almost entirely Muslim city – didn't get the memo. Against the backdrop of the waves on the shoreline, oblivious to the other couples dotted around them and the occasional angler, they sit in various degrees of intimate embrace, with some kissers seemingly ready to 'get a room', as the expression goes, if a room were available to consummate their young love. Rather than running away from intimacy, for many young, unmarried Muslim lovers, finding a place to be alone and to get intimate is a monumental challenge, particularly in overcrowded urban areas.

In heaving Cairo for instance, where the only private space many people own is inside their own heads, every possible available intimate or romantic space is occupied. At night, along the quieter stretches of the Nile corniche, couples sit embracing on the wall, at discreet intervals, while they look out over the river, with its sometimes infernal cacophony. Those who are fortunate enough to own a car head off to one of the quieter neighbourhoods where they park in dark side streets or drive out to the edge of the desert where they can have even more privacy. But couples who seek private space in the public domain run the risk of being questioned or arrested by the Vice Police. One of the reasons going all the way tends to occur more among the upper classes is not because poorer people are necessarily more pious but is often simply a question of space. Wealthier youth can afford to rent a place, their families may own an empty property somewhere, or they can sneak their lovers into their large homes while their parents are out.

I recall the rush of adrenaline when kissing a girlfriend by the river, in a darkened backstreet, in a girlfriend's car, or in the countryside surrounding Cairo, not just due to the excitement of intimacy but also due to the risk of getting caught.

One consequence of society's repression of sexual expression is that, paradoxically, it transforms sex into an obsession. The repressed sexual energy surging through public spaces, such as markets, malls and educational campuses is perceptible. Young friends talk and fantasise about the opposite sex (and, for a minority, their own gender) with far greater passion than their counterparts in more sexually liberated societies. This surprised me when I returned to Egypt from England as a teenager. My parents had led me to believe that Egyptian youth were pious and lived traditional Muslim lifestyles. What I found was considerably different. Boys and girls showed very un-Islamic levels of interest in each other: they regularly went out together, albeit often under the safe cover of a large group; and some dated and more. This contrast between a non-existent moral utopia and reality helped trigger my own incipient sexual liberation.

In England, I had reached the age where girls stopped being girls and became women in my eyes. This caused me no small measure of moral confusion, with the voice of my conscience (which I now understand was not the voice of God but rather that of my mother) warning me to beware. Although I couldn't comprehend why something that felt so good could be so bad, I tried to keep my urges under control. Towards the end of my time in London, I had almost overcome my moral reservations about dating girls, which may partly explain why my dad suddenly decided it was time for us to move back to Egypt – though I suspect such pre-emptive concerns probably related more to my younger sister than to me. Given my father's authoritarian tendencies, I suspect England's culture of youth independence worried him, as it does other Arab and

Muslim parents in the diaspora, more than our potential sexual liberation. But in both cases, his calculations were in vain. Being forced to move to Egypt at such a volatile, sensitive age unleashed my till-then largely latent rebellious tendencies. Not only did I revolt against the patriarchal authority of my father, I also overcame many of my moral qualms about girls and had my first sexual experience, with an English girl in Cairo, months after touching down in my native city.

Double lives

There comes a time everywhere when budding adults start dreaming of boy meets girl. However, in most European countries, boy can easily meet girl and, if they fancy each other, they can decide to date and move together through the various euphemistic bases with relative ease. As a young man, I sometimes wished that I had not moved back to Egypt and was still living in the UK, where gender relations are more honest, straightforward and open. In Egypt, the barriers are much higher. "Young people might look young but they were born defeated, restricted, and gagged," contends Marwa Rakha, a prominent Egyptian expert on relationships and author of *Poison Tree*, a novel about the toxic sexual environment into which young Muslim women, as well as men, are too often thrust.[6] "They will revolt in secrecy, adding a new number each second to the hypocritical population."

While paying lip service to the conservative sexual values of society, many young people will seek to escape them in private, away from the prying eyes of their families and communities. But maintaining such double lives requires them to mislead or lie to their parents about where they are going, what they are doing there and who they are spending their time with, which can result in serious cognitive dissonances for the young minds involved. In such a context, honesty between men and women is often not appreciated. In order to deal with society's double-standards by leading duplicitous lives, many young people caught in this predicament weave an elaborate web of fiction to their families and half-truths to their lovers. This, along with the difficulty of the intergalactic leap required to reach Venus or Mars, to borrow a metaphor, means they expend an immense amount of time and energy on dreaming of, building or maintaining their illicit love lives. This conflicts with the popular myth that keeping young women and men apart and away from the path of temptation, as well as making them fearful of "sinful" behaviour, will somehow stop them from dwelling on and pursuing their sexual urges. In fact, friends spend an inordinate amount of time thinking and talking about the opposite sex with their peers and inner circle, and strategising about what to do with their aching hearts or pulsating hormones. This forces many young people to find proxies for their affections. These include intense levels of flirtation in places where both genders meet, virtual dates and even virtual sex on phones or via social media. Interestingly, weddings are also famed venues to pick up, either a date or a prospective spouse, depending on one's inclination, at least that is the case in Muslim communities where the party is not gender segregated. Outside of discos, weddings in Egypt are one of the few places where public displays of eroticism between members of the opposite sex are tolerated, with even older aunties and uncles smiling on as young men and women swivel their hips, shake their shoulders and gyrate their sweating bodies perilously close to each other, often separated only by the width of a fluttering hair.

This frustration even makes it into popular music and helps explain the lasting appeal of certain themes in Arabic love songs: unrequited emotions; endless sleepless nights; flirtation and innuendo; the torment of being kept apart; the intoxication of infatuation; the irresistible appeal of dreamy eyes; silken hair and razor-sharp eyelashes that cut to the very quick of the soul. Even the decorous Egyptian diva, the legendary Umm Kulthoum, was not above swooning about lovers drunk on their emotions, while the more youthful Abdel-Halim Hafez would lament the inferno of love and how pain had caused him to repent of love... until the next time. One of Abdel-Halim's songs, *Sawah* (*Wanderer*)[7] poetically expresses the frustrations caused by the enforced separation caused by gender segregation. In the song, Abdel-Halim (who was known popularly as the "Dark Nightingale"), likens a lover to a wanderer of the world or a nomad in the wilderness whose path never crosses that of his lover. Towards the end, he, like the famous mad lover of classical Arabic literature, Majnun Laila,[8] starts conversing with the moon, becoming literally a lunatic, asking the luminous rock to light his path to his lover and imploring the moon to tell his lover what it has witnessed of his torments from its perch in the night sky.

At the lighter, and more modern, end of the musical spectrum, pop songs talk about the meandering grace of a lover's walk, chance encounters, eyes meeting across crowded spaces and some go as far as sexual innuendo but, rarely, do songs explicitly talk about sex. That is the preserve of films, which often show kissing, embracing and some suggestive, but not explicit, bedroom and shower scenes. Literature tends to enjoy the greatest freedom of sexual expression, but even here authors can fall foul of the censor or of public indignation. This is precisely what happened to Egyptian novelist Ahmed

Naji, when an excerpt of his novel was published in a local literary magazine. A reader filed a lawsuit that the explicit sexual content of the chapter which he found offensive had caused him heart palpitations and psychological damage. Rather than dismiss this spurious case, the judge sentenced Nagi to two years for "violating public modesty" in a verdict which goes against both the letter and spirit of the constitution.[9]

Across the Arab world, conservatives and older people like to complain about the perceived over-sexualisation of art and pop music, with Lebanese performers often bearing the brunt of this outrage. A leading example of this is Haifa Wehbe, the "Arab Kim Kardashian" (though Wehbe's fans would say it's the other way around). The Lebanese sex goddess's skimpy dresses[10] and suggestive music videos, including one in which she breathes in an astronaut from space while being touched up by male dancers with rippling muscles,[11] have provoked outrage mixed with awe and admiration for years. Critics pine back to a time of supposedly greater decorum in music, censoring from their minds the fact that skimpily dressed performers and dancers have been a staple of Arabic music and film ever since motion pictures were invented. The uncrowned queen of seduction that was streetwise and native, known as 'baladi' in Egyptian colloquial, was perhaps the innovative Egyptian dancing legend Tahiya Carioca (1915-1999), whom was described by the late Edward Said as "the finest belly-dancer ever" who was also a versatile actress who defied typecasting and "a political militant [who was] the remarkable symbol of a national culture".[12]

As I explored in the chapter on Muslim women, belly-dancers are at once adored, revered, respected, despised and feared. This reverence is reflected in the colloquial name accorded to the head belly-dancer, alema, which, as explained earlier, derives from the Arabic word for female teacher. Like the Japanese *geisha* (though perhaps with less constraint and subtlety than the understated and restrained Japanese culture), the Egyptian *alema*'s art utilises the promise of sex, sensuality rather than sexuality, to tantalise male audiences, and often mixed ones too. Some *alema*s double as prostitutes, not just dancers. However, unlike street prostitutes, the way they commodified sex was subtle and indirect. This was certainly the case in the bygone heyday of the *alema*. These artistic women were reminiscent of the elite *hetairai* of ancient Greece, and often become long-term sexual, romantic and even intellectual companions of wealthier men, entertaining them as much with their lively, uninhibited and oft-cultured conversation as with their sexual prowess. Traditionally, some *alema*s also ran brothels alongside their dancing operations, in the days when prostitution was still legal in Egypt. Although many Egyptians are convinced that it was the British who legalised prostitution in Egypt, it was actually legal long before the British arrived and was a handsome source of revenue for Muhammad Ali, a former Ottoman solider of Albanian descent who ruled Egypt in the first half of the 19th century. However, he discovered that prostitution was affecting the health and discipline of his newly formed and highly coercive conscript army, which prompted him to ban the trade from Cairo and from around military camps, as Egyptian historian Khaled Fahmy demonstrates, forcing many *alema*s to relocate to the provinces.[13] The Egyptian Nobel laureate Naguib Mahfouz was skilled at bringing the traditional prototype of the *alema* and the men she captivated to vivid life, such as in his famous Cairo trilogy.[14] In it, Mahfouz's archetype of the tyrannical family patriarch, known to his family as Si Sayyid, lived the dual and hypocritical life of stone-faced disciplinarian with his obedient wife and kids at home and soft and pliable lover-boy at an *alema*'s brothel at night.

Although progressive on social issues and generally more open-minded towards women than previous generations of Arab writers and intellectuals, Mahfouz was unable to shake off the traditionalist influence on his view of women. "Woman in the literary works of Naguib Mahfouz… remains a 'woman'," wrote the outspoken Egyptian feminist Nawal Al Saadawi. "Throughout, she is fundamentally the same since her honour does not go further than an intact hymen and a chaste sexual life."[15] And Mahfouz reflects a broader attitude; dancers, *alemas* and actresses are granted a greater licence to defy social conventions regarding dealings with the opposite sex and the open expression of sensuality and even sexuality, (though they are judged as being morally inferior for it), while women who abide by public displays of modesty and chastity are "*banat nas*" ("daughters of [decent] people").

When boy meets girl

For the many 'respectable' women, and the men who want to get involved with them, interactions with the opposite sex can be an ordeal. Navigating the overlap between religion, tradition and varying attitudes to gender relations can be a minefield when boy meets girl. The contrast between this and mainstream Western norms was humorously detailed in the Egyptian parody of the YouTube sensation, *First Kiss*.[16] In the original short film by Tatia Pilieva, what are billed as perfect strangers are paired up and asked to kiss one another. Awkwardness and discomfort ensue, but the newly introduced couples, including homosexual men and women, overcome their inhibitions and kiss. In the Egyptian parody, also called *First Kiss*, the strangers, all apparently heterosexual, also stand around making awkward conversation, trying to get to know each other.[17] At first, the film gives the impression that the newly formed pairs are also going to kiss but it eventually becomes clear that what has been asked of them is to shake hands, which some very religious Muslims refuse to do. While the discomfort and awkwardness is exaggerated for comic effect, it is not a million miles away from the truth of interacting across gender lines for some young people in Egypt.

Sexual frustration and repression is a staple of the Egyptian screen, with treatments ranging from psychological thrillers and socially aware dramas to melodrama and (tragi) comedies.[18] One humorous treatment of the subject was the youth flick *Film Thaqafi* (*Cultural Film*), with the title an Arabic euphemism for porno film. Released in 2000, it features a hapless group of young friends who have managed to get their hands on a blue movie and the comedic action revolves around their frustrations as they try to locate a video player, a TV and a place to watch the porno, with one of the magical ingredients always missing.[19] But the fundamental element that is missing for the frustrated young men in the film is a real-life woman, which explains their visible dismay when they discover that the brother of one of the characters actually has a breathing, sleeping, walking, talking, living girlfriend. Finding a romantic or sexual partner is a common frustration for young people in Egypt and other Muslim countries, even in liberal circles. For example, in Cairo, the attendance at parties and in the city's nightlife is often male-heavy, which is tedious for both genders – women get sick and tired of the seemingly endless male attention and the long line of men trying to hit on them, while the surfeit of men, especially those who are more reserved or do not wish to come across as being overbearing, stand around in frustrated huddles.

The apparent gender imbalance at the more sexually liberated end of the spectrum does not, in my opinion, reflect a fundamental difference in how Muslim men and women view sex and sexual relations, there are women and men located across the entire spectrum of sexual attitudes. However, social attitudes towards men who are sexually active are much more accepting and forgiving than they are towards women – a global phenomenon, but particularly intense in conservative Muslim cultures – and this inevitably has an effect on the number of women willing or able to express their sexual liberation. Even though the theological concept of *zina* (adultery), which in Islam means any extramarital sexual relationship, applies both to men and women,[20] the social reality is very different. Even ultraconservative parents who disapprove of premarital sex will give their sons extra leeway and tolerate their transgressions, while keeping their daughters on a very short leash – a double-standard which has always infuriated me. Many families take this double-standard to extremes, with fathers and even mothers taking pride in their sons' prowess while any suggestion of sexual proclivity on the part of their daughters would be seen as a serious or even unforgivable stain on the family's collective honour. "Across the Arab world, female virginity – defined as an intact hymen – remains what could best be described as a big fucking deal," writes Shereen El Feki in *Sex and the Citadel*.[21]

Many young men also entertain similarly contradictory attitudes, which is not only hypocritical but also self-defeating. Just as it takes two to tango, it also takes two to be sexually free. Over the years, I have encountered too many men who are frustrated by the relative scarcity of women willing to date or sleep with them, while expressing disrespect and contempt for just such women, without realising the fatal contradiction and the breakdown in logic involved. "I would never marry a woman who slept with me," I have heard lads say on countless occasions. The more conservative version is, "I would never marry a woman who dated me or dated another man." When quizzed as to why, the two most typical responses were both highly insulting.

The first reason often given boils down to possessiveness. "A woman's honour is like a matchstick; you can light it only once," is a common opinion I have heard, equating 'honour' with the hymen, as if that flimsy and fragile membrane is more important than a woman's brain, personality or achievements.

Moreover, modern technology has made this outdated and regressive adage obsolete, as the large number of women who undergo surgery to repair or rebuild their hymens attests – surgically restoring the fake 'honour' society links to their genitalia. This kind of surgery has become a fad in many Muslim societies, including in Lebanon and Tunisia. Rather than admitting that sexual liberation is required and necessary for the Muslim woman, many segments of society prefer to repair tattered and outdated traditions with a hypocritical, superficial and cosmetic fix to the body of tradition. This allows some women (at least those who can afford the operation) to satisfy their natural sexual desires, while maintaining the social illusion that they are the virgins their family, community, spouse and in-laws so desire, or pretend to desire. This phenomenon of 're-virgination' has become so common in Tunisia that it prompted Tunisian psychoanalyst Nédra Ben Smail to write an entire study on this social coping mechanism. Despite the liberation of Tunisian women in so many spheres in life, which constitutes a veritable rupture with tradition, for the vast majority of Tunisian women extra-marital sex remains a taboo, Ben Smail notes. This is partly because the weight of cultural identity is placed on women's shoulders. "The attachment to virginity is, today, considered to be an element of Arab identity and a prescription of the Islamic faith," she writes. "In contrast, trivialising virginity amounts to a cultural transgression, to a dissociation from the group."[22] This leads to a situation where many Tunisian women are compelled to maintain a conservative sexual discourse and appearances in public, while experiencing the sexual liberation that should be their right in private and secret.

A cheaper, and equally controversial option is the 'artificial hymen', a cheap Chinese import which was essentially a squishy bag filled with red liquid. Even before the advent of modern surgery and paraphernalia, women, who also have sexual needs and urges, have found ways to stick to the letter of society's virginity codes but not their spirit, by having sex and sexual intimacy in ways that do not involve vaginal penetration.

The other justification given for avoiding women who have had sex before marriage revolves around the hypothesis that a woman who has given herself to you cannot be trusted to be faithful, that she may well give herself to another man once you tie the knot. Rather than the prospect of being betrayed, what this attitude betrays is a severe lack of self-esteem, trust issues and a profound misunderstanding of how human relationships work. Moreover, it raises the question of how many self-respecting women would be willing to defy social convention, take the risk of being alienated from their family or ostracised from their community for a guy who will not respect them and, even if they are madly in love, is unlikely to commit to a long-term relationship? Guys who hold these convictions are often after only sex, but they do not believe a woman should be extended the same privilege of engaging in carnal pleasures simply for pleasure's sake; they want to have their cake and eat it, in other words. For that reason, there are men who express passionate, even undying, love and promise the moon, in order to get a woman into bed with them, while privately regarding her as a 'slut' for having done precisely that.

Moreover, there are some men who refuse to marry a woman they have dated or slept with, who actually do love the partner in question but do not desire a marriage of equals, as love matches are more likely to be. They want the best of both worlds, to love a dynamic, electrifying woman in their youth, and to 'settle down' with a predictable, reliable, obedient wife when they are older. Of course, there are plenty of men who pay lip service to these social conventions, or fail to challenge them, while not actually believing or subscribing to them. These men may profess such beliefs to appease their peers, yet marry their girlfriends after sleeping with them or end up marrying a woman who had prior sexual experiences with other men. Rather than using their own experiences to challenge prevalent stereotypes, they decide that discretion is the better part of valour and keep a diplomatic silence about the woman's sexual past. Luckily, as we will see later in the chapter, there is a growing trend to challenge these fossilised social norms.

Sinless sex

Far from sex in its entirety being regarded as dirty, as alleged by some Western critics of Islam, the question for the majority of Muslims relates to the conditions which cleanse sex of its supposed sinfulness. The most significant battleground regarding sex in Islam is the framework within which it should be performed, i.e. when intercourse counts as *halal* (licit) and when it is to be condemned, or even punished, as *haram* (illicit or prohibited),[23] especially with the emergence of new types of relationships that go against perceived Islamic tradition, even though temporary 'marriages' have been common in numerous Muslim societies over the centuries.

The idea that the only purpose of sex is procreation does not really exist in Islam, which has recognised the recreational aspects of intercourse since the very beginning. Even the most conservative families and scholars do not condemn the sexual act in itself but rail against adultery, while welcoming sex when conducted as an expression of lawful wedlock. Religious scholars who suggest otherwise are quickly cut down to size. This was the case back in 2006 when Rashad Hassan Khalil of Egypt's al-Azhar, probably the most revered religious institution in Sunni Islam, issued a *fatwa* (a religious opinion or edict) that nudity during intercourse rendered a marriage invalid. This sparked widespread outrage, condemnation and ridicule. "Nothing is prohibited during marital sex, except, of course, sodomy," another cleric weighed in, (his views on anal sex, as we will see later, do not in fact reflect a consensus amongst Islamic scholars). To drive the point further, yet another scholar suggested that, "Islam is not embarrassed to talk about sex."[24] As with Donald Trump's assertion that "Islam hates us,"[25] you may wonder how exactly Islam can 'talk' about anything, let alone sex.

Even if Islam can broach this topic, millions of Muslims around the world feel they cannot, with the subject rarely brought up in polite society, which spans the bulk of parents and older family members, elders in society, including the clergy and Islamic scholars, the education system and much of the media, in many countries. Of course, parents in the West also find it difficult to have 'the talk' with their children about the 'birds and the bees' – hence the euphemisms. But when it comes to many Muslims, it is not just a question of awkwardness, it is also a deep-seated taboo. "I'm thankful to my parents for instilling in us the value of respect towards each other. However, I still wish that we were talked to about sex in the family... That would have made life much easier," writes Shahamat Hussain, a Muslim blogger in Hyderabad, the Indian city now famed as a tech hub.[26] This sense of coyness and shame is not limited to Muslim societies but is a common phenomenon in societies where patriarchal traditions and/or religions, or interpretations thereof, still dominate, including in the more traditional sectors of western society. This is the case, for example, in mainstream Indian society, regardless of faith or caste. "Sex happens to top the list of tabooed subjects in India," observes an Indian blogger. "You dare talk about sex at home and your parents will give you a lecture on how you should concentrate on your studies or they might just chide [you] and walk off."[27]

This results in another form of dissonance. "Such logic practically manifests into expecting a young man and woman to know basically nothing the day before marriage, but expecting them, the day after, to be an expert ready to pop out children at the nine-month mark," writes Zoha Qamar, a Muslim-American student at Columbia University.[28] Whether through osmosis or intuition, a couple of newly weds must overcome the years of official silence towards the sexual act that they lived through when they were single and to dive straight in and indulge in these previously forbidden fruits on their wedding night, when what was previously a distasteful sin is suddenly reinvented as a delicious virtue.

In a few short hours, the nervous young couple, probably stressed by all the long and exhausting wedding arrangements, must shed the habit of saintly virtue, as symbolised by the wedding veil, and enter the domain once known as vice. This leap is even greater in old-fashioned, conservative arranged marriages, which are becoming increasingly rare across the Muslim world, where the newly weds must go from barely knowing each other to knowing each other in the Biblical sense of the word, without the social foreplay of having gone out together to get more intimately acquainted on the emotional plane. This sudden change is likely to be more shocking for the woman because, in a traditional setting, her leading *raison d'etre* is to get married. This is reflected in how, for example, Berber brides-to-be on the Tunisian island of Jerba used to go into seclusion a month before the wedding to avoid exposure to the sun in order to remain as pale as possible and to go on a diet, to pile on the pounds, plumpness being considered a sign of beauty because, as used to be the case in the West, it signified affluence and plenty. I remember visiting a museum display about this pre-wedding confinement, and trying to imagine what it must have been like to give over your entire existence, including your freedom to go outdoors, to this single-minded pursuit of wedlock, and what kind of nerves it caused on the big night itself.

The name of the wedding night in Arabic, *laylet el-dokhla* (Night of Entry or Penetration), is symbolically pregnant with these possibilities. The classic wedding night from hell has to be that of Shahrazad (also spelt Scheherazade), from the ancient *1,001 Nights* story collection, which embodies society's long-standing anxieties towards virginity, sex and the arbitrary exercising of male power. In the frame story, Shahrazad risked the looming shadow of the executioner's sword each night as she sought to stay the murderous hand of the tyrant king, Shahriyar, who succumbed to murderous jealousy after being sexually betrayed by his beloved queen and resolves to marry and then kill a virgin each night, and does so for 1,000 nights, to avenge his broken heart, shattered ego and damaged honour, prompting Shahrazad to put herself forward as his 1,001ˢᵗ victim, despite her family's protests, and regales him for 1,001 nights with her cliffhanger tales (in earlier editions, 1,001 nights meant a 'long time').

Although most people today, including Arabs, have a Disney view of the *1,001 Nights* – linked to the 'children's stories' of Sindbad, Ali Baba and the 40 thieves, and Aladdin – the original was a much darker commentary on the human condition, on traditional gender relations, on jealousy, on autocracy, on the corrupting influence of absolute power, on rebellion and revolt and on one of the most powerful weapons of the weak: their wits and wiliness. "[Shahrazad] was supposed to be [Shahriyar's] prisoner, another of his wives to be used sexually and murdered in the morning," Hanan Al-Shaykh, who authored an adaptation of the classic tales,[29] explained in an interview. "But I believe that he becomes her prisoner – because he was addicted to [her] stories, to her voice, to sitting up with her through the night." Moreover, the enchanting tales Shahrazad recounts do not just entertain her king but also educate him about tyranny, the oppression of women and their inevitable revolt. "These female characters become cunning to overcome the men who oppress them," observes Al-Shaykh. "They fight to make their own choices and live according to their beliefs about freedom, sexuality, and love."[30]

As for the happy couple in a conventional wedding, they must not only endure being the centre of constant attention (according to some customs, they sit on throne-like seats raised on a dais and, in many cases, stand quite literally in the spotlight) but once all the guests are gone, they have only a few hours of privacy to themselves before the arrival of their families to wish the happy, or perhaps terrified, couple a *"sabahiya mubaraka"*, a "blessed morning (after)", before they sate their curiosity. In

117

very traditional, usually rural settings, before the couple can be left alone, the bride must endure the demeaning intrusion of her groom's finger or that of a strange woman, often a village midwife, who pierces the hymen and emerges from the room with a bloodied cloth to reveal to the world that the bride is a 'virgin'. In such traditional settings, this makes the wedding night doubly stressful and also traumatic for the bride, as the Egyptian feminist Nawal al-Saadawi so vividly portrays in her writings (such as in her memoirs),[31] for she must satisfy her in-laws about her 'virtue' and satisfy the oft-raging hormones of her groom.

In addition to the possible psychological shock, this can be a painful introduction to the world of sex, since an inexperienced and oversexed groom may not be aware of the pain he may be causing his bride. Of course, even traditional families can work around traditions. For example, a small amount of blood may be extracted from a cut and substituted for that of the bride, or some grooms may pretend to sleep with their brides on the wedding night, but actually wait in order to help her overcome her anxiety and also to overcome his own. Luckily for Muslim women, as they become more educated, independent and empowered, these intrusive, unjust traditions have been dying out in many Muslim countries, particularly in cities, and they remain important only in very remote rural settings. This has led to "new generations of Arab youth where the males no longer judge a girl by her hymen, or the flow of blood on the night of marriage," noted El Saadawi, though she acknowledged that the "vast majority of Arab men still insist on virginity in their partner at marriage".[32]

The ignorance created by the refusal and failure to talk about sex have many serious, life-changing and even life-threatening consequences. With little to no information about sex provided at home or in school (perhaps surprisingly, Iran does provide some sex education to youngsters),[33] many young Muslims are forced to turn to alternative sources, not always reliable, including their friends and peers, the internet and even pornography. In addition, whereas Islamic customs were established at a time when most women and men were married off in adolescence, today, it is common for young people to marry in their 20s or even their 30s. For those who decide or are compelled to abstain from sex until marriage, this means that they may not have their first sexual experience until up to two decades after they reach sexual maturity. On top of the undoubted frustration this causes, it can also result in profound psychological difficulties and performance-related anxieties when the time does come. This can sometimes manifest itself in vaginismus, when the vagina contracts during stimulation making intercourse painful or impossible, or in erectile dysfunction, when the penis fails to become erect, according to some sexologists.[34]

Lack of or inaccurate knowledge may also lead people to engage in unsafe or unhygienic sexual practices or unwittingly cause a sexual partner pain. Paradoxically, in many cases, ignorance, or 'innocence', as advocates like to regard it, is more likely to lead to the outcome least desired. With patchy knowledge about the biology and consequences of sex, the chances of an unwanted pregnancy occurring are multiplied. But rather than educate young people about responsible sex, the traditional response has been to up the fear factor. This is reflected in the extraordinary fertility of the 'fallen women' of the Egyptian silver screen. In countless old black-and-white films, some naive, innocent woman is seduced by a lying manipulator (presumably he has sex with her during the fade out), only to fall pregnant before the very next scene, leading her to become ostracised from her family and society. Of course, this is hardly an exclusively Muslim problem but afflicts conservative communities across the world. This is dramatically and outlandishly illustrated by the study which found one in 200 women in America claiming to have experienced a 'virgin pregnancy'. The researchers found that many of these women had signed chastity pledges or had received little in the way of sexual education from their parents.[35]

That said, in the absence of formal education, many young Muslims do gain awareness through informal channels, especially friends and peers. The understanding gleaned from hearsay, gossip and friendship network is often, though not always, surprisingly sound. "There is a vast social safety net that explains what is expected and the mechanics," points out the British-Arab writer and journalist Faisal Al Yafai. "Young women in particular discuss sex constantly, endlessly, just as they do elsewhere." This was certainly the case with Holly Dagres, the Iranian-American journalist, during her teen years in Iran. "During senior year in high school, we had a friend that was our classroom sex and relationship guru," she recalls. "When it was break time, we'd gather around and ask all sorts of questions since she had lost her virginity."

Here be dragons

Why are traditional Muslims and traditionalists of other religions so reluctant to talk about sex? At one level, it could relate to the notions of privacy and decorum that are common across the world. In addition, the sacredness of private space in Islam means that the place of sex is in the bedroom, and mentioning it in the living room or classroom oversteps perceived propriety. Another reason is that since sex out of wedlock is considered *haram* or sinful, people may fear that they are legitimising or encouraging, or being seen to encourage, that kind of behaviour by speaking candidly about the subject. "There is huge confusion between sex education and promiscuity," Marwa Rakha told me in an interview some years ago. "There is a difference between knowing and understanding your body, organs, and needs, on the one hand, and throwing yourself into a maelstrom of meaningless physical encounters that will only add to the dilemma."

The main reason, however, is fear of releasing the serpent of sexuality onto the virgin isles of paradise. "Most families want their children virgins until they get married," observes Rakha. "To fulfil this 'beautiful' dream, they will minimise sexual education and awareness to the bare minimum, lest the sex dragons awaken and ruin the plan," hence the ignorance into which young people are flung. Rakha also points to the overall poor level of education in societies like Egypt. "Education and awareness are weak in general in Egypt and many other Arab/Muslim societies," she explains. "Those in charge of the education process do not want generations of knowledgeable and curious children, teens, and adults."

This hints at another factor at play. While in capitalism, sex sells, in the patriarchal order, sex both sells and compels. By controlling access to it, parents (including the greatest parent of all, the state) exercise a potent form of intergenerational soft power and influence. Licit sex is tied to marriage, and marriage is often tied to the parents' (especially the father's), willingness to bankroll the lavish requirements of tying the knot. These vary according to means but are almost invariably beyond the means of the young couple. This affords the older generation power to dictate the behaviour and choices of their offspring, whether consciously or subconsciously. In fact, at the most traditional and conservative end of the spectrum, like in other traditional cultures, young people are often regarded almost as a kind of family 'property', with the father and patriarch the effective CEO of Family Inc.

Once you strip away all the moral and religious embellishments traditional arranged marriages are essentially social and commercial transactions between two families in which the futures of young people are traded. This is especially the case for women, who go from belonging to their fathers to belong to their husbands, while, in contrast, young men go from belonging to their fathers to, in a manner of speaking, 'owning' their wives. Muslims who bemoan how materialistic marriage has become in the modern age overlook the fact that the transactional nature of wedlock, if anything, was more pronounced in the past than today, as love has become widely, though not universally, recognised as an essential prerequisite for marriage. This helps illuminate why love matches are traditionally frowned upon, because love can throw into disarray the family's ability to pick or approve a suitable match for its younger members. Seen in this light, romantic poetry and love songs are not just sentimental ballads but can be potent acts of subversion and rebellion against the traditional social order. Of course, many parents are so submerged in the system that they do not observe its mechanics and machinations, don't realise the manipulative power social and religious convention grants them over their children, and believe whole-heartedly that they are looking out for their children's best interests and acting out of love, even if that makes their children miserable.

Sexy Islam and classical foreplay

With all the ignorance, misinformation and misconceptions in the air, people are left to take matters into their own hands.

In addition to the informal networks mentioned above and online support groups on social media, a new generation of sex advisers and therapists has emerged, aided by the emergence of satellite channels, the internet and social media. For example, among her many manifestations, Marwa Rakha has worked as a relationship and dating expert, both online and in the broadcast media, with the aim of demystifying sex and challenging society's conservative mores and attitudes towards virginity and sex.

In a similar vein, Alyaa Gad, an Egyptian medical doctor based in Switzerland, runs her own incredibly popular YouTube channel which tackles intimate sexual themes, including female orgasms, ideal penis size, premature ejaculation, female genital mutilation and much more. Gad's video giving nervous young couples tips on what to do on their wedding nights went viral and had over 4.5 million views at the time of writing.[36] Gad is careful not to rock the boat excessively, and steers clear of talking about sex outside marriage in her videos. "Even if I want to change people's mindsets about sexuality in the Arab world, I am not trying to disrupt local traditions," she pointed out in an interview. "I just want to share the message that sex is beautiful and that we shouldn't feel shame in talking about it or doing it."[37]

Alongside ignorance, shame is a powerful emotion felt by most of the people who contact Gad for help. "Even the ex-Muslims still have loads of mental struggles between the deep-rooted crap and the truth," she told me. Meanwhile, the religious sometimes seek escape from the chains of 'decency' imposed on them by their faith. "The funny, sad thing is, I receive loads of messages from religious wives who cheat only because the sex is better on the other side," Gad says. "I know a guy whose wife was forced to wear the veil under pressure from his Islamist father, and when she did, he totally lost desire in her to the extent that he lost his erections most of the times they were together," Gad recalls. "At a certain point she took it off (his dad passed), and their sexual life was back to normal in one day."

Even when conservatives are open to discussing sexual topics, the notion that certain aspects of sex are impure or dirty (*najassa*, in Arabic), can lead to the unhealthy outcome in which people regard their bodies and desires as somewhat unclean. "The idea of *najassa* has become so dominant that it can make enjoying sex impossible," Gad asserts. She offers the example of oral sex, including both cunnilingus and fellatio, which are regarded as permissible by certain religious authorities, though many do warn that swallowing the 'filthy' fluids is sinful.[38] When Gad attempted to challenge this view, she opened up a can of worms. "I became known as the 'woman who swallows'. I don't know why I bother, sometimes," she joked.

On the conservative end of the spectrum, recent years have seen the emergence of sexologists who give advice on sex and relationships within an Islamic framework. A pioneer and trailblazer in this regard was Heba Kotb, a professor at Cairo University who claims to be the Arab world's first licensed clinical sexologist and who has hosted a number of popular TV programmes and has written numerous columns about sex.[39] Despite being dressed in a hijab (often a cultural indicator of coyness), Kotb is not shy to discuss the most intimate details in front of millions of viewers. In her view, a married couple should be creative and daring in their sex life, and that anything goes, except what is explicitly prohibited in the Quran, which, according to her, is sex during menstruation and anal sex.[40] She has repeatedly highlighted the importance of foreplay and the female orgasm. "The biggest chapter of the Quran is called *The*

Cow. There is a verse talking about the woman's rising pleasure. It's an order to the man to give the woman the right to have pleasure," Kotb said in an interview, though she did not clarify which verse she was referring to and when I checked I could not find such a reference.[41]

Unfortunately, for viewers who wish to have sex out of wedlock, with people of the same sex, or with themselves, Kotb does not have much time or tolerance. She eventually overcame her original reservations and now advises men to masturbate, warning of the potential health consequences of not doing so. However, Kotb does not believe her sisters in Islam should be extended the same right. "The woman, by means of instinct, does not need masturbation. She's not like the man whatsoever," she claimed dubiously in the same interview. "So that's why I'm not very sympathetic with young women and girls choosing to masturbate. They're ruining their sexual future – a woman has to remain blank until she gets married." Despite being a medical doctor who received part of her medical training in the United States – or perhaps partly because of it, given the influential sway in conservative America of the notion that gay people can be cured of or 'converted' into homosexuality[42] – Kotb maintains an unscientific and intolerant view of homosexuality, likening homosexuals to alcoholics and drug-takers, even claiming to have 'cured' dozens of homosexuals, as if a person's sexuality was a disease or psychological disorder, and not part of their make-up.

Sex gurus of yore

But Kotb's regressive views on sex out of wedlock and homosexuality have not shielded her from outrage and criticism from ultra-conservative clerics. One radical sheikh,

Youssef al-Badri, went so far as to claim that one of Kotb's TV shows "invades the privacy of our bedrooms" and "increases the number of sex perverts".[43] This idea that sexual openness is a perversion and corruption has been common among modern-day Islamists. "Lust, unseemly dedication to pleasure, new ways of self-indulgence, uncontrolled freedom of the lower instincts and bodily desires, the equipment of women with every technique of seduction and incitement," the founder of the Muslim Brotherhood Hassan al-Banna lamented, were "destroying the integrity of the family and threatening the happiness of the home."[44]

Unfortunately for al-Banna and al-Badri but fortunately for Islam, earlier generations of clerics and theologians had no such hang ups. In fact, there was a time when Islamic scholars played the role of veritable sex gurus. For instance, Abu Hamid al-Ghazali, the 11th-century philosopher and mystic who is among the most influential figures in Islam, known for both popularising Sufism and launching a frontal attack on rational philosophy,[45] not only wrote widely about theological issues but also dispensed plentiful sex tips to the faithful, including on the importance of the female orgasm and how it differs from its male equivalent. "Her orgasm may be delayed, thus exciting her desire; to withdraw quickly is harmful to the woman," the sage observed. "Congruence in attaining a climax is more gratifying to her because the man is not preoccupied with his own pleasure, but rather with hers."[46]

It may seem odd that one of the most revered religious scholars in Islamic history, an ascetic who spent many years in seclusion, would speak with authority not just about male ejaculation, but also about the female orgasm and the joy of a couple coming together. But unlike in Catholicism and some other branches of Christianity, Muslim clerics and scholars never had to take a vow of chastity, and hence could gain first-hand, as well as second-hand, sexual knowledge. Moreover, the founders of Islam and Christianity had a radically different relationship with sex. With the canonical gospels silent on the subject, Jesus is generally assumed to have been so pure as to have been above not only sexual gratification, like his mother, but also above marriage itself. In contrast, Muhammad appears to have enjoyed an active sex life, first, for a quarter of a century, as the monogamous husband of an older woman and love of his life, Khadija, then as a polygamous older man who married about 10 women in the space of a decade, for a wide range of political, social and romantic reasons, perhaps most controversially, Aisha, who was pre-pubescent when she was married to Muhammad.

Faced with present-day Muslim coyness about sex and the more open nature of sexual discourse in previous centuries, some modern Muslims undergo their sexual awakening at the hands of long-dead Islamic scholars. This was the case for Ali Ghandour, an academic at the University of Munster in Germany. Just as many teenage boys come across their father's secret porn stash, Ghandour happened across a book by an Ottoman theologian, historian and poet, Imam Ibn Kamal Pasha, secreted in a discreet corner of his father's library. "There were stories in there that today you might compare with *50 Shades of Grey*," Ghandour explained in an interview.[47] This early exposure aroused a desire in Ghandour in later life to write a book on the subject to tackle the taboo surrounding sex in many Muslim communities.[48] One ancient scholar who captured Ghandour's imagination was the 15th-century Egyptian scholar of Persian and Circassian origin, Imam Jalaluddin al-Suyut, who was known as *Faqih al-Hubb* (the Jurist of Love) and was perhaps the most prolific erotologist in the classical Islamic tradition, penning books on the "science" and health benefits of sexual intercourse.[49] Despite the more explicit and open nature of medieval Islamic culture, they are a poor guide for the present. "If you want to know anything about sex today, you read the old legal texts. But that causes problems, because you can't compare pre-industrial society with that of the present day," Ali Ghandour observed. "At that time, people got married not long after they reached sexual maturity and single parents and small families were simply not envisaged."

Of course, these Islamic scholars did not operate in a vacuum. As you might expect, the wider culture of the time was replete with overt sexuality, despite what Muslim traditionalists might like to imagine about an idyllic past of piety and purity. This can be seen in the *Encyclopedia of Pleasure,* written in Baghdad by one Ali ibn Nasr al-Katib, who "sounds like just the sort of man I'd like to meet," admits Shereen El Feki. "Its forty-three chapters cover every conceivable sexual practice: heterosexual, homosexual (male and female), bisexual, animal, vegetable, and mineral—you name it, it's all there," she explains. "Ali ibn Nasr's message is clear: sex is God's gift to mankind and we are meant to enjoy it." Surprisingly for many modern Muslims, the author dedicates considerable space to female pleasure and how to attain it. "What's remarkable about his work, seen through twenty-first-century eyes, is not whether women actually behaved in this way in the eleventh century," El Feki concludes. "But the fact that it was considered desirable that they should express their sexuality – at least in private – and that it was socially acceptable to write about it in such a free, frank, and detailed fashion."[50]

This more open attitude is also made abundantly clear in the explicit sexual content of the older editions of the classic *1,001*

Nights, the most popular collection of stories in Islamic history. The tales touch on numerous erotic themes, including desire, the unparalleled pleasure of sex, sexual power dynamics, sexual blackmail, sexual addiction, prostitution, homosexuality, bisexuality, cross-dressing, sex changes and even bestiality. Like mainstream eroticism today, the sexual imagery is aimed primarily at titillating and arousing the male fantasy, and is often demeaning to women, though the tales do feature many sexually experienced and confident women who initiate young men into the world of physical desire. "This permissiveness reflects the life of the urban elite under the Abbasid caliphs, whose luxury, refinement and pleasures are elaborately described in literary sources," notes *The Arabian Nights Encyclopaedia*.[51]

And erotica was not just literary, it was also visual. Despite the Islamic aversion to graven images, Muslim artists over the centuries have produced paintings, including exquisite Mughal, Persian and Ottoman miniatures and paintings that are explicit and pornographic in nature, featuring couples in various states of undress and intoxication; some even show exposed genitalia and copulation. Despite the naked sexuality of these images, some scholars bizarrely insist on moving beyond the flesh and insisting that under their erotic skins these images are actually spiritual. "A certain uneasiness to accept the presence of erotic motifs... combined with a general hesitancy, or even prudishness, to speak about sexual matters resulted in the persistent adoption of the rhetoric of carnal experiences as mere metaphors for spiritual ones," note Francesca Leoni and Mika Natif in a rare study on the subject. Of course, there is no reason for erotic images not to be both carnal and spiritual; as many Sufis believed you could reach the latter through the former.[52] In a similar vein to how orientalists objectified and fantasised about harem beauty or the *alema*, Persian artists of the 16th and

17th century eroticised Christian Europeans in what you might call an occidentalist fantasy. "Safavid visual and textual sources indicate that both the male and the female European were loci of sexual curiosity and interest," notes Amy Landau. "Depicted scantily clad and in uninhibited postures, the European female became a subject of eroticisation and fantasy."[53] A 16th-century public mural in Isfahan, the Persian capital during the Safavid dynasty, depicts a scene of revelry involving Europeans which includes erotic vignettes containing naked female breasts, bare male buttocks and suggestive poses.[54]

Gay Islam

In contrast to modern Islamic mores, which tend to regard homosexuality as a sin to be either ignored or punished, the permissiveness of the *1,001 Nights* extended to gay love. For example, in one tale, Abu Nuwas, who in real life and in the stories was an outrageously camp poet in Caliph Harun al-Rashid's court, cooks up a sumptuous banquet and takes to the streets to find a worthy companion with whom to dine. He eventually encounters what he, borrowing Quranic imagery, describes as "three handsome beardless young men, as if they were youths of the gardens of paradise," whom he takes home. Even though the caliph is scandalised by Abu Nuwas's exploits when he barges in on the poet's drunken revelry, he refrains from beheading the artist on the strength of a joke.[55]

In real life, Persian-Arab Abu Nuwas was more than a joker and court jester. He was one of the most innovative and original Arab poets, revolutionising Arabic poetry, in terms of its themes, styles and manner, taking it out of its nostalgia for the romanticised Bedouin life and thrusting it into the cosmopolitan, multicultural urbane world which was his element in Baghdad. More irreverent than Oscar Wilde, always ready with a witty and scathing riposte, and a proud hedonist, Abu Nuwas was the original rebel without a cause – or more correctly, his cause was to extract as much pleasure out of life as he could, often employing scriptural allusions to describe his pursuit of sex and booze, likening them to worship. When it came to his substantial body of erotic poetry, Abu Nuwas dedicated an estimated two-thirds to young men and the third he wrote in apparent praise of women often employed masculine grammar or described cross-dressing women.[56] Although Abu Nuwas's preferences for pubescent youth and his attitudes to forcible sex with slave-boys are reprehensible by our modern standards of equality, consent and protecting the weak and vulnerable, the frankness and unapologetic nature with which he expresses his sexuality is something rare in modern Islamic societies (and only recently became acceptable in liberal Western circles). But being a male-dominated society, traditional Muslim culture did not produce a female Abu Nuwas. Even today, many have difficulty getting their heads around lesbianism, partly because it does not involve penises and (rarely) penetration and, if noticed at all, tends to be viewed as a temporary substitute for male love,[57] though modern Arab writers and artists have broached the topic, both indirectly and directly.[58]

Abu Nuwas fell out of favour, had to seek refuge in Egypt and wound up in prison a couple of times. However, when the poet fled Baghdad, this had little to do with his homosexual exploits and his homoerotic verse but had everything to do with a political miscalculation, when he decided to lament in verse the downfall of the Persian Barmakid family, the most powerful and wealthiest family after the caliph's, which Harun al-Rashid had eventually eliminated.[59] Upon his return from exile, Abu Nuwas resumed where he left off, and with even greater gusto, passion and indulgence. Under the patronage of Harun's son and successor, al-Amin, Abu Nuwas found a kindred spirit, and reportedly penned most of his erotic verse during his reign. Surprisingly, al-Amin did imprison him, but this seems to have been due to a political power struggle with his half-brother, al-Mamum, who used al-Amin's reputation as a drunkard to undermine his legitimacy. Even in prison, Abu Nuwas does not seem to have been particularly cowed and reputedly penned a number of irreverent poems while languishing behind bars.[60]

This is a far cry from current reality in many parts of the Muslim world. This is tragically embodied in how the 21st-century entity which calls itself the 'caliphate' compares to its medieval and pre-modern predecessors. While Abu Nuwas stumbled through the streets of Baghdad, drunkenly pursuing his latest infatuation and metaphorically shouting about it in eloquent poetry from the rooftops, the Islamic State (ISIS) literally hurls men accused of homosexual acts from the rooftops.[61] Shockingly, at least half the countries which outlaw homosexual acts have a Muslim majority, while 13 of these prescribe the death penalty, according to the International Lesbian, Gay, Bisexual, Trans and Intersex Association (ILGA), though some rarely if ever put it into practice.[62]

The shift does not appear to be theological, as many medieval and classical scholars regarded *liwat* (sodomy) to be sinful, but it marks change social and legalistic norms. "Whatever textual sources reveal about the presence of same-sex intimate relations, the fact that some Muslims have engaged in homoerotic activities does not mean it is religiously legitimate to do so," notes Kecia Ali, professor of religion at Boston University. "Despite the widespread medieval acceptance of same-sex desire between men and attractive male youths, Muslim thinkers took for granted that such sexual relations were neither licit nor possible to legitimise." A number of classical Islamic scholars, including Ibn Hajar and al-Dhahabi, included sodomy as a mortal or major sin (*al-kabair*). However, unlike those modern Muslim societies which punish homosexual acts, classical scholars did not generally regard *liwat* as a punishable sin and prescribed no penalty for it. This is partly because the Quran is silent or ambiguous on the topic and partly because they viewed same-sex desire, mainly between men, as being natural.[63]

In contrast, many modern Muslims regard homosexuality as unnatural and an expression of Western hegemony aimed at corrupting or destroying Islamic civilisation by undermining its supposed moral rectitude. Paradoxically, this is both a product of European imperialism, (mainly British imperialism, as France had decriminalised consensual homosexual conduct in 1791), and a by-product of resistance to it. During the period of direct British colonial rule, Britain found it unacceptable that many of its imperial possessions possessed no laws against sodomy and so introduced them, in British India (now India, Pakistan and Bangladesh), Malaysia, Singapore, Nigeria, Somalia, Sudan, and many other Muslim majority and non-Muslim countries.[64] "Half the world's countries that criminalise homosexual conduct do so because they cling to Victorian morality and colonial laws. Getting rid of these unjust remnants of the British Empire is long overdue," said Scott Long of Human Rights Watch.[65] Even in places not directly ruled by Europe, European homophobic attitudes of the time began to be seen as virtuous in Islamic societies that had hitherto been ambivalent, indifferent or tolerant towards same-sex desires and relationships. This was the case in the Ottoman empire in the mid-19th century, when, influenced by European mores, homosexuality became a social stigma in the large cities, though it was never outlawed.[66] Paradoxically, these European mores became so ingrained into local attitudes that today they are regarded as 'authentic' Islamic or national values, while homosexuality is considered a newfangled Western import. This is reflected in the popular 'alternative fact' propagated by many Muslims that homosexuality does not exist in Muslim societies, which requires turning a wilfully blind eye to the society around them and ignoring their own literature and history. This sentiment was memorably expressed by former Iranian President Mahmoud Ahmadinejad, when he told an audience at Columbia University in the United States: "In Iran, we don't have homosexuals like in your country. In Iran, we do not have this phenomenon."[67] This, naturally, leaves one wondering if homosexuals do not exist in Iran, why does the Islamic Republic threaten this imaginary demographic group with the death penalty?

Foreign agents or individual agency?

A more nuanced and intelligent variation on the 'Western import' hypothesis is the notion that same-sex desire and sexual activity does exist among Muslims but that homosexuality as an identity is a modern Western construct. One prominent advocate of this theory is Joseph Massad, professor of modern Arab politics and intellectual history at Columbia University. In Massad's view, homosexuality (and by implication heterosexuality) are Western ideas forced, by local Westernised elites and foreign neo-imperialists (whom he dubs the "Gay International") on Arab and Muslim societies where sexual identities have traditionally been more fluid. "In contradistinction to the liberatory claims made by the Gay

International in relation to what it posits as an always already homosexual population," he writes, "it is the very discourse of the Gay International, which both produces homosexuals as well as gays and lesbians,[68] where they do not exist and represses same-sex desires and practices that refuse to be assimilated into its sexual epistemology."[69] Instead, Massad opts for the more obscure and very unsexy term, 'practitioners of same-sex contact'. "By lumping them all together, [Massad] sidesteps the question of whether any of these 'practitioners' have a right to identify themselves as gay, lesbian, etc., if they so wish," maintains Brian Whitaker, the author and former Middle East editor at *The Guardian*. "Massad simply dismisses such people as unimportant victims of Western influence."[70]

Although Massad is right that different societies define sexuality in divergent ways and that traditional Muslim conceptions of sexual identity differ from modern Western ones, his disingenuous line of argument conceals more than it reveals. Despite being lauded as a worthy successor to Edward Said, Massad unwittingly perpetuates the Orientalist myth identified by Said in which: "The West is the actor, the Orient a passive reactor."[71] Massad not only robs Arabs and Muslims who identify as homosexual (or heterosexual for that matter, of agency), he also appears to distort the nature of traditional Muslim sexual identity and contemporary Western categories. When it comes to terminology, just because no exact equivalent for the neutral term 'homosexual' has existed in Arabic until recently, that does not mean that no terms to describe homosexual identity exist. In fact, Arabic has numerous, albeit usually derogatory, terms, such as *luti* ('sodomite') and others which equate gayness with passive effeminacy (including *khawal*, which originally referred to transvestite male dancers, and *mukhannath*, which means 'effeminate men'), and *shadh* (or deviant). Besides, even if a term does not exist that does not mean that which it describes is non-existent, especially when it comes to desires and behaviour. Just because the term 'genocide' was coined in the 20th century that does not mean the inhabitants of previous centuries did not wish or attempt to wipe other peoples off the face of the Earth.

Moreover, sexual orientation is far more than a social construct, it is a biological fact, as a substantial body of scientific research has proved rather convincingly,[72] and exists in the animal kingdom too.[73] Questions of nature versus nurture, and how much homosexuality is one or the other aside, the main reason why gays often construct their cultural identity around their sexuality is because society has forced them to do so with its prejudice and discrimination against alternative sexualities. In addition, it is inaccurate to claim that current Western sexual identities offer only a 'hetero-homo binary'. In reality, contemporary definitions of sexuality, like gender, view it as a spectrum or continuum, and even posits that the individual's sexual identity is fluid and can shift with time. In fact, over 200 scales have been developed to measure sexuality.[74] This non-binary view is clear in the mostly inclusive, if cumbersome, name for the non-heterosexual movement: Lesbian, Gay, Bisexual and Transgender (LGBT). In fact, the Arab/Muslim sexuality which Massad claims does not comply with the 'hetero-homo binary' does fit rather neatly into the bisexual category, or some of the others identified by the dozens of available scales.

In bygone centuries, some Muslims tended more towards the homosexual end of the sexual spectrum. Abu Nuwas, for instance, who seems to have been forced into an unhappy marriage, not only dedicated most of his erotic poetry to beardless male youth, as noted earlier, but he also often derided the love of women in his verse and once even vowed never to travel by sea again (a euphemism for sex with women), but would stick to travelling by land (a metaphor for men). There are reports that Abu Nuwas's wife also preferred women, which suggests they were in a marriage of convenience.[75]

It also strikes me that the Muslim world did not need to import a restrictive hetero-homo binary from the West, as Islam recognises only a heterosexual bond as being legitimate (*halal*), which has meant that, throughout the centuries, men and women who preferred sex with their own gender generally had to do so discreetly. And, ultimately, it is in the closet where Massad seems to want the Muslim LGBT community to remain or return to, by romanticising the tradition of society turning a blind eye as long as gays exercised discretion. "This argument is troubling because it again idealises the private world of Arab sexuality without interrogating why individuals might seek to identify with western taxonomies," noted one generally positive review of Massad's book. "Even if society tolerates sexuality in private, it does not follow that oppression is absent from these private spaces and that western liberation discourse would not offer a new language for confronting oppression."[76]

However, like the classic orientalists whom Massad despises, his conception of Arab and Muslim identity appears to be one of apparent unchanging, monolithic stagnation, in which Muslim societies must choose between the indigenous or the foreign, rather than picking, reshaping and fusing various influences, as confident societies have done throughout the ages.

This restrictive view also deprives the individual of the right to choose their identity. After all, not so long ago, Western conceptions of sexuality were not so unlike those of Arabs and Muslims. For example, Oscar Wilde, in his impassioned defence of the "love that dare not speak its name" sounded remarkably like a classical Arab poet. "It is beautiful, it is fine, it is the noblest form of affection. There is nothing unnatural about it," Wilde said during his trial. "It is intellectual, and it repeatedly exists between an older and a younger man, when the older man has intellect, and the younger man has all the joy, hope and glamour of life before him."[77] Like Islamic jurisprudence, British law did not trouble itself with orientation or sexuality but with sexual acts. The key difference was that Islamic jurisprudence did not generally regard it as a punishable offense, while English law considered 'buggery' to be a capital crime from the 16th to the 19th century,[78] and sodomy was only decriminalised in the 20th century. A similar gradual process took place in other European countries and in the United States.

This raises the question of why Muslims should not be entitled to embark on their own process of reform. Even if they have borrowed (and adapted) sexual identities from elsewhere, or even imported them wholesale, when will their identities, beliefs and convictions come to be regarded as legitimate by the gatekeepers of acceptable identity? After all, the notion of the modern nation state is also a western import, yet Massad has no problem defending the Palestinian right to a state and self-determination, and rejects efforts to blame the victim for the occupation. "Palestinians have every right to fight for the simple right of statehood, yet when they are homosexual they are merely the puppets in a plot created by the 'Gay International'," lamented a young Palestinian I know who lives in Europe and identifies as "queer". He is at pains to point out that he is not "the imaginary product of the West. Born and raised in the Arab world, I have taught myself the 'white man's tongue'." He is also distrustful and sceptical of those western LGBT activists who take a condescending, supremacist view of their Arab comrades or advocate destructive warfare as a means of 'liberating' the natives. "The gay scene today as it stands, is a cesspool of fascist ideas and imagery," he maintains. But the LGBT community and LGBT activists are not a monolithic 'Gay International' with some kind of central command. There are many LGBT activists who are anti-war, oppose western foreign policy in the Middle East and believe change should be driven by locals, with their own role being that of solidarity or support.

The elders of Sodom

Robbing Arab and Muslim gays of agency is bad enough but depicting them as witless or intentional agents of a foreign conspiracy is far worse. Efforts to gain acceptance by the LGBT community are stymied by the notion that these vulnerable communities are either hapless copycats blindly emulating the West. Being simultaneously portrayed as part of a sinister Western conspiracy makes life potentially dangerous for them. Massad extols the virtues of discreet, private same-sex activity, but that offers people very limited protection. It is true that most Muslim countries possess a vibrant underground gay scene, which can often hide in plain sight. In fact, (relative) sexual segregation can sometimes make homosexual love easier than its heterosexual variety, especially as physical intimacy between people of the same gender, such as holding hands and walking arm in arm, is a heterosexual norm in many Muslim societies. However, this bubble can easily be burst. Even if we accept that homosexuality is a constructed identity, homophobia is a very real and present danger.

This was dramatically and tragically demonstrated around the turn of the millennium. Egypt's gay community once kept a low public profile and kept themselves to themselves, most keeping their identities secret even from their families. But the state refused to respect this privacy and, in May 2001, vice police and state security raided a venue that was popular with gays but also drew many straight customers, the Queen Boat, a floating night club on the Nile. Of the 52 arrested and tried, only 30 had actually been on the boat, while the rest had been rounded up earlier. Women (benefiting from the perceived non-existence of lesbianism) and foreigners (protected by their non-Egyptian passports) were not arrested. In order to whip up public passion, the pliant Mubarak-era scandal sheets described the defendants as being members of a satanic cult who were caught, naked, conducting a mock wedding ceremony. The authors of this fiction were not the media but state security, which claimed it had found a pamphlet in the supposed ringleader's home, (who was arrested sometime before the Queen Boat raid), which allegedly outlined the cult's creed, "Our religion is the religion of Lot's people, our prophet and guide is Abu Nuwas".

The men arrested during the Queen Boat round-ups represented a broad cross-section of Egyptian society, including at least one who was illiterate and many who had little to no exposure to Western society and could hardly be classed as part of the westernised elite. When asked to use the English word "gay" in his confession, one confused defendant asked the officer what the word meant. The accused men were stripped of their dignity and rights, kept from communicating with their families for weeks, and physically and verbally abused by prison guards and other inmates, who constantly mocked them and expressed disgust towards their presumed sexuality.

Outside the prison walls, large segments of the Egyptian media had abandoned all ethical constraints, not only shaming the arrested men using the vilest language, but some also naming them, as well as propagating the outlandish conspiracy theories surrounding the men without making the slightest attempt to fact-check or express scepticism. Years before Massad coined the term 'Gay International', the Queen Boat defendants were not only portrayed as a satanic cult worshipping Lot's people but as members of a non-existent foreign conspiracy, vaguely represented as the 'globalisation of perversion', or as an American or Israeli plot. One magazine, *al-Musawwar*, ran a doctored photo featuring the alleged ring leader wearing an Israeli army helmet and sitting in front of an Israeli flag as part of an exposé of "Lot's people" – a conspiracy theory you could call the Protocols of the Elders of Sodom. The men who were caught up in the Queen Boat were not only deeply traumatised by the affair; their lives were ruined, even those who were not convicted. In addition to the shame their families experienced and the stigmatisation they experienced in their communities, many were unable to find work, while some saw their families broken and their marriages destroyed. Class and education made a difference, not in terms of sexuality or trauma, but in terms of capacity to shield oneself from the fallout or to set up life elsewhere, either in Egypt or abroad. Yet so many seem to blame these men for what happened to them, as if their private sexual preferences were public property.[79]

At this point, I must confess to a personal interest in the Queen Boat travesty and fiasco. I knew one of the men who got caught in the dragnet. To respect his right to forget and be forgotten, I will not name him in these pages. A carefree party animal, my friend was out having fun that fateful night. He was one of the least politically minded of my Cairo circle. His greatest worry in the world was his family's repeated attempts to get him to marry his cousin and his insistence to them on remaining a bachelor. He lived in a spacious closet for family and the outside world which had a transparent door only for his close friends. Though he steered clear of politics, politics decided to veer towards him and run him over in zealous pursuit of cynical self-interest (i.e. government attempts to outflank the Islamist opposition and distract attention from growing economic hardship). My friend became a prisoner of conscience (spending more than a year in jail). Like the other defendants, he was maltreated and exposed to humiliating medical examinations. The contrast between the terrified image of him trying to mask his face in the defendants' cage and the last time I saw him, a few weeks previously, on the beach in South Sinai, carefree and nursing his tan, was saddening.

About a year after the initial arrests, the president's office overturned the original convictions and called for a retrial. Our carefree friend came out a broken man. His life and career ruined, this friend, who had once confided in me that he had no desire, unlike so many other young Egyptians, to leave Egypt because he liked his life there, had no more reason to stay. Although his application for immigration to Canada had cleared and he could leave, still he hesitated. Despite all that had happened to him, he still loved Egypt, even though the state did not reciprocate the emotion and many of his fellow Egyptians expressed nothing but contempt and hatred towards him. He wasn't so keen on the idea of leaving his homeland, his family, and the people he loved. Reluctant, he nevertheless moved to Canada in the nick of time. He was retried in absentia, receiving a three-year sentence. He has now regained some of his old spirit and a hint of his previous optimism. Some years after his move to Canada, we regained contact. He was in the process of rebuilding the career he enjoyed and had bought a flat with a boyfriend he had made since arriving there.

At the time, I was a novice hack working for an international news agency with few avenues open to me beyond reporting straight news, which made me feel powerless in the face of this injustice. When I suggested I work on a feature about the arrests and the precarious situation of the gay community, my bureau chief adopted a wait-and-see approach, arguing that until something concrete happened, and not just speculation and hearsay, there was no story – and by the time there was a story, I had already left the country. I also found stonewalling within the Egyptian human rights community. Hafez Abu Saada, the head of the Egyptian Organisation for Human Rights, told me on the telephone that his organisation would only speak up for these men if allegations of torture emerged. He admitted to me that the EOHR was embattled enough due to government allegations that it was a foreign-sponsored agitator and they didn't want to alienate popular opinion too much by appearing elitist. Journalist Hesham Qassem, who was with EOHR at the time, expressed this point: "Taking up such a case will jeopardise our credibility with average Egyptians and other cases of human rights [violations] are more worthy of our attention."[80] In public statements, Abu Saada went further: "Personally, I don't like the subject of homosexuality, and I don't want to defend them."[81] One journalist and human rights defender who broke the silence and wrote robustly and critically about the affair was Hossam Bahgat. For his pains, he was dismissed from the EOHR two days after his piece was published.[82] Some months later, Bahgat set up his own NGO, the Egyptian Initiative for Personal Rights, which included sexual rights as part of its mandate.[83]

Another journalist who resisted the self-righteous wave of incrimination and prejudice was Rana Allam, who covered the case unsensationally and critically, highlighting the plight of the arrested men, for the semi-official *Al Ahram Weekly*, but it was like walking a tightrope, even though Cairo's English-language media was generally more enlightened and balanced than its Arabic counterpart. "I was backed by our editor in chief, the late Hosni Guindy,[84] who was an amazing journalist and human being," Allam told me. "Other colleagues from the organisation [i.e. the Arabic *Al Ahram*] mocked me. They never really had a serious conversation with me." Allam's troubles did not end at the office or in the public domain; her coverage caused her difficulties at home too, "In my close circle, and within my family, I had many long ugly arguments. I was accused of wanting to shed my skin and become a Westerner, of denouncing religion and values, of being 'disgusting'… and how I am ruining my reputation and risking my son's future (I had a one-year old baby at the time)." This reflects just how, despite their relatively gay-friendly past, Egyptians have internalised the notion that homosexuality is a foreign import, one spread by a pliant and willing local elite, designed to 'corrupt' Egypt and weaken the moral fabric that once supposedly made it strong.

The right to choose

In the years since the Queen Boat debacle, the situation has changed considerably in Egypt and some other parts of the Muslim world, with the social landscape growing more polarised over time. "There is more awareness now, and talking about it is less of a taboo than it used to be," says Brian Whitaker, who wrote a book about homosexuality in the Arab context which was first published in 2006 and updated in 2011. "In practical terms, though, little has changed."

In Egypt, the government continues to round up allegedly gay men, in a bid to portray itself as a moral arbiter, and this has stepped up under the tutelage of the current Egyptian president Abdel-Fattah al-Sisi. However, criticism and opposition to this has also become more vocal. For example, some Egyptian human rights organisations found their voice during the Queen Boat retrial. The Hisham Mubarak Law Centre, Bahgat's EIPR and the Nadeem Centre for Rehabilitation of Victims of Violence issued a joint statement expressing their "astonishment and outrage" over "the conviction without trial of people tried for consensual homosexual conduct in the Queen Boat case".[85] On the fifth anniversary of the Queen Boat fiasco, I was able to publish an article in *Al Ahram Weekly* on Egypt's culture of denial towards homosexuality which caused remarkably little controversy.[86]

EIPR has not shied away from challenging public prejudice. The organisation's Dalia Abd El-Hameed published a piece in 2015, in both English and Arabic,[87] on the hard-hitting *MadaMasr* website in which she condemned the police and judicial persecution of gays and the "discriminatory and inflammatory" position of some human rights activists. "Homosexuality is not a disease. Homosexuality is not a crime," she concluded.[88] When 'investigative journalist' Mona al-Iraqi filmed and broadcast a raid on a bathhouse, which she alleged uncovered a den of male prostitution, the public outrage, non-existent during the Queen Boat trial, at the invasion of these men's privacy and the miscarriage of justice was immense, forcing the judiciary to do its job and acquit the men.[89] As for al-Iraqi, her show was taken off the air and she received a six-month sentence for defamation and broadcasting false news (though she successfully appealed against it later).[90] This hints at how the public mood is shifting, pitting greater tolerance against a vicious conservative backlash, and revealing an intergenerational conflict in which the young are teaching their elders a thing or two about values. "The more the world accepts and legalizes same-sex relationships, the stronger the push against it in our societies," notes Rana Allam, who went on to become editor-in-chief of *Daily News Egypt* and has been a vocal advocate of equal rights for all. "I also see that the younger generations have less negative attitudes towards homosexuality. The teens of today, in my view, are much more accepting of all gender diversities than the older generations."

Some Muslim-majority countries have long had a legal system which tolerates homosexuality. Turkey has not only never outlawed homosexual acts, its LGBT community is vibrant and combative, holding regular pride parades, even when they are banned for 'security' concerns.[91] A number of Muslim-majority countries have even debated legalising gay marriage. For instance, Albania introduced a draft law on same-sex marriage in 2009,[92] but it has faced stiff opposition from conservatives, both Muslim and Christian, ever since.[93] In addition, gay rights groups have popped up in some countries, such as Lebanon, as have LGBT-friendly mosques. Islamic scholars in a number countries are re-examining Islamic scripture and theology and attempting to reinterpret it in a more gay-friendly fashion. These include Kecia Ali, who was mentioned earlier in the chapter and Scott Siraj al-Haqq Kugle, a professor of Islamic studies at Emory College.

In addition to unleashing the spectre of Islamist violence and jihadism in the areas where power vacuums have been created, the Arab revolutionary wave, which began in 2011, also increased the space for, awareness about and tolerance of the LGBT community. This is noticeable in Tunisia, for instance. On the one hand, Tunisia continues to outlaw homosexuality with its colonial-era Article 230 on 'sodomy',[94] homophobic outbursts (including by government officials) are common place, and arrests and prosecutions, including intrusive anal examinations, continue periodically.[95] On the other hand, Tunisia's LGBT community is slowly coming out of the closet, establishing at least one advocacy group, called Shams (Arabic for 'Sun') and a number of online publications, which has provoked both rabid homophobia and a growing base of supporters. Representatives of the LGBT community are now appearing in the media to put their case to the public, which arouses hostility and fury but has also forced society to examine its prejudices. Activists and their supporters have been mounting a concerted campaign to repeal Article 230, a move designed to protect their privacy, dignity and human rights.[96] A tentative step towards protecting the dignity of the LGBT community was the Tunisian Medical Council's decision to ban forced medical examinations of homosexual men, which was described by Human Rights Watch as "A courageous step in opposing the use of these torturous exams."[97] Support sometimes comes from unexpected quarters. For instance, Riad Chaibi, the spokesman for Ennahdha, the moderate Islamist party which helped lead Tunisia's transition to democracy, vowed to respect the rights of gays and atheists, who possess a "right to exist", and admitted that homosexuals suffered from a lack of dignity because society regards them as "worthless".[98]

When I moved to Tunisia in 2017, some of the first people I got to know were a Tunisian-French gay couple who were co-habiting and raising the Tunisian partner's adopted son from an earlier relationship. More impressively still, they lived in an apartment in the family home above the parents of the Tunisian partner. Now, the son and the parents are all artists, and artists have a reputation for greater tolerance and permissiveness than mainstream society. Nevertheless, when I expressed my admiration of this arrangement to the mother, her response was, "We're believers. There is nothing in Islam that says this is wrong. God wants his creations to be happy." And the family appears radiantly happy, and their little boy loves his father and step-father. But they have to be discreet. While open about their relationship to their inner circle, they do not go around advertising their relationship in public. But they are confident about the future. "The situation has changed a lot in Tunisia," the Tunisian partner told me. "People have become much more open and accepting of gays since the revolution and things are moving forward."

Sexual (r)evolution

In the wider realm of sexuality, a tide of greater freedom and respect for individual choice is building up momentum. This is reflected, for instance, in the greater public openness to talk about sex, discussed earlier in the chapter. It is also reflected in the efforts by young people to challenge society's prejudices and broaden the scope of publicly accepted sexual relationships. And some youth are unapologetic in their demands for greater tolerance, even of public displays of affection. This was reflected in Moroccans posting photos of themselves and organising a 'kiss in' in the Moroccan capital Rabat in solidarity with three teenagers who were arrested for posting photos of themselves making out on Facebook. "Our message is that they are defending love, the freedom to love and kiss freely," said one participant.[99]

Then, there is the growing phenomenon of *urfi* (or 'customary') marriages in places like Egypt,[100] in which young couples who wish to co-habit without the hobbling financial demands of family and society, simply sign an unofficial, unregistered 'marriage' document (which the couple can simply tear up should they wish to break up). Young people enter into such arrangements to give their cohabitation a sheen of social legitimacy or, simply, as a way to get around the restrictions imposed by many landlords on renting only to married couples. Of course, such 'marriages' carry certain risks, such as the issue of paternity if a child is born,[101] or how some men have been known to not tear up their copy and use it to claim a woman has no right to marry another person because she is already married to him. Perhaps surprisingly, many *salafists* also support and encourage *urfi* couplings, as they do in Tunisia;[102] partly as a way to help young believers deal with their sexual frustration in a *halal* manner; as a countercultural rebellion against the huge materialism of marriage in mainstream society; and as a way to forge marriages between 'brothers' and 'sisters' in the movement of which their families may disapprove.

Although there has long been greater tolerance of premarital sex for men, an increasing minority of women are openly calling for a levelling of the playing field and demanding that society accept their sexuality. Defying society's conservative sexual norms can be deadly, as Pakistan's Qandeel Baloch discovered. The Pakistani model and social media star, (born Fouzia Azeem), made a name for herself with her provocative videos and stunts, including offering to strip for her nation if the Pakistani cricket team beat India. She was also an outspoken advocate of women's rights. Mocked by his friends for the 'dishonour' his sister was bringing on the family, her brother murdered her. Although applauded by ultra-conservatives,

Baloch's murder sparked public outrage and a campaign to stiffen the punishment for so-called 'honour' killings. Baloch's parents defended their daughter and condemned their son. "She was an amazing daughter. I have no words that do her justice, and she took care of us much more than our sons, including financially," her distraught mother said.[103] Combating the dishonourable practice of honour killings has become a top priority for activists in Muslim countries where this phenomenon is prevalent. A daring Palestinian-Jordanian journalist, Rana Husseini, has written a hard-hitting book on the topic.[104]

Despite the risks of ostracisation (or worse), an increasing number of young women are standing up for their right to control their own sexuality. One group of Egyptian women challenged the taboo surrounding virginity by going public with their first sexual experience. None of the women expressed regret about having premarital sex and all were defiant towards social prejudice regarding what they had done. "I think a lot of the guys I know will disrespect me and look at me as an easy hook up because I'm not a virgin. Many of my childhood friends will judge me and talk about me behind my back and a few will probably give me the cold shoulder," one of the women confessed. "I know I'd definitely be judged for not being a virgin before marriage... I would rather remain unmarried than marry someone who is incapable of accepting my past, lifestyle, and way of thinking," another asserted defiantly.[105]

Whether the battle for greater sexual liberation and tolerance eventually wins and Muslim societies grow to accept the notion that sex and sexuality are not collective concerns but a matter of individual rights is anyone's guess. But achieving this will require the de-coupling of sex and sexuality from politics and successfully defeating the myth propagated by social conservatives that the root of society's ills lies in people's genitalia, especially women's vaginas. In reality, freedom of sexual choice is good for everyone. It allows the individual to grow into a balanced and healthy citizen. On a more global scale, it enables society to channel the energies wasted on sexual frustration and sexual intrusiveness to more useful and productive ends. I hope to see a future in which every Muslim can decide for him- or herself whether they want to be sexually liberal or conservative. That, to me, is the true meaning of sexual liberation.

CHAPTER FIVE

Alcohol and Islam: Fermenting rebellion?

Alcohol in Islam is not just sinful; it is the source of all the Muslim world's troubles. Alcohol is like a mighty evil genie who has been trapped in a bottle for centuries until modern Muslims, under the influence of a decadent West, decided to uncork that bottle, unleashing the malignant, if delicious, spirit on the sacred body of Islam, causing it to rot from within.

"Drinking is what has set us back so much," a pious Tunisian recently told me. "All our problems come from *khamr*:[1] all the accidents on the roads, the laziness of workers, corruption and the numbing of people's senses towards their fellow believers." Alarmed, I desired to get to the bottom of this mystery. I have drunk alcohol for the greater part of my adult life, yet it has done me no perceptible harm. Not to me, nor to my drinking friends, nor even to some of the greatest minds Islamic civilisation has produced. While I haven't fulfilled all my dreams and desires, life has generally been good to me. What was I missing? Was alcohol perhaps blurring my vision? Had Satan so intoxicated me with the illusion of success and happiness that I could no longer tell harm from *haram*? Another question that nagged like a swaying shadow in the middle of my foggy consciousness was, how could such a relatively small group have such a disproportionately devastating impact on society? I know many Tunisians like their drink and alcohol is not prohibited in this largely secular country, but still they make up only a sizeable minority of the country's population – nearly 95% of Tunisians are lifetime teetotallers or ex-drinkers.[2] Perhaps the pious Tunisian had in mind the reported 50% of Tunisian students who drink and/or do marijuana,[3] or the growing demand for booze in Tunisia, despite the large hikes in what in the Anglosphere is referred to as "sin tax".[4]

My confused stupor was intensified by another thought. What about the bulk of humanity for whom alcohol is not prohibited? They count the most successful societies in the world in their number, from Europe and the Americas, to Japan and China. By this reckoning, it is a miracle that Europeans ever managed to pick themselves up off the tavern floor, dust-off their vomit-smeared clothes, conquer and colonise most of the world, set in motion the industrial revolution, and continue to be one of the wealthiest, most technologically advanced regions in the planet. When I put this to the Tunisian sage, his response was profoundly bewildering to my faculties. "It's because they are not Muslims and we are," he countered. "God gave us a different moral code and they have learned to live with and handle alcohol. When a Muslim drinks, he drinks to excess." It is unfair, you may think, that God should use one measure for Muslims and another for non-believers, allowing one party to have all the fun while the other party must stick to his fundamentals, foregoing the intoxicating pleasure of booze until they reach heaven, where there flow "rivers of wine, a delight to the drinkers."[5] Even more confusingly, I have heard other Muslim sages explain that God is actually 'punishing' Westerners with sex, booze and rock'n'roll. Or then again, maybe God is not testing Muslims but punishing them for their transgressions. Muslims lost their powerful empires, and became subject to foreign domination because "they succumbed to comforts and luxuries, discarded the Quran and *hadith*, resorted to oppression and cruelty of their subjugates [*sic*], became power-drunk and arrogant and indulged openly in wine and women," warned Muhammad Faruq Meeruti, an Indian scholar of Islam. And, centuries on, the Muslim *umma*, or nation, like a snoring drunkard in the gutter, still refuses to wake up. "The Muslims continue to lead a sedentary existence of listlessness, heedlessness, indulgence in luxuries and pleasures."[6]

Duty-free Islam

Among conservative Muslims, the theory that alcohol – alongside sexual promiscuity – has contributed to the demise and downfall of Islam is a surprisingly common one. One reason for this is the myth that what once made Islam great was the piety of believers and how closely they followed Islamic precepts. In order to make Islam great again, the theory goes, Muslims need to revert to 'true' Islam and live according to its 'authentic' spirit – which certainly does not include alcoholic spirits, wine, beer and other intoxicating drinks. Booze is a visible and symbolic sign of the departure from this supposedly pristine original condition, and a staggering exhibition of dereliction of Islamic duty.

Apparently unaware of the paradox that the very word 'alcohol' is an Arabic one and that Muslims were the first to distil potent spirits,[7] Islamists and Muslim conservatives are fond of depicting drinking as a foreign vice exported by the West and imported by immoral secular Muslim elites as part of a conspiracy to lead Muslims drunkenly off the precipice into a dazed oblivion, from which they cannot rise to claim back their rights or be productive members of the community. It is this liquor-induced decadence, rather than religion, that is figuratively the true 'opium of the masses'. Even if the masses, according to Muslim conservatives, do not actually drink, they are rendered prostrate by the waft emanating from the elites who do, although, as I shall show later, drinking is in fact a centuries-old pursuit for the common Muslim too. "The Europeans worked assiduously in trying to immerse (the world) in materialism, with their corrupting traits and murderous germs, to overwhelm those Muslim lands that their hands stretched out to," wrote Hassan al-Banna, the founding father of the Muslim Brotherhood, the most influential Islamist group in Egypt and numerous other countries, implying incorrectly that Muslim countries were not materialistic before the arrival of Europeans. Although Banna was writing at a time of direct European colonial rule, he did not see military occupation as the greatest danger or evil. Rather, he regarded the cultural invasion of the Muslim soul as being "far more dangerous than any political or military campaign" because it appealed to the mind.

And how was this occurring? In addition to altering the "basic principles of government, justice, and education," Europeans "imported their semi-naked women into these regions, together with their liquors, their theatres, their dance halls, their amusements arcades, their stories, their newspapers, their novels, their whims, their silly games, and their vices," Banna asserted, as though none of these things had existed in Egypt or the wider Muslim world before the arrival of those cunning, corrupting Westerners. Banna reserved his choicest venom for the local (secular) elites, whom he believed were aping Europe blindly. "The enemies of Islam can deceive Muslim intellectuals and draw a thick veil over the eyes of the zealous by depicting Islam as defective in various aspects of doctrine, ritual observance, and morality," Banna railed.[8] One of Banna's disciples and an intellectual cornerstone of the Muslim Brotherhood at the time, Sayyid Qutb, would, in his path to radicalisation, take these ideas even further and declare that true Islam no longer existed and Muslim societies had reverted to a phase of post-Islamic '*Jahiliyyah*' (the supposed state of pre-Islamic ignorance) full of imported western vice – including drink. When outlining the case for banning alcohol in Egypt, Qutb states that "alcohol is undeniably forbidden, and the Islamic community can never countenance its use." In case any of the faithful was in any doubt, Qutb explains that Islam prohibits drinking because, "It is related to luxury and the idleness that arises from luxury... and the watchfulness that Islam prescribes can never be reconciled with alcohol or any other drug. Islam does not accept any cowardly escape from reality or distortion of life."[9]

Odes to wine

The trouble with Sayyid Qutb's conception (and that of other Islamists) of a pristine and 'virtuous' Islam in which Muslims did not drink is that it never really existed. However, it is not only Islamists who believe that drinking is an imported habit in Islamic societies. Many mainstream Muslims, even those who do not read a moral or political dimension into alcoholic beverages, also regard drinking as a manifestation of 'westernisation', quite literally a form of 'westoxification'.[10] As a child in London, I grew up with the impression that because drinking was *haram*, it was a European habit, even though some Muslim friends of the family did drink. On the way to the UK, when I was too young to know what alcohol was, we travelled in Lebanon and Syria, where I have a recollection of hours spent on long meals outdoors, and while the kids played, I now realise some of the adults, but not my parents, drank booze.

As I got older and my English friends started to express interest in drinking, alcohol was an intriguingly exotic notion but one that was not for me as a Muslim who was still at the stage of believing that what his mother told him was gospel. With time, I began to loosen up gradually. The first step was to order drinks at the pub for my English friends. Although none of us were yet old enough, being very tall for my age, and perhaps my skin tone, tended to fool those pulling pints. I moved back to Egypt just as my English peers were discovering alcohol. Had I continued to live there, I would have likely eventually joined them, especially as I was growing up at a time and place where the Muslims in my life did not primarily identify as Muslims – their primary identities were based on nationality or nation of origin and secular political ideology. This may help explain why it did not take me too long to take up drinking after arriving in Cairo. I was helped in this through my discovery that, *haram* or not, many Muslims drank, although most did so with varying degrees of guilt because of drinking's religious status as a 'sin', though they saw it as a largely harmless one. My first sips of forbidden fermented fruits and grains was accompanied with a strong sense of guilt and doubt, but this lapsed with time. My eventual loss of faith and growing awareness of history alleviated any residual uncertainty, clearing my conscience of the dregs of doubt.

The history of drinking in Islam is a little bit like an eccentric old relative who occasionally turns up at family events, gets a bit tipsy and starts embarrassing your parents with anecdotes about the drunken indiscretions of their youth. Despite the formal prohibition of alcohol in Islamic jurisprudence, as far as I can ascertain, there has never been a time in Islamic history in which Muslim societies imposed a universal ban on alcohol. Throughout Islam's one and a half millennia of existence, there has always been at least a significant minority of Muslims who have consumed alcohol. Contrary to contemporary convictions, this was especially the case in the early centuries of Islam. Despite the image of the so-called *jahiliyya* period as being pickled in alcohol, there was actually very little wine in the Arabia of the time and most of it was imported from other, more fertile regions of the Middle East, such as Syria, Mesopotamia and Persia. This may provide some historical context for why Islam developed the notion that consuming alcohol was a ruinous indulgence, not only because of the dangers of intoxication but of the huge financial burden it placed on those who drank, and by extension their families, clans and wider society. During this largely undocumented period shrouded in historical mystery, the rarity of wine was reflected in pre-Islamic poetry, where wine was often employed as a symbol of the abundant wealth of a chieftain and his excessive Arab generosity, not to mention, his manly ability to hold his drink. As Islam spread from Arabia to the more urban, cultivated areas of the Middle East, a shift in poetic attitudes to wine was perceptible. Boozing went from being an incidental feature of the traditional *qasida* (a classical Arabic poem which follows a single, elaborate metre throughout) to become a genre of witty and oft-humorous poetry in its own right, with romantic and spiritual sub-genres, which was known as *khamiriyat* (from the Arabic for grape or date wine, *khamr*).[11] For many poets who indulged in wine and sang its praises in verse, it was a till-death-us-do-part sort of bond. Abu Mihjan al-Thaqafi, a companion of Muhammad who was so fond of his tipple that he went into battle drunk, reportedly wrote:[12]

> *If I should die bury me by a vine*
> *Whose roots after death may slake my bones' thirst*

This was parodied by a wine poet from the Umayyad era, the first hereditary dynasty in Islam, which developed a reputation for boozing in the Islamic imagination. Abu al-Hindi asserted:

> *When I die make vine leaves my winding-sheet [shroud],*
> *with the wine press as my grave;*
> *I hope in future to have from God the boon of pardon,*
> *after all the wine I've drunk*

Given our ISIS-imbued image of the caliphate today, it may surprise us that not just raunchy poets but also caliphs could take poetic licence to sacrilegious and blasphemous excess. Alluding to the Quran's banishment of poets to the desert wilderness,[13] the Umayyad Caliph Walid ibn Yazid (Walid II), who ruled for just over a year (743-4 AD),[14] wrote:[15]

> *How I wish today that*
> *My share of life's provisions*
> *Was a wine on which to squander*
> *My earnings and inheritance*
> *In every dry river valley*

But it was not until the dawn of the Abbasid caliphate, also filled with big drinkers, that wine poetry came into its hedonistic own. The man who perfected the genre was none other than the Persian-Arab poet Abu Nuwas, whose homoerotic poetry we encountered in the chapter on sex. Abu Nuwas often likened wine to a beautiful woman and wrote more fondly,

159

lovingly and convincingly of wine's feminine allure than he did that of any real woman. Abu Nuwas also employed Quranic and Biblical imagery and allusions in his wine verse, including Noah and Adam.[16] Despite the irreverent wit and mock heroism of the genre of *khamiriyat* developed by Abu Nuwas and his contemporaries, these Muslim poets continued the ancient tradition of *in veno veritas*. Wine poetry was not only about pleasure-seeking and finding, it often covered serious social and political issues, such as the inferior status of Persians and other non-Arabs in the early caliphates. Wine poetry also possessed a spiritual dimension. Sufi mystics often alluded to wine and inebriation in their verses describing the spiritual intoxication they felt in the divine presence. Although most Muslims today argue that such references were allegorical – and for some mystics they probably were – there is no reason to doubt that when some Sufis or mystical poets wrote about wine, they simply meant wine. In fact, some Sufi sects, such as the Malamatis, certainly did drink wine.[17] Like present-day hippies and their use of 'mind-expanding' substances, there were Sufis who saw intoxicants as a tool for enlightenment. For instance, Fuzuli, a 16th-century Sufi poet from Azerbaijan, compared the spiritual effects of hashish and wine. In this conception, hashish was the master of Sufi teaching, while wine was a mere disciple who could set the world on fire.[18] Many of the best practitioners of this genre of mystical *khamiriyat* were Persians or wrote in Persian. A shining example of this is the legendary 14th-century Persian poet Hafez, who remains the most popular poet in Iran and among Persian-speakers elsewhere, even though his verse is dominated by two things banned in the Islamic Republic, i.e. wine and women. which may partly explain the desire to reinterpret his verse as spiritual allegory, rather than a celebration of sensuous pleasure. The

Islamic Republic of Iran has a Hafez Day, which Supreme Leader Ali Khamenei has described as "the commemoration of Islamic and Iranian culture and pure thoughts." No mention is made of Hafez's infatuation with the bottle (unless this is what Khamenei meant by 'pure thoughts') and his love of women is swept under the carpet of mysticism. One Iranian professor went so far as to claim that Hafez shifted Persian poetry away from odes to the earthly beloved to express devotion for "God Almighty as the Supreme Beloved, and using metaphors to express his love for God and faith in Islam."[19] But it is incredibly hard to discern such mysticism in a lot of his verse. Take this example:[20]

> My breast is filled with roses,
> My cup is crowned with wine,
> And by my side reposes
> The maid I hail as mine.
> The monarch, wheresoe'er he be,
> Is but a slave compared to me!
> ...
>
> How blest am I! around me, swelling,
> The notes of melody arise;
> I hold the cup, with juice excelling,
> And gaze upon thy radiant eyes.
> O Hafiz!---never waste thy hours
> Without the cup, the lute, and love!

That verse does not appear in the slightest mystical, unless by 'mystical' is meant the shrugging off of the superficial trappings of life in favour of the simplicity of loving wine, women and music. If so, then we should also classify today's rock stars as mystics. "In the absence of reliable biographical data, the safest way to understand Hafez and fathom his beliefs and attitudes is to go by his own poems. To impose views not sanctioned by his poetry is to make Hafez a mirror of the views of his interpreters," urges the exasperated author of the entry on Hafez in the *Encyclopaedia Iranica*. "Making an oracular saint and a mystic out of him, rather than a superb and truly great poet, will mean ignoring the transparency of his language and the lucidity of his diction." In fact, Hafez, who appropriately enough came from the Persian wine capital, Shiraz, wrote biting satire about those Sufi mystics who disguised themselves in cloaks of poverty while secretly consuming wine. The irreverent wit also mocked the Islamic clergy, which is conveniently overlooked by today's clerics. He especially ridiculed those who forbade their flocks from drinking while being drunkards themselves. In one poem, Hafez disparages a *faqih*, or scholar, who issued a *fatwa* prohibiting alcohol, which he wrote while drunk.

In addition to biting satire, Hafez also regularly employed irony. His contempt for religious hypocrites, rather than honest drinkers and lovers like himself, is anything but subtle in his poetry. "I would rather choose an abject wine-seller or a debauchee as my spiritual guide and mentor than one of you liars and cheats," Hafez declares in one verse. "Let us have wine, since the *shaikh*, the *hafez* [memorizer], the *mofti*, and the *mohtaseb* [the bazaar supervisor] are all cheats when you look closely," he urged in another.[21] Reading verses like this, I wonder what Hafez would have made of the reported spat, in 2016, between Iran and France over whether wine would be served during a luncheon in Paris for the Iranian president Hassan Rouhani, which ended with the cancellation of the event because neither side was willing to capitulate.[22] Would Hafez have sided with the clerics ruling modern Iran or would he have sided with the French, or would he have pronounced a curse on both their houses, deriding their dogma, which they let get in the way of more important issues? After all, the affair was ultimately about anything but wine. It was about identity politics, with both France's socialist president François Hollande and Iran's reformist Rouhani conscious of the political mileage their conservative enemies would gain if either showed signs of pragmatism.

In the spirit of the times

While all these Islamic odes to wine and the actual drinking they portrayed may seem peculiar from our 21st-century vantage, they made a lot of sense in the context of the time. When Islam broke out of Arabia, it spread into areas where alcoholic beverages were a millennia-old integral part of the culture. In Egypt and Mesopotamia, beer brewing stretches back to the very dawn of civilisation, with its origins shrouded in the mystery of pre-recorded history. The ancient Egyptians believed that beer had been invented by the chief god, Osiris, and though wine was also produced and consumed, beer was the Egyptian poison of choice until Greco-Roman times, and was used as a substitute for water, for entertainment and as divine offerings.[23] As for wine, it was arguably invented in what we today call the Middle East, most likely in the Fertile Crescent.[24] By the time Islam arrived, wine was a long-established aspect of daily life, from the profane to the sacred, and a pivotal sector of the economy. Rather than spoil the fun with an Islamic prohibition in this ocean of alcohol in which they were a minority, the conquering Arabs seem to have simply chosen to join the party.

During the classical Islamic period, the main action the rulers took against alcohol was to limit its production to non-Muslims, mostly Christians, Zoroastrians (Zoroastrianism had been the dominant religion of Persia), and Jews. However, as the *khamiriyat* and other Arab sources attest, the consumption of alcohol was not limited to non-Muslims. In fact, Muslims may have even made up the bulk of business in many drinking establishments. "The Jews and Armenians prepare wine on purpose for the Mohamedans, by adding lime, hemp and other ingredients, to increase its pungency and strength," observed one bewildered 19th-century European traveller in Persia, "for the wine that soonest intoxicates is accounted the best, and the lighter and more delicate kinds, are held in no estimation among the adherents of the prophet."[25] In many Muslim countries today, this still appears to be the case. When per-capita alcohol consumption is calculated based on the entire population, Muslim-majority countries consistently come out at the bottom of the league. But when you remove abstainers from the equation, the picture becomes very different. According to this measure, the top alcohol consumption per head in the world is in, of all places, Chad, which also defines what constitutes an alcoholic beverage as starting from 5.2% alcohol content.[26] This attitude, which can still be found to the modern day among some Muslim drinkers, may stem from the notion that, since alcohol is considered a sin, there is no point to sinning in half-measures. It could also be a function of the taboo attached to drinking, which results in many Muslims not receiving an education in how to drink responsibly. Rather than theological questions, these excesses, especially by the idler segments of the upper classes, may have contributed to the stigma which eventually attached to drinking in Muslim societies. The demand for potent drink among the drinking minority in the Islamic world was quickly quenched by medieval Muslim scientists, fuelling one of the greatest paradoxes in

Islamic history: the invention of 'alcohol', which originally meant only distilled spirits, or the Water of Life, as it is often poetically referred to in Arabic. "It may be that the single most pervasive legacy of Islamic civilisation is not holy scripture, but the rather unholy art of distilling alcohol," observes Max Rodenbeck, the veteran Middle East correspondent and author of an acclaimed biography of Cairo.[27] "Not only were Arabs the first to make spirits. The great trading civilisation of Islam spread the skill across the globe, and in its lands some of the world's finest alcoholic concoctions are still made to this day." It is unclear whether medieval alchemists or chemists set out with the express purpose of creating more potent brews or whether this was simply an accidental, some would say serendipitous, side effect, of the quest to distil wine and other liquids for their medicinal and military uses, as well as for creating perfumes, as outlined in, for example, the famous treatise on *The Book of the Alchemistry of Perfume and Distillation* by the 9th century polymath al-Kindi. But I cannot help suspecting that some of these scientists did not just have healing, on their minds. In fact, the line between the medical and recreational could be, and remains, truly blurry (as the history of gin and tonic demonstrates). For example, Ibn Sina (Avicenna), the scientist often credited with first inventing a successful distillation process, relied on the odd cocktail (for a Muslim) of prayer and wine when he needed to ponder a difficult question.[28] In his 11th century seminal canon on medicine, Ibn Sina relates the various health benefits of drinking and recommends different wines for various desired effects: white wine is great for cooling down and doesn't cause headaches, thick sweet wine is ideal for those who wish to put on weight and gain in strength, while red wine is good for people with a "phlegmatic temperament". He recommends that people do not drink while eating, but after the food has been digested, unless they are accustomed to it. Modern Arab drinkers, accustomed to drinking with their *mezzes*, will scoff at this notion. He also advises those who intend to go on a bender only to eat fatty soup or porridge, gives tips on how to slow down the intoxicating effects of alcohol, and even, for those in a rush, how to accelerate drunkenness. The good scientist also offers remedies for intoxication. "The right thing to do for someone who has drunk excessively is to induce vomiting, if it is easy," he suggests, "otherwise, have them drink a lot of water, alone or with honey, then bathe in a bathtub, spread oil on the skin and put them to sleep."[29] Whether or not medieval Muslim scientists set out with the express purpose of developing effective technology for the development of potent spirits, the net effect was the same: distillation techniques spread like liquid fire across all the domains of Islam, where it was used to develop potent local spirits, often called *araq* (from the Arabic for the beads of "sweat" produced during distillation), and from there they conquered the world, as Rodenbeck highlighted in an entertaining article he wrote on the gift of Arab spirits.[30] Moreover, distillation proved to be something of a godsend in those times and places where Muslim rulers decided to ban the production of alcohol or punish those who consumed it. During periods like this, as during the prohibition years in America, drinking did not stop, it simply went underground. In addition to smuggling, a thriving cottage industry of bootleg spirits bubbles up wherever alcohol has been banned, even in Islam's land of origin, Saudi Arabia. For instance, when Iran or Sudan banned the consumption of alcohol, Sudanese and Iranian drinkers became amateur chemists, brewing up their own potent concoctions at home or buying them from illegal distillers. But this has attendant dangers, such as when the poisonous methanol is not distilled away, which can lead to death or blindness, as occurred in the southern Iranian city of Rafsanjan in 2013.[31] Many Sudanese are furious with the ban, which was introduced in 1983, and insist that drinking does not contradict their traditional Sufi culture.[32] As a sign of how prevalent boozing was in Sudan prior to the 1983 introduction of strict Islamic law, then president, Jaafar Nimeiri, used to be a drinker himself. A few years before the prohibition was introduced, he reportedly ordered members of his government, in 1976, either to give up drinking or to give up their positions.[33] For Iranians, who possess one of the oldest wine-making traditions in the world and who continued drinking for most of their Islamic history, prohibition since the 1979 revolution has been particularly tough, creating a lively if concealed underground party scene.

Alcohol-free Islam?

For generations, Muslims were actually a minority in much of the territories governed by the early Islamic empires. Contrary to popular myth, early Arab rulers had little appetite to spread their faith, with the Umayyads, for instance, mostly considering Islam the faith of the ruling Arab elite. In fact, the empire's economy was underpinned by the tax paid by non-Muslims and so conversions were costly to the state coffers.[34] Even when the Abbasids defeated the Umayyads, opening the gateway fully to conversion and filling its elite with Persians, it still took at least two centuries for Islam to become the majority religion in Persia.[35] In very Christian Egypt, this process took at least three or four centuries, possibly longer.[36] In this early stage of Islam, the wine produced in Islamic dominions, which was regarded as the best in the world before Charlemagne developed the French wine industry, was an important component of the

167

Abbasid economy and, in a reverse of the current reality, was exported to Europe, and the later Fatimid dynasty, which ruled out of Egypt, derived considerable revenue from taxing alcoholic beverages.[37]

Theologically, too, the idea that Islam prohibits the consumption of alcohol was not as clear-cut as it seems now, living as we are centuries after the establishment of rigid Islamic orthodoxy, when the religion has lost much of its original fluidity. This is hardly surprising since, rather than presenting a consistent view on intoxicating beverages, the Quran sets out a dizzyingly confusing array of views on the topic. In an early mention of fermented drink, the Quran exalts it, informing the faithful: "And from the fruits of the palm trees and grapevines you take intoxicant and good provision. Indeed in that is a sign for a people who reason."[38] In other words, God is promoting grape and date wine as the choice of sensible people because it gives them a buzz and is nutritious at the same time. After numerous incidents of Muslims behaving badly while drunk, the Quran commands them: "O you who have believed, do not approach prayer while you are intoxicated until you know what you are saying."[39] This verse seems to imply that as long as a Muslim does not slur his or her words, they are welcome to join the faithful in worship. Later, the Quran starts to sound stricter, but still God does not seem to want his followers to jump on the wagon. "They ask you about wine and gambling. Say, 'In them is great sin and benefit for people. But their sin is greater than their benefit.'"[40] Finally, God commands: "O you who have believed, indeed, intoxicants, gambling, [sacrificing on] stone altars [to other than Allah], and divining arrows are but defilement from the work of Satan, so avoid them that you may be successful."[41] Calling wine "the work of Satan" is much harsher but still God's heart does not really seem to be in it. Why is *khamr* grouped together with a miscellaneous list of random sins? The use of the words "avoid" and "successful" sounds more like a sober friend giving an alcoholic some life-changing tips than a thou-shalt-not type of divine deity commanding obedience. In addition, unlike the major sins outlined in the Quran, nowhere is there a punishment prescribed for drinking or even being drunk.

Irreverence aside, it is not just me who finds the Quranic verses confusing, early Muslims did too. Although today's generally accepted interpretation of the dizzying cocktail of contradictory Quranic verses on *khamr* is that alcohol is forbidden, there was heated controversy amongst the scholars and jurists of classical Islam as to whether their religion prohibited intoxicants or just advised against intoxication. For example, jurists from the Hanafi school of Islamic jurisprudence, including its founder Abu Hanifa, were convinced, following exhaustive textual analysis, that it was intoxication that was proscribed and that some alcoholic drinks, including *nabith* (a term which today is another word for wine, but which in classical Arabic meant a fruit-based beverage which could be drunk fermented or unfermented), was, in fact, permissible.[42] Even today, there are dissenting voices who disagree with the prohibition on religious grounds. Khaled al-Gendy, a prominent cleric and TV personality in Egypt, where the consumption and sale of alcohol is legal under secular laws, stirred controversy amongst conservative Muslims when he asserted that "If the same alcoholic drink was consumed by one person without getting drunk, it is not *haram*, while being consumed by another person to drunkenness makes it *haram*."[43]

It was possibly after Islam became the majority faith that attitudes to alcohol began to shift more radically. Part of the issue was demographic. In some parts of the Muslim world,

169

the non-Muslim communities who could produce alcohol for Muslims to consume dwindled over the centuries. In addition, Islam had begun life simply as a manifestation of the "true faith" correcting the "distortions" in Christianity and Judaism, but as it matured it needed to distinguish itself from its predecessors, to become a religion in its own right. Recommending moderation sounded too much like the rest, but forbidding alcohol was one way to give Islam a more distinctive brand identity. Moreover, Islamic philosophy has generally valued harmony and feared discord, or *fitna*, because it can disrupt the peace of the community, something that has been common in the unruly history of Islam, with or without the added ingredient of booze. Of course, social 'peace' is often just code for the peace of mind of the ruler and *fitna* can often be interpreted as disobedience of or rebellion against the ruler. In addition to being dens of 'vice', taverns and other drinking establishments are places where the disaffected can gather and plot, fuelled perhaps with some variety of Dutch courage or other.

Science-proofing prohibition

Modern Muslims often seek out a science-based argument for the prohibition of alcohol, citing statistics on the detrimental effects of alcoholism on the individual and the costs to society. "Statistics bear witness to the fact that the devastating impact of alcohol consumption on human civilisation is no myth and is becoming increasingly apparent as society continuously fails in its attempts to control drinking," one article in a publication which seeks to present Islam's "rational, harmonious and inspiring nature" asserted. "As the world acknowledges the harmful impact of alcohol and scrambles to minimise its detrimental effects, many are unaware that in the history of human civilisation there does indeed exist a time when a society was purged of the troubles that accompany alcohol consumption."[44] While nobody can doubt the negative side effects of alcohol addiction and abuse – including a host of diseases and the carnage caused by drunk driving – this line of argument is disingenuous for a number of reasons. Not only does it claim incorrectly that Islamic societies have been purged of the troubles that accompany alcohol consumption, it also presents a black-and-white picture of drinking. Although a minority of drinkers do fall prey to alcoholism, the majority drink in moderation. It also overlooks the large body of scientific evidence pointing to the health benefits of moderate drinking. For instance, dozens of studies have proven that moderate drinking reduces the risk of cardiovascular disease by 25% to 40% because it raises the levels of high-density lipoprotein (otherwise known as 'good cholesterol'), according to the Harvard School of Public Health.[45] Young and old alike benefit from moderate drinking, with young women in particular showing clear signs of better health than not just heavy drinkers but also abstainers.[46] Another extensive study of women found that moderate, regular drinking reduced the risk of hypertension, myocardial infarction, stroke, sudden cardiac arrest, gallstones, cognitive decline, and mortality in general. "Women with low to moderate intake and regular frequency (> 3 days/week) had the lowest risk of mortality compared with abstainers," the researchers concluded.[47] Thus one could argue that, while Islam's prohibition of alcohol benefits the minority of drinkers who become alcoholics by keeping them out of harm's way, it harms the far larger number of people who drink in moderation. Besides, even if science proved alcohol to be 100% healthy, devout Muslims would still not drink, because they believe God ordered them to, and God has reasons for asking things which are often beyond our comprehension, or so the reasoning goes.

When weighing up the pros and cons of prohibiting alcohol, one must also consider the substitutes Muslims consume in place of alcohol, even though a drinker may not regard them as adequate substitutes and may see them rather as complements. Although the consensus amongst most Islamic scholars is that any substance that intoxicates or causes bodily harm is *haram*, the social stigma and taboo attached to other soft drugs, namely cannabis, is usually lower.[48] This explains why the use of the various cannabis derivatives, including *bungo*, *keef* and *hashish*, is more prevalent than alcohol in many Muslim societies. In past centuries, *hashish* was even known among Sufis as the 'wine of the poor'.[49] I have met lots of Muslims over the years who would not touch a drop of alcohol but would happily roll a joint, and for similar motives to drinkers: to relax, to unwind, to overcome social anxiety, etc. While cannabis, like alcohol, has many beneficial aspects, it also comes with a small risk of addiction and other health issues, especially for long-term users, such as temporary hallucinations and paranoia, cognitive problems and the same dangers as smoking tobacco.[50] Indeed, for those who do not indulge in any kind of soft recreational drug, tobacco is often the poison of choice, which partly explains why smoking is so prevalent in many Muslim communities (the absence of effective anti-smoking campaigns is also a factor). While tobacco does not have the same intoxicating effects as alcohol, except for the buzz caused to those who smoke rarely or have just begun, its long-term health effects are devastating. In the United States, for instance, smoking is linked to more preventable deaths each year than alcohol abuse, illegal drug use, HIV, road accidents and shootings.[51] Another substitute is *qat*, which goes by various local names, a mild stimulant chewed or drunk in the Horn of Africa and southern Arabia. It is especially popular in Yemen. Although it is not physically addictive, some users develop a psychological dependence on the plant. It causes a mild high, usually triggering a sense of euphoria, heightened sociability and excitement in the user. In the long term, however, it can lead to feelings of depression, anorexia, as well as infrequent hallucinatory or psychotic episodes, and oral cancer.[52] Another major impact of *qat* is environmental. In Yemen, for instance, demand is so enormous that almost 40% of the country's agricultural water resources are used to grow the popular plant, whose production now swallows up 15% of farmland, exacerbating the current food crisis.[53]

Despite the spread and prevalence of other soft recreational drugs in Muslim societies, drink still occupies pride of place in the popular imagination for its perceived corrupting effects. In times of turbulent change or violent upheaval, alcohol takes on a special poignancy, as the root of evil, a marker of the corruption of the elites or the corrosive effects of 'imported' customs. For instance, the periods when Egypt's normally hard-drinking Mamluk rulers cracked down on alcohol often coincided with outbreaks of plague or the failure of the Nile waters to rise during the critical flooding season.[54] This can also be seen in Ibn Taymiyyah's war on drinking. Ibn Tawmiyyah, an accomplished but bigoted scholar who came from a long line of scholars (including a celebrated female one), was born and lived during the destructive and turbulent times of the Mongol invasions of the Levant in the 14th century. His upbringing was a traumatic one, as he became a refugee when his family fled the Mongol forces before they destroyed his birth town of Harran, on today's

Syrian-Turkish border. Not only did he join the resistance against the Mongols in Syria, he was the first Islamic scholar to conclude that it was permissible to declare jihad against Muslims if they were living in a state of 'jahiliyya', inspiring modern radical Islamists, like the jihadist in Syria and Iraq, as well as Sayyid Qutb, as outlined earlier in the chapter. Ibn Taymiyyah puritanism saw him campaigning against the sale and taxation of alcohol and conducting vigilante attacks against taverns.[55]

Alcohol was sometimes banned due to the deranged whims of an unhinged ruler. This occurred a couple of times during the erratic rule of the Fatimid caliph, al-Hakim bi-Amr Allah, the Nero or Donald Trump of his day. But Egyptians are nothing if not resourceful. Taken by surprise by the novelty of his first ban, when he, on a whim, decided to reverse his reversal of the prohibition, the city's inhabitants somehow got advance warning and bought up most of the wine stock before the caliph's men could destroy it. However, for the most part, Egypt's Fatimid rulers had no qualms about alcohol and only restricted its sale during important religious festivals.[56] This still lives on in modern times. While the majority of Muslims go without food or drink from dawn to dusk during Ramadan, some Egyptians suffer a special kind of thirst because the law prohibits Egyptians from purchasing alcohol during the holy month. This is hypocritical and contradictory on so many fronts. This means that an Egyptian Christian cannot order a drink at a bar during Ramadan but a European or Arab Muslim can. This has led to preposterous situations, for instance, a teetotalling foreigner who buys a beer for a drinking Egyptian, and surreptitiously passes it on disguised as a non-alcoholic beverage. This temporary, partial prohibition is also the ultimate in nanny-statism. If the state permits the production and sale of alcohol, it must leave it up to the individual citizen as to how (s)he relates to its moral dimension – it is not the state's role to be our moral guardians. There was a time when I, like many Muslim drinkers, voluntarily gave up drinking for Ramadan, rather like how some lapsed Christians give up certain 'vices' for Lent. When I fasted, particularly in the final years, it was only mildly out of a sense of religious duty, since I didn't practise any of the other pillars of Islam, but more as an act of self-discipline and for the unique spirit of the month. I would often join drinking friends for a last drink before the month-long road which lay ahead. Though fasting got much easier physically, it became much tougher philosophically and eventually I was no longer willing or able to square the philosophical circle or cognitive dissonance of performing just one ritual of a faith I no longer believed in and had abandoned, except for certain of its cultural trappings. For years, I have drunk during Ramadan. In Tunisia, which despite being more secular also shuts down the sale of alcohol during Ramadan, I make sure to build up a minimum stockpile to help quench my thirst, as foreign friends and Egyptians I knew who continued drinking did in Cairo. This can make you feel a little like a closet alcoholic. Having had no car at the time, I went to the supermarket a couple of times to stock up. As luck would have it, I got the same woman at the checkout, which made me feel a little awkward. I wondered what this pious-looking lady in a hijab made of the clanking of the bottles as I packed them into my backpack. Perhaps she thought nothing and, veteran that she was, had grown accustomed to the pre-Ramadan rush of the unholy to empty out the alcohol aisle.

Champagne Muslims

As is clear from the above, traditionalists and fundamentalists have tended to portray, and condemn, drinking as an elite indulgence and sin. But, in my view, this is more wishful thinking than a reflection of any actual reality. The majority of Muslims around the world do not drink, but those who do come from a diverse patchwork of backgrounds, social groups and socio-economic classes. The myth is a blatant and transparent attempt, in my analysis, to 'other' drinkers and put them beyond the pale of the community. In this mythology, an authentic citizen is an upright, noble Muslim who dispenses his religious duties, while those who drink are part of a detached elite who cannot stand upright because they stagger too much from all the alcohol they pour down their gullets. Of course, it does not help that corrupt or authoritarian ruling elites have a tendency to indulge in alcohol, often while professing piety. The worst example of this is the Saudi royal family, which is regularly hit with with drinking-related scandals. This was demonstrated by the Wikileaks cables containing details of parties thrown by certain Saudi princes featuring sex, booze and rock 'n' roll.[57] For me, the issue here should not be the drinking, which conservatives latch on to, but the utter hypocrisy of a ruling family which tells its subjects to do as they say, not as they do, and the Wahhabi clergy which hypocritically turns a blind eye to the excesses of the royals while turning the screws against the mass of the population for even minor 'moral' infractions. Being from a secular pan-Arabist family, the excesses of the Saudi royals were a popular topic of conversation for my parents and their friends.

But it is not just the royals and the upper classes who indulge in forbidden (fermented) fruits, common Saudis do too, but the risks they run are far higher and their access to prohibited substances is far lower, forcing them to rely on oft-dangerous bootleg brews, which are colloquially known as *Sadiqi* or *Sidiqi* ('my friend'), often abbreviated to 'Sid', and a variety of other monikers. *Sadiqi* can be up to 80% alcohol and is sometimes made using sewage water, according to one report in the Arabic-language media. Despite the huge risks involved, the underground booze business is thriving. Most Saudi either do not believe that this is going on in the kingdom, or think it is exclusively limited to foreigners, "liberals" and the stigmatised Shi'a community. Callers-in to a radio show claimed that Saudi youth would not drink because they are "proud of the religion and traditions", according to the same report. Saudi's morality police are more honest about the real extent of the underground drinking culture. In the space of a single month, they shut down 50 illegal 'factories' in southern Riyadh alone, and though the producers tend to be illegal immigrants, the consumers include many, many Saudis. Although one figure in the morality police described this as a "foreign conspiracy" to corrupt the kingdom's youth, young Saudis disagreed and some even suggested that alcohol consumption should be decriminalised.[58]

In more secular Muslim countries where alcohol is legal, consumption is much more evenly spread. In Tunisia, where I am currently living, people from all walks of life and economic classes drink. When I go to buy wine, I see people of all ages and walks of life queuing outside the narrow, grill-encased windows of the dispensary or perusing the wine aisle at the supermarket. Once, shortly after arriving in Tunis, a scruffily dressed man approached my son and me at a street-side teahouse and invited himself to sit down. Amiable, if somewhat odd, the man related his story as an illegal immigrant in Europe and his deportation some months earlier back to Tunisia, where he had been struggling to find employment ever since. I made sympathetic noises and offered to buy him a drink, which he declined, explaining that he preferred something stronger. When it came time to go home, my new 'friend' asked if that was wine in the bag by my feet. When I answered in the affirmative, he asked: "Are you going to drink it now? If you are, I can come home with you and join you." Now it was my turn to decline his generous offer and explain that I didn't drink that early in the day, and I had to take my son somewhere. He then offered to come by later, an invitation I politely turned down.

This hints at the key difference between the less-privileged and the moneyed elites – it is not a question of piety but of ability. Owing to low overall demand, high taxation or prohibition, alcohol can be an expensive luxury in many Muslim societies. Some may abstain altogether because of the financial constraints, as I once did when going through money troubles.

To take the case of my native Egypt, those who can afford it may drink upmarket local wines or imported spirits. Meanwhile, poorer drinkers may knock back potentially deadly local imitation brands or home-made concoctions, even though alcohol is legal in the country. In Cairo, there are drinking establishments to suit a wide range of budgets and there was a time when people could sit out on the pavement at street-side cafes and drink, but now it generally has to be done inside the establishment, behind frosted glass. Wealthier city dwellers drink at trendy bars, posh restaurants or fancy clubs, while those on tighter budgets frequent dingier, spit-and-sawdust locales, known as 'baladi' bars. Cairo also, of course, has bars that are local institutions in their own right, bringing together drinkers and thinkers from across the socio-economic spectrum, such as Hurriya in downtown Cairo, or the Café Riche. The former place is a cross between a traditional, smokey Cairo ahwa (coffee-shop or tea house) and a belle époque cafe.

As Islamists and traditionalists perceive it, Egypt was a dry and pious land until it was contaminated, polluted and defiled by Western imperialism, followed by native, 'Godless' liberalism, socialism and pan-Arabism, and with their proposed bans they want to return Egypt to this pure, unsullied past. The inconvenient truth, however, is that this utopian past never existed. While living for a couple of years in Egypt in the first quarter of the 19th century, before the country had been influenced much by Europe, the British orientalist Edward Lane wrote about the widespread, if private, drinking habits of many of the Egyptians he encountered of various classes and occupations, "thinking it no sin to indulge thus in moderation".[59] This Egypt contrasts with some other Muslim drinking cultures we have considered, where excess seemed the object. This, and the fact that numerous Egyptians Lane met found it "no sin" to drink could relate to the fact that the Hanafi school, with its relatively benign attitude to the permissibility of drinking without intoxication, predominates in Egypt. While elite Egyptians drank wine, both fermented and distilled, poorer Egyptians, Lane informs us, drank what they called '*boozah*', (which is interestingly the contemporary Levantine word for ice-cream). The two words may not be as unrelated as they seem. In Turkey, *boozah*, which is a word of Turkic origin, is a sweet, barley- or millet-based drink which can be drunk fermented or unfermented. The *boozah* Lane came across was made of crumbled barley bread with added water, which was left to ferment, and was drank by Nile boatsmen and other poorer Egyptians. Lane, who ironically did not drink wine himself, described the practice of pre- or post-meal wine-drinking engaged in by his Egyptian friends during the elaborate ritual of the "wine table".[60] Like other ancient

Mediterranean peoples, Egyptians indulged in a separate *majlis al-khamr* ('wine session') after dinner, where the booze was accompanied by music, conversation or debate, and light snacks.[61]

This permissive Egyptian attitude was also prevalent in medieval times, long, long before any perceptible European influence had arrived in the Nile valley. "In Cairo of the Middle Ages alcoholic beverages were never universally scorned," writes Anna Paulina Lewicka, a professor of oriental studies at the University of Warsaw, in a history of food and drink in the Egyptian capital. "Neither the local population nor the members of the foreign ruling elites nor the multinational soldiery garrisoned within the city area were avowed abstainers." The difference between the classes, like today, was in what kind of booze they indulged in: the upper classes drinking wine and the masses drinking beer, which was known as '*mizr*' at the time, and later *boozah,* though medieval *boozah* may have been different to the one Lane encountered, and more akin to the Turkic original, which was made of millet grain. The favourite wine of medieval Cairo was known as *shamsi* (meaning 'sunny'), a long-lasting vintage made of imported raisins and honey which were left to ferment in the sun, hence its name. Amazingly, a 15th-century theologian by the name of Shams al-Deen al-Nawaji wrote a book in praise of the common Cairene practice of early morning drinking, known as *sabuh* (from the Arabic for morning). While the pious headed for the mosque to pray, Cairo's revellers started a different type of devotion at the crack of dawn. There were also the quasi-alcoholic drinks, like the elusive *fuqqa',* which medieval chroniclers were ambiguous about whether it was an intoxicant or not. It appears that there were numerous recipes for the concoction and one of them may have been a fizzy, frothy, mildly intoxicating drink, a kind of 'champagne' of medieval Egypt.[62]

Colonial or patriotic boozing?

The arrival of European imperialism in the latter part of the 19th century did not teach Egyptians to drink, as the above clearly demonstrates. The key difference it made was in what Egyptians drank and how they drank it. Egyptians developed a taste for imported European wines, spirits and beers, and for consuming them in European-style cafes and bars. In addition, European entrepreneurs established Egypt's modern alcohol industry. For instance, Stella beer, one of the most popular brands in the country, was first established by entrepreneurs from Belgium and named for the Belgian equivalent. With growing nationalism, a unique thing happened, Egyptian Muslims became officially involved in alcohol production for the first time since Islam had arrived in the country.[63] Not only was beer openly advertised for much of the 20th century, buying Egyptian beer was promoted as the 'patriotic' thing to do by Egyptian nationalists in a newspaper ad from the 1920s – a tradition pursued during the Nasser years.[64]

During Egypt's state-controlled socialist era, Stella deteriorated to become a kind of magical potion of variable strength and quality – sometimes the drinker could get tipsy from a single bottle and at other times a crate might just about give you a buzz. The local wine of choice (pretty much the only wine in fact) was Omar al-Khayyam, named for the Persian polymath, poet and *bon vivant* whose love and wine poetry was rediscovered by Muslims thanks to its popularity in the West. Sadly, the wine is not as sublime as Khayyam's poetry. Today, after liberalisation, Egypt produces a wide range of quality alcoholic beverages, some of which have won international prizes, and off-licences, have sprouted up everywhere, including specialised chain stores. As with just about everything else in Cairo, you can have your booze delivered directly to your home at almost any hour of the day or night. Nevertheless, the status of alcohol is precarious, caught as it is in a polarised landscape of greater tolerance pitted against growing puritanism.

Personally, I do not object to Muslim conservatives viewing drinking as a sin; that is entirely within their rights. What I object to is the insistence amongst Islamists to politicise alcohol by depicting it as one of the main causes of Islam's malaise, which also makes it, inevitably, a mode of rebellion against stifling religious authoritarianism. Not only is this simplistic formulation a serious misdiagnosis of the Muslim world's problems, it also infringes on the rights of those who wish to be left alone in peace to enjoy their drink without fear of retribution. Even if it is a sin and a form of cultural *jahiliyya*, let us drown in our sinful ignorance while you swim in the ocean of your virtue. Isn't it enough for you to know that we will burn in hell while you drink from rivers of heavenly wine? And if we do not become toast, we will toast your good health.

CHAPTER SIX

Jesus v Muhammad: Of prophets and messiahs

Although I am an atheist and was raised a Muslim, I have been touched by Jesus. And I don't mean figuratively. The past two millennia had not been particularly kind to him. Dressed in a white toga and trademark sandals, with a woollen blanket draped over one shoulder, he had piled on the pounds, his long brown hair was streaked with grey and his progress through the streets of the old city of Jerusalem did not elicit the slightest interest, neither from locals nor even pilgrims. One time, I mustered up the resolve to approach him. "I enjoyed seeing the Pope in Bethlehem," the friendly Jesus figure told me, referring to Pope Francis's visit in May 2014. "I am a devout Christian but also a Jew at heart."

Of course, Jesus, during his first coming, saw himself as nothing more than a Jewish reformer, but I wasn't about to quibble with such a friendly eccentric who may have been suffering from what some psychologists have dubbed the 'Jerusalem syndrome'. I felt awkward about asking him if he was actually *the* Jesus Christ. I felt it would be rude, as he seemed so confident in his assumed identity that he appeared to assume

I knew who he was. For ordinary believers, such delusions (whether of grandeur or paranoia) seem incomprehensible, somewhat unsettling and even pitiful. But looked at rationally, they are not all that weird. After all, there is a fine line between spiritual rapture and emotional or psychological rupture, especially for the already disturbed or troubled.

An inkling of this can be seen in Sufi devotees during a religious ceremony of trance-like swaying and dancing known as a *zar*, when they temporarily lose their connection with the world and believe they are floating through various states of consciousness, which they believe include *qurb* (nearness), *wajd* (ecstasy), *sukr* (intoxication) and *wudd* (intimacy).[1] Many Christian pilgrims in Jerusalem feel ecstasy because they are convinced that the spirit of Jesus is all around them; on the Via Dolorosa, where, in emulation of Jesus, some carry crosses of their own, in the Church of the Holy Sepulchre, in the Cenacle, the presumed venue of the Last Supper. There is even a nondescript rock face just outside the old city's wall, in the Garden Tomb, near Damascus Gate, that is believed by quite a few Protestants to be the visage of Jesus. The leap of faith required to go from seeing Jesus (or any other religious figure) to being Jesus may be far smaller than most of us appreciate. It could start with discerning the eyes and the nose of your saviour instead of a cliff face. It may then graduate to feeling ecstasy at the divine presence, and such an intimacy and union with the Son of God that the line separating worshipper from worshipped begins to blur, until the saved may start believing he has become the saviour.

I witnessed this at a coffee shop popular with evangelicals and Messianic Jews in Jerusalem's old city. One woman, a Messianic Jew who was also somehow a Seventh Day Adventist, was talking loudly about her vision. The prophetess was following in the footsteps of her prophet, William Miller, who predicted that the Second Coming, and the end of the world, would occur in 1844.[2] Seemingly undeterred by Miller's failure and the Great Disappointment it unleashed,[3] the divinely guided woman prophesied, based on her reading of the Bible, that the Messiah would come down to Earth and build the Third Temple before Yom Kippur in 2016. Needless to say, the end times passed and time continued to march on stubbornly and defiantly. Stubborn and defiant, those awaiting the end times march on undeterred, seeking out the next sign that Jesus is coming. In fact, the prophetess I met may have been onto something, but her clairvoyance clock was set a few minutes fast. Don't take my word for it. There is a group of end-time pastors who are convinced that Donald Trump is the messiah who will not only defend Israel (despite the anti-Semites he seems to attract) but will also build the Third Temple.[4] 'The Donald' is not only the most unlikely US president ever, he is also the most improbable Christian messiah ever. Vulgar, semi-literate, unforgiving, vindictive, elitist, privileged and racist, Trump cuts a very Christ-unlike figure, as reflected in the photos from his encounter with Pope Francis II. He may indeed have felt like some sort of messiah following the legendary welcome he received on his first foreign tour as president, which took him to the holiest places for Muslims, Jews and Christians. Had Trump not been a Republican willing to bend to the Christian right's will, I suspect rightwing evangelicals would have condemned him as the 'anti-Christ'. While the billionaire messiah opined that not paying taxes was "smart" and constantly boasts about how rich and successful he is, Jesus held a Communist-like disdain for the wealthy, with his conviction that: "It is easier for a camel to go through the eye of a needle than for a rich man to enter the Kingdom of God."[5] The extra preposterousness of

the notion of Trump as messiah appears in a blaze of glory if
you try to imagine The Donald delivering his own version of
the Sermon on the Mount; the Sermon at the Trump Tower
(perhaps delivered by tweet). This is how I picture what Trump
would tell the assembled Trumpians:

Cursed are the leftists and liberals
For theirs is the prison cell
Cursed are the poor
For they are lazy Obamacarists
Cursed are the scientists and experts
For demanding facts and evidence
Cursed are journalists and the media
For being the most dishonest of the Earth
Cursed are the women
For having pussies I want to grope
And then suing me afterwards
Cursed are the niggers
Cuz black lives don't matter – they really don't
Cursed are the Muslims, Mexicans and Jews
For being terrorists, criminals and the Elders of Zion
And blessed is this freak
For I shall inherit the Earth
And it'll be great
Better than great
It's going to be amazing

Make Jesus Great Again

Lands of prophets

It is probably no coincidence that the harmless Jesus figure
I met in Jerusalem and the menacing messiah of Trump are

both Americans. Although America is known the world over for turning profits into a religion, it also appears to surpass the Holy Land in its generation of religious prophets – at least in the modern era. There was Joseph Smith, the founder of Mormonism, Wallace Fard Muhammad, the founder of the Nation of Islam who, along with his successor Elijah Muhammad, were the prophets of this 'Islamic' sect, and perhaps the most profitable prophet of all, the saviour of the elite, Scientology's L Ron Hubbard.

Likewise, Jesus himself did not emerge in a prophetic vacuum. The time he was born in was a period of huge social, religious and political upheaval, and was replete with people claiming to be prophets and even messiah. Likewise, in Arabia at the time of Muhammad and before he was born, another period of immense upheaval, prophets constituted an influential subclass of the population. Many Muslims acknowledge this, though they put their own spin on it. "During these long centuries, many prophets called their tribes to the worship of God alone. The Arabs gave them little hearing and continued with their paganism," wrote the celebrated Egyptian author Muhammad Husayn Haykal, referring to Hud and Saleh, in his biography of Islam's prophet.[6] In a nod to this pre-Islamic reality, the Quran mentions a handful of pre-Muhammadan Arabian prophets, including the mysterious Hud and Saleh,[7] whose two tribes were destroyed in typically brutal divine fashion, the first for rejecting monotheism and the second for stringing up an animal God deemed sacred, which echo a number of Biblical stories. Other prophet-like figures in Arabia included the *arraf* (Seer) or *kahin* (priest), which the Quran regards as 'false prophets'.[8] They were believed to be in the grip of genies and spoke, like *jinn*-possessed Arab poets, in beautiful verse, often delivered in trances. They also supposedly performed miracles and solved people's problems with oracular visions.[9] As an indication of just how crowded the prophetic scene was, there were even proto-Islamic prophets, known as *hanifs*, i.e. those who turn away (from idolatry), who emerged in Mecca not long before Muhammad, and included a number of relatives of Muhammad and his first wife Khadija,[10] such as Waraqa ibn Nawfal, who was a Nestorian priest.[11] The Quran considers Ibrahim (Abraham) to be the first *hanif* and uses the term to describe pre-Islamic Arabian prophets who battled against polytheism.[12]

Likewise, around the time Jesus is believed to have lived, there were numerous Jewish claimants to prophethood. "There were a number of prophetic figures that appeared among the people around the time of Jesus," wrote the late Richard Horsley, a professor of liberal arts and the study of religion. "The peasantry, from whose ranks the popular prophets and their followers came, were probably acquainted with the expectations of an eschatological prophet." These popular prophets were so numerous that Horsley subdivided them into two groups, oracular prophets and action prophets.[13] However, the literate class of Jews at the time, such as as those belonging to the sect of the Essenes (who left behind actual written records, most famously the Dead Sea Scrolls), do not appear to have expected a popular prophet in the classical Biblical mould. For them, "prophetic activity was channelled primarily into (inspired) interpretation of traditional Biblical prophecies," noted Horsley.[14] Keen to escape the combined oppression of the Romans and their vassal kings, the Herodian dynasty, Jewish peasants began following a number of action prophets in large numbers, including some that made it into the New Testament, such as John the Baptist. Dismissed as "impostors and demagogues" by the pro-Roman Jewish historian Flavius Josephus, he bemoaned how these prophets "provoked revolutionary action and impelled the masses to act like madmen."[15] But these peasants were not simple madmen. In addition to being primed to await a prophet who would deliver them to freedom and root out evil from the world, they had simply had enough of the hardships and exploitation of their lives. "There is plenty of evidence that a strong apocalyptic mood pervaded the society during this period of acute distress and tension," explained Horsley.[16] This mood crescendoed just before and during the Jewish revolt against Rome, as non-violent and violent prophets emerged who believed they would liberate their people. The included "The Egyptian", a Jew who moved to Jerusalem from Egypt, and another Jesus, son of Hananiah, who wandered the streets of Jerusalem, crying his laments for the city, even when he was tortured.[17] Other revolutionary prophets who led the Jews against the Romans, some of whom claimed to be messiahs, included Simon of Peraea, who was a slave of King Herod and had risen up against his son when the monarch died, burning down his palace in Jericho and claiming the title of king for himself. He was killed by a joint force of Herod's men and the Romans.[18] Another, Judas of Galilee, not to be confused with Jesus' disciple, led a rebellion against Roman taxation by encouraging peasants not to register for the census and punishing those who disobeyed.[19] Yet another was Judas of Galilee's son or grandson, Menahem ben Judah, who, in an echo of the stabbing attacks occurring nowadays, led the Sicarii, a group of assassins which, quite literally, employed cloak-and-dagger tactics to murder Romans and their Jewish allies.[20]

Unlike these prophets of yore, there is a chance that the modern-day Son of Man whom I encountered in Jerusalem did not actually believe he was the reincarnation of the Son of God. But there are numerous others who believe wholeheartedly that they are the second coming, sometimes in open rivalry. Ibrahim Abu el-Hawa, the proprietor of the House of Peace hostel on the Mount of Olives, once claimed to have hosted, at the same time, two tourists convinced they were Jesus. Needless to say, the conversation at the breakfast table between the two wannabe messiahs was awkward. In all my time in Jerusalem, I have never met nor heard of anyone who believes that he is Muhammad, which may be partly because of the founder of Islam's claim that he was the 'seal of the prophets', i.e. the last one. That does not mean that Muslims who believe they are the reincarnation of Muhammad do not exist. They do, but only the most unhinged or deranged will reveal their convictions to their community. While laid-back Muslims are likely to take such self-proclaimed holy figures with a pinch of salt and a smile, in many Muslim societies, if the state does not prosecute someone claiming to be Muhammad, they stand a good chance of being persecuted by self-appointed defenders of the faith in their communities. This is exactly what happened to Mohammad Asghar, who was both prosecuted and persecuted. A mentally ill grandfather from Scotland with paranoid schizophrenia who travelled to his native Pakistan in 2010 where he stopped taking his medication, Asghar was reported shortly after his arrival to the authorities by a neighbour who alleged that Asghar had written letters in which he claimed he was the prophet Muhammad. After spending four years behind bars, Asghar was sentenced to death in 2014, with the court rejecting his defence's claims that he had serious mental health issues, even though he had been sectioned in Scotland shortly before he took flight. Since Pakistan has a moratorium on the death penalty, a zealous police officer (who is supposed to uphold the law), took it into his own hands when he smuggled a gun into the prison and shot Asghar in the back. Luckily, the then 70-year-old survived.[21] "It's gone on for so long that it's hard to have a normal life," Asghar's daughter, Jasmine Rana, told *The Guardian*. "I can't sleep. I have to tell my kids to write down what they want to tell me and put it on Post-it notes, otherwise I don't remember."[22] Although Rana, many in the British Muslim community, (including Sadiq Khan, before he became mayor of London), and other prominent Brits, such as the irreverent stand-up comic Frankie Boyle,[23] have campaigned for Asghar's release, he remained on death row at the time of writing.[24] But even if Asghar is released, he may not make it much further than the prison gate, given the profusion of pious vigilantes in Pakistan. Unless he is taken under armed guard straight to the airport, Asghar's fate may be like that of Abid Mehmood, another Pakistani claiming to be the prophet, who, in 2015, was gunned down shortly after being released from prison for mental health reasons.[25]

Reviving prophecy

Despite such displays of murderous intolerance, some Muslims not only get away with claiming to be a prophet, but even gain themselves substantial followers – which, after all, is the key to prophetic legitimacy. The pivotal difference between Muhammad, Jesus and other pretenders to prophethood or messiah-hood is that they managed to win the popularity, or even popular, vote, either during their lifetime or posthumously.

Despite Muhammad's insistence that he was the seal of the prophets, Islam does possess a concept of the returned messiah, the mysterious figure of the *mahdi* – and many have claimed this crown over the many centuries since Muhammad died, especially in the ranks of rebels and revolutionaries. One spectacular example who created a nation of supporters emerged in Sudan. On 29 June 1881, a zealous Sufi mystic named Muhammad Ahmad ibn al-Sayyid Abdullah announced that he was the *mahdi* and declared war on Sudan's hated foreign rulers, Egypt and Britain. With a speed that would make ISIS look like junior league, he led an 'army', initially armed with just sticks and spears, that within just four years had overwhelmed almost all of the Egyptian-occupied Sudan. In the process, this motley crew wiped out three Egyptian armies sent to put down the insurrection, and captured Khartoum from Major General Charles George Gordon, which led the indignant British to dub him a false prophet.[26] Several Islamic spin-off religions were established by men claiming to be *mahdis* or prophets, including the Druze and Bahai faiths. The prophetic founder of Ahmadiyyah Islam, Mirza Ghulam Ahmad, went so far as to claim that he was the living fusion of the spirit of Muhammad, Jesus and the Hindu god Krishna.[27] The notion that Ahmad was a prophet and that he combined the spirit of Muhammad and Krishna outrages many mainstream Muslims to this day. As the Ahmadiyyah sect emerged in pre-partition India, Pakistan is the most hostile country towards this version of Islam. The public hostility towards Ahmadiyyah Islam is such that the controversial second amendment to Pakistan's constitution, passed in 1974, effectively ex-communicated Ahmadis by declaring that "a person who does not believe in the absolute and unqualified finality of the prophethood of Muhammad (Peace be upon him)…is not a Muslim."[28] This was followed up a decade later with the notorious and openly fascistic Ordinance XX of 1984, which bars Ahmadis from publicly practising their faith or using Islamic texts while worshipping, depriving them even of their Qurans.[29] This has led to the prosecution and persecution of Ahmadis by the state and vigilante violence against them by religious fanatics. Unsurprisingly, Pakistan's Ahmadi population has plummeted and some must regret their forefathers' support for the disastrous partition of India.

The Ahmadi story of Jesus sounds a bit like the Bollywood version of *The Last Temptation of Christ*. In the Martin Scorsese adaptation, Jesus discovers on the cross that he is not the messiah and elopes with Mary Magdalene, only to discover in old age that it was Satan who had tempted him off the cross, and he returns to the site of his crucifixion where he implores the Lord to crucify him again and to let him be "God's son". In the Ahmadi version, Jesus survived crucifixion and decided to put as much distance as possible between himself and his persecutors. With his mother, Mary, his wife, Mary Magdalene, and Thomas – which places this disciple's doubts that Jesus had been resurrected in an entirely different light – Christ fled to, of all places, Kashmir. There, he died at a ripe old age in beautiful Srinagar, chilling with the lost tribes of Israel, which seems to suggest that the Himalayas were as popular with the ancient Israelites as they are with modern Israelis.[30] Despite the Ahmadiyyah's bizarre founding myths and its founder's extremely lofty opinion of himself, its theological positions are generally tolerant, rejecting any punishment for apostasy[31] or blasphemy,[32] and accepting other faiths, including Christianity.

Although people in the modern West, if they know anything about the Ahmadiyyah sect at all, are only aware of its reputation for tolerance, earlier generations of Christians were not so enthusiastic. As you might expect, the idea that Jesus, rather than 'dying for our sins', lived in domestic bliss with Mary Magdalene in India, and that Mirza Ghulam Ahmad was some kind of Muhammad-Jesus combo did not go down well with devout Christians of the time, especially the British missionaries working in India, who attacked Ahmad despite his rejection of jihad against the British in India.[33] This attitude continues amongst the devout. Calling him another "false Christ", the anti-Islam site Answering Islam accused

Ahmad of seeking to "dishonour Jesus" because "he denied the sinlessness, physical ascension and return of Jesus... reducing him to the level of common prophethood".[34]

One believer's prophet is another believer's fraud

For the non-believer, the idea that Jesus was sinless, rose up to heaven and will come back a second time to save humanity from itself (again) sounds almost as far-fetched as Mirza Ghulam Ahmad embodying the Ahmadi trinity of Muhammad-Jesus-Krishna. The fact that the Jesus story sounds more credible to me is probably because I grew up exposed to every facet of Christ's official biography – his prophesied birth, his rebellious youth, and his untimely, sadistic death – usually presented as though it were fact, whether in morning assembly at school, in Religious Education classes or during the Christmas play.

The religious snobbery of getting riled by claims of "common prophethood" is also baffling. "The Bible reveals that the Father is God, that the Son is God, and that the Holy Spirit is God," wrote Albert Mohler, president of the Southern Baptist Theological Seminary. "Jesus is not merely a prophet, as acknowledged by Muslims, He is God in human flesh."[35] For rationalists who neither believe in prophets nor demigods, this whole debate can seem rather perplexing. But given the centuries of conflict and schism over the nature of Christ (later known as Christology) within Christianity itself, ever since at least the Arian heresy,[36] and all the many Christians who have been ex-communicated or executed for holding heretical or blasphemous views, it should really come as no surprise that Islam's sacrilegious view of Jesus should meet with such hostility. "Jesus is a controversial prophet," observes the Palestinian historian Tarif Khalidi. "He is the only prophet in the Quran who is deliberately made to distance himself from the doctrines that his community is said to hold of him."[37] In his Quranic incarnation, Jesus vigorously disowns the Trinity when God interrogates him on whether he claimed godly status for himself.[38] "Muslim scholars regard the Christian churches as having gone seriously astray in their interpretation of Jesus," explains Carl Ernst, a professor of Islamic studies. "For them, the unity of God was absolutely essential, and calling a human being divine was a kind of idolatry amounting to polytheism."[39] But was it? And was it all that absolute?

An Islamic trinity?

As someone who was raised a Muslim, I used to wonder, like many of my co-religionists, how Christians managed to square the figurative circle of believing in the trinity, i.e. three divinities, residing in the single God. However, it is always easy to see the contradictions, inconsistencies, irrationalities, circular logic and logical fallacies in another's faith. It is far harder to see the holes in one's own belief system, partly because self-criticism is the hardest form of criticism and partly because, since religion is founded on faith, the believer does not want to introduce a level of doubt that will shake that belief.

But as I discovered with time, despite Islam's view of Jesus as 'merely a prophet', it places him as close to godliness as humanely possible. Christ is the nearest any of God's earthly envoys, including Muhammad himself, comes to immortality and divinity. Not only was Jesus born a "boy most pure",[40] according to the Quran, he is also the only character in Islam's sacred book who is described as the "Word" of God.[41] The Quran even quotes God as claiming that "We blew into [Mary] of Our Spirit".[42] This is perplexing, to say the least.

Although Islam passionately rejects the trinity, here is its holy book placing the "Son of Mary" at the righteous angle where God, his Holy Spirit and Jesus intersect, but apparently do not form a triangle. To the sceptic, this sounds remarkably like the hair-splitting, and futile, theological debates for which the Byzantine Empire was notorious. Did Jesus have one nature (monophysite) or two, both divine and human (dyophysite)? Did the human precede the divine or the divine precede the human? Were Christ's human and divine natures distinct or intertwined? Does it matter? Should anyone really lose sleep over such issues, let alone establish competing churches and religions to dispute them?

To add to the confusion, not only was Jesus' start in life exceptional, so was his death, according to the Islamic tradition. It is generally accepted in Islam that Jesus is the only human to have the distinction of entering eternal heaven without the intermediate nuisance of suffering death. Following the *deus ex machina* tradition of ancient Greek tragedies, a stunt double is placed on the cross at the last moment and the Romans are led to believe that this common criminal is Christ, while the real Jesus is surreptitiously raised up to heaven.[43] While this plot device has the benefit of ridding the believer of the heavy burden of guilt (that symbolic cross Christians must bear to atone for Jesus dying for their sins), it does effectively turn Jesus into an immortal human, like the demigods of the bad old days of classical polytheism. Although Islam does not accept that Jesus is the Son of God and Christianity rejects the notion that he is just a prophet, it strikes me that the dispute is far more about semantics – and, as with most schisms, about politics – than any actual substantive differences between the two religions' vision of the Son of Man.

Muhammad: The prince of darkness

The reverence with which Jesus is held by Islam and the Muslim mainstream stands in stark contrast to the centuries-long contempt and vilification Muhammad has experienced in Christendom, which is still popular in conservative circles today. "The fact that Muhammad engaged in battle and was married to a number of women seems to many Christians clear proof that he could not be on the same exalted level as Jesus," notes Carl Ernst. "Christian critics of Muhammad generally describe him as motivated by a combination of political ambition and sensual lust." This causes dismay amongst Muslims who feel that Christians do not respect their founder of their faith in the same way they revere Jesus. "Muslims are often bewildered by the extreme hostility that Christians have shown towards their beloved prophet."[44]Although there are Christians nowadays who show a profound respect for Islam, such as Pope Francis, preachers and televangelists tend to continue the negative tradition. "Jesus taught peace, love and forgiveness. He came to give His life for the sins of mankind, not to take life," wrote controversial evangelist Franklin Graham in a popular Facebook post,[45] responding to the likening of ISIS to the historical crimes committed in the name of Christianity, by then President Barack Obama,[46] whom Graham has hinted may be a closet Muslim.[47] One wonders where this Jesus of "peace, love and forgiveness" was when Graham beat the war drum by supporting the invasion of Iraq, then cynically used the ensuing chaos to send in his missionary soldiers of Christ to "reach out to love [Iraqis] and to save them, and as a Christian, I do this in the name of Jesus Christ."[48] Despite the modern view of Jesus Christ as some kind of ancient olive tree-hugging, pacifist hippy who preached a new testament of love and forgiveness, he himself claimed otherwise. His injunctions to "love thy enemies" and "turn the other cheek" notwithstanding,[49] Jesus, like Muhammad would centuries later, preached both peace and violence. "Think not that I am come to send peace on earth," Christ briefed his disciples before sending them out to spread the gospel. "I came not to send peace, but a sword."[50] Like with other giant religious figures, including Buddha, what Jesus actually preached or did not preach is ultimately neither here nor there. In a similar vein to their Islamic counterparts, Christian warmongers have always found a way, by selectively quoting Jesus and drawing on the Old Testament, to claim they possess Christ's blessing for their bloody projects. This can be seen in the term *crusade*, which is still invoked in modern times – by the likes of the divinely guided George W Bush,[51] for instance – and the number of 'Christian armies' and 'soldiers of Christ' the world has witnessed over the centuries, right down to the modern day.

In contrast to the supposedly peace-loving Jesus, "Muhammad on the contrary was a warrior and killed many innocent people," added Franklin Graham, the son of the founding father of televangelism Billy Graham, in his Facebook post mentioned earlier.

This view of the Islamic prophet as blood-drenched warmonger stretches back to the misty dawn of Islam, when rumours of the Muslim armies' conquests were beginning to filter through to an anxious Christendom. "He is false, for the prophets do not come armed with a sword," a purportedly learned Jewish sage is supposed to have said in a Byzantine polemic, composed around the time of Muhammad's death.[52] Of course, this overlooks entirely the numerous Biblical prophets who were both men of war and holy men, including Moses[53] and Joshua,[54] to name but two.

As the rivalry, clash and animosity between the new religion and its older cousin escalated, Muhammad graduated from being a false prophet to become the antichrist and even Satan's envoy.[55] For all these alleged sins, Dante, in his *Divine Comedy*, sentences Muhammad to the ninth *bolgia*, or ditch, of the Eighth Circle of Hell, where he dwelt, in sadistic, eternal torture, among the "sowers of scandal, schismatics, and heretics". In Dante's *Inferno*, Muhammad stood "torn from the chin throughout…Down to the hinder passage", i.e. his anus, while his entrails dangled between his legs.[56]

"Muhammad is always the impostor (familiar, because he pretends to be like the Jesus we know) and always the Oriental (alien, because although he is in some ways 'like' Jesus, he is after all not like him)," wrote Edward Said in his seminal work, *Orientalism*.[57]

And despite a generally more positive and informed view of Islam in the contemporary West,[58] this image of Muhammad as the devil's diplomat lives on. Claiming that the angel Muhammad saw was not Gabriel but Satan disguised as "an angel of light", Robert Jeffress, pastor of the First Baptist megachurch in Dallas said: "It was Satan himself who delivered those delusions to those people to lead people by the millions away from God… [Islam] is based on a false book that is based on a fraud. It was founded by a false prophet."[59]

This extreme and irrational contempt and aversion to Muhammad is not just limited to Christian fundamentalists and fanatics, it has seeped through to many secular commentators who uphold the values of science and/or the Enlightenment. Today, we are familiar with every brand of evil being compared to Hitler and the Nazis. But during the Führer's ascendancy, he was sometimes likened to Muhammad. Rather than making the more obvious link between Nazism and Christianity, Carl Jung, the founding father of analytical psychology, wrote as the clouds of war massed over Europe in 1939: "We do not know whether Hitler is going to found a new Islam. He is already on the way; he is like Muhammad. The emotion in Germany is Islamic; warlike and Islamic. They are all drunk with a wild god."[60]

Muhammad: The lord of light

Needless to say, Muhammad as false prophet, impostor, devil's advocate and even Hitler is the polar opposite of how Muslims view the founder of their religion. All through my life, I have heard Muslims extol Muhammad's wisdom, intelligence, peaceable nature, diplomatic prowess, statecraft and even his physical beauty. This reverence is clear in the Islamic declaration of faith in which the believer professes their belief that there is no god but God and Muhammad is his messenger. Most Muslims also do not refer to their prophet as just "Muhammad". They either attach the prefix *Sayedouna* (Our Lord) or the suffix "*Sallallahu alayhi wa sallam*", which is usually translated as "Peace be upon him", but literally(and bizarrely in the context of puritanical monotheism, it means "God pray upon him".

While Christians traditionally viewed Muhammad as the prince of darkness, Muslims depict him as the lord of light. "The light of Muhammad has become distributed in millions of pieces and has encompassed the entire world," the 13th-century Persian Sufi mystic Rumi wrote in one of his poems. "When Muhammad's light came, unbelief put on its black clothes... Last night, there was a big commotion among the stars because a peerless star had descended to the Earth."[61]

This light of humanity, this peerless star occupies a similarly exalted place in Islam as Jesus does in Christianity. And though Muslims steer well clear of describing their prophet as the

Son of God, they do unconsciously bestow upon him what are essentially godly attributes. Foremost among these are the implicit and explicit moral infallibility and sinlessness of Muhammad's reported words and deeds (*hadith*), upon which many Islamic laws are based. This stands in stark contrast to Muhammad's own reported insistence that, "I am a man like you. I eat food like you and I also sit down when I am tired like you."[62] This is backed up by the Quran, which commands Muhammad to "say, 'Glory to my Lord! Am I aught but a man – a messenger?'"[63] and "say, 'I am but a mortal man like all of you.'"[64]

Religious pop icons

It is one of those paradoxes of religion which somehow make perfect sense to the believer, but leave those of other religions or none confusedly scratching their heads in bewilderment. Drawing on the Ten Commandments both Christianity and Islam have an Old Testament aversion to 'graven images'.[65] Despite this common injunction, Islam and Christianity have developed radically different ideas on how to depict Jesus and Muhammad. Although they regard Christ as the Son of God, Christians have developed a centuries-old, intricate and diverse tradition of depicting the human image of Jesus, from cradle to grave, from resurrection to ascension. As religion has declined in many parts of the West, this tradition has expanded to include images mocking and lampooning Jesus, not just revering him – though these do still elicit controversy, protest, self-censorship and even occasional violence.

In contrast, in spite of Muhammad's status as "but a mortal man", Muslims have traditionally refrained from creating visual iconography to represent him. In the modern age, where visual imagery is ubiquitous, this has resulted in some absurd situations. Take cinema. While Jesus Christ superstar struts in his full divine glory across European and American cinema screens, Muhammad, like some sort of postmodernist anti-hero, is nowhere to be seen in biopics or TV dramas of which he is the peerless star.

Instead, Muhammad is either depicted as a disembodied voice or, for the more puritanical director, his actions and statements are reported, like Godot's, by the other players in the drama. The big budget Iranian production, *Muhammad: The Messenger of God* – described by *Variety* as clichéd, overlong and old-fashioned[66] – employs both techniques, showing only the back and voice of the prophet as a child and his uncle Abu Talib repeats the words of the adult Muhammad. While this is supposed to avoid idolatrous behaviour, I am sceptical that, after a millennium and a half of avoiding idol worship, the appearance of Muhammad in human form on their screens would suddenly cause Muslim viewers to idly worship his image. In addition, I cannot help feeling that this selective exercising of the conventional Islamic prohibition on depicting life forms may actually have the opposite effect to the desired one, i.e. that it makes Muhammad appear more divine and otherworldly than human.

Moreover, Muslims may generally veer away from graphical iconography, but there is a long tradition of transforming Muhammad into a literary and poetic icon. Though pictures may often speak a thousand words, a word can evoke a thousand images. For example, imagine trying to paint Rumi's description of Muhammad's light "in millions of pieces" that "encompassed the entire world", or unbelief putting on its "black clothes" because the prophet had caused "commotion among the stars" by falling to earth from the heavens.

That said, iconography in Christianity and iconoclasm in Islam are not as straightforward as they appear at first sight. The graphical depiction of Jesus in early Christianity was controversial, and did not really seem to take off in earnest until Christianity became the official religion of the Roman empire. Historians attribute this opposition to iconography to the large number of Jews who followed the new faith in its infancy, the early persecution of Christians and the need of converts to distance themselves from the polytheistic traditions surrounding them.

In early icons, Jesus was depicted as a beardless young man with short hair.[67] Later, as Christianity became more Hellenised, drawing on classical portrayals of Greek philosophers and young miracle workers, the iconic Jesus grew his beard and hair.[68] And regional, ethnic and racial variations notwithstanding, this is the dominant image of Christ we have today. That said, and perhaps influenced by its rival Islam,[69] Christianity has experienced periods of iconoclasm, during the eighth and ninth centuries in Byzantium and during the Protestant Reformation, including the ISIS-like Beeldenstorm in 16th-century Holland. Then, as now, the reasons for the unleashed religious fury were as much, and perhaps more, social, economic and political as they were theological.[70] Likewise, there have been periods of Islamic history where some Muslim societies have embraced the visual depiction of Muhammad, namely from the 13th to the 17th centuries. Some of this was perhaps inspired by Christian tradition, as the Jesus-like halo on some icons of Muhammad suggest, or expressed a nostalgia for pre-Islamic artistic traditions, as in Persia. Interestingly, as is the case with the local variations in the depiction of Jesus, Muhammad often does not look in the slightest bit Arab in some of his Islamic iconography; for instance, Mongol artists portray him as Chinese-looking. One of the most ambitious of these efforts was Siyer-i Nebi, a 14th-century Ottoman epic about the life of Muhammad, which consists of 814 miniature illustrations.[71]

Conservative Muslims are bound to insist that these episodes were anomalies and fads which run contrary to Islam. However, such fundamentalist attitudes display a fundamental misunderstanding of Islamic theology. "The Quran does not prohibit figural imagery. Rather, it castigates the worship of idols," notes Christiane Gruber, an academic specialising in Islamic book arts, paintings of Muhammad, as well as Islamic ascension texts and images. "If we turn to Islamic law, there does not exist a single legal decree, or fatwa, in the historical corpus that explicitly and decisively prohibits figural imagery, including images of the Prophet."[72]

However, depicting Muhammad reverently is one thing but insulting and disparaging the prophet is something else entirely, it would seem, as the Danish cartoon controversy, the French satirical magazine *Charlie Hebdo*, and others have done. But matters are not always how they appear. Despite the apparent widespread outrage among Muslims towards everything from Salman Rushdie's *The Satanic Verses* to the Muhammad cartoon controversies, millions of Muslims were not offended or did not feel the urge to act on any offence they felt. Author, lecturer and broadcaster Kenan Malik outlines how it took months of incitement by Muslim religious radicals, as well as the intervention of disappointed journalists looking for sensation, before any semblance of an outraged reaction to the Danish cartoons or Rushdie's novel could be provoked. And as is so often the case, the outrage was politically, not religiously, motivated. "Those that were [offended] were driven by political zeal rather than theological fervour," Malik elaborates.[73] Political motives can include a wide range of grievances, from the local to the global: anger at domestic policies projected onto an external target; rage at Western hegemony and the legacy of colonialism; the jostling between Islamist and secular political forces in the Muslim world; the geopolitical rivalry between Iran and Saudi Arabia; the tussle between Islamophobes and Islamic fundamentalists, and many more.

Of course, Muhammad's self-appointed defenders who, took it upon themselves to avenge their prophet's honour by committing an act of bloody terror by murdering, in cold blood, staff and visitors at the offices of *Charlie Hebdo* believe they are acting in accordance to their religion's principles. While many atrocities can be and have been justified religiously, I am not convinced that there is a persuasive theological case to be made for slaughtering those who insult the prophet.

In actuality, ridiculing Muhammad is not just a Western pastime, Muslims have centuries of form in this regard, albeit mostly in written not drawn caricatures. While Christians traditionally derided the Islamic prophet from a rival religious vantage point, within the Islamic world itself, Muhammad was criticised and mocked from a secular, rationalist, anti-religious perspective. One example is the religious sceptic and scholar Ibn al-Rawandi (827-911), who spent a significant part of his life in Baghdad, believed that intellect and science supersede all else, and religion was illogical and irrational. In his writings, he attacked Muhammad and the other prophets as "fraudulent tricksters", "magicians" and "liars" (see chapter on atheism).[74]

Devout Muslims who feel they are duty-bound to defend the honour of Muhammad through violence or intimidation should take a deep breath and recall the Quranic injunction: "For you is your religion, and for me is mine religion."[75]

205

CHAPTER SEVEN

Clash, mash or crash of civilisations?

Before he became the Trump administration's chief strategist, Steve Bannon expressed his belief that the West was in a monumental struggle against state-sponsored crony capitalism and fascism. While liberal citizens of 'Leftistan' may nod their heads in vigorous agreement, they would be sorely mistaken to think that Bannon was referring to the man who would become his boss, Donald Trump, or France's Marin Le Pen, or Geert Wilders of the Netherlands, or Hungary's Viktor Orbán, or any of the other members of the far-right vanguard sweeping across Europe and America. Bannon was, of course, referring to the only fascism that matters, the Islamic variety. "I think we are in a crisis of the underpinnings of capitalism, and on top of that we're now, I believe, at the beginning stages of a global war against Islamic fascism," he told, via Skype, a conference hosted by a conservative Catholic organisation, held in the Vatican in 2014.[2] Fortunately, the West had an ally in this cosmic struggle in the form of India, Bannon argued, whose right-wing Hindu nationalist prime minister Narendra Modi he likened to his hero Ronald Reagan, according to an Indian blogger whom Bannon wanted to run Breitbart India.[3] The consequences of inaction would be dire, Bannon warned his audience, urging them to "fight for our beliefs against this new barbarity that's starting, that will completely eradicate everything that we've been bequeathed over the last 2,000, 2,500 years." The stakes couldn't have been higher nor more staggeringly terrifying: this presumably covers the West's Christian heritage, from the Dark Ages to the Renaissance and Enlightenment, as well as its earlier Greco-Roman legacy, not to mention World Wars I and II. Bannon not only foresees a Christian apocalypse but a Hindu one, because of the dangerous global imbalance of *dharma* (the righteous actions which keeps the very cosmos in balance),[4] which is not to be confused with *karma* (actions, words and deeds and their spiritual consequences).

How, you may wonder, could a rag-tag 'army' of 100,000 jihadis scattered around the world,[5] poorly trained and armed, members of groups more at war with Muslim societies and one another than with the 'infidel', defeat and bring down the mighty West, with its fighter jets, 'smart' bombs and nukes? Why, simply asking that question shows how naive and gullible you are. The anti-Western jihadist fighting force should not be measured by active fighters alone. There are hundreds of millions more sympathisers, or even sympa-fighters, in reserve. According to Donald Trump, some "27%, could be 35%" of the world's 1.6 billion Muslims, are keenly awaiting the opportunity to go to war and kill the Western *kafir*, citing a Pew poll[6] that was so horrifying in its implications that it had shaken the Pew Research Centre to the very core of its being. The shock was so acute that it had led to a collective amnesia amongst Pew researchers, who claimed to have never conducted nor heard of such a survey.[7]

Revealing his remarkable foresight and gift for seeing the bigger picture, Steve Bannon made a similar point during his

Vatican talk in 2014. He did not just refer to the "outright war against jihadist Islamic fascism", in the form of ISIS, al-Qaeda or the Taliban, he seemed to imply that Christendom was, and had always been, at war with Islam, before the West lost its way to extreme secularisation. "If you look back at the long history of the Judeo-Christian West's struggle against Islam, I believe that our forefathers kept their stance, and I think they did the right thing," Bannon told his audience, though his ancestors would have been surprised to learn that Jews were their allies rather than the 'killers of Christ' they had believed them to be. "I think they kept it out of the world, whether it was at Vienna, or Tours, or other places," Bannon added, the mysterious, mystical 'it' referring to a timeless Islam. A couple of years later, Donald Trump summed up Bannon's assertion, which seemed to presage the president's repeatedly attempted Muslim ban, with his typically succinct eloquence. "I think Islam hates us," he told CNN's Anderson Cooper,[8] revealing either that inanimate ideas also have feelings or that Islam is actually a hydra with 1.6 billion heads.

Crusaders "R" US

While Donald Trump[9] and many others in the Birther movement were absolutely convinced that Barack Obama is a closet Muslim, jihadis believed the exact opposite, that the former US president is not only a practising Christian, as he asserts, but no less than the "Dog of Rome", in the words of Jihadi John, who added for good measure that "tomorrow we will be slaughtering your soldiers. With Allah's permission, we will break this final and last crusade."[10] Barack Obama is not a crypto-Muslim and is actually a crusader? This can't be right. This must be another of those wily tricks of Muslim deception. This must be *taqiyya* of the highest order, right?[11] But it does not stop there. In their war against the infidel, jihadist groups are convinced that Donald Trump is not a curse who will destroy them but a Godsend and useful idiot, or psychopath, who will help advance their cause. "This guy is a complete maniac," one Abu Omar Khorasani, was quoted as saying of Donald Trump following his victory at the ballot box. Being a top ISIS commander in Afghanistan Khorashani presumably knows a lot about what constitutes a "complete maniac". "[Trump's] utter hate towards Muslims will make our job much easier because we can recruit thousands," the ISIS commander claimed.[12] "Our leaders were closely following the US election but it was unexpected that the Americans will dig their own graves and they did so," admitted Khorashani, echoing the dismay of Western pundits following Trump's victory. Sympathisers with jihadist organisations rejoiced at his anti-Muslim policies and discourse, calling his attempted bans on Muslims from certain countries from entering the United States a "blessed ban".[13]

Who knows, maybe irony will have the last laugh and Trump, the birther-in-chief, will also become the subject of outlandish conspiracy theories. After all, if you sow illusion and paranoia, you will reap paranoid delusion. There are enormous signs of discontent among Trump's radical core of voters, the movement which calls itself the Alt Right, especially following his first foreign trip,[14] during which he was treated to a sultan's welcome in Saudi Arabia, praising perhaps the most oppressive Islamic regime in the world and calling Islam "one of the world's great religions", after years of browbeating Obama for his alleged ignoring of Islam's inherent evil. Disappointed conspiracy theorists at the *Daily Stormer*[15] and other far-right sites have woven conspiracy theories starring Trump, with

Paul Joseph Watson, editor of the far-right Infowars, calling the president "another deep state/Neo-Con puppet".[16] David Duke, the former Imperial Wizard of the Ku Klux Klan and one of candidate Trump's greatest supporters, managed to perceive a massive Zionist-Islamist conspiracy behind Trump's foreign policy shifts.[17]

A brief history of the clash of civilisations

With all these declarations of jihads and crusades, coupled with fears of cultural infiltration and annihilation, it is unsurprising that many people are convinced that we are in the throes of a monumental war between the West (or Christendom, if you prefer) and Islam. Advocates of this idea on both sides believe they are not only in the right but also on the defensive in this confrontation between good and evil, or more accurately, us and them. For many in the West, the rise of ISIS, al-Qaeda, homegrown Islamic extremism and, above all, the 9/11 attacks, in their monstrous audacity and nihilistic novelty, are the smoking gun that shows that Muslims are out to destroy the West because they hate our freedoms. "This is not a grievance-based conflict. This is a clash of civilisations, for they do not hate us because we have military assets in the Middle East," opined Republican presidential hopeful Senator Marco Rubio, in November 2015, following the multiple terrorist attacks which struck Paris, claiming the lives of 130 people. "They hate us because of our values. They hate us because young girls here go to school. They hate us because women drive."[18]

Many Muslims disagree and see the clash as very much grievance-based, as well as civilisational. They regard the West's cultural, political and economic hegemony, its support of some of the most repressive and tyrannical leaders in the Muslim world and its invasion and occupation of Muslim-majority countries, such as the 'shock and awe' wholesale destruction of Iraq at the hands of the United States and Britain, founded on sexed up claims of weapons of mass destruction and imaginary links between Saddam Hussein and al-Qaeda, as crystal clear evidence that the West wishes to wipe Islam off the face of the Earth. For instance, Osama bin Laden, while not taking direct responsibility for 9/11, claimed that the atrocities committed were in self-defence. "This is something we have agitated for before, as a matter of self-defence, in defence of our brothers and sons in Palestine, and to liberate our sacred religious sites," the al-Qaeda founder told *Al Jazeera* in October 2001. "If inciting people to do that is terrorism, and if killing those who kill our sons is terrorism, then let history be witness that we are terrorists."[19]

This apparent clash was given intellectual and academic expression by the American political scientist Samuel P Huntington, who published an incredibly influential essay on the "clash of civilisations"[20] in 1993, which he later expanded into a book.[21] Although he did not single out Islam and the West as being the only protagonists in this cultural collision, Huntington argued that the fundamental source of conflict in the post-Cold War era would be not ideological or economic but 'cultural' wars between civilisations – as if culture were somehow distinct from ideology and not interrelated and intertwined, or that civilisations could somehow be separated from their political and economic underpinnings and interests. "The clash of civilisations will dominate global politics. The fault lines between civilisations will be the battle lines of the future," the Harvard professor argued. Huntington divided the world into some half a dozen major civilisational groups which, he posited, would clash at two levels: local "fault line conflicts" where civilisations overlap and "core state conflicts" between the major states of different civilisations.

Huntington gave the fault line between Islam and the West special historical prominence, which could have been, in part, inspired by the conflict consuming the Balkans at the time, which appeared to revolve around religion. "Conflict along the fault line between Western and Islamic civilisations has been going on for 1,300 years. This centuries-old military interaction between the West and Islam is unlikely to decline. It could become more virulent," he wrote. "On both sides the interaction between Islam and the West is seen as a clash of civilisations."[22] Referring to the Muslim world's fault lines, or frontiers, with other cultures, Huntington concludes that: "Islam has bloody borders," as though there were a civilisation or nation in the world whose boundaries – both internal and external – are not blood-soaked.[23]

Although the clash of civilisations theory has become associated with Samuel Huntington, he was not the first to posit it, nor did he coin the term. A few years before him, the prominent British-American historian and scholar of Islam Bernard Lewis wrote an essay in which he foresaw a far more specific clash of civilisations, namely between the West and Islam. "It should by now be clear that we are facing a mood and a movement far transcending the level of issues and policies and the governments that pursue them," Lewis, the historian of choice for the neo-conservative movement, wrote in 1990, in what has proved to be one of the most influential essays of recent decades. "This is no less than a clash of civilisations – the perhaps irrational but surely historic reaction of an ancient rival against our Judeo-Christian heritage, our secular present, and the worldwide expansion of both."[24]

Unlike Christian fundamentalists, the far right and the alt-right, Bernard Lewis, who turned 100 in 2016, was an accomplished and knowledgeable scholar of Islamic culture. One may disagree with the conclusions he draws from the historical and political evidence, with his political bias, especially in latter years, and with the omissions he makes, but one cannot doubt his profound understanding of the subject upon which he pens his polemics, especially in his earlier scholarship. This is evident in his urging of caution and sensitivity in his 1990 essay. "We must take great care on all sides to avoid the danger of a new era of religious wars," he counselled. "To this end we must strive to achieve a better appreciation of other religious and political cultures, through the study of their history, their literature, and their achievements. At the same time, we may hope that they will try to achieve a better understanding of ours."

Clash of values or clash of value?

Although Lewis and Huntington gave us the modern term's current ideological contours, the notion of a 'clash of civilisations' between those two age-old rivals, Islam and Christendom, has ancient pedigree, stretching back centuries, as far back as the very birth of Islam, when the nascent religion established itself as a direct rival to Christendom in both the sacred and the secular spheres. Examples include the historical notions of jihads and crusades, not to mention the idea of 'civilisation versus barbarism' espoused by dominant powers and influential voices on both sides throughout the centuries.

This would seem to be corroborated by the early history of Islam, when it swept like wildfire through the Christianised Greco-Roman and the Zoroastrian Persian worlds, both of which had been severely depleted due to the endless internecine Byzantine-Sasanian wars, the last of which, from 602 to 628, left the two empires weak and impoverished, paving the way for the so-called "human tsunami" of the Arab conquests.[25] When the Muslim armies landed on the shores of Europe, their legendary commander Tariq ibn Ziyad, who gave his name to Gibraltar (a bastardisation of Jabal Tariq), the rock separating Iberia from North Africa, reportedly after burning his ships and warning his troops that "Behind you is the sea, before you, the enemy," urged them on with this pledge: "The one fruit which [the Commander of True Believers, Alwalid, son of Abdalmelik] desires to obtain from your bravery is that the word of God shall be exalted in this country, and that the true religion shall be established here."[26]

Each crusade launched against Islam was framed in such overtly religious terms. "Freshly quickened by the divine correction, you must apply the strength of your righteousness to another matter which concerns you as well as God. For your brethren who live in the east are in urgent need of your help, and you must hasten to give them the aid which has often been promised them," urged Pope Urban II in 1095, paving the way for what would become known as the First Crusade. "On this account I, or rather the Lord, beseech you as Christ's heralds to publish this everywhere and to persuade all people of whatever rank, foot-soldiers and knights, poor and rich, to carry aid promptly to those Christians and to destroy that vile race from the lands of our friends."[27]

With this long history to draw on, it is, therefore, unsurprising that when former US president George W Bush likened his "war on terrorism" to a "crusade"[28] and claimed that he was on a "mission from God" when he invaded Iraq,[29] many took it to mean that a centuries-old religious war had resumed. Bush's arch-enemy Osama bin Laden – who had earlier been an ally of the Reagan-Bush Snr administration against their common enemy, the Soviet Union in Afghanistan – concurred about the religious dimensions of the emerging conflict. "This battle is not between al-Qaeda and the US. This is a battle of Muslims against the global crusaders," the Al Qaeda chief said in an October 2001 interview, in a desperate bid to internationalise his disparate movement and fringe ideology.[30]

But are Bush, bin Laden, Huntington, Lewis and others right? Is there really a clash of civilisations in motion or are we simply witnessing a more mundane clash of geopolitical and economic interests – not so much a clash of values but a clash of value – be it manifest in the form of resources, export markets or control over territories of geostrategic importance?

Although culture and ideology can, on some occasions, lead to conflict, for the most part, societies enter into conflicts for other reasons, foremost among them are avarice and the pursuit of perceived strategic interests. For instance, to motivate his own troops, the vast majority of whom were, like him, not Arabs but Berbers, and were recent converts to Islam, Tariq ibn Ziyad informed his men that if they conquered Iberia, "The Commander of True Believers, Alwalid, son of Abdel-Malik... promises that you shall become his comrades and shall hold the rank of kings in this country."[31] This hints at how, even at times when ideology and faith are supposedly at the forefront, material interests and greed are not far from the surface – in this case, the promise of loot and positions of authority as a reward for conquest. In many cases, it would seem that booty trumps belief.

Critics of Huntington's clash of civilisations, like the dissident American scholar Noam Chomsky, see the theory as simply the symptom of the avarice of an empire, i.e. *Pax Americana*, in search of another justification for its imperial and economic aspirations after the Cold War paradigm fell apart with the collapse of the Soviet bloc.[32] That would explain, for instance, why the United States decided to invade Saddam Hussein's secular Iraq, even though it was a sworn enemy of al-Qaeda and Jihadist Islam, yet is bosom buddies with Saudi Arabia, the hotbed of reactionary Wahhabism, which it exports with dire consequences around the region and the world. Indeed, Saudi Arabia happens to be the home of most of the hijackers who took part in the 11 September 2001 attacks,[33] not to mention the long-standing allegations that members of the Saudi government and royal family supported the 9/11 plot.[34]

Even the most fanatical and ideologically driven groups and nations can be motivated by *realpolitik*. For example, following the November 2015 Paris attacks, ISIS released a statement sprinkled with references to "a faithful group of the soldiers of the Caliphate" who attacked "crusaders" in Paris, a city described as the "the carrier of the banner of the Cross". However, buried amid its jihadist rhetoric of fighting the 'infidel' was a clear indication that the choice of Paris as a target was not coincidental and was largely motivated by France's military involvement against ISIS in Syria. "The smell of death will never leave their noses as long as they lead the convoy of the Crusader campaign... and are proud of fighting Islam in France and striking the Muslims in the land of the Caliphate with their planes," the statement asserted.[35]

Civilisational lines in the sand

The fact that clashes of interest trump clashes of culture more often than not is reflected in the counter-intuitive alliances that cut across civilisational lines and which have been commonplace since the very dawn of Islam – as they have been in many other contexts. For instance, Tariq ibn Ziyad, capable military commander that he was, did not conquer Andalusia by himself. He had the help of the very Christian Julian of Septem (Ceuta) and Visigothic opponents of Roderick, who at the time was the (unpopular) ruler of most of Spain. It even appears that the overstretched Arabs were not at first interested at that point in crossing the Straits of Gibraltar and it was Roderick's Christian opponents who persuaded them that it would be a cakewalk and provided them with vital intelligence and logistical support.[36] And this was to be no exception. The subsequent history of medieval Spain was replete with shifting alliances, across highly permeable ideological lines, between its various Muslim and Christian rulers, often guided by little more than the expediency of the moment.

Perhaps the most remarkable medieval collaboration of all was what modern-day historians call the Abbasid-Carolingian alliance, which was a spectacular example of the adage that the enemy of my enemy is my friend. The common Muslim enemy was the Umayyads, the remnants of whom had fled their capital Damascus after the Abbasid revolt and set up a rival, if weaker, caliphate in Iberia, which was a political threat to the Abbasids and a territorial threat to the Carolingians. The common Christian enemy was the Byzantine empire, which was a political rival to the Carolingians for leadership of the Christian world and a territorial rival to the Abbasids. As part of this multi-generational alliance, two legendary leaders of Islam and Christendom, the Holy Roman Emperor Charlemagne, who is credited with having halted Islam's northward advance in Europe, and Caliph Harun al-Rashid, the Abbasid dynasty's most famous monarch, sent each other several embassies in the mid-eighth century.[37] In a bid to demonstrate the importance they attached to this relationship, as well as their own prestige and might, the two rulers exchanged lavish gifts, with the caliph once dispatching a huge shipment of luxury perfumes, spices, rich fabrics, a chessboard, a clock and an elephant called Abu al-Abbas.[38] This diplomatic relationship was underpinned by a massive, two-way flow of trade, which saw the reverse of today's roles, with Charlemagne's Europe importing luxury goods from Harun al-Rashid's Middle East and exporting various raw materials and primary goods in return.[39] In addition, there was a military component. Charlemagne allied himself with pro-Abbasid rulers in Iberia and ventured on an unsuccessful expedition to take Zaragoza, which failed partly because of the forces sent by the Abbasid caliph did not reach the place to aid the Holy Roman Emperor's troops.[40]

In more modern times, examples include the Arabs allying themselves with the British and the French against the Turks, the Muslim League's alliance with the British Raj in India, Pakistan's later alliance with America against the USSR, Nasser's Egypt in the non-aligned camp of Nehru's India against pro-Western Pakistan, or the Ottomans fighting alongside the Germans against the British, French and Russians during World War I, sitting out World War II and joining US-led NATO thereafter. In fact, throughout its centuries as a major power, the Ottoman empire built alliances with various Christian European states, including France, Poland, Elizabethan England and modern Germany. The Ottoman empire even sought to exploit the schism brought about by the Reformation in Europe by allying itself with the Protestant movement. For their part, though they had a dim view of Islam, Dutch Protestants were willing to collaborate with the Turks in their battle against the church and the Habsburgs, employing the derogatory slogan 'Liever Turksch dan Paus' ('Rather Turkish than Pope').[41] Europeans also sought to exploit the fault lines and schisms in the Ottoman empire. The first to try this was Napoleon Bonaparte, when he assured Egyptians upon his arrival in their land: "They have told you that I come to destroy your religion, but do not believe it... I come to restore your rights, punish the usurpers and I respect God, his prophet and the Quran more than the Mamluks."[42] During his disastrous sojourn in Egypt, the eccentric French general tried to convince a sceptical Egyptian population that he was a Muslim (of sorts) and that the French republic and its revolutionary ethos reflected the true spirit of Islam (sort of). He even did his utmost to recruit the *ulema,* or clergy, to his cause, setting up a special *diwan* (council), for the purpose.[43] But his project failed and Napoleon, the *de facto* sultan of Egypt, returned to France to become its emperor, while the Ottomans and Egypt's Mamluks, with British help, survived for a while longer.

Turkey's relationship with the European Union is now perhaps at its worst since the European integration project began in the 1950s, evidenced by the escalating dispute between Turkey and its long-standing ally, Germany, with Berlin accusing Recep Tayyip Erdoğan's regime of "intolerable" levels of spying on Turks in Germany and human rights abuses.[44] But it would be a mistake to view this through a civilisational prism. Angela Merkel's government, to its credit, has been critical about the rise of ultra-nationalism and fascism in Europe and the United States. Some will point, as proof of a civilisational clash, the numerous rebuffs Turkey has received over the decades to Ankara's ambition to become a full member of the EU, which have often been framed in civilisational terms, such as the regular references to the Gates of Vienna and the controversy unleashed over whether the EU is a Christian club during the drafting of the Lisbon Treaty,[45] led by former French president

Valéry Giscard d'Estaing, who believed Turkey's entry would spell the end of Europe.[46] Although many people believe this rhetoric, it is also an emotive mask for calculated political manoeuvring. Beyond the appeals to identity lies a home truth troubling the Union's big hitters; if Turkey were to become a full member, with its current population only second to Germany's, it would rapidly become the largest country in the EU, in light of its higher population growth.[47]

A century ago, Germany became the first modern country to declare a global jihad against her enemies, literally so. During World War I, Germany entered into a military alliance with the Ottomans, despite their empire's chronic weakness, in order to get the Sultan, who was officially also caliph, to declare a pan-Islamic jihad which, the Germans calculated, would hurt its enemies, Britain, France and Russia, all of whom possessed vast Muslim territories and had hundreds of thousands of Muslim soldiers fighting on their side of the trenches. "In a great European war, especially if Turkey participates in it against England, one may certainly expect an overall revolt of the Muslims in the British colonies," predicted the pioneering Arabist, historian, diplomat, archaeologist and German spy, Max von Oppenheim, in 1908.[48] Oppenheim went on to lead the German pan-Islamic propaganda effort during the war, which contrary to plan, had almost no effect in inciting a mass Islamic uprising. Given Oppenheim's profound and wide-ranging knowledge of Islamic history, he should really have foreseen this. If Muslims rulers have never successfully managed to launch a pan-Islamic jihad, how did the Germans expect to succeed?

But it was not just the Germans who wished to tether their imperial flag to the ship of jihad. The British were ultimately more successful. The use of the concept of jihad by the German-Ottoman alliance had its desired effect and set off alarm bells and panic in Britain and France, who did all they could to counter it, through such efforts as backing and provoking revolt in Arabia, and promoting the Sharif of Mecca, who was an Arab, ruled over Mecca and was supposedly descended from Muhammad, as a more legitimate heir to the title of caliphate than the Sultan in Istanbul. The British counter-jihad was more effective but they, too, overestimated its utility. "Perhaps there is a caution in this narrative," Eugene Rogan, the prominent historian of the Middle East,[49] warned western leaders of the 21st century. "When they overreact to the threat of religious war, they concede power to the very enemies they seek to overcome, with consequences impossible to predict."[50] The impossible to predict consequences of the Middle East theatre in World War I, during which religious and nationalistic passions were unleashed, were the sudden and disruptive collapse of the Ottoman empire, and its final death as a multicultural, multi-ethnic, and multi-confessional entity, the ramifications of which continue to this day. If the Ottomans had not entered World War I and the empire had been given the time and space to crumble in peace, might we have ended up instead with a democratic superstate or confederation of autonomous peoples combining the benefits of a borderless empire with those of freedom and equality for all?[51] We will never know.

Despite the repeated warnings from intellectuals and dissidents over the decades, the major western powers have generally ignored the cautionary tale offered by World War I and have continued to exploit Islamic religious forces for the sake of short-term political expediency, without paying heed to the dangerous, formidable and cumulative blowback of such policies. This was especially the case during the secular post-colonial and Cold War era. Islamic fanatics were willing to play the role of western power brokers' useful idiots, or, had decided that their greater enemies were the godless in their midst rather than the godless in the West. Perhaps the most unlikely current alliance is the long-standing Anglo-American relationship with Saudi Arabia, which has stood rock-solid since the 1915 Anglo-Saudi Treaty (Darin Treaty).[52] In terms of values, culture, political philosophy and religious ideology, such an improbable union should not exist, and if it did, it should be a shortlived marriage of convenience, not an enduring alliance that has lasted for more than a century. The special relationship between Riyadh, London and later Washington has withstood two world wars, a cold war, the global exporting of Wahhabism, Western hegemony over the Middle East, 9/11, the Anglo-American invasion of Iraq, the Saudi-led invasion of Yemen, the current mayhem in the region and even the rise of Donald Trump. After meeting with the famously Islamophobic US president, the then Saudi Deputy Crown Prince Mohammed bin Salman made the unimaginable claim that Trump was a "true friend of Muslims who will serve the Muslim world in an unimaginable manner".[53]

The clash within

The late Edward Said, author of the controversial, groundbreaking critique of Western imperialistic philosophy, *Orientalism*, saw in Huntington's clash of civilisations theory an extension of the pseudo-scientific Orientalist scholarship which had been used for at least a couple of centuries to justify European and western hegemony. In an essay entitled "The Clash of Ignorances," published shortly after 9/11, Said argued that Huntington ignored the internal dynamics and plurality of every civilisation and the fact that the major contest in most modern cultures concerns the definition or interpretation of each culture.[54]

Proximity is often a greater cause of friction than culture. No matter how much politicians and social leaders talk about 'our values', a common set of values to which everyone in a society subscribes simply do not exist. The diversity of opinion and views within any single society, even supposedly homogeneous ones, is mind-blowingly broad. Imagine, then, how wide-ranging values will be within a supposed civilisational bloc. For these reasons, conflicts within self-identified cultural or civilisational groups can be greater than those between them. Over the centuries, Christians and Muslims have gone to war and possibly killed more of their co-religionists than each other, as the unprecedented carnage of two world wars in Europe and the current devastation in the Middle East highlight all too clearly. This distrust of one's brothers and sisters in faith is succinctly summed up in an old Byzantine adage about their co-religionists to the west: "Have a Frank as a friend, never as a neighbour."[55] And this fear must have appeared justified to the Byzantines during the Fourth Crusade when, instead of coming to their aid against the infidel Muslims, western crusaders sacked Byzantium itself. Instead of turning back the tide of Islam, the leaders of the crusade divvied up the Byzantine empire, with Baldwin of Flanders crowned Emperor Baldwin I of Constantinople in the Hagia Sophia.[56] "For the occasions past and present, when sons and daughters of the Catholic Church have sinned by action or omission against their Orthodox brothers and sisters, may the Lord grant us the forgiveness we beg of him," the late Pope John Paul II said in 2001, by way of apology. "It is tragic that the assailants, who had set out to secure free access for Christians to the Holy Land, turned against their own brothers in the faith. The fact that they were Latin Christians fills Catholics with deep regret."[57]

Of course, there has not just been rivalry and clashes between Western and Eastern Christianity, but conflict has plagued both camps, as can be gleaned from the bitter stand-offs between Catholics and Protestants, or between the Orthodox and Coptic churches. This can be seen in how the Crusader kingdoms of the Middle East were often at war with one another, sometimes even allying themselves with the supposed Muslim enemy. One notable example of this was how Raymond of Tripoli, who spoke fluent Arabic and was widely read in Islamic literature, forged a shortlived peace with the legendary Saladin until the crusader hawks took flight. A baffled Andalusian traveller who passed through the Levant during this time of crusade/jihad, wrote: "There is complete understanding between the two sides, and equity is respected. The men of war pursue their war, but the people remain at peace."[58]

What this reveals is that the kinks, inconsistencies, contradictions and even randomness of history as an actual lived experience are too often ironed out or justified with the benefit of hindsight to fit into a particular ideological mould. Centuries after the event, many Muslims and Christians, for instance, look back on their past interactions as a clash between Islam and Christendom. That said, two terms in Arabic, which Muslims have lamented for generations, give lie to this convenient half-truth: *ta'ifiya* (factionalism) and *fitna,* which means 'sedition' and is used to refer, among many other things, to the civil wars and conflicts which afflicted and hobbled the rapidly expanding Muslim community during the early history of Islam. Divide and conquer and divide and rule have been widely recognised strategies for the powerful to dominate the weak for centuries. But there is a flip side to this which can too easily be missed; the lure of power and riches can divide the rulers as they battle for influence and affluence. This is visible in the fates of three of the first four caliphs of Islam (Umar ibn al-Khattab, Uthman ibn Affan, and Ali ibn Abi Talib, who reigned during the so-called First Fitna), who were assassinated as a result of various political intrigues. Ali's supporters, known as Shi'at Ali (Ali's party), initiated the longest-lasting schism in Islam, giving birth to the Shi'a and Sunni branches of Islam.

During the course of the seven-century-long Muslim presence in Iberia, there was as much infighting on each side as there was fighting between them. An example of this was the Berber revolt, which started in Tangiers in 740 and spread to Iberia, and involved newly converted North African Muslims who rose up against the racism of Arab Muslims and the brutality of their Arab governors.[59] After the collapse of the Iberian Umayyad dynasty (whose survivors had fled to Spain in the first place after the dynasty had been defeated, not by Christians, but by its rival claimants to the caliphate, the Abbasids, in 750 AD) following a civil war which ended in 1031 AD, centralised Muslim power in Spain crumbled and enduring factionalism set in as rival emirates and city states, known as *reinos de taifa*, jockeyed for ascendancy. Militarily weak, these small emirates often relied not only on North African fighters but also on Christian mercenaries.[60] The most famous of these is probably Rodrigo Díaz de Vivar, better known as El Cid, a soldier of fortune for both Christian and Muslim monarchs alike. El Cid began his career by fighting for the Christian kingdom of Castille against its Christian and Muslim rivals. Alfonso VI of Leon (whom El Cid had earlier helped defeat, leading to his imprisonment then exile in Islamic Toledo under the protection of its sovereign, al-Mamun) then assumed the Castillian throne. Now it was the turn of El Cid (the name comes from the Arabic Sayyid, meaning master or lord) to seek refuge and employment in a Muslim *taifa* (Zaragoza), on whose behalf he battled against its Christian and Muslim enemies. El Cid ended his career by going into business for himself, carving out a territory centred on multicultural Valencia, where he became the *de facto* ruler of a mixed population of Muslims and Christians, and for that matter, Jews.[61]

Christianity has also not been immune to factionalism. Indeed, Christendom set an unenviable example for Islam to follow. Long before Muhammad was born, the Byzantine empire was not only weakened due to the endless series of wars it fought with the Persians but also due to its internal, schism-ridden divisions, with many churches considered heretical. This helps partly explain how it was that the relatively small Arab armies were able to conquer and govern so much territory, where Muslims were a tiny minority, in such a short space of time. In Egypt, for example, many of the indigenous Copts were glad to see the back of the Byzantines and the hated emperor Heraclius, who had overtaxed and persecuted them as heretics.[62] Some even appear to have assisted the Arab invaders. "This expulsion (of the Romans) and victory of the Muslim is due to the wickedness of the emperor Heraclius and his persecution of the Orthodox through the patriarch Cyrus. This was the cause of the ruin of the Romans and the subjugation of Egypt by the Muslim," many Egyptian Christians at the time believed, according to John, the Bishop of Nikiu.[63]

Crash of civilisations?

If there has not been a clash of civilisations, what have we been witnessing in recent years?

It is possible that we are experiencing a crash of civilisation. I do not mean the collapse of civilisation and the end of technologically advanced human society, but rather the more mundane and periodic collapse of the dominant political, economic and social orders.

At one level, we are experiencing the crumbling of the post-Cold War world order in which America is no longer the sole global superpower, and its pre-eminence is being challenged by other global powers. But this is no Huntingtonian civilisational clash over cultural values but is rather about economic value and crude, raw political power, with the emphasis on crude oil and raw materials, as the major economies seek to satisfy their voracious appetites for the world's finite and dwindling resources. This has led to brewing geostrategic clashes of interests between the great powers, as America tries to hold on to its waning global reach, Russia tries to claw back the influence it lost following the implosion of the Soviet Union and China, after years of quiet growth in the background, begins to flex its muscles on the foreign stage, both to defend its emerging strategic interests and for prestige. So far, these clashes have been indirect or by proxy, and the "core state conflicts" Huntington foresaw have not really materialised. However, Syria – where all the permanent members of the UN Security Council and regional powers are involved in one way or another – is one hotspot that could set off a wider direct conflict between the major powers – but this would have little or nothing to do with values. Like Congo at the turn of this century or Spain in the 1930s, Syria has become the theatre not only of a local civil war but of a global and regional scramble for influence.

Another major factor fuelling instability worldwide, and one swept under the carpet or underplayed by Huntington, Lewis, neo-cons and neo-liberals is the intensifying struggle between the haves and the have-nots, as corporate power has globalised but the mechanisms to defend workers' rights and protect citizens have not. Locally and globally, economic inequality, both between nations and within them, is rising, despite recent falls in absolute poverty, and with it, stark social inequalities. Statistically, this is eloquently expressed in the fact that just eight billionaires own as much wealth as the poorest half of humanity, i.e. 3.6 billion people.[64] Even the World Economic Forum has recognised the high stakes related to inequality, blaming the rise of populist politicians like Donald Trump and policies such as Brexit on the disenchantment associated with growing inequity. "Rising income and wealth disparity is… the most important trend in determining global developments over the next 10 years," it forecasted in 2017.[65] This far-right populism does not tackle inequality but tends to exacerbate it.[66] Likewise, Brexit is leading to a situation which is the worst on record for income growth in the bottom half, resulting in the greatest rising in inequality since the Thatcher years in the 1980s.[67]

In addition to populist 'solutions' that will only worsen the divide, this inequality has led to the global rise of simplistic and polarised identity politics being used as an alternative to building a profound understanding of why people are becoming worse off and more vulnerable and as a substitute for meaningful change and reforms. Rather than the fault line clashes between civilisations that Huntington foresaw, this has resulted in fault line cracks and clashes appearing at the very heart of every civilisation and their component societies. In the West, this can be seen in the growing polarisation of society, growing nativism and tribalism,[68] the stigmatisation of minorities, the emergence of muscular far-right populism and racism, as well as social protest movements, from years of street battles in Greece to Occupy Wall Street.

The excesses of global corporatism have led many to throw the baby out with the bathwater, and disparage even the positive social and cultural aspects of globalisation and multiculturalism. In America, this has led to the surreal situation where a billionaire has been elected to be the champion of right-wing anti-globalisation. This distrust of multiculturalism was expressed by British Prime Minister Theresa May when she told her fellow Brits, "If you believe you're a citizen of the world, you are a citizen of nowhere. You don't understand what the very word citizenship means."[69] As someone who counts himself as a citizen of nowhere, but more vitally a citizen of everywhere, I can only conclude that this Little Englander clearly misunderstands what symbolic global citizenship means. It signifies the willingness to reach across artificial cultural and political divides, not out of a sense of treachery to your supposed own, but out of a sense of shared humanity with the rest of the world. The true citizen of the world understands very well the meaning of citizenship, and lives it. We not only pay our dues to the nations of our birth and heritage, we are also responsible members of the societies we have adopted or have adopted us (even if temporarily), not to mention the rest of humanity. We are loyal to the places we come from and the places we move to, but our primary allegiance is to humanity. Narrow patriotism of the 'my-side-right-or-wrong' variety is not only destructive to the world, it tears apart the societies which adopt it, as has been demonstrated too many times to mention, as occurred in Europe in the build up to the two world wars, or is happening in the Middle East today. So, by owing our primary loyalty to humanity, we are actually the ultimate patriots because our so-called 'divided allegiances' are what will save us from our greatest enemy, ourselves.

Inequalities, both economic and social, were a major factor behind the revolutionary and counter-revolutionary waves which have swept across the Middle East in recent years, with bread, jobs and social justice major rallying calls for protesters. Even in Tunisia, which has had the most successful post-revolutionary transition, failure to tackle socio-economic inequality effectively is threatening the impressive political gains the country has scored. Some disappointed Tunisians I have encountered even go so far as to express nostalgia for the repressive and corrupt Ben Ali years, lionising the former dictator as some sort of man of the people, rather than the crook he was who took the country to the cleaners. These nostalgists also fail to see that the troubles that Tunisia and the wider region are experiencing are a consequence of what went before; of the corruption, dictatorship and mismangement, which hollowed out the state and rendered it dysfunctional. What we see today is not some new disease which the region has contracted but the symptom of a malaise that had been festering for years. A sick body can appear externally stable and even seem to grow stronger for years while it is actually being demolished and consumed from within.

Across the region, states were failing spectacularly in their mission to underpin the social and economic welfare of their citizens, with the main service they provided being security for a small elite (and for their foreign sponsors) at the expense of the majority. Even the unwritten social contract by which citizens kept their mouths shut in return for security and stability has unravelled. With one state after another failing its burgeoning populations in education, healthcare, social security and job creation, the former mix of persuasion and coercion gave way to large-scale repression. And when states fail their citizens so spectacularly, this is likely to lead to state failure, as has occurred in Syria, Yemen and Libya, to name three extreme examples. One major symptom of failing or failed states is the accentuation of difference. In the Middle East, there has long been polarisation between modernisers and traditionalists, between secularists and religious conservatives, between moderates and fundamentalists, between leftists and rightists, between majorities and minorities, between universalists and nativists, between conservatives and liberals, and more. The recent seismic shifts in the region's social and political landscape have thrown these contrasting and conflicting tides into sharp relief, where once they were swept under the carpet, transforming mere tension into open conflict.

Whereas the global clash of civilisations posited by Huntington does not exist except in the illusions of extremists hitherto on the fringe (yet who are sadly becoming increasingly mainstream), clashes over culture are widely occurring on the national level, within individual societies. This clash within is currently playing itself out most visibly in the Middle East. For instance, though ISIS's 'jihad' has been about territory and resources, its main ideological enemy has been what it regards as errant Muslims – 'the near enemy' – who are worse than the infidel, in ISIS's reckoning, because they claim to belong to Islam but walk the path of *kufr* or unbelief.[70] Despite ISIS's merciless persecution and ethnic cleansing of minorities,[71] such as Yazidis and Christians, the group systematically targets and persecutes fellow Muslims, including Shia, Kurds, Turks, Shabaks,[72] Turkmen,[73] Sufis,[74] secularists and fellow Sunni Arabs who simply happen to reject its murderous creed. And ISIS is no exception. A US government report found that "Muslims suffered between 82% and 97% of terrorism-related fatalities over the past five years."[75] The fact that the vast majority of victims of Islamic terrorism are fellow Muslims may shock many but it has its own illogical logic to it. One major factor is the institutional weakness of governments in many Muslim states, who are sometimes unable but more often unwilling to make the necessary efforts to protect their citizens' lives and livelihoods. This creates a level of relative lawlessness that can be exploited by extremists. Another factor is ideological. Many Islamic extremists believe that modern-day Muslim societies have reverted to *jahiliya*, i.e. a state of pre-Islamic 'ignorance'. The most influential modern Islamist thinker to advocate this view was the Egyptian Sayyid Qutb, who developed a nihilistic form of Islamic radicalism while he was being tortured in one of Nasser's political prisons. "We are also surrounded by *jahiliyyah* today, which is of the same nature as it was during the first period of Islam, perhaps a little deeper," he wrote in his landmark thesis, *Milestones,* which mentions the word 'jahiliyya' almost 200 times, by my count. "Our whole environment, people's beliefs and ideas, habits and art, rules and laws is *jahiliyyah,* even to the extent that what we consider to be Islamic culture, Islamic sources, Islamic philosophy and Islamic thought are also constructs of *jahiliyyah!*"[76] Though this idea has existed on the fringes of Islam for centuries, with the term first coined by the godfather of salafists Ibn Taymiyyah (1263-1348),[77] during a period of massive upheaval and destruction caused by the Mongol invasions of the Middle East, Sayyid Qutb expanded and enlarged it to encompass pretty much every Muslim who did not agree with his views, with far-reaching and devastating consequences. Qutb paved the way for a version of Islamic salafism which would become known as *takfir wel hijra* (meaning excommunication and migration), which regarded pretty much all Muslims as beyond the pale of Islam, making them legitimate targets, and urged, as Qutb did on numerous occasions in his book, true believers to withdraw from society until such time as they could change it.

In addition to the jihadist conflict with mainstream Muslim society, a kind of global jihadist civil war[78] is in motion, both in Syria and elsewhere, between al-Qaeda, its more radical, gruesome and murderously sectarian offshoot, ISIS, and other jihadist outfits, each of which condemns the others as godless and not true to Islam, whereas their real motivation is greed for power and influence, and envy of one another's successes. This was illustrated in the assassination by al-Qaeda-allied al-Nusra Front of Abu Ali al-Baridi, the commander of the ISIS-affiliated al-Yarmouk Martyrs Brigade.[79] In a statement about the killing, al-Nusra placed al-Baridi firmly outside the community of believers.[80]

Decoding the West's Islamic DNA

What gets left bleeding by the wayside in these polarised times is what I like to call the 'Mash of Civilisations'. Judaism, Christianity and Islam have so influenced one another over the centuries, and been influenced in turn by the same traditions (including the Greco-Roman, Mesopotamian and Egyptian), that it is impossible to speak of them as separate, discrete civilisations. They are sub-groups of a single civilisation, and the diversity within each is greater than the differences between them. I would go so far as to posit that the Middle East and the West belong to the same Judeo-Christian-Islamic tradition, which is merely a subset of human civilisation. Muslims and Christians further east in south and southeast Asia share more in terms of culture or civilisational with their non-Abrahamic neighbour than they do with their co-religionists further west.

There are plenty of conservative Muslims, Christians and Jews who will disagree with my assertion. Like Muslims who fantasise about an ahistorical caliphate, conservative Europeans who dream of a bygone utopia of a Europe uncontaminated by Islam miss the reality that the 'Islamisation of the West' occurred centuries ago. Islamic civilisation is so hardwired into Europe's cultural, social and intellectual DNA that it would be impossible to expunge its influence. The same applies in the other direction, in light of Christendom's and the West's powerful influence on Arab and Islamic society.

In addition to the philosophy, science, literature and art of the Muslim world which profoundly shaped the European Renaissance and have received much public attention in recent years, Islamic culture had some far more unexpected and surprising influences on Western civilisation. One man in particular, for whom no statues or memorials stand anywhere in Europe and of whom very few westerners have heard is possibly the most unsung cultural, style and musical icon in European history. In the ninth century, Ali Ibn Nafi (789-857), known to his contemporaries as *Ziryab* (or Blackbird), was Cordoba's most sought-after hipster, who moved to Spain from then trendy Baghdad, and brought into vogue the idea of seasonal fashions, steering history's catwalk towards the fashion slavery of the 21st century. This sultan of style also added a fifth pair of strings to the Arab *oud*, paving the way to the European lute, which in turn would become the modern guitar, and, like a medieval rock star, he revolutionised Andalusian music forever. He also introduced Europe to the idea of dining etiquette, from table cloths and crystal decanters to the three-course meal.[81] Perhaps finding the new continent where he now dwelt displeasing to his refined nose, Ziryab is credited with having introduced deodorant to Europe. To top it all off, Ziryab was (like many of the Arab elite of the period) a polymath, with wide-ranging knowledge in astronomy, philosophy and medicine.[82] "We might consider him some charming... if outlandish mixture of Oscar Wilde, Andy Warhol, Salvador Dali, Orson Welles, Christian Dior, Phil Spector, Terence Conran and Tony Wilson," was the verdict of one historian.[83]

The impact of Muslims on European and Western culture does not begin nor end with Ziryab. In fact, you could go so far as to say that the French Enlightenment, computer geek-speak (including Java), and even Starbucks would not have been possible without Muslims. Of course, I'm not talking about the significant Islamic contributions to mathematics, the sciences and free-thought. I'm talking about coffee, which the legendary French historian Jules Michelet called the "auspicious revolution",[84] and coffee shops. Although today coffee is often seen as a rather bourgeois indulgence, an antidote for late nights, or the workaholic's friend, it was once a revolutionary drink drunk by revolutionaries. So much so that authorities feared not only the mystical powers of this newfound super substance, but its potential for sedition, when the hyper-alert, from all walks of life gathered in the new-fangled coffeehouses. These started in earnest in Cairo and Damascus, in the 16th century, spread across the Ottoman empire and from there to Europe, via Italy – where they talked about culture, society and politics. Not only was coffee banned in Mecca for a time, England's Charles II decided to outlaw it too. This followed a petition from disgruntled women whose husbands went to the tavern till they were "Drunk as a Drum and then back again to the Coffee-house to drink themselves sober" returning home with "nothing *moist* but their snotty Noses, nothing *stiffe* but their Joints, nor *standing* but their Ears". Sniffing an opportunity to suppress these dens of "idle and disaffected Persons", the king set about, in 1675, to shutter the country's coffeehouses, not out of moral rectitude, but to suppress dissent, as these innovative establishments had become places where "false, malitious and scandalous reports are devised and spread abroad to the defamation of his Majestie's Government." But the revolution he hoped to forestall was actually fomented (or perhaps fermented), by the potential absence of coffee, leading Charles II to change his mind at the eleventh hour and not enforce the ban.[85] Across the channel, where cafes were more inclusive establishments, drawing women as well as men from many backgrounds, coffeehouses became intellectual, cultural and political melting pots, enabling such luminaries as Voltaire, Rousseau, and Diderot to debate their Enlightenment ideas and ideals, and was a meeting place of those agitating for political change in pre-revolutionary France.[86]

The Turks may have failed to penetrate the gates of Vienna militarily in 1529 and 1683, as is widely recalled by European anti-immigration nationalists today, but they did manage to invade it culturally, namely through the introduction of coffee and coffeehouses. Vienna's first registered coffeehouse was opened, in 1685, by an Armenian Ottoman named Johannes Diodato, who also managed to obtain a 20-year royal monopoly on selling the lucrative substance.[87] In fact, Armenians, who shared the culture of the Ottomans and the religion of Europeans, played a pivotal role in the spreading of the new wonder drug across Europe. An Armenian immigrant established London's first coffeehouse in 1652 and the first entrepreneur to sell coffee to ordinary Parisians was also an Armenian immigrant at the St Germain annual fair in 1672, where he pitched an Ottoman-style booth at a time when all things Turkish were trendy in France.[88]

Coffee was not the only drug Europeans imported from their Muslim neighbours. Centuries before, in early medieval times, before France had established its own indigenous high-quality wine industry, the taverns of Gaul were full of wines from the Abbasid caliphate, including, of all places, Gaza.[89] This is bound to strike the modern reader as counter-intuitive, as both the words caliphate and Gaza are associated, in the 21st century, with teetotalling puritanism, but this wasn't always the case. Medieval Muslims even invented 'alcohol'. Back then, alcohol (the term is probably derived from the Arabic 'al-kohl'), meant a distilled spirit, a technique invented and perfected by medieval Arab chemists and exported across the world by Muslim merchants (see chapter 5, on alcohol).

At the other end of the spectrum, there are definite parallels between the Protestant attitudes towards temperance and abstention from alcohol and mainstream Islamic theology. Whether or not Protestant puritans were directly inspired by the Islamic precedent, the net effect was similar: a number of Protestant countries have imposed partial or complete bans on the production and consumption of alcoholic beverages at one time or another. The most famous example is the United States and its Prohibition, which began in 1920 and ended, a failure, in 1933. One of the longest lasting prohibitions was in Iceland, where beer was only legalised in 1989, when jubilant Icelanders ordered the amber nectar legally for the first time in 74 years.[90]

And the similarities between Christian Protestantism and Sunni Islam do not stop at the beer vat. Like Islam, many Protestant theologies are iconoclastic against all 'graven images', whereas Catholicism is only iconoclastic against pagan imagery, and the Iconoclastic Fury of the 16th century, in which 'idols' were smashed in many parts of Europe, especially the Low Countries, presaged ISIS by several centuries. Both Protestantism and Islam champion the idea that work is a form of worship, though the modern Protestant work ethic appears to exceed its Islamic counterpart by an order of magnitude.

However, judging by the common saying 'al-'amal 'ibada' (i.e. Work is Worship), the long hours many people work in Muslim-majority countries and the fact that Friday is just another working day for millions might suggest otherwise.

These similarities, along with political and economic interests and expediency, might explain why Protestant political movements and even monarchs sought to ally themselves with the Ottomans, namely by highlighting how much in common they had which they did not share with the Catholic church or the Habsburgs. England's isolated Queen Elizabeth I even entered into a long correspondence with the then Ottoman sultan, Murad III, with both extolling their ideological common ground, while building strong trading and political ties, including the export of English tin and lead, some removed from the roofs of Catholic monasteries, for use by the Turks to build cannons.[91] In correspondences with Protestant rebels in Flanders, the Turkish sultan, Suleiman I ('The Magnificent'), promised military and financial support to the Protestants because they did not worship idols, believed in the oneness of God and fought against their emperor and pope. Presumably the latter fact, dressed up in ideological garb, was the main imperative behind the sultan's interest in Protestantism: the defanging of his European rivals. Whatever Suleiman's actual motives, some historians argue that the success of the Reformation and the spread of Protestantism hinged on this Ottoman support.[92] Although Suleiman was almost certainly driven by imperial considerations in his attempts to forge alliances with the European Reformation, he and other sultans did provide Protestants with protection, allowing them to practise their religion freely in Ottoman-controlled Transylvania. In addition, in moves that carry resonance in today's debate over refugees, persecuted Christians, not just

Iberian Jews and Muslims, found refuge in the Ottoman empire. These included a hodgepodge mix of Huguenots, Quakers, Anglicans, Jesuits and Capuchins, who may have been sipping primitive versions of cappuccinos by the Bosphorus.[93]

Islam's veiled westernisation

Whereas the Islamic influence on the contemporary West is largely historical and so hard-wired into its cultural and social DNA that it often goes unnoticed and unacknowledged, the Western influence on Muslim societies is possibly even profounder and, because it is continuing and ongoing, far clearer to see and more obvious. In terms of technology, knowledge, science, philosophy, political systems, legal codes, and culture, Europe and America have exerted an immense and perhaps unprecedented influence on Muslim societies. This process, commonly known as 'westernisation', tended to be imposed by the European imperial powers during the colonial era, and was actively embraced by most modernising elites in the early post-colonial period as an essential component to true liberation. While, westernisation may be ostensibly resisted in many parts of the Muslim world today, truth be told, western influence has become so deeply woven into the social, political and economic fabric that it has become, to all intents and purposes, irreversible, indigenous even, and cannot be undone without renting society completely apart.

Even in areas not directly under European rule, such as the Ottoman Empire and Egypt during the 19th century, local reformers looked to Europe for inspiration. The *tanzimat*, which sought to reform and modernise the Ottoman empire, emulated Western European systems, centralised the traditionally decentralised administration of the Ottoman state, and granted legal equality to all Ottoman subjects, regardless of religion or ethnicity. This top-down effort was not organic and dynamic enough and proved to be too little, too late to save the ailing empire, the original 'Sick Man of Europe', especially with the vultures of other European empires circling in for prize chunks of the sultan's dominion.[94] Its influences endure, however, in legal and administrative legacies across the former Ottoman territories.

In the first half of the 19th century, what became known as the Arab *Nahda* or Renaissance was born. Like its earlier European counterpart, which borrowed heavily from Arab sciences and philosophy and tried to recast them in a European light, the Egyptian Renaissance sought to create a fusion and synthesis between the best of modern Western ideas, sciences and technologies and the best of the earlier Islamic tradition of free-thought, as well as drawing on pre-Islamic achievements. This Renaissance took off with Rifa'a al-Tahtawi, a French-educated reformer and scholar, who was the first modern Egyptian to write first-hand about European society and oversaw the translation into Arabic of some 2,000 European works at the School of Languages he established.[95] Peculiarly, al-Tahtawi and other 19th-century reformers who followed him, such as the highly influential Muhammad Abdu, were former or continuing Islamic scholars, *ulema*, who, nevertheless, were committed to the secularisation of their societies, as well as the education and political systems. This is not as strange as it may at first sound. Many of these men believed that Europe had captured the genuine spirit of Islam, while Muslims had lost it, so it was only natural that Muslims should look west to regain this essence.

This is rather like what happened in Europe during the Renaissance and Enlightenment. Although much of the foundations of Europe's modernisation were directly taken from the Islamic tradition, European thinkers saw it as a return to the essence of ancient Greece and Rome. For instance, the notion of the separation between church and state is generally regarded as a quintessentially European innovation and many even see it as being alien to Islam, yet European thinkers were strongly influenced in this regard by Ibn Rushd's theories on the separation of reason and faith,[96] a fact that has largely fallen into oblivion. Although Ibn Khaldun, widely regarded as the father of modern sociology and political science, saw in Islamic law and the caliphate the ideal form of government, he recognised the importance of separating religious from political authority and acknowledged that virtuous government did not have to be based on divine laws, as religious fanatics and fundamentalists insist even today, because justice and good governance had been achieved by "heathens and other nations who had no scriptures and had not been reached by a prophetic mission".[97]

The drive for westernisation and secularisation picked up momentum in the first half of the 20th century partly because pro-independence leaders and modernisers sought to overcome European domination by emulating what they regarded as the best aspects of Western civilisation and partly because of broad admiration for the achievements and success of European powers, their imperial injustices notwithstanding. At a certain level this was unsurprising as many liberation leaders were western-educated and often rubbed shoulders with Europeans. For instance, Habib Bourguiba, who led Tunisia to independence, moved to Paris to pursue his higher education in order to arm himself intellectually against France. While there, he fell in love with a French widow, moved in with her and they had a child together. Upon returning to

Tunisia, Bourguiba married his French girlfriend (who was over a decade his senior) and she eventually became Tunisia's first first lady.[98] Bourguiba's vision for post-independence Tunisia was profoundly affected, amongst other things, by the contrast between the repression of French rule at home and the empowerment and liberalism he had witnessed in Paris under France's Third Republic, not to mention one of his brothers, Mohamed, who worked as a medic and lived with an Italian nurse, and was a radical secularist and modernist. Turkey's Mustafa Kemal Atatürk, India's Gandhi, as well as Bourguiba's own experience of social, economic and gender inequality.[99]

The progressive nation-building which occurred in the Middle East during the first half of the 20th century was conceived along largely secular lines, especially in countries like Tunisia, Turkey, Egypt, Syria and Iraq. The political ideologies which shaped the modern Middle East and much of the Muslim world were also of European or western origins, including liberalism, socialism, communism, ethno-nationalism and even Islamic fundamentalism, which borrowed liberally from its Christian counterparts, particularly the American religious right.

When secular experiments failed to deliver tangible results, despite early gains, and resulted in renewed despotism, dictatorship and economic stagnation, Islamists seized the opportunity, employing a simplistic, yet appealing argument: the reasons for these failures were not complex and multifaceted but were down to society's alleged deviations from Islamic principles and true Islam. In addition, the abuse of such principles as democracy, equality, individualism and human rights by the western powers to advance their narrow political interests and hegemony helped Islamists and conservatives to depict these concepts as destructive imperialist ploys and inauthentic western imports. Despite this rhetoric, even Islamists have internalised and integrated many modern western concepts, such as a commitment to parliamentarianism and the ballot box, albeit subordinating them to 'God's will'. The most modernist example of this is Tunisia's Ennahda party, which worked to build consensus with secular parties following Ben Ali's ouster, facilitated the transition to democracy,[100] and allowed the formulation of a secular constitution for the country.[101]

In some other countries, such as Egypt, the failure of Islamists to deliver a viable alternative, and the discovery that Egypt's complex mess of problems could not be reduced to a simple question of piety and faith have turned the country's Muslim Brotherhood from the most popular opposition figures to a generally unpopular movement opposed by millions (but still supported by a dwindling, if significant, hardcore). This reality was exploited by Sisi to overthrow Mohamed Morsi, seize power for himself, outlaw the Brotherhood, persecute its members and attempt to crush any form of opposition.

It is my conviction, paradoxically, that the violent wave of Islamism which is setting many parts of the region ablaze is not a sign of success nor strength. Having failed to gain the level of support they had hoped for, through which the masses would willingly and voluntarily embrace 'divine laws', radical Islamists and jihadists decided to exploit the power vacuums and mayhem in places like Syria, Iraq and Libya to become God's self-appointed agents, representatives and defenders on Earth. Ironically, perhaps, ISIS and the other jihadist outfits are the biggest single advertisement for the virtue of separating religion from affairs of state, and for keeping the spiritual private.

CHAPTER EIGHT

Rationalising Islam: Muslim sceptics, heretics, apostates and atheists

In the West, my ethnicity, name and presumed religion can result in my being regarded as a potential terrorist. But it does not end there. Suspicion surrounds me in Arab countries too, and not just for my critical journalism. In Saudi Arabia, for instance, I am a terrorist.

I happen to be an atheist and, according to Saudi regulations issued in 2014, terrorism includes, in Article 1, no less than the following: "Calling for atheist thought in any form, or calling into question the fundamentals of the Islamic religion on which this country is based."[1] Needless to say, this move left me bewildered and confused. Perhaps the world had neglected the news of the worrying territorial gains made by the other ISIS, the Impious State in Iraq and Syria, known to its enemies as the Infidel State, not to mention the advances made by Hizbullah. Maybe the Atheist Brotherhood or the leftist guerrilla group, the Popular Front for the Liberation from Islam, is rolling its tanks into Riyadh to overthrow the divinely elected Al Saud family.

The grave danger posed by atheists was expressed in crystal clear terms by the Saudi ambassador to the United Nations Abdallah al-Mouallimi, who said on *Al Jazeera*: "Any calls that challenge Islamic rule or Islamic ideology are considered subversive in Saudi Arabia and would be subversive and could lead to chaos." But interviewer Mehdi Hassan refused to comprehend the gravity of the situation, one in which gravity itself might grind to a halt if Muslims ceased to believe. "Somebody who says, 'I don't believe in God and others shouldn't believe in God' is equivalent to Osama bin Laden?" Hassan asked in disbelief. But the good ambassador was ready, firing back: "If he is going out in the public, and saying, 'I don't believe in God,' that's subversive. He is inviting others to retaliate."[2] Now it all makes sense. If an atheist's words cause a Muslim extremist to commit an act of violence, this terrorism is the atheist's fault, not that of the fanatic who committed it. By his logic, I imagine al-Mouallimi will have no objections if a Saudi citizen or European Muslim is attacked by an Islamophobe neo-Nazi – after all, the Muslim's beliefs 'invited others to retaliate,' a fascist would argue. What awes me the most is just how powerful atheists are. We can wreak all this panic and havoc, despite apparently only numbering in the handfuls. "We are a country that is homogeneous in accepting Islam by the entire population," insisted al-Mouallimi, which raises the question: if everyone accepts Islam, how can there be atheists?

Our subversive, destructive collective power is made all the more remarkable by our utter uselessness as individuals. "An Arab atheist is usually a parasite – someone who claims to be knowledgeable but is not and will probably eventually commit suicide," wrote a columnist in a Saudi newspaper. "An Arab atheist is usually a drunk, certainly a degenerate and has definitely nothing to offer."[3] Panic over then. We're so intoxicated and decadent, and will probably end up offing ourselves, that we pose no threat to anyone but ourselves. See, there is nothing to worry about, Saudi Arabia. Can you please remove us from your terrorism list now? Egyptian religious authorities have assigned a figure to this evil. According to Ibrahim Negm, an adviser to the Egyptian Mufti, a survey, in 2014, found there to be exactly 866 atheists in Egypt, the highest number in the Arab world, apparently. Saudi Arabia, in contrast, has just 178, according to the same survey.[4] But do not let our small number deceive you. Though we do not believe in supernatural powers, we possess them. Atheists, as we all know, are, in reality, Satanists. Don't believe me? Ask Gamal Mohie, the chief of a Cairo municipality in which a Satano-atheistic cult was shut down. "There was no sign reading 'atheists' café' outside, as nobody would put up such a public announcement," explained Mohie. "However, it was popularly known as a place for Satan worship, rituals and dances. There were also Satanic drawings at the entrance."[5] Truly, "*al-shitan shater*, the devil is clever," as we say in Egypt. This is probably because he is always found hiding in the detail, concealed behind a semicolon or, far more sinisterly, placing question marks where there should be statements of certainty. But the ever-alert authorities are vigilant and they are fighting these demonic dens. In Saudi Arabia, they are catching the virus of unbelief early. In 2016, the Ministry of Education launched a moral 'vaccination' programme to build up and strengthen the theist immune system of the kingdom's pious but vulnerable schoolchildren against the triple threat of atheism, secularism and liberalism.[6]

Dangerous demonisation

The often quite literal demonisation of atheists that goes on in Saudi Arabia and some other Muslim countries has serious repercussions for those who do not believe but have the misfortune to be trapped in such a religiously fundamentalist and intolerant society. At the extreme end of the scale, this leads to open, unapologetic persecution. In Saudi Arabia, those found guilty of atheism or 'apostasy' can receive capital punishment or be flogged pitilessly. For example, in 2017, one man who allegedly renounced Islam and Muhammad on social media was reportedly sentenced to death.[7] A year earlier, another man was sentenced to 10 years in prison and 2,000 lashes for expressing his atheism in hundreds of social media posts, after the young non-believer reportedly refused to 'repent'[8] – surely something he should be rewarded for because he refused to be a hypocrite.

The fast lane to hell is paved with the state's declared pious intentions. In Saudi Arabia, you do not need to be an atheist in order to be charged with being one; often, it is enough simply to oppose the state or criticise the regime. This is what liberal reformer Raif Badawi learned after he launched a website to enable liberals in Saudi Arabia to debate various issues. Badawi was eventually sentenced to 10 years in prison and an unbearable 1,000 lashes over 20 sessions (most of which, mercifully, have yet to be delivered), for 'insulting Islam' and 'apostasy'.[9] Judging by his writings, Badawi's crime seems to have been advocating the secularisation of politics in Saudi Arabia and his ridiculing and deriding of the Wahhabi clergy, such as when he urged "NASA to abandon its telescopes and, instead, turn to our Sharia astronomers," following the demands of a Saudi televangelist that astronomers be punished for creating scepticism about Islamic law.[10] Badawi's "harsh and inhumane sentence", as his wife, Ensaf Haidar, described it, "was meant to send a clear message to all those who might dare stand up against Saudi Arabia's religious hard-liners".[11] Human rights campaigners agree, with Amnesty International calling Badawi's trial a "bid to stifle political and social debate".[12]

247

Other people who have fallen foul of the Saudi thought police include the Palestinian poet Ashraf Fayadh, who was initially sentenced to death for 'apostasy' based on a complaint filed by a rival artist following a dispute with Fayadh. Though later commuted to a still-severe eight years and 800 lashes of the whip, the initial news that Fayadh would be beheaded caused his father in Gaza to have a stroke and the poor man died before his son could see him.[13] The self-righteous mob can also play a part in inflaming public passions against those who step out of line, even a little bit. This is what happened to Saudi poet Hamza Kashgari who posted rather mild tweets on an imaginary encounter with Muhammad during the prophet's birthday (*mawlid*) in which he declared, among other things, "I have loved aspects of you, hated others" and that "No Saudi women will go to hell, because it's impossible to go there twice."[14] An online campaign of hatred and death threats prompted Kashgari to flee the country. Giving the state's self-declared role as protector of Islam, it had to act, launching an international manhunt which led to Kashgari being deported back to Saudi Arabia from Malaysia. After more than one and a half years in prison for his 'blasphemous' outburst, Kashgari was released in October 2013.[15] But punishing atheists and non-believers in Saudi Arabia is not just about silencing opposition and stifling freedoms, there is also a survival factor. Since the establishment of the Saudi state, its royal family has drawn its supposed legitimacy not from below, i.e. the support of its subjects, but from above, from Islam and God, as the protector of the religion's holiest sites and the upholder of Wahhabi orthodoxy. Even if non-believers are politically inactive and do not seek to overthrow the regime, their very existence is regarded as a mortal threat by the authorities, because by not believing, they undermine the basis of the state's legitimacy. "In Saudi terms, equating atheism with terrorism does have a certain logic since atheism presents a challenge to the most fundamental principles of the Saudi state," writes Brian Whitaker, former Middle East editor at *The Guardian*, in his book on Arab atheists. "The Saudi state cannot accept non-belief without changing the basis on which it has been constructed."[16]

Crypto-atheism

As the birthplace of Islam and a strict Wahhabi theocracy, Saudi Arabia, like ISIS's maturer older brother, projects a holier-than-thou image to the rest of the Muslim world. Not only does the regime view the country as more Islamic than the rest, it does not tolerate freedom of belief for other religions and even other branches of Islam, especially the much-maligned Shi'a and Sufi Muslims. Both conversion and atheism are considered 'apostasy' and are potentially punishable by death.[17] In such an environment, and in light of the convictions mentioned above, it is unsurprising that Saudis and foreigners living in the kingdom are very careful when expressing their views about religion. Despite this, there has been an apparent explosion in the ranks of atheists and non-practising Muslims, a phenomenon which caused a veritable sense of panic in the Saudi media. This was driven home by a poll in 2012 in which 5% of Saudis were revealed to be self-professed atheists. This may not sound like much but this was the same percentage as the United States and only 1% behind Finland, while in secular Muslim Turkey, only 2% of Turks admitted to being atheists.[18] In addition, it is possible that the real number is considerably higher, as respondents in repressive regimes often do not admit, even in anonymous polls, their true convictions, given the paranoia surrounding being outed as a non-believer in Saudi and the enormous risks involved.

This sense of terror was summed up succinctly by a Saudi atheist who agreed to speak anonymously to a journalist: "Please bear in mind, that people are witch hunting for us... so be careful which details you use." Jabir (not his real name), spoke of the great difficulty involved in hiding his collection of books on atheism and rationalism, which put me in mind of the early Christians in the Roman empire who had to hide their faith in order to avoid persecution. But, perhaps surprisingly, he said that finding fellow non-believers was not difficult, particularly in the age of social media. In fact, there has emerged an anonymous and secretive atheistic underground, albeit a small one, meeting mostly online but sometimes also in the real world. "We non-believers have meetings and groups in a lot of Saudi cities," Jabir was quoted as saying. "If you go into them, then you will be shocked by the numbers and elements of society represented." The thing which surprised Jabir the most was the large number of older atheists in these groups who had kept their convictions secret for decades until the young started to convene. Like other atheists in Saudi Arabia, Jabir projects an outward semblance of piety to his family and society, not just out of fear of being jailed or executed by the state, but because of the ostracisation from the community and likely vigilante action he would face.[19] This model of secret or discreet atheism is common not just in Saudi Arabia but in many conservative Muslim societies. And some even defend it as a sign of concealed pluralism. "Muslim societies are quietly tolerant of rebellious acts of all kinds, from the sexual to the religious," wrote Nesrine Malik, the London-based Sudanese columnist. "But because religion, family, society and politics are built around community, to be a declared atheist in the public space is to make a stand against the fabric of society."[20] While it is true that Muslims tolerate much in private that they would not countenance in public, the argument that atheists should be neither seen nor heard because they challenge the dominant social order does not stand up to scrutiny. America is generally a very pious country and communities there, especially in 'Middle America', are built around a strong public belief in God and the church remains the centre of life for many millions of Americans. Does that mean American atheists should keep their mouths shut because in God they do not trust? "I would make the distinction between individual atheism as a matter of belief, and the position of publicly declaring oneself atheist – or, more potently, 'ex-Muslim'," Malik explains. "The former is a personal position, the latter a political one that seeks to challenge authority." I too do not like the term 'ex-Muslim', partly because it has become politicised through appropriation by Islamophobes to present a distorted picture of reality and partly because 'atheist', 'agnostic' or 'convert' are better ways of describing someone who leaves Islam, and avoid using it to describe myself. In addition, someone may not believe in God or religion but may be culturally Muslim, as I feel I am, at least in part. I do not object to people who choose the label of their own volition. Beyond this, there are multiple problems with Malik's assertion. In countries which draw their legitimacy from religion and build the social order based on, it is the state which is politicising belief, not atheists. Of course, some Muslim atheists are politicised, but in Muslim societies this role is generally forced upon them, not one they adopt out of choice, because many governments and Islamic fundamentalists insist on making faith an integral part of their definition of citizenship. Moreover, for the majority of atheists who go public, their motivation is not political, but personal, cultural and social. They wish simply to be accepted and respected for who they are and they do not wish to be dishonest about their convictions – but it seems that, like with sex and drinking, too many conservative Muslim societies and communities prefer hypocritical 'Muslims' to honest atheists.

This is rather like Muslims in the West. A tiny minority is politicised along faith lines, such as the fringe Islamists who campaign for special legal dispensations for Muslims, but the majority simply practice their faith and believe, correctly, that they should be respected for who they are, yet the far-right hates any public displays of Islamic faith or culture out of a conviction that it supposedly threatens the (Judeo-)Christian fabric of western society. I doubt that Malik would argue that Muslims in Europe should conceal their faith because bigots find them threatening for no other reason than their existence and use the rare incidents of Islamist terrorism to vilify the entire community. And even if going public with one's atheism is a political statement, so what? The peaceful expression of one's political beliefs is a fundamental human right. Moreover, though atheists have historically committed political violence in other parts of the world, even the most politicised Arab or Muslim atheist has not killed in the name of his or her convictions, which gives society even less of an excuse to marginalise, prosecute or persecute this minority. "It is still possible to be an atheist without necessarily rejecting a Muslim cultural identity and heritage," Malik points out. Although a minority of non-believers do reject their community and cultural heritage, the majority of atheists I have encountered acknowledged that their cultural reference is, at least partly, Islamic and many are proud of this.

Malik does conclude that Muslims need to expand tolerance for non-belief into the public sphere. However, her apparent defence of closeting atheism, even while acknowledging the "severe mental toll" caused by all the "dissimulation and tongue biting" involved, is baffling.

Unique paths to faithlessness

Just as people who find religion follow their own unique path, there is also no single course to losing it. For some, the undermining or loss of belief comes early, in childhood. An acquaintance of mine, Amira Mohsen, a journalist and political analyst, whose father was an Egyptian Muslim and her mother a British convert, is a case in point. "As a kid, I was always confused about how my mother's family (who were Christian and Agnostic) were perfectly nice, lovely people and yet were supposed to go to hell," Mohsen recalls. "My mum would explain to me that in their hearts they were really Muslim or that my Grandmother became Muslim on her death bed but I was never convinced. I guess that's what got me thinking that it's possible to be a decent person and not a Muslim." Mohsen attempted to silence these doubts, because of her religious upbringing. "I remember thinking [religion] was pointless but I was convinced that these thoughts were just Satan whispering in my ear," she confesses . And Satan does lead some Muslims to unbelief, but not in the way that the religious think. This was the case with Waleed Mansour, a young Egyptian from Alexandria with a master's in environmental science, whom I met recently on the sidelines of a conference. Amongst the things which caused Mansour to decide that Islam was unconvincing was the figure of the devil, or Ibliss, as he is often referred to in Arabic. "It's not logical at all to have someone blamed for everything," he told me. "It is also not logical that there is no pardon for him." Mansour does not like labels and prefers not to describe himself as an atheist. Judging from his comments and our chats together, deist or agnostic may be closer to capturing his views. For Mansour, his beliefs are in a continuous state of questioning and flux. "I am in a constant [process] of debate and discussion to either proof myself right or wrong," he notes. He also admits that he is not opposed to religion *per se*, but just finds what is currently on offer unsatisfactory and that "sooner or later there will be new religions other than the ones we have now". Mansour is fond of telling his friends that one day in the distant future the Bibliotheca Alexandrina would house sections featuring the then dead religions of Islam, Christianity and Judaism, alongside the ancient Egyptian and Greco-Roman religions. Visitors would marvel at what their ancestors used to worship and wonder how and why, Mansour imagines.

For others, finding atheism is a process of questioning with no clear beginning and no likely end. "I did not become an atheist," explains Milad, a young atheist who grew up in a Coptic family from Imbaba, a poor Cairo suburb that was gripped by an Islamist insurgency in the 1990s, whom I interviewed, like many other Arab and Muslim unbelievers, in the context of my research into the subject. "Atheism is a state of thought. It has no specific starting point." For others, it starts with questioning their given identities. "I was born into a family which inherited the beliefs of its parents and handed those same beliefs down to their children," remarks Alber Saber, an Egyptian atheist now living in exile after he was sentenced to serve prison time for expressing his beliefs online. At university, Saber began to question his hereditary identity. "When I was born they wrote in my birth certificate a religion I did not believe in nor knew anything about. If I had been born into another family, I would have had a different religion," he explains. This, Saber found, was unsatisfactory, so he decided to explore his own Christian faith, Islam and other religions, to see where his mind, rather than his heritage, would lead him. After about five years of investigation, Saber had not yet made up his mind until a friend asked him what conclusions he'd reached. Upon analysing his own response, it dawned on Saber that he was an atheist.

For a surprising number of atheists I know and have spoken to in the context of my research and journalism, their abandonment of faith was, paradoxically, actually the product of an attempt to deepen it, understand religion better or silence the doubts plaguing their consciences. "When I started university in the 1980s, I realised that I was very knowledgeable about lots of things, except my own religion. So I decided that I was going to delve deep into it and be as expert as possible," Ayman Abdel-Fattah, a socially minded businessman and affably outspoken atheist, told me in a noisy watering hole in upscale Zamalek. However, instead of confirming and reaffirming his faith, this exercise, Abdel-Fattah admits, "gave me the shock of my life."

"When you start to study it verse by verse, and you start to examine the words of God and the directions God used to give to his so-called prophet, that's shocking as well," Abdel-Fattah elaborates. "You get this impression that this God wants to make this guy's wishes, whatever they may be, come true." The early Muslims, who are generally depicted as faithful continuers of Muhammad's mission, did not impress this young seeker of truth either. "What removed any doubt is how the people around the prophet acted, both during his lifetime and the day after he died. They were at each other's throats," notes Abdel-Fattah. "This is a sign that they knew he was a fake and they saw that, through this new religion, they will succeed in ruling the [Arabian] Peninsula and beyond, so that's why they went along." Studying other monotheistic traditions gave Abdel-Fattah no solace either, and he found the New and Old Testaments to be just as flawed and perhaps more so. "There was nowhere else to go, except to really go even further back and study ancient mythology," he recalls. "Once you read and you see the origins of every single story in the three books, you discover that there isn't a single story that is not rooted in pre-religious, pre-monotheistic times." This was a realisation that Saber also reached during his quest.

It is remarkable how the monotheistic religions managed both to kill off polytheism, and to appropriate many of its stories, ideas and traditions. The Genesis story of the worldwide flood God sent to destroy humanity – starring Noah, his family and an ark full of animals – bears a remarkable resemblance to several earlier Mesopotamian myths. The Epic of Gilgamesh features a boat carrying "living creatures of every kind" that endures six days and nights of violent storms from which "not could brother look after brother", after which "all mankind had turned back into clay", with the ship eventually running ashore atop a mountain. Several birds were sent out to scout for land, including a dove and a swallow, which returned, while a raven did not, a sign it had found land (another interpretation could have been it had fallen into the sea out of exhaustion).[21] Even the idea of the One God we are so proud of in monotheism is not as singular as we like to believe and polytheism is not as pluralistic as we may think. Polytheism is buried in monotheism, and vice versa, as the Danish existential philosopher Søren Kierkegaard described.[22] Muslims are fond of pointing to the trinity but Islam too contains residues of polytheism. To my mind, the 99 names or aspects of God come across as almost like a direct appeal to the polytheistic tendencies and beliefs of many of the early Muslims, with Allah symbolically swallowing up the competition, like a giant corporation taking over small local businesses. Moreover, numerous scholars have likened the angels and demons of monotheism to the minor deities of yore, with God in a position similar to the chief deity, such as Zeus.

Unlike Abdel-Fattah, some atheists in Muslim societies begin their journey as deeply conservative believers. "I was a very religious person when I was a teenager. I used to teach kids in church and remote villages about Christianity and Jesus," recalls Mena Bassily, a young Egyptian computer scientist now living in New Zealand. Unsatisfied with the responses to his doubts given by the Coptic clergy, who tend... conservatism, and their stock response of God "knows what is best" and that He has "a plan we cannot question," Bassily embarked on a journey of spiritual self-discovery which eventually led him to jettison his faith.

Soulless existence

Many believers assume we unbelievers suffer a God-shaped emptiness and hollowness inside our souls which strips our lives of meaning and purpose. And this sentiment is not just restricted to Muslims. Cardinal Cormac Murphy-O'Connor, for example, once colourfully warned that Britain was drifting towards becoming a "God-free zone", with religion banished to the private sphere, causing mass "spiritual homelessness"[23]. The extremist Islamist Hizb ut-Tahrir in the UK seems to agree with this estimation and smells an opportunity in the 'spiritual vacuum' that Britain is purportedly experiencing. "As Christianity is becoming less of a feature in Britain, there is a need for people to consider Islam as an alternative to atheism," the Hizb asserts on its website, apparently unaware of the significant minority of 'Muslims' who are also atheists.[24]

Of course, there are Muslims who have abandoned their faith and this led to confusion and a profound sense of having become spiritually homeless in the God-free zone of their making. "I know I don't need religion to be happy, but I don't know how to be happy without religion," wrote one Muslim atheist, who admitted to having been depressed before he left Islam, to the advice section of a humanist website. "I'm craving for religion even if I know it's completely human-made. I don't know how to defeat my depression without religion."[25]

But for many others, quitting religion brought with it greater happiness and relief. I do not feel that my own loss of faith has left me suspended in a dark, terrifying void, nor am I like a spiritual refugee slumming it out in some frontier camp for exiled souls. There is so much around us to instil a sense of wonder and mystique. The modern world has its own special magic and, as far as our knowledge of human civilisation goes, we are truly living in the age of 'miracles'. Jesus could supposedly restore sight to the blind, so can our doctors.[26] If Muhammad were alive in the 21st century, his night flight from Mecca to Jerusalem would not be considered a miracle in the slightest, except perhaps a political one, given there is no legal way to fly between the two enemy states. Other examples abound. Modern technology enables us to do so many things that would have been considered superhuman miracles or plain impossible a couple of centuries ago and the gap between science fiction and fact vanishes at an ever-accelerating rate. When I was a child, the idea of handheld video phones was the stuff of space-age sci-fi. Today, most of us carry supercomputers in our pockets that can connect us to a web of billions of humans, and for my son, this 'miracle' is totally unremarkable. With the explosion of computing power and the rapid development of artificial intelligence, we are on the path to developing technology that knows and sees things about us that were formerly reserved for deities. In addition, the facts of nature we have uncovered are often stranger than the myths of religion. Instead of the seven heavens, we have an infinite number in which float billions of galaxies and trillions of stars. At the other end of the scale, science has uncovered entire quantum universes on the head of a pin. For the truly mind-boggling, there is the possibility that multiverses exist, in which the possibilities that do not occur in our universe may take place elsewhere.

Others assume that deprived of religion, the non-believer loses his or her moral compass, suffers a lobotomy of his morals and exists in an ethics-free nihilistic haze. But this notion is frankly insulting to humanity, and to non-believers, as it is built on the assumption that we are errant children who have to be coerced into doing right and avoiding wrong. "That's not taking responsibility for your own actions. It's a very infantilised way of living," contends Amira Mohsen. "I am responsible for my actions and don't need some artificial construct to tell me how to live my life."

The main difference between the morality of the faithful and faithless is that the non-believer is much freer to exercise reason to decide which ethics to uphold, which new ethics to add and which outdated ones to jettison. I can detect no correlation between faith and ethical living, as many religious people believe, and some of the most moral people I have met in my life have been atheists, agnostic or non-practising. Morals did not grow out of religion, as some religions claim, though religion does have influence on a society's moral compass. Religion grew out of 'morals', in my view. And recent scientific research appears to provide evidence of this. One large-scale study found that people of vastly different backgrounds and faith systems appeared to operate according to a rather universal moral code when deciding on the 'right' choice for certain dilemmas.[27] "Morality is far more ancient than religion," said Marc Hauser, one of the study's authors. "Most, if not all, of the psychological ingredients that enter into religion originally evolved to solve more general problems of social interaction."[28]

I have also met believers who are convinced that atheists and non-believers are arrogant because, by dethroning God, they have usurped the role of divinity and deity for themselves. But this is a misconception. Modern science-based secularism is, in many ways, far more humble than religion. Although it sometimes entertains excessive faith in human ingenuity, it has knocked us off our mantle at the centre of creation. Now we know that we are collectively less significant than a grain of sand – albeit one with a big ego – in the infinite desert of the universe, which was not created to revolve around us and is likely as oblivious of our existence as we are of the individual particles which make up our bodies.

Many believers are also convinced that atheists are more materialistic and hedonistic because they are not 'spiritual'. However, religion does not immunise against the material and despite the wealth of the modern world, it is not more materialistic than the more God-fearing past.

Jekyll and Hyde reactions

What atheists say causes them to lose their faith and what the mainstream media and authorities say is the cause often bear only a passing resemblance. The emergence in recent years of an increasingly visible and assertive atheistic minority in a conservative country like Egypt has presented society and the state with a dilemma. On the one hand, Egyptians have traditionally had something of a live and let live attitude. However, prior to 2011, mainstream society chose wilful blindness. Before the revolution, Ayman Abdel-Fattah says, Egyptians preferred to adopt a deathly silence on the subject. "There was not a single attempt for any serious academic study or genuine analysis of the social repercussions of the trend, despite the fact that it was easily observable through the blogosphere and social media at large," he points out. Meanwhile, spurred by Islamist radicals the state sought, on occasion, to shut up and shut down those vocal atheists who dared to break the silence, such as Abdel-Kareem Nabil, the blogger known online as Kareem Amer, who was imprisoned in 2007.[29] At the time of Amer's imprisonment, I wrote about Egypt's "Jekyll and Hyde approach to freedom of expression" in which "its claims of being a democratising state means that it periodically loosens the reins, often allowing an impressive breadth of criticism – until it panics when the space is used to demand reform."[30] One noteworthy aspect of the Amer case was the large number of Muslims campaigning for his release. "Despite what Kareem said about our religion. Free speech doesn't mean speech that you approve of. It includes criticism," the organisers of the campaign said, challenging the public with: "You may be disgusted at what he said, even angered. That's okay, so are we! But we will defend with all our might his right to express such opinions, because it is his basic, inalienable human right."[31]

The 2011 revolution and uprising has widened people's acceptance of and demands for pluralism and tolerance of varying opinions, convictions and ways of life, while the state's Jekyll and Hyde tendencies have deepened. However, rather than create intolerance, the wild crackdowns of the state and the random violence of Islamists have deepened tolerance of unbelief in the popular mind. When I first started writing about my atheism, in English for non-Arab media, I felt that my voice was an isolated one in the wilderness. Following 2011, I felt I had many kindred spirits in the public sphere and, even when I started writing about my convictions and about atheism for Egyptian and Arab outlets, I got plenty of positive reactions and did not harvest a storm of anger or condemnation.

Others have not been so lucky. One example is Alber Saber, who had to battle being part of two vulnerable minorities, a Copt by birth and an atheist by conviction. On 12 September 2012, a mob of angry neighbours gathered outside the apartment building where Saber lived with his family, angered by false rumours that the boy next door had posted on his Facebook page the controversial, tasteless and revolting anti-Islam YouTube video, *Innocence of Muslims*, described as a "bigoted piece of poison" in *The Guardian*.[32] Instead of protecting the blogger from the mob and defending his freedom of expression, especially against this false charge, the police returned the next day to arrest him. Saber was insulted during his interrogation and a junior officer incited fellow prisoners against him, provoking one of them to cut him with a razor on his throat, he told me. In December 2012, Saber was sentenced to three years for "insulting" and "disdaining" religion on social media.[33] "This made me feel that anyone who thinks differently to the religion or ideology of the state is a criminal," Saber insisted. "But I will not give up my right to think."

During his appeal, the young activist fled Egypt. "I really miss my life in Egypt because I am now living in Switzerland far away from my family, friends and country," he told me from his exile, "even if my country does not respect my rights and has caused me a lot of trouble." Saber admits that despite the dangers he faced in Egypt, he did not want to flee, but did so to protect his family.

Egyptians tend to pride themselves on their profound faith, and so the emergence of a minority which undermines this self-image is traumatic and troubling. This explains the ridiculous attempt, mentioned earlier in the chapter, to understate the number of atheists in the country by al-Azhar, while at the same time depicting it as an existential societal problem requiring special programmes to combat atheism. It is visible in Abdel-Fattah al-Sisi's defence of freedom of belief and his calls for a "revolution" within Islam, on one side of the equation, and his government's National Plan to Fight Atheism,[34] on the other side. This same dissonance is palpable in the 2014 Egyptian constitution. "Freedom, human dignity, and social justice are the rights of every citizen," the document informs us in its lengthy preamble. Towards that end, Article 54 of the constitution describes personal freedom as a "natural right", while Article 64 says, in no uncertain terms, that "freedom of belief is absolute." However, other parts of the constitution reveal that this freedom of conscience is actually absolute in an extremely relative sort of way, and that the state is society's self-appointed moral guardian. For instance, Article 10 states that: "The family is the nucleus of society, and is founded on religion, morality, and patriotism. The state shall ensure its cohesion, stability and the establishment of its values."[35] This appears to imply that citizens are free to be non-believers and even to raise their children as such, but the state reserves the right to prosecute and even persecute them, if it so wishes. This contradiction manifests itself in how there are atheists who publicly profess their convictions and face no retribution for it, while others are thrown behind bars. The arrest of a student described as an atheist in 2015 for allegedly insulting Islam prompted Human Rights Watch to declare Egyptian atheists to be "one of Egypt's least-protected minorities" and urged the authorities to be "guided by the constitution and stop persecuting people for atheism".[36]

This dualism is also evident in some of the media treatment of atheism. An episode of the popular talk show *90 Minutes* ran an episode with the lurid title: 'Penetrating the secret world of atheists in Egypt'.[37] Despite assertions that she wished to give a guest atheist, Ismail Mohamed (who has his own YouTube channel[38]), a fair hearing and a podium to air his views, the programme's presenter Riham el-Sahly exhibited clear and unprofessional bias throughout, starting with the very first words she uttered. As I watched in dismay, el-Sahly brought on one hostile guest after another, such as a psychiatrist who suggested that atheism was caused by – as is similarly suggested about homosexuality in the Arab world – psychological, financial and family problems and so atheists deserved patience and pity, and an Islamic cleric. When callers-in expressed sympathy for atheists or suggested that Ismail Mohamed was not alone and that there were large numbers of atheists in Egypt, she shouted them down.

So what prompted the media to wake up to this phenomenon? "[Everything] changed after it became apparent the Islamists were going to take over," Ayman Abdel-Fattah explains. "[The media] concluded there was one, and only one, reason for this 'atheism tsunami.' It was the Islamists' rule."

Sea change in attitudes

A 'tsunami of atheism' evokes images of a Biblical god flooding the world with atheists rather than the more conventional water, fire or brimstone, was an expression memorably used by

Amr Adeeb, the loud-mouthed host of the popular talk show al-Qahira al-Youm (Cairo Today).[39] The 'experts' on Adeeb's show concluded that young people were turning to atheism as a reaction to the reactionary brand of Islam that had taken hold in Egypt. Adeeb was taking his cue from the Sisi regime, of which he has generally been a loud cheerleader. The military regime has manipulated the widespread fear that Egypt could become the next Saudi Arabia or ISIS caliphate to demonise the Muslim Brotherhood, blaming every ill in the land on them, thereby justifying its persecution of the movement. In addition to the propaganda purposes it serves the state, holding radical Islamism responsible for atheism appeals to religious moderates by allowing them the comfort of believing that it is not the contradictions within religion that are causing people to leave it but the way it is abused by extremists.

According to my own reading of the situation, I doubt there are significantly more Muslim atheists today than there were a decade ago or even half a century ago. The main factor is their increased visibility as a product of the huge gradual changes in the social and political landscape since the turn of the millennium, and the seismic shifts that have taken place since the 2011 revolutions, which may have largely failed politically for now, but have revolutionised people's consciousness, with ordinary people more willing to accept difference and minorities more assertive in their demands to be seen, heard and respected, despite the obvious risks involved. The greater openness and debate this has engendered has brought atheism and other alternative belief systems out into the open. Rather than constituting a tsunami, society had tried to keep atheists hidden behind a dam of wilful ignorance, but the wave of popular desire for freedom and openness eventually breached the floodgates. This can also be seen in the case of Tunisia, where atheists have become more open since the revolution, which has led to anger from conservatives and violence from salafists, as occurred with the attack on a cinema screening *Ni Dieu, Ni Maitre* (*No God, No Master*) by Tunisian-French director Nadia El-Fani.[40]

I would argue that the Muslim Brotherhood, salafist Islamists and the radical jihadists bringing mayhem and destruction in Syria, Iraq, Libya and elsewhere have had a far more profound and traumatic impact on the Muslim mainstream than they have on those who have drifted to the outer limits of belief and beyond. Political Islam is based on the simplistic illusion that 'Islam is the solution' and that if we use the Quran as our 'constitution'[41] all the wrongs in the world will be righted. This myth helped many people find a comfortable answer as to why secular Arab experiments had stalled or failed, that God was punishing Muslims for having drifted too far away from the fundamentals of their faith. Despite the evidence that pretty much every modern example of a state that was supposedly 'Islamic' has failed to outperform its secular predecessors or rivals, has not stamped out corruption or nepotism, and has often delivered intolerant and regressive rule, prior to Morsi's presidency, millions of Egyptians believed, nonetheless, that piety counted more than competence. The belated and disheartening realisation that people who are pious can also be power-hungry, incompetent and focused on narrow self-interest has led to the related realisation that people who are not pious or religious can be of moral standing and driven by the greater good. The holier-than-thou attitude of Islamists towards other Muslims, as if they are the only ones who know what is right, and the persecution of ordinary Muslims by extremists for being 'un-Islamic' or for worshipping in a different way have made many ordinary Muslims aware that anyone could potentially be branded a *kafir* and, so, many are now more hesitant to use such terminology themselves and are more accepting of the right of the individual to choose their belief system. In other words, Islamists have made more Muslims committed secularists rather than atheists, which in the minds of many Islamists are one and the same thing, despite the large difference between the two words.

This shift in mentality was expressed by the Egyptian political cartoonist Andeel and his mixed feelings towards a militant atheist who called himself Masry Molhid (i.e. Egyptian Atheist) and whose YouTube videos derided and insulted every tenet of Islam. Noting how "the majority of non-political Egyptians, who elected the Brotherhood out of religiosity, experimentalism or even fear, started regretting it," Andeel wrote that "my dislike for the cruelty in Masry Molhid's narrative easily faded away every time I was slammed with a video of those sheikhs on TV defending Morsi or the Brotherhood, or attacking what they called liberals and secularists or their favourite customer, the Christians." At one point, Andeel felt Masry Molhid work involved some heroism because he was "opposing a terrible authority, an authority gaining its legitimacy from how much of the Quran its president had memorised." However, Andeel's newfound respect for Masry Molhid's defiance of the Islamists rapidly soured when Masry Molhid hypocritically went from being the persecuted to becoming the cheerleader of persecution. "Masry Molhid was at the peak of his brutality. His celebration of violence against the Brotherhood was exceptional and worrying," Andeel observed. "Masry Molhid sat and dwelt on scenarios in which he imagined possible ways to kill the [Brotherhood] protesters."[42]

When it comes to atheists themselves, I think the bad press given to Islam and the warping of its more tolerant and humane aspects by extremists, if anything, only helped confirm to them their fears and worries about mixing religion with politics, about Islamising politics and politicising Islam. That is not to say that the excesses and abuses of Islamists and Muslim extremists do not play a part, but for most atheists it is at most only a marginal contributor. The main exception are atheists who used to be radical Islamists, such as occurred in the highly publicised case of Noha Mahmoud Salem. Trained as a doctor, Salem had been raised in a pious family and went on to marry a salafist and wear the full face veil, or *niqab*. When her husband slapped her face and her father defended his right to do so, Salem started questioning her religion and delving deeper into its various tenets, and what she discovered shattered the foundations of her faith, even the comforting spiritual aspects, such as the notion of the soul. "A human being is a series of cells with DNA that generate, get old and then die," she observed in an interview. "After death is like before being: simply nothing."[43] One TV host who interviewed her, the sensationalist Riham Said, kicked Salem off her show after Salem had asserted that the Quran was authored by Muhammad and there was no such thing as divine revelation. Ironically, Said, who dresses in tight and revealing clothing and once removed, on-screen, a headscarf she had worn to be able to interview a salafist sheikh to highlight his hypocrisy, claimed to support Islamic law and expressed her wish to implement it fully, including the stoning of adulterers, even though puritanical interpretations of *sharia* would have her out of her job, because TV is *haram,* a woman's voice should not be heard in public, and she must be confined to the house.[44]

Atheists old and new

Whether conscious or subconscious, one motive behind viewing atheism as a new phenomenon in Muslim countries is, as is the case with alcohol and sexual liberation (see relevant chapters), to depict it as something alien and imported from the West, that those who do not believe have been corrupted by western ideas and are no longer genuine or authentic. But a cursory look at history would rapidly dispel any illusions that atheism and religious scepticism are anything new. In fact, they stretch back to the very dawn of Islam. As if to prove this point, the prominent Egyptian existentialist philosopher and poet, Abdel-Rahman Badawi, who clashed with Egypt's Nasser and was imprisoned by Libya's Gaddafi, published, in 1945, an encyclopaedic history of atheism in the Islamic context, which he described as "one of the most fascinating and fertile international currents of atheism in the spiritual history of humanity". According to Badawi, the difference between the West (Christendom) and Islam is not in the existence of atheism but in how it is generally expressed. In Christianity, with its trinity, it centres more around the death of God, as Nietzsche puts it, while atheism in Islam, with its central focus on Muhammad as the 'seal of the prophets' and its holy book supposedly composed in heaven, centres around the refutation of prophets, prophethood and divine revelations. However, there is "no difference to the ultimate outcome of both tendencies," Badawi pointed out.[45]

The bad boy of this form of medieval atheism, and one featured in Badawi's encyclopaedia, was Ibn al-Rawandi, who probably lived between 827 and 911. Only fragments of Ibn al-Rawandi's works have survived, which is a pretty clear indication of the hostility with which many of his contemporaries and

269

later orthodox scholars viewed him. Described by one Sarah Stroumsa, a professor of Arabic studies, as a "true freethinker, in the sense that he rejected the authority of any scriptural or revealed religion,"[46] scholars are divided over whether he was a sceptic or an out-and-out radical atheist. Ibn al-Rawandi penned numerous polemics against the irrelevance of religion in the presence of human intelligence and religion's inherent contradictions. What seems clear is that al-Rawandi originally belonged to the rationalist Mu'tazilite school of Islam but then broke away from them because he felt they did not take human reason to its logical conclusion. The most infamous of these works was the colourfully named *Kitab el-Zumurrud* (*The Book of the Emerald*) in which Ibn al-Rawandi, according to one outraged Islamic scholar, "disputed the reality of [prophetic] miracles and claimed that they were fraudulent tricks and that the people who performed them were magicians and liars; that the Quran is the speech of an unwise being, and that it contains contradictions, errors and absurdities."[47]

The case of Ibn al-Rawandi was an extreme manifestation of a centuries-old battle in Islam. On one side were the forward-looking rationalists, the scientists and philosophers, who advocated human agency and the continuity of human progress. On the other were the backward-looking traditionalists who believed that humanity reached a utopian state of perfection in the age of Muhammad and his immediate successors and has been in a constant state of decline, a fall from grace, since then, and that the only way to elevate mankind was by emulating the prophet.

Like some modern-day scientists who speak of "God" in an abstract sense, the Islamic philosophers' conception of a deity tended to be very different to the micro-managing God of scripture. The Persian scientist and philosopher Ibn Sina

(980-1037), who established many of the logical principles upon which the modern scientific method is based, conceived of God as a kind of supreme intellect. Ibn Sina viewed existence not as the work of a capricious deity, but of a divine, self-causing thought process, which can be traced through a long chain of cause and effect to the First Principle, which exists outside time and is auto-reflective and is "in opposition to the theological conception of creation in time".[48] The implications of this were immense for believers. Ibn Sina's deism, in which God knows what unfolds but only in a universal manner,[49] effectively excluded the existence of the personal God of scripture who monitors our every act, judges them and intervenes directly in the running of the world. For Ibn Sina, not only was God rational, but so was the human soul, and his conception of paradise for this eternal soul was that of a place where it could fulfil its full intellectual potential, potential (perhaps while sipping on a glass of wine, which he did often to get his intellectual juices flowing – see chapter on alcohol). While he differed from other Muslim rationalists in that he did not reject prophecy, Ibn Sina regarded prophets simply as gifted individuals who could see the underlying truth of the cosmos, and not individuals with whom God communicated.[50] Unsurprisingly, Ibn Sina's conception was rejected by traditionalist scholars, who went on the offensive. The most effective of these attacks was the 11th-century polemic *The Incoherence of the Philosophers*,[51] which was penned by the Persian theologian al-Ghazali who also had a sideline in writing about sex (see chapter 4). Ironically, despite charging the philosophers with heresy and even unbelief, al-Ghazali was an admirer of many aspects of Ibn Sina's work, so much so that some later philosophers thought him to be a secret follower who felt compelled to dissimulate so as to appease his peers. Some modern academics have found signs of al-Ghazali plagiarising significant portions of Ibn Sina's works without crediting him.[52] In defence of the metaphysical aspects of rational philosophy, the 12th-century Andalusian philosopher and polymath Ibn al-Rushd (Averroes) attacked al-Ghazali's treatise in his *The Incoherence of the Incoherence*.[53]

From our 21st century scientific perspective, Ibn Sina's metaphysics appear incoherent but nowhere near as incoherent as al-Ghazali's. The centrality of the world in Ibn Sina's conception of the cosmos conflicts with our scientific knowledge of how the universe actually is. For a modern-day rationalist, Ibn Sina's attempts to explain away evil as an incidental by-product of a benign creator and his defence of prophecy will strike us as somewhat irrational and even quaint. But his efforts, along with those of Ibn Rushd, to square the circle of faith and science and to build up a coherent and complete metaphysics of rationality and science was revolutionary and had a profound influence on Europe right up to the Enlightenment, as did Ibn Sina's works on medicine.

As the case of Ibn Sina, Ibn Rushd and al-Ghazali illustrate, the existence or non-existence of God was also a central philosophical question in Islam, in contrast to Badawai's assertion above that Islamic atheism and scepticism were primarily focused on the question of prophets and prophecy. In Islam, you have atheists who also focus on the existence of God, while there are atheists in the West who focus on questions of prophethood and divine revelation. Moreover, there is something which unites atheists in both cultural groups – a tendency towards rationality and science. Of course, not all atheists are equally rational or scientific, some are even downright dogmatic and fall into the same trap they criticise supposedly naive religious folk for being caught in.

For instance, when it comes to the modern movement popularly referred to as 'New Atheism' in the West, many of its proponents differ from the majority of Muslim atheists in one critical regard, their attitudes to Islam. While Muslim atheists tend to see Islam as part of a continuum of irrational mythology and make-believe, a surprising number of New Atheists, despite being scientists, regard Islam as being uniquely dastardly and view Christianity and often Judaism, despite their rejection of both, as being more virtuous faiths. This sentiment was explicitly spelt out by Richard Dawkins, the evolutionary biologist, pop science author and commentator on ethics, who describes himself as a "secular Christian" due to a "feeling for nostalgia and ceremonies".[54] Given Christianity's centuries-old hostility towards its upstart cousin, Dawkins' Anglican upbringing may explain why the supposedly rational scientist reserves a special, irrational place in hell for Islam. "I regard Islam as one of the great evils in the world," Dawkins contended,[55] which echoes the conservative Protestant attitudes of leading American televangelists, such as Franklin Graham, who has repeatedly described Islam as "wicked and evil". "I don't believe this is a wonderful, peaceful religion," the inflammatory preacher said, adding, in reference to the 11 September 2001 attacks in America, that: "It wasn't Methodists flying into those buildings, it wasn't Lutherans."[56]

And why does Dawkins take an especially dim view of Islam? In the same interview, he claimed it was because, "There is a belief that every word of the Quran is literally true." While I agree that this is highly problematic, Dawkins conveniently glosses over the fact that a quarter of the citizens of the world's most powerful nation believes the Bible should be taken literally and another half believes it to be the "inspired" word of God, which makes three-quarters of Americans in total.[57]

Fortunately, the New Atheism's distorted vision of Islam do not accurately reflect the views of the people for whom they are presumed to speak, but mirror those of the Christian right. Some 39% of evangelical Christians in America have a very unfavourable perception of Islam, compared with just 7% of agnostics or people with no faith, according to a poll conducted by a religious research group.[58] This is probably because mainstream atheists are more reasonable than televangelist New Atheists, whose outspoken and outrageous views help them capture the limelight, rather like how radical preachers make the front pages of newspapers, while tolerant Muslims are hardly heard. In addition, a measure of unspoken, even unconscious solidarity may be involved, given that the only group as despised or more so than Muslims in contemporary America are atheists, with both Catholic and Protestant Christians actually preferring Muslims to non-believers.[59] This means that, whether as an atheist or a Muslim, I cannot win in America – I will be disliked and distrusted by the mainstream either way.

Unbelievers' paradise

It should be noted that the contempt is mutual. According to the same survey, American atheists held the religious in low esteem, especially evangelicals, but they respected Jews – though perhaps they were thinking more along cultural than religious lines, more Woody Allen than ultra-conservative Haredi Jews. And this disdain towards believers has a long pedigree.

"The inhabitants of the earth are of two sorts: those with brains but no religion, and those with religion but no brains," was said not by Richard Dawkins but by Abu al-Ala' al-Ma'arri (973-1057), the blind Syrian poet, philosopher, rationalist and hermit who was both a vegan and an early advocate of extreme birth control, that is, that humans should not reproduce at all.[60] Despite the strident and uncompromising irreverence of this statement, al-Ma'ari was actually an extremely humble, hospitable, generous and forgiving ascetic. This Syrian was a highly respected scholar of his day, who is still admired by secularists in Syria, and, after a brief period in Baghdad, turned his small hometown of Ma'ara, near Aleppo, into a magnet for poets, philosophers, students, princes and other legion admirers. A cynic in the original Greek sense of the term, al-Ma'ari was a study in contrasts. He was reportedly wealthy but lived the frugal life of a hermit. He was a recluse, yet received his many admirers with an open heart. He rejected all religion, yet was regarded as a spiritual guru, even by the religious he derided in his verse. Although he was one of the biggest pessimists history has known, the maverick al-Ma'ari was, throughout his long life (he lived to 84), admired as one of the greatest poets Arabic has ever known and as an accomplished, incisive philosopher who worshipped reason, and did so wittily.[61] In a verse typical of his scepticism, al-Ma'ari describes faith thus:

> *Now this religion happens to prevail*
> *Until by that religion overthrown,*
> *Because men dare not live with men alone,*
> *But always with another fairy-tale.*[62]

In some of his poetry, al-Maari expresses a vague belief in a deity but rejects religion and posits heaven is not only on earth but inside everyone of us.

> *"There is no God save Allah!"—that is true,*
> *Nor is there any prophet save the mind*
> *Of man who wanders through the dark to find*
> *The Paradise that is in me and you.*[63]

Despite al-Ma'ari's irreverence and rejection of religion, the critics of his age gave him rave reviews. It was only much later that certain Muslims began to rave against him. Luckily for al-Ma'ari, he did not live to see what would happen to his homeland a millennium later, in the 21ˢᵗ century, where the jihadist Nusra Front (now known as the Conquest of Syria Front) beheaded all the statues of the blind poet it could find,[64] and would have probably beheaded, or at least flogged him and tortured him until he 'recanted', if he were still around.

One of al-Ma'ari's most creative and multifaceted works is *The Epistle of Forgiveness*, which was written ostensibly as a letter to a bigoted sheikh and poet who had attempted to initiate a correspondence with the old sceptic. Composed a number of centuries before Dante's *The Divine Comedy*, al-Ma'ari sends his hypocritical correspondent on a similarly fantastical journey to paradise and hell. Whereas Dante's later work was full of reverence and piety, and no comedy in the modern sense, al-Ma'ari's fictional journey to the afterlife was irreverent, sceptical, satirical and deeply ironic, mocking the Quranic and Islamic conceptions of heaven, placing pagan and irreverent poets in paradise, and transforming entry into heaven into a bureaucratic process tied up in red tape, with a gatekeeper who explains that "for humans I cannot intercede" and would only allow the new arrival in with a certificate of good conduct or the intercession of the "prophet of the Arabs",[65] which he attempts by meeting Muhammad's companions and family, until the prophet himself finally intercedes.[66] In addition, for al-Ma'ari, hell was other people's imperfect command of Arabic and heaven was a place for the intellect to run free.[67]

Intifada in hell

Centuries later, al-Ma'ari influenced numerous secular Arab thinkers. The Iraqi poet, reformer and atheist Jamil Sidqi al-Zahawi (1863-1936) published, in 1931, *Revolution in Hell*, an epic poem inspired by *The Epistle of Forgiveness*. In this subversive interpretation, humanity's most daring and original thinkers have been condemned to eternal damnation as punishment for their courage, while the obedient and pro-establishment are rewarded with everlasting paradise, in a remarkable parallel to how Arab patriarchal dictatorships operate. The subversive inhabitants of hell, led appropriately enough by al-Ma'ari, storm heaven and claim it as their rightful abode.[68]

And al-Zahawi was not alone. The *Nahda*, or 'Renaissance', which occurred in places like Egypt starting in the second half of the 19th century not only included reformers who attempted to modernise Islam and bring it into the age of modern science, but it also included a significant minority of sceptics. Paradoxically perhaps, al-Azhar University, the world's leading seat of orthodox Sunni learning, produced numerous sceptics, secularists, doubters, closet non-believers and fully declared atheists. One example of the sceptics was the man who would become known in Egypt as the 'Dean of Letters', Taha Hussein (1889-1973),[69] who began life by going to Quranic school and al-Azhar, and then went on to study at the Sorbonne in France. Despite having been blinded as a toddler, Hussein managed to overcome his disability in an age with little support for the handicapped and to write some of the most influential works in Arabic of the 20th century. Hussein was a pioneer in applying modern scientific methodology to Islamic studies, and his 1926 work on *jahiliyya* (pre-Islamic) poetry was groundbreaking. In it, he developed an evidence-based theory that what is taken to be pre-Islamic poetry was a later fabrication intended to support the Quranic narrative, some of which he cast into doubt, and to give the Arabs the claim to a glorious past.[70] This led to enormous controversy among conservative Muslims and in al-Azhar, and his book was banned. Nevertheless, Hussein maintained his pre-eminence as a literary figure and educational reformer, introducing free primary education in 1950, when he served as education minister. Arab atheists often regard Taha Hussein as a kindred spirit, but whether he was a conditional Muslim, an Islamic reformer, a sceptic or an outright non-believer is a secret he took to his grave.

Whatever his views about Islam, Taha Hussein was a strong believer in pre-Islam. He was the leading advocate of 'Pharaonism', which espoused that Egypt should align itself with its pre-Islamic heritage and use its Mediterranean legacy as a cultural bridge to connect itself to modern Europe.[71]

Ali Ahmad Said Esber, an innovative Syrian literary figure who is widely considered to be the most influential living Arab poet, has not only liberated Arabic poetry from the stifling chains of tradition, which he believed stemmed from al-Ghazali's and other traditionalist scholars' focus on emulation being superior to innovation,[72] he has also sought inspiration in the Levant's pre-Islamic past, in the wider Mediterranean region and in Europe, as well as the present and future. That explains why he adopted, at the age of 18, the pen name Adonis, a Greek god closely related to the Phoenician Adon, the Cannanite Baal, the Egyptian Osiris and other gods from the Fertile Crescent.[73] "The East and the West are economic and military concepts, and were created by colonialism... But in art there is no East and West," Adonis told an interviewer. "The creative ones are from one world, regardless of what country they come from or where they went. They live together beyond geography, beyond languages and nationalism, and they belong to the creative world of humanity."[74] Like his fellow Syrian spiritual non-believer al-Ma'ari, Adonis is both areligious and anti-religion but follows his own form of mysticism, one based on *sufism* – he once went so far as to claim spuriously that poetry was only written by atheists.[75] That said, artists are often of a sceptical and questioning disposition, and this can result in them rejecting faith, even if they do not consciously express it in their art. An example of this is the Egyptian revolutionary artist Ganzeer, regarded as one of the two dozen most influential street artists in the world.[76] "I don't think atheism has been expressed directly in any of my artworks, but I suppose the way I have expressed certain perspectives on matters may possibly be taken that way," he mused. One example he cites, which offended a handful of conservatives, is a painting of a naked Muslim imploring God to make her husband satisfy her sexually.[77]

Adonis, who was born into the Alawite sect, is easy for radical Islamists and the religious establishment to hate, and has received numerous death threats over the years. However, when one of their own professes unbelief, the situation becomes much thornier. This is especially the case when graduates of al-Azhar become open atheists. One of the most prominent examples of this was Abdullah al-Qasemi (1907-1996), colourfully described by one writer as the "godfather of modern Gulf atheists".[78] In his youth in Saudi Arabia, al-Qasemi was a fairly typical pro-salafist scholar and even stirred up controversy while studying at al-Azhar for attacking the more moderate Egyptian establishment from a radical Wahhabi perspective, for which the university punished him with expulsion.

After moving away from Saudi Arabia, he became exposed to different cultures, religions and ways of life, and this seems to have fuelled al-Qasemi's scepticism, until he publicly became an outright non-believer. For conservative theologians and salafists who had previously eulogised him, al-Qasemi's transformation was particularly problematic and traumatic, as he could not be dismissed as a godless liberal, leftist or secularist. Perplexed, they sought out reasons for his abandonment of his faith. Some put it down to his poverty and unimpressive lineage, which, they claim, made him bitter about his religious heritage. Others saw in it a severe psychological disorder. In a bid to discredit him, there were allegations that he was doing it for the money (this made no sense, in light of the fact that Arab leftists were poor and the petro-dollar sheikhs were rich and willing to pay salafist defenders). Yet others regarded it as a sign of Qasemi's opportunism, riding fashionable intellectual waves, not to mention his alleged self-aggrandising arrogance and hubris, which led him to believe that he was greater than Islam and God.[79] Almost no conservative critics saw in his 'conversion' a genuine, courageous and painful process of questioning and inquiry. Rather than debate and challenge al-Qasemi's ideas, the outraged religious establishments caused his books to be banned in most Arab countries, and a couple of attempts were reportedly made on his life. This is rather odd considering believers say that the truth of Islam is self-evident, which implies that being exposed to opposing ideas should not pose a challenge to the faith. The efforts to suppress al-Qasemi's appear to support to support one of his notions about the survival strategies employed by the religious: "Religions triumph in the battles they avoid, they don't fight against reason nor through reason. They never go in free fights against reason," al-Qasemi is quoted as saying.[80]

In the course of the 20th century, the trend of religious scepticism and rejection expanded in many parts of the Muslim world, especially amongst communists, leftists and secular liberals. At one level, this was a manifestation of confidence; confidence in modernity and its ability to deliver independence from European colonialism, prosperity and dignity. Sometimes it was imposed by the state, as occurred in the Muslim-majority republics of the former Soviet Union. Although Islam was tolerated to a limited extent following the Bolshevik revolution, Stalin, in his bulldozer efforts to create the New Soviet Man (who was supposedly free of the shackles of history and superstition), shut down mosques, persecuted Islamic leaders and outlawed Islamic endowments (*waqfs*) , not to mention ethnic cleansing campaigns during World War II.[81]

The Soviet experience highlights the dangers of the state adopting any kind of official religion, including atheism, and how destructive dogma is, even dogma which claims to be scientific and rational. Following the collapse of the Soviet Union, both Christianity and Islam enjoyed a resurgence in the post-communist regimes. The main exception to this was Albania, where citizens in this small but multi-confessional country tend to be non-practising or outright atheists, with Albania one of the least religious countries in the world[82] and the least religious Muslim-majority country[83] (which partly helps explain why it escaped the sectarian conflicts which engulfed other parts of the Balkans in the 1990s). In Albania, the process of de-religionisation actually began before the communist era, and was a central plank of is first post-independence republic and the subsequent monarchy. Instead, language and nationalistic chauvinism became the state's religion. "Let us all, as brothers, swear an oath not to mind church or mosque. The faith of the Albanians is Albanianism," wrote Pashko Vasa, a central figure in the 19th-century Albanian National Awakening.[84] This very long process helps explain why Albania emerged from the communist era as the most secular of the Balkan countries and the one where the revival of religion was the weakest, much to the consternation of foreign

Muslim and Christian missionaries.[85] Albanians I have met in the Middle East find the central role of religion there hard to fathom, Albanian I knew, whose father was Catholic and whose mother was Muslim, with their daughter being both and neither, could not could not understand why Arabs found this remarkable. In contrast, in the Arab world, communism tended to be a hybrid ideology which often did not overtly reject religion. The People's Democratic Republic of Yemen, for instance, propagated a communist-friendly version of Islam in which Muhammad was portrayed as the champion of the proletariat – interestingly, the regime appears to have done so on the advice of East Germany.[86]

Seismic shifts

Religious scepticism and anti-religion could also be partly triggered by seismic political and social shocks which sent the traditional order into a tailspin. One example of this was the routing Arabs received at the hands of what had not yet become Israel in 1948, which became popularly known to Palestinians as the *Nakba* (Catastrophe). Many Palestinian nationalists were communists and secular leftists who were extremely sceptical of religion or outright non-believers. Mahmoud Darwish, Palestine's national poet, navigated the fine line separating scepticism from unbelief, both in his life and in his writings. In his writings, Darwish deals with shaken or shattered faith following the traumatic loss and destruction of his homeland, attacking both God and religion. "God does not come to the poor," Darwish declares in one of his poems, "because God does not come without a reason."[87] One zealous Palestinian woman posted a fairly exhaustive list of verses from Darwish's poetry which are sceptical, mocking or derisive of religion to show how Darwish "put himself above God" and was a "*kafir*".[88] Whether or not he was an atheist is open to question, but he certainly appears to have been a doubter and a romantic rationalist. "He was spiritual, but not a conventional believer. He saw in scripture poetry, not texts to live by," the Syrian poet and writer Rana Kabbani, who had been Darwish's first, told me. "But that was common among young communists of his generation. A huge shift of perception has taken place since."

Ghassan Kanafani was similarly sceptical and bleak. After being expelled from Palestine as a child, Kanafani played a pivotal role in setting the literary tone of Palestinian exile in his novels and short stories and was a prominent member of the leftist Popular Front for the Liberation of Palestine, until this "commando who never fired a gun" was assassinated by the Mossad, the Israeli secret service, in 1972.[89] In his acclaimed novella *Rijal fi al-Shams* (*Men in the Sun*), Kanafani bemoans the defeatism, fatalism and passivity of exile which ends in Palestinian refugees dying inside the boiling hot tank of a water truck at the Iraqi-Kuwaiti border without exhibiting any kind of resistance. Although many see in this scene an allegory for the devastating effects of defeat, despair and corruption, I see in it a declaration of a shattered faith in God and a rejection of religion – something which does not sit easily with the growth in religiosity amongst contemporary Palestinians. Symbolically, the journey across the Iraqi desert bears a striking resemblance to the "straight path" in Islamic thought, on which the virtuous walk up to heaven, while the sinners fall by the wayside, into hell.[90] One character in the novel explicitly spells out this lack of faith when he declares: "The curse of almighty God be upon you. The curse of almighty God, who doesn't exist anywhere, be visited upon you."[91]

Scepticism was often mixed in with ambiguity, sometimes due to a profound confusion felt by Muslim and Arab intellectuals, a sense of non-alignment, or at other times, spurred by a need to distort or dissimulate their actual views. A dialogue in a novel by Halim Barakat, the Syrian novelist and sociologist who was raised in Beirut, captures this ambiguity and confusion, this alienation:[92]

> "You're a Muslim!"
> "No, I reject and am rejected. I'm not a believer, but not an atheist either."
> "You're a communist?"
> "No, but not a capitalist."
> "You're a rightist?"
> "No."
> "You're a leftist?"
> "No."

Some writers fluctuated between scepticism and doubt to a critical form of faith, but even as open-minded believers they could fall foul of conservatives. Egyptian novelist and Nobel laureate Naguib Mahfouz counted in their number. When he was younger, he experienced profound doubt which he says he resolved as he grew older. In the late 1950s, Mahfouz published an allegorical novel on the history of faith and doubt. Set in an imaginary traditional quarter of Cairo rather like the one Mahfouz was born and grew up in, *Awlad Haretna* (Children of the Alley) traces the history of God, the Abrahamic faiths and their relationship with modern-day secularism and science by depicting them as neighbours in one alleyway. The editors of Egypt's largest daily *al-Ahram* felt confident enough to serialise Mahfouz's as-yet unpublished novel in 1959. Muslim conservatives were up in arms and – rather like their Christian counterparts who managed to get Life of Brian banned in many parts of the West when it was first released – they bullied the government into banning the book version, forcing Mahfouz to go and publish it in liberal Beirut. In the twilight of his life, Mahfouz defended the novel. "I wanted the book to show that science has a place in society, just as a new religion does, and that science does not necessarily conflict with religious values," he told an interviewer. "I wanted it to persuade readers that if we reject science, we reject the common man."[93]

But the verbal opposition of conservatives did not intimidate Mahfouz. So relaxed was he in generally placid Egypt that the exact movements of this creature of habit were known to millions of Egyptians. Sadly, in 1994, the ailing novelist was stabbed in the neck as retroactive punishment for his irreverence. Ironically, the attack was spurred by the call of an Egyptian firebrand who likened Mahfouz's *Awlad Haretna* to Salman Rushdie's *Satanic Verses,* to which Iran's Ayatollah Khomeini had issued a *fatwa* and reward calling for Rushdie's death.[94]

Ironically, a couple of years before the attempted assassination, Mahfouz expressed harsh criticism towards Rushdie. "I have always defended Rushdie's right to write and say what he wants in terms of ideas. But he does not have the right to insult anything, especially a prophet or anything considered holy," he claimed.[95] This strikes me as an untenable position and a surprising one given Mahfouz's own experience. Not only do I believe that freedom of expression includes the right to pillory what is sacred, even if one accepts that causing insult is unacceptable, the notion of offence is extremely elastic, as Mahfouz learnt for himself.

In fact, *The Satanic Verses* bears a remarkable resemblance to Mahfouz's *Awlad Haretna*, in the sense that it is an allegorical novel about faith, alienation and how religion relates to the modern world. *The Satanic Verses* was not even about Islam, Rushdie insisted but about "migration, metamorphosis, divided selves, love, death, London and Bombay," not to mention "a castigation of western materialism. The tone is comic."[96] At the time of the Khomeini *fatwa*, Rushdie, describing himself as a "lapsed Muslim" who no longer believed, noted that *Satanic Verses* was "about a dispute between different ideas of the text. Between the sacred and the profane ideas of what a book is" and that this debate "existed within the life of the Prophet Muhammad between himself and other kinds of writers, which I didn't make up," noting wryly that "it's rather strange that a book which discusses that dispute, immediately becomes surrounded by exactly that dispute."[97] It is unsurprising, in light of the hysteria his novel provoked amongst radical Muslims and the years he spent in hiding, that this lapsed Muslim became a self-described "hardline atheist".[98]

One significant turning point which paved the way to the religious revival which swept through the Arab world, and with it, the widening cultural and religious polarisation, occurred half a century ago, in 1967, when the secular Arab regimes, led by Nasser's Egypt, suffered a devastating, humiliating defeat at the hands of Israel in just six days. But while it propelled many into the arms of rigid religiosity, it pushed others away from faith and into profound doubt and scepticism, intensifying their critique both of religion and of incomplete Arab secularism and freedom. This occurred not only with the likes of Adonis but also with the Egyptian novelist Sanallah Ibrahim. One of the most outspoken writers in this regard was the late Sadiq Jalal al-Azm, the prominent leftist intellectual and academic from Syria. In the wake of the crushing defeat, he pointed the main finger of blame not at Israel's military superiority or at superpower support, but at the absence of deep modernity and science in the Arab world. "The Arab armies were not lacking in military weapons and equipment," he wrote in a post-mortem of the war and its fallout. "What they lacked was the human element, capable and trained at a high level – technically, militarily and in leadership."

And why was this? According to al-Azm, this was because Arab societies had not allowed science to "penetrate to its roots [and] achieve a serious understanding of its generative powers." In observing the superficiality of integrating science, he wrote, "We have opened a space in our life for the refrigerator, television, oil well, MIG, radar, and so on. However, the mentality that uses these imported achievements is still a traditional mentality that belongs to the nomadic and agrarian stages and which clings to the supernatural."[99] Al-Azm gave a thorough analysis of the detrimental effects of this clinging to the supernatural in his subsequent *Critique of Religious Thought*,[100] which caused an uproar when it was published in 1969, leading to his imprisonment in 1970 for supposedly inciting sectarianism in Lebanon, and to the banning of the book in most of the Arab world. In this work, al-Azm called on Arabs to jettison religion and to embrace scientific socialism whole-heartedly, by placing science, technology and the immediate emancipation of women at the heart of reforms. He described as a myth the notion that religion and science were compatible, and argued that society could not be organised on both bases. He ridiculed the idea of 'concordism', i.e. the theory that any new scientific knowledge could be found retroactively in scripture. He blamed the Arab world's secular regimes for striking a kind of Faustian bargain in which they tried to reconcile scientific modernity with religious tradition.[101]

In keeping with his fierce secularism and defence of human rights and plurality, al-Azm came out as an outspoken defender of Salman Rushdie during the *Satanic Verses* controversy, not only criticising Muslims but also the condemnation which Rushdie received from some Catholic and Jewish clergy, as well as what al-Azm perceived as the lukewarm defence from western liberals. "My impression is that Rushdie has been defended by the concerned segment of the Western intelligentsia, formalistically, legalistically, detachedly and at arm's length," he wrote in a scathing essay. "Perhaps the deep-seated and silent assumption in the West remains that Muslims are simply not worthy of <u>serious dissidents</u>, do not deserve them, and are ultimately incapable of producing them; for, in the last analysis, it is the theocracy of the Ayatoallahs that becomes them." But a dissident Rushdie was, al-Azm insisted: "Rushdie's fiction is an angry and rebellious exploration of very specific inhuman conditions and very concrete wicked social situations and rotten political circumstances." And the reaction to Rushdie and other acts of religious iconoclasm and rebellion had "far more to do with the affairs of state than with the affairs of faith," he noted. [102]

Believe and let live

Like selective religious outrage, charges of 'unbelief' or 'apostasy' (*ridda*, in Arabic) are almost invariably far more about politics than religion. Islamic jurisprudence tends to regard apostasy as a crime and, in many cases, one that is potentially punishable by death. But the arguments put forward for harsh punishment justify it not because renouncing Islam is a sin but because of its supposed potential to sow *fitna* or sedition among the community of believers. This was explicitly spelled out by classical scholars and jurists. "The reason to kill an apostate is only with the intent to eliminate the danger of war, and not for the reason of his disbelief," opined Ibn al-Humam, a 15th century Egyptian jurist and theologian. "Therefore, only such an apostate shall be killed who is actively engaged in war; and usually it is a man, and not a woman… [but] an apostate female could be killed if she in fact instigates and causes war by her influence and armed force at her disposal."[103] Of course, this fear of *fitna*, whether real or imagined, is not limited to Islam or Muslims, especially when it comes to atheists. Historically, it has been a common element in European thought too, stretching back to Plato, all the way to modern thinkers like John Locke, with atheists excluded from public office in England until the twilight of the 19th century, as Brian Whitaker demonstrates.[104]

In most of the relatively rare but periodic episodes when apostasy was punished by death in Islamic history, this was due to fears of or actual acts of sedition and rebellion, rather than unbelief. This explains why charges of apostasy have been far more frequently levelled against other sects of Islam and minority religious groups than against atheists and agnostics. This was particularly the case in the early decades following the death of Muhammad, when the nascent and still small community looked at risk of unravelling and the new religion expiring. A prime example of this were the so-called *Ridda* or Apostasy Wars, which Islam's first "caliph" or "successor", Abu Bakr, launched immediately after Muhammad's death to place rebellious Arabian tribes under his control. Some of these had in fact remained Muslim but did not recognise his authority or the legitimacy of a caliphate, while others had reverted to their former beliefs or found their own local prophets.[105] But for the most part Muslims of other sects, lapsed Muslims and atheists were largely left alone, even if conservative scholars liked to throw around allegations of apostasy willy-nilly, something which irked al-Ghazali, because of what it implied; that only "a small clique of theologians" would make it to paradise. "Charges of apostasy were not unusual... [but] such accusations had little practical effect," wrote British-American historian and academic Bernard Lewis. "The accused were for the most part unmolested, and some even held high office in the Muslim state... As the rules and penalties of Muslim law were systemised and more regularly enforced, charges of apostasy became rarer."[106]

This helps to illuminate how it was that, for example, the Abbasid caliphate produced some of the greatest free thinkers in Islamic and human history, yet also instigated some of the bloodiest inquisitions (*mihna*) Islam has known. The longest such *mihna* was instigated by Caliph al-Ma'mun (786-833), son of the legendary Harun al-Rashid. Unlike our regular ideas of inquisitions as being efforts to enforce regressive religious ideas, al-Ma'mun's *mihna* supported the rationalist Mu'tazilite school of Islam, forcing conservative scholars to recant their belief that the Qu'ran was eternal and not created.[107] This rationalist and scientific bent was expressed in the central role al-Ma'mun played in establishing Baghdad's Bayt el-Hekma (House of Wisdom) as one of the greatest centres of learning in the medieval world.[108] In reality, the supposedly pious al-Ma'mun's inquisition had little to do with religion and everything to do with power. Not only was al-Mam'un embroiled in a bloody succession struggle and civil war with his half-brother, the extravagant playboy al-Amin, who was (in)famous for his homoerotic affairs and patronage of the camp court poet Abu Nuwas (see chapter on sex), in addition, al-Mam'un wanted to force the clergy to accept his authority and supremacy on spiritual matters, a battle the Abbasid caliphs ultimately lost.

Moreover, al-Mam'un was facing uprisings across the empire and was at war with the Byzantines.

Throughout much of Islamic history, when charges of apostasy have arisen, they have been motivated almost entirely by political considerations. Rulers have used them to combat dissent, to quash opposition, to put down uprisings or to distract attention away from their failings. The religious establishment and radical ideological groups have used the charge to establish their authority, mount insurrections against the ruler of the day or to silence opponents. Paradoxically, and as manifestations of the rule of unintended consequences, suppressing or punishing apostasy to avoid *fitna* has too often resulted in sedition and conflict. Moreover, the notion that apostasy is a punishable crime stands in stark contrast not only with modern notions of human rights but with the Quran's own assertions that freedom of belief is sacred. Islam's holiest book clearly states that there is no compulsion in religion[109] and insists that *kafiroun* (unbelievers) and believers each have the freedom to choose their faith.[110] Although the Quran does condemn apostasy, it appears to mean those who adopt Islam for opportunistic reasons and then reject it,[111] or yo-yo between believing and not believing, as reflected in the word *irtidad* which means 'reverting' or 'backsliding'. Most importantly, though the Quran identifies apostasy as a sin, it does not define it as a crime and prescribes no worldly punishment for it.

It is in the interest of both the individual and society as a whole, and is also theologically sound, that those Muslim countries which still outlaw apostasy and punish it end these inhumane practices. It is also high time that the self-appointed defenders of the faith realise that Islam, Muhammad and God do not need human bodyguards and assassins. This does not mean they should not condemn and dislike those they regard as unbelievers – by all means, that is their human right. But if God does exist and is as almighty as they believe, then he will be more than capable of avenging his good name in the afterlife by condemning us insolent non-believers to eternal damnation and its all-consuming fires. However, if God is a figment of our collective imagination, we heathens will find rest in the eternal oblivion we suspect is our lot anyway. Alternatively, sensible believers and atheists can respect one another's hard-gained convictions.

In my view, doing away with the criminal offence of apostasy is only a first step. Equally importantly is formalising freedom of belief and conscience for Muslims and the citizens of Muslim countries. A significant step in that direction would be to remove religious affiliation from birth certificates and identity documents in those Muslim countries that mention them. Another important step would be to abolish, or leave to personal choice, the religiously based family and personal status courts still operating in many Muslim countries. Perhaps the most necessary and most radical step is to stop considering everyone born into a Muslim family as being a Muslim by birth. Despite being a devout Muslim, my late mother was of this view because she was also a staunch believer in freedom of choice and conscience. In addition to being better for the individual, she argued it would be better for Islam. "It is far better for the Muslim community to have millions of true believers than hundreds of millions of accidental believers," she once told me.

I and many others had no choice in my designation as a 'Muslim'. My Egyptian birth certificate, ID and passport all inform me that I am one. Not only the state regards me as a born Muslim but so do the vast majority of Muslims, yet I was never asked my opinion on the matter. We do not want our son to suffer the same fate, especially as he has a triple heritage: the secular humanism of his parents, as well as his father's Islamic and his mother's Christian heritage. At seven, Iskander is reaching the age where he is beginning to have rudimentary questions about faith. A confused European friend of his recently asked whether Iskander was Muslim or Christian. I informed him cryptically that, in a way, he is both and he is neither. It would be up to him, as an adult, to decide what he wanted to be. And this should be a fundamental right enjoyed by every 'Muslim' and every human.

CHAPTER NINE

Memo to a jihadist

Dear Aspiring Jihadi,

Young Muslims who abandon their lives and homes to go and fight in Syria, Iraq, Libya or Yemen inspire terror, fear, incomprehension and even ridicule in wider society.

Perhaps to shield ourselves from our anxiety and discomfort, many of us have found solace in laughter. The more surreal aspects of the jihadist presence on social media have been quite entertaining, and have made us wish that, instead of executions and mass murder, these fighters would decide to go home and declare that the greater jihad is the 'jihad of the selfie'.[1]

Many jihadists have posted selfies and images of themselves on social media bearing arms, Rambo-style, or swimming, as if they were on some sort of Club Med holiday for self-styled holy warriors.[2] Some appear inexplicably to be endorsing evil western consumer products, including Nutella.[3] There is even a sideline in cute and cuddly 'mewjahideen' kittens.[4]

Yusuf Sarwar and Mohammed Ahmed – two young British jihadis who went to Syria and were sentenced to 13-year jail terms upon their return[5] – caused a wave of mockery, and a sigh of relief from mainstream Muslims, when it was revealed that they had ordered *Islam for Dummies* and *The Koran for Dummies* before their departure. "You could not ask for better evidence to bolster the argument that the 1,400-year-old Islamic faith has little to do with the modern jihadist movement," concluded the prominent journalist and TV presenter Mehdi Hasan. "If we want to tackle jihadism, we need to… start highlighting how so many of them lead decidedly un-Islamic lives."[6]

I can understand where Hasan is coming from. Throughout history, no conflict, not even those classed as 'religious', has ever been solely about religion. Religion often provides a convenient shell or cloak for political, social, cultural, economic and other drivers. Individuals who engage in religious conflict can be motivated by the secular, profane or even personal, or, as is usually the case, by a complex interplay of factors.

Hasan appears too keen to counter the prominent narrative in many western circles that Islam is intrinsically violent, that radicalisation is not the exception but the rule, and that there is no such thing as a moderate Muslim – in short, the kind of rhetoric Donald Trump and other bigots have relied on. But in his zeal to counter the crude narrative of Islamophobes, Hasan has fallen into the trap of pedalling his own simplistic storyline. This approach is about as disingenuous as saying that the Crusades had little to do with Christianity, that the Tories did little to create the Euroscepticism that led to Brexit and that the Republican right is innocent of Donald Trump.

Moreover, I know many Muslims who lead "decidedly un-Islamic lives", and none of them feel in the slightest bit attracted by jihadist ideology. In fact, they are mostly terrified, not just by jihadists but by Islamists who wish to curb their freedoms. In addition to already having to live with being deemed 'not Muslim enough' by conservative Muslims and having to watch their backs in conservative Muslim countries, 'un-Islamic' Muslims are bound to be alarmed by the implications of Hasan's insinuation that society should keep an eye on them.

While I agree with Hasan that there is plenty of evidence that "long beards and flowing robes aren't indicators of radicalisation," if we must be so superficial about it, I would counter that they are far greater indicators than boozing, going to nightclubs, dating or having pre-marital sex.

For their part, those drawn to radical Islamism and jihadism will also take issue with Hasan's assertion that they are uninformed, that they have "little to do with" Islam and that they lead "un-Islamic lives". One recruit to the Islamic State (ISIS) who defected from the Free Syrian Army (FSA) claimed this was because of ISIS's "intellectualism and the way it spreads religion and fights injustice".[7] Local civilians who support ISIS often do so out of pragmatic considerations rather than any particular attraction to the organisation's ideology – because they think ISIS will bring them security and stability when war is blazing all around, end corruption through their piety, and defend their rights as Sunnis and guard their honour.

The reality is there are and have always been many forms of Islam – not all of them equal or equally valid – from place to place and from one era to another, some tolerant and peaceable, others intolerant and violent, some rational and others superstitious, with all drawing, to varying degrees, on the accepted Islamic sources. In actuality, ever since the dawn of Islam, there has been a constant battle between rationalists and literalists, between traditionalists and innovators, between progressives and reactionaries, and between those who wish to build a different future and those who want to reconstruct an idealised past. The tone of any given Islamic age or place was set by who had the upper hand.

And radical Islamism, dear would-be jihadists, has attracted both believers who know little about their religion and those who are extremely well-versed. Which are you?

Similarly to how racists and neo-Nazis can be mere stupid thugs, but can also often be intelligent, highly educated and well-versed in the language of democracy, so many Islamic radicals and jihadists have a thorough and deep knowledge of Islam, even if most of their co-religionists disagree with them.

For example, Abdullah Azzam, the Palestinian founding father of the Arab jihadist effort in Afghanistan and the later al-Qaeda movement, was a qualified Islamic scholar who studied Islam in Damascus and Cairo and afterwards taught in Jordan and Saudi Arabia. Despite this thorough theological grounding, Azzam believed in "jihad and the rifle alone" and mocked peaceful Muslims by insisting that "those who believe that Islam can flourish [and] be victorious without jihad, fighting, and blood are deluded and have no understanding of the nature of this religion."[8] We can disagree with Azzam on whether this was actually the case in Islamic history or not, but we cannot doubt the depth of his knowledge and learning.

Despite making no active plans to build a caliphate, Azzam, nevertheless, looked forward to its eventual emergence. "We shall continue the jihad no matter how long the way, until the last breath and the last beat of the pulse – or until we see the Islamic state established," he wrote.[9] Of course, compared with ISIS and other al-Qaeda spin-offs and affiliates, Azzam was a relative moderate, who saw jihad as largely confined to the battlefield and was generally against *takfir*, i.e. ex-communicating, and resisted calls to condemn Muslim governments as comprised of "unbelievers".[10]

Perhaps foreseeing the shape of things to come at the hands of his unscholarly rival, Ayman Zawahiri, and other, future jihadist incarnations, Azzam warned against fervour without scholarly knowledge: "They, because of their lack of knowledge, are simply youth with much zeal, and the hearts of these youth were made to follow their desires."[11]

But murderous zeal is not just limited to unscholarly youth. After all, ISIS's self-proclaimed caliph, Abu Bakr al-Baghdadi, born Ibrahim al-Badri, is the son of a Quranic teacher and a qualified Islamic scholar (even though his original dream had been to study law and he was a talented footballer, nicknamed 'Messi' and 'Maradona') and who has a PhD from the Saddam University for Islamic Studies. Yet Baghdadi presides over the world's most violent and murderous jihadist outfit.[12]

Some dismiss modern-day salafism and violent jihadism as some kind of newfangled innovation in Islam. But many salafists and jihadists draw their ideological inspiration from the man they reverently refer to as 'Sheikh al-Islam', otherwise known as Taqiudin Ahmad ibn Taymiyyah, who lived some eight centuries ago and was regarded by admirers and rivals alike as a powerful thinker and highly intelligent. However, in his own time, just like today, ibn Taymiyyah was a marginal figure and never represented Islam's theological mainstream. Interestingly, like his modern disciples in the Levant, Ibn Taymiyyah, who was a refugee from Iraq who fled to Syria, was born in and lived through a period of great upheaval sparked by the Mongol invasions, whose devastation was comparable, in many ways, with the 'shock and awe' of the 2003 US invasion and occupation of Iraq and the post-2011 total war spearheaded by the Assad regime and its allies in Syria.[13] To varying degrees ISIS and other jihadists movements base their ideas of jihad, *takfir*, salafism and the imposition of Islamic law on the *fatwas* and books of Ibn Taymiyya, with some additional innovations of their own.[14]

That said, ISIS is also manned with members, including ex-Baathists and some Sunni tribal leaders, who have no interest in religion or establishing an Islamic state but are in the game for other grievances, namely the Anglo-American occupation and destruction of their homeland and the loss of their livelihoods. One of these was Hajj Bakr (real name: Samir Abd Muhammad al-Khlifawi), the ex-Iraqi intelligence officer and mastermind of ISIS's military strategy and intelligence apparatus. Like American neo-cons, he had no strong religious convictions of his own but believed that the faith of others could be exploited to achieve victory.[15]

Rebels without a hope

There are numerous theories about what leads people to become jihadis. At one end of the spectrum, it is all the fault of Islam, the religion of violence, and has nothing to do with geopolitical or socio-economic grievances. At the other end of the scale, Islam, the religion of peace, is completely innocent of these murderous radicals and it is all a reaction to neo-colonialism, racism and economic inequality.

A popular theory at present is that, faced with a secular ideological void, we are witnessing the "Islamisation of radicalism," as argued by Olivier Roy of the European University Institute, who calls other theories "inadequate to account for the phenomena".[16] However, this description applies equally well to Roy's own theory. If European Muslims and converts are running into the arms of jihadist recruiters because they need an outlet for their radicalism in the absence of alternative ideologies, this fails to explain why many young whites and Christians in Europe and America are embracing white supremacy, Christian fundamentalism, fascism, neo-Nazism and authoritarianism, with some committing terrorist atrocities. How does that fit in with the 'Islamisation of radicalism'? Or are we also witnessing a 'Christianisation of radicalism' or the 'Nazification of radicalism'? And further afield, how do we explain the rise of violent and intolerant Hindu or Buddhist ultranationalism? Is that the 'Hinduisation of radicalism' or the 'Buddhaisation of radicalism'?

There is no single formula that can explain why people are drawn to violent radicalism today, but important factors include the massive and widespread exploitation of young people all over the world, the huge inequalities between nations and between the haves and have-nots, wide-scale repression, the unresponsiveness of political elites to people's needs and grievances, and bland centrist politics that seek to appease the markets than to defend the rights of citizens.

So dear would-be jihadist, what motivates you?

Perhaps you look at the state of the Muslim or Arab country you live in and feel anger, despair and powerlessness at the tyranny, corruption, poverty and lack of opportunity there. You may gaze in disbelief at the wider region, and how every ideology and experiment in self-government seems to have failed or come up short, at least for ordinary citizens. Pan-Arabism has delivered disunity, defeat and despotism. Conservative monarchies have used religion to claim a God-given right to rule and use the clergy and the morality police to guard their palaces and keep their subjects down. You may be a young person who had huge, ambitious personal dreams and aspirations for the future – or even just simple ones, like getting married and starting a family. But large or small, you gape in dismay at the shattered fragments of your dreams, crushed by the heavy boot of unemployment, underpayment, disempowerment, corruption, cronyism or plain incompetence.

This may make you feel that your life is pointless, that you have no mission. This could leave you craving for a higher purpose, to find self-actualisation through selflessness, to become a hero.

Alternatively (especially if you live in the West), you may feel aggrieved by the racism and disrespect for your religion and culture which you experience or witness in Europe and America, especially as the far-right continues its ascendancy, or that the much-fabled equality of the West does not extend to you due to the invisible hand of discrimination. Or you may feel rejected by and alienated from both the society in which you were born and grew up and the society of your forebears, leaving you with a desire to become, in a manner of speaking, more Catholic than the Pope.

It is quite possible that you are outraged and angered by western military misadventures in Muslim lands, such as the wholesale destruction of Iraq, the West's global economic and political hegemony, not to mention all the dictators and tyrants whom major western powers support. This may even lead you to conclude, erroneously, that democracy, modernity, freedom and secularism are just the Trojan horses of the new crusaders bent on destroying Islam once and for all.

You may be infuriated by all those Arab and Muslim leaders for whom the life of their citizens has become so cheap and their countries so expendable that they are willing to sacrifice both at the altar of their power hunger and greed.

So, dear aspiring jihadist, as you can see, there are many paths to jihad, just as there are many paths to wisdom. Unlike with wisdom, however, there is nothing wise, intelligent, edifying or noble about taking part in the modern, blood-drenched jihadist enterprise to restore the caliphate, which, as you shall see, is itself nothing but a massive illusion. I advise you to steer well clear.

Here are five simple, but not simplistic, reasons why:

1. Jihadist regret

In a similar vein to those who took part in the Spanish civil war or ran off to join the French Foreign Legion, many lured by the call to jihad arrive on the battlefield filled with high ideals, a sense of empowerment and the feeling that they are changing the world and saving their fellow Muslims. However, a large number end up broken, disillusioned, traumatised, shell-shocked, and live to regret their decision. Some express their sense of betrayal when they discover that what they are asked to fight for is in fact so different to what they thought they were going to fight for.

"We came to fight the regime and instead we are involved in gang warfare,"[17] one British jihadi, who said he spoke on behalf of 30 others, told the International Centre for the Study of Radicalisation and Political Violence, which has issued reports on jihadist defectors[18] and other issues related to radical Islam.[19] "There was neither a holy war nor any of the preachings in the holy book were followed," echoed one disaffected Indian recruit, Areeb Majeed, upon his return home. "ISIS fighters raped many a woman there." [20]

And it is women, whether local or those who came to the 'caliphate' of their own volition, who have paid the heaviest price for ISIS's presence. The media has carried numerous reports of women who went off to join ISIS and ended up trapped. Two Austrian teenagers were reportedly desperate to return home because they were forced into marriage, got pregnant feared their lives. Others have been reportedly made to run brothels in which women from Iraq's minorities are prostituted to ISIS fighters.[21]

Even some of those tasked with brainwashing and recruiting jihadis have expressed regret. Abu Muntasir, dubbed the 'godfather' of the British jihadist movement, fought in numerous conflicts across the world and recruited hundreds of young jihadists. But today he is full of regret for infecting so many with the jihadist "virus" and getting them involved in "unwinnable wars".[22] "I cannot hate. Hate is not what Muhammad taught," he said in an ITV documentary by British filmmaker Deeyah Khan.[23]

This may explain why young Arabs are turning away from ISIS in droves, with half now seeing it as the biggest problem facing the Middle East, up from 37% a year earlier, according to the 2016 Arab Youth Survey.[24]

2. The caliphate illusion

The caliphate which ISIS claims to be constructing, or restoring, in no way actually resembles its historical namesakes.

For instance, the Abbasid caliphate centred in Baghdad (750-1258), may be just down the road geographically from ISIS territory, but is centuries away (and centuries ahead) of its backward-gazing ISIS counterpart. Abbasid society was an impressively dynamic and diverse empire which, in sharp contrast to ISIS's violent puritanism, thrived during its heyday on multiculturalism, science, innovation, learning and culture, including odes to wine and racy homoerotic poetry.

With the Bayt al-Hekma (House of Wisdom) at the heart of its scientific establishment, the Abbasid caliphate gave us many sciences without which the modern world would not function, including that bane of every pupil, algebra, devised by Muhammad ibn Musa al-Khwarizmi. Even the modern

303

scientific method itself was invented in Baghdad by the 'first scientist' Ibn al-Haytham, who also made major advances in optics.[25] This era of medieval free thought – by the standards of the time – and innovation underpinned the Muslim world's success. Contrast this with ISIS's school curricula, which have reportedly banned numerous topics and focus almost exclusively on ideology and indoctrination.[26]

In fact, it is this very free-thinking and 'decadence' which causes ISIS and other salafists of the modern-day to harken back to an even earlier era, that of Muhammad and his first 'successors' (Khulafa', whence the English term 'caliph').

Driven by ambition, rivalry, jealousy and power, as much as faith, the early Rashidun ('rightly guided') caliphs bear almost no resemblance to jihadist mythology. For the most part, these first caliphs were forward-looking and future-oriented, whereas today's wannabe caliphates are stuck in a past that never was. In addition, they did not persecute those of other religions, guaranteed freedom of worship, and learnt and adopted from the other cultures they came into contact with.

Under the Umayyads, whether centred in Damascus or Cordoba, and the early Abbasids, Islam's 'golden age' was characterised, rather like today's America, by a complex synthesis and symbiosis between cultures. It incorporated Christian, Jewish, ancient Greek, Byzantine, Persian and even Chinese ideas and added to them to create a new, dynamic whole. Later, the Ottoman and Mughal empires were also at their most successful when they tolerated and promoted diversity.

3. There is no crusade

The US invasion of Afghanistan and Iraq – with George W Bush's declaration of a "crusade"[27] against terrorism and the revelation that he believed God had told him to invade the two countries[28] – has bolstered the conviction among many Islamists that not only is some kind of neo-crusade in motion but that the West is bent on destroying Islam.

"There is no evidence of the involvement of the people of Afghanistan in what happened in America," Osama bin Laden said in 2001. "The campaign, however, continues to unjustly annihilate the villagers and civilians, children, women, and innocent people," he added, tapping into popular anger at the US-led slaughter. "This clearly indicates the nature of this war. This war is fundamentally religious," the head of al-Qaeda concluded.[29]

Despite his crusading language, Bush insisted that his War on Terror was not a war against Islam, though he did, as noted earlier, regard it as a "crusade" and that his decision was divinely inspired. He was at pains, rhetorically at least, to establish a firewall between America's wars in the Middle East and America's relationship with its own Muslims and the Muslim world. "Here in the United States our Muslim citizens are making many contributions in business, science and law, medicine and education, and in other fields," Bush said in December 2002. "America treasures the relationship we have with our many Muslim friends, and we respect the vibrant faith of Islam which inspires countless individuals to lead lives of honesty, integrity, and morality."[30]

There is nothing new in Bin Laden's conclusion. Decades before him, the spiritual father of violent Salafism, Sayyid Qutb, was convinced that Western imperialism was not a secular, greed-driven enterprise but "a mask for the crusading spirit".[31]

This "crusading spirit" also looks inwards, not just outwards, according to the Qutb-inspired al-Qaeda leader, Yemeni-American

Anwar al-Awlaki, who became the first US citizen to be killed by a drone strike, one ordered by Barack Obama in 2011.[32] "Muslims of the West, take heed and learn from the lessons of history: there are ominous clouds gathering in your horizon," he warned. "Yesterday America was a land of slavery, segregation, lynching and Ku Klux Klan and tomorrow it will be a land of religious discrimination and concentration camps... The West will eventually turn against its Muslim citizens."[33]

The rise of Donald Trump, with his crude attacks on Muslims, has given credence to al-Awlaki's warnings and Trump's efforts to ban foreign Muslims from entering America have been greeted with euphoria among jihadist groups. Pro-ISIS social media dubbed the ban "blessed" and concluded that it would be the "the best caller to [jihadist] Islam".[34]

But is there any truth to this alleged crusade against Islam?

The short answer is no. The Christian right may think there is a jihad against Christendom, and the Muslim right may believe that there is a crusade against Islam, but there is no clash of civilisations, only clashes of interest (see chapter 7). The wars in Iraq and Afghanistan can be explained fully and satisfactorily in terms of strategic interests, geopolitical rivalry, competition for resources and so forth, without recourse to religion. The same model of destruction, disruption, political meddling and military interventions America is using in the Middle East was earlier mobilised to devastating effect in Latin America, even though these countries are Christian.

Even al-Awlaki admitted as much. "Americans need to stop looking at themselves from their own lens, but look at themselves from the lens of the world," the senior al-Qaeda leader urged. "America is not despised only by Muslims, but by many millions of people around the world, and in America itself."[35]

However, al-Awlaki seemed unaware of, or unconcerned about, the contradiction between his allegation that America was waging a crusade against Islam and the fact that non-Muslims around the world were suffering under US hegemony, not to mention the disempowered within America itself.

The jihadist leader undermines his own argument further when he tells Americans: "Your decision-makers, the politicians, the lobbyists and the major corporations are the ones gaining from your foreign policy, and you are the ones paying the price for it." This suggests that Washington's wars and interventions in the Middle East are not a war against Islam's prophet but a war for massive corporate profits.

A similar situation exists domestically. As American Muslims face the intensification of negative and othering rhetoric against them, perhaps leading in time to real and serious persecution, it is tempting to connect this to their Islamic faith. But Islam here is incidental. It is because they are a minority, and in troubled times minorities are a convenient and easy scapegoat for society's ills. They could worship the Flying Spaghetti Monster and still face a major threat. In fact, if the influence of ultraconservative Christians continues to grow apace, atheists in America also face real danger. In addition, Muslims are only one of many groups at risk in nativist America today. African-Americans arguably face an equally threatening, if not significantly more threatening future, given their painful history. Mexicans and other Latin Americans are also on the chopping board, and Jews, with the rising tide of anti-Semitism, are likely not to be far behind, as historical amnesia sets in again. Academics, intellectuals, journalists, artists and leftists are among the groups at potential risk if the ongoing vilification campaigns do not cease.

4. Islamic state of mind

Ever since Mustafa Kemal "Atatürk" and his Turkish nationalist movement abolished the Ottoman caliphate in 1924, Islamists of various stripes in different parts of the world have striven to revive the institution.

And even before ISIS and Abu Bakr al-Baghdadi, there were earlier claimants to the throne. There was the short-lived Arab Sharifian caliphate in 1924-5 and the Taliban's Mullah Omar was the 'Prince of the Faithful', but only over Afghanistan.

But what these nostalgists and restorationists overlook (or do not seem to realise) is that the caliphate has a questionable foundation in Islam, and reflects more the desires and ambitions of the leaders of the Muslim community following Muhammad's death than the prophet's wish or any blueprint in the Quran. In fact, contrary to what millions of Muslims and non-Muslims believe, Islam is not a complete guide to living nor is it a more political religion than Christianity. It can and has been separated from the state on numerous occasions.

Muhammad never nominated a successor (caliph) nor spelt out a method for identifying one – and the Quran also provides no model for a state.[36]

This could have been out of fear of having his authority challenged or Muhammad, aware that his mission was largely spiritual, not political, and realising that the situation of his community was on the cusp of altering radically, and even out of respect for the freewill of future generations, he refused to lay out a model for Islamic governance. The clear proof that Muhammad bequeathed no prescription for the future form of his community were the so-called 'Ridda Wars' (or Wars of Apostasy) during which the first caliph, Abu Bakr, went to war with those Arab tribes who rejected his authority. While today, Muslims tend to view this as a sign that these tribes were hypocrites (considered worse than unbelievers by many Muslims) who had reverted to their old beliefs after Muhammad's death, many of them were actually devout Muslims who simply rejected the idea of a caliphate (succession), or the authority of Abu Bakr, even if he was chosen by *shura* (consultation). Even though the first four caliphs were retroactively given the title *rashidun*, or 'rightly guided', by later Muslims, they themselves were left after Muhammad's death with zero guidance on succession, let alone righteous guidance. This is reflected in the in-fighting, *fitnas* and civil wars which beset the early Muslim community and the fact that three of the four 'rightly guided' caliphs were killed by assassins: Umar, Uthman and Ali. It is the very political question of who deserved to be caliph and on what basis succession should occur which led to the split between Sunni and Shi'a Islam. But rather than keeping temporal power in the temporal sphere, and leaving the Islamic leadership open to all candidates, Muhammad's companions and relatives sought to found the legitimacy of their claims to leadership on their proximity and/or familial ties to the prophet, and through him, to God.

There was also massive opposition to the Umayyads' transformation of the caliphate into a dynastic monarchy governed by an Arab elite in which even non-Arab Muslims were second-class citizens, with the once adamantly anti-Muslim Quraish tribe, to which Muhammad had belonged, the *crème de la crème*. The Abbasids cleverly manipulated the bubbling discontent amongst non-Arab Muslims, non-Muslims and Arabs of excluded tribes with one of the most sophisticated propaganda and revolutionary campaigns the medieval world had ever seen, depicting the now Muslim Umayyads as still-pagan enemies of Islam who had destroyed the original, inclusive meaning of Islam in which all Muslims were considered equal. The Abbasids also cleverly and deviously concealed how they intended to rule in the post-revolutionary order.[37] Despite having stoked and ridden the wave of opposition to the Umayyads, the Abbasids also struggled to assert their legitimacy. Though they had constructed an empire in which Muslims, regardless of ethnicity, and non-Muslims, regardless of religion, had a role, the flimsy foundations of Abbasid legitimacy, which was founded on the concept of *dawla* (which now means 'state' but used to mean 'revolution' or 'cycle') and *da'wa* (which means 'calling to' or 'invitation' but effectively meant propaganda in this context), came back to bite the caliphs. The *dawla*'s cyclical nature provided opponents with a conceptual framework to challenge the Abbasids using their own tools and toys.[38]

But the generally savvy Abbasids managed to remain in charge for centuries, until the caliphs were relegated to mere spiritual figureheads by their own military commanders, who took on the title *Amir al-Umara* (Commanders of the Commanders). When the Mongols swept across the region, annihilating, in 1258, the magnificence of Baghdad and slaughtering its citizens, including Caliph al-Musta'sim, who had the hubris to believe his own propaganda and tell the invaders that they were "drunk" on success and that he "could muster" all of Islam against them,[39] the caliphate became a portable talisman. In Egypt, the *mamluks*, an elite and highly trained slave army whose status was above that of ordinary citizens, needed to legitimise their rule, so they brought al-Mustansir, a surviving member of the Abbasid family to Cairo, and crowned him a toothless caliph: For his part, al-Mustansir legitimised the *mamluk* Baybars as sultan and "restorer of the caliphate", which helped Baybars gain the upper hand over rival claimants and cover up the brutality of his rise to power.[40]

When the Turks defeated the Mamluks and marched into Cairo in the early 16th century, they kidnapped what would prove to be the absolute last Abbasid caliph, Al-Mutawakkil III, and brought him to Constantinople for a time, seizing the prophet's alleged relics, such as his sword and hair, which are still on display at the Topkapi museum. Since the 14th century, the rising Ottoman sultans had also claimed for themselves the title of caliph, but being non-Arabs and not descended from Muhammad's family or tribe, they interpreted it differently, as meaning the most powerful and capable defenders of the faith, rather than the commanders of the faithful. However, when the empire began its decline, the Ottoman sultans began a more serious campaign to be viewed as caliphs in the more traditional sense.[41]

Since pretty much the first day of the first caliph, the concept of the caliphate, though it derives its ultimate legitimacy from Islam, has stood on fragile, precarious and questionable theological grounds. While some caliphs may have governed out of a genuine belief in the sacredness of their role, the whole edifice was essentially a device used for centuries to anchor the ruler's legitimacy in the heavens, even though his ambitions were worldly and most caliphs took a very worldly approach to power, no different to secular rulers. In addition, the caliphate often resulted in instability due to the absence of clear rules for the transfer of power, and contributed to the absolutist attitudes the region's leaders traditionally held towards power, and towards their own subjects, as opposed to the 'people power' upon which Muhammad seems to have attempted to build his community.

What all this shows is that neither Muhammad nor the Quran prescribe any form of government, nor does Islam need a caliphate.[42] The implication of this is that the only truly Islamic state, is a spiritual state, a state of mind.

5. Secularism is the solution

When Muhammad arrived in the city of Yathrib, later to become known as Medina, he drew up a bill of rights which was, by the standards of its time, an enlightened document. This Constitution of Medina stipulates that Muslims, Jews, Christians and even pagans all have equal political and cultural rights.[43]

Surprisingly for modern Muslims, Muhammad's definition of the *umma*, i.e. the 'community' or 'nation', in the document extends to include all the Oasis of Medina's inhabitants, not just the followers of Islam, but also Jews and Pagans.[44]

This implies that, for Muhammad, the 'nation' was a geographically bound multicultural entity, not a borderless community of believers in a single faith. This is a far cry from ISIS's attitudes towards even fellow Sunni Muslims who do not practise its brand of Islam, let alone Shi'a, Christians or other minorities.

In addition, since Islam, as shown above, does not appear to stipulate any form of governance or government, this leaves Muslims free to select the method of self-rule which best serves their interests and needs.

Since every experiment in modern Islamic governance has varied widely in its nature and failed to deliver the kind of success it promised, and since Islam's ancient success was based largely on secular rule and free inquiry, I propose that the best form of government for Muslim societies is secular democracy. Of course, no form of government, not even democracy, is perfect. But the advantage of democracy is that it does not claim to be timeless, infallible or unchangeable, and so can be adapted, enhanced and improved as the times and circumstances change.

CHAPTER TEN

Memo to the alt-right

Dear Alt-righter,

You pride yourself on your profound understanding of the truth about Islam and the lies spread about the Religion of Peace® not just by Muslims but also by the politically correct mainstream media, as well as the liberal and progressive political and intellectual classes.

Well, bravo, you are politically incorrect. But not in the way you think. Your views about Islam and Muslims are largely incorrect, not just politically, but also socially, culturally and theologically. The only enduring reason that such fallacies carry weight is because they are emitted, received and bounced around in echo chambers which enable untruths and half-truths to parade as facts, and circular logic to masquerade as rational discourse. In the West, the true political correctness of our time is not Islamophilia, as you are convinced, but Islamophobia. Over the years, the mainstream and tabloid media in many parts of America and Europe have carried far more content vilifying and stigmatising Muslims than apologia for or the whitewashing of Islam. The trouble with the mainstream media is not that it is Muslim-friendly but that it is not hostile enough for your liking.

You bemoan the moral relativism of the allegedly self-hating left and multiculturalists. Instead, you argue that the entire world must adhere to the same standards, though what you often mean by this is your muddled interpretation of 'Western values'. I would love nothing more than to live in a world in which the universal values of individual human rights, equality, non-violence and tolerance of others are the norms. However, my experience is that those who inveigh the loudest against 'moral relativism' and say that we cannot allow non-Western societies to operate by different rules, are generally the first to insist on a lack of moral equivalence because the West is benign and, hence, gets an exemption from adhering to the same standards they insist must be applied to everyone else.

In this moral universe, the universal does not reign. The Soviet Union invading Afghanistan is evil and malignant. The United States invading Afghanistan is noble and benevolent, though the execution may have been wrong, you insist. A Muslim who commits an act of political or presumed political violence is a terrorist, while a white man or woman who does the same is a 'lone wolf' – as if whites never join packs and Muslims never go it alone. Muslims are expected to loudly condemn and disown the extremists in their midst, while white people can just get on with life without having to say anything about the extremists in their midst. Christian fundamentalists loudly decry Islamic theocracies while demanding the establishment of Christian nations in the West. And the examples go on and on.

My dearest alt-righter, if you have read this far, I congratulate you. You have a more open mind than many of your peers. Although you are likely seething by this stage, I urge you to bear with me as I analyse and deconstruct some frequently asserted questionable statements about Islam. You never know, you may learn something and may perhaps change or question some of your views, even if just a little bit.

1. The Christian God is not the Muslim Allah

You are probably used to hearing people speak of 'Allah' when referring to the god whom Muslims worship. Although some do so innocently, out of a conviction that it is more authentic to use Arabic terms when speaking about Islam because the Quran is in Arabic, people on the far-right and conservative Christians and some Jews do so because they believe Muslims worship a different god. "Confusing the God of the Bible with the Allah of the Quran is not only a mistake, it is a dangerous distortion of the Gospel of Christ," writes Albert Mohler, president of the Southern Baptist Theological Seminary.[1]

And this is not just a Protestant position. There seems to be agreement among the fanatical fringes of the Catholic and Orthodox churches too. One Orthodox Christian blogger went so far as to condemn the practice of saying Muslims and Christians pray to the same God as heresy. "In Islam, Allah is classically presented as being so 'other', so utterly transcendent and beyond, that he is ultimately beyond the grasp of humans to know him, let alone love him," he claims. "Islam calls man [sic] to be slaves of Allah, not to love him."[2]

A minority take this quite literally to the lunatic fringe, alleging that Allah is not a monotheistic God at all, but the moon god,[3] an idea popularised since the early 1990s by Robert Morey,[4] the unhinged pastor who runs the website Faith Defenders. Responding to people who called him crazy, Morey advocated destroying Mecca because "without that old pagan temple to pray toward and make a pilgrimage to, Islam will collapse. Terrorism will be cut off at the roots."[5]

Of course, no religion has a monopoly on nuttiness. There are non-Arabic-speaking Muslims who also believe that 'Allah' is a word reserved only for Muslims. In multi-ethnic, multi-confessional Malaysia, growing religious bigotry led the government to ban Christians, who lost their appeal in the high court, from referring to Allah in their Bibles and services, even though they have been doing so, unremarked and unharassed, for generations.[6] As I pointed out at the time of this ridiculous ruling, this confusion only occurs with non-Arabic speakers. For Arabic speakers, the issue is not and has never been controversial: Allah is used by Arabic-speaking Muslims, Christians and Jews to refer to the singular God of monotheism, and it takes on plural form to refer to polytheistic gods (lower-cased in English), such as the deities of the Greek, Roman and Egyptian pantheons.[7] The Arabic word *Allah* resembles the word for God in other Semitic languages, including Hebrew and Aramaic (which is the language Jesus spoke). Most historians and grammarians now agree that Allah derives from the Arabic for 'The God'.[8] In fact, the word 'Allah' predated Islam and was used by Arabic-speaking Christians and Jews to refer to the monotheistic God and by pagan Arabs to refer to their supreme god, who begot a holy trinity of goddesses: his daughters al-Lat, al-Uzza and Manat.[9] The Semitic Biblical names for God also have their roots in pre-monotheism, including Yahweh, who started life as the 'tribal' or 'national' god of the Israelites, and whose name was likely imported along the caravan route from, of all places, northern Arabia.[10]

English took a similar semantic root. 'God' is a Germanic word whose origins predate the arrival of Christianity and whose original meaning has been lost to the mists of time. However, it was almost certainly rooted in ancient polytheism and was likely originally a neuter plural in form (i.e. it referred to genderless 'gods') and may have its roots not with the higher gods of the Germanic pantheon but with the "multitudes" of "the highest beings in control of the world" which included dwarves, elves, giants and trolls (not to be confused with our modern conceptions of them), according to prominent etymologist Anatoly Liberman.[11]

And if an elf can semantically morph into the almighty, all-seeing, universal deity of Christianity and Judaism, there is no reason this evolution should not include Islam. So, please, stop using Allah in English and say God instead. It is more accurate and more inclusive. Quite a few conservative Christians and even neo-cons agree. One major voice advocating this unity is Miroslav Volf, professor of theology at Yale Divinity School, who argues that Muslims and Christians believe in the same God, but just conceive of him in slightly different ways, but that this difference in the conception of God occurs within Christianity and Islam, not just between them.[12]

"The God=Allah equation means that, however hostile political relations may be, a common 'children of Abraham' bond does exist and its exploration can one day provide a basis for interfaith comity," writes Daniel Pipes, a Middle East commentator and the founder of the conservative Middle East Forum and the right-wing Campus Watch. "Jewish-Christian dialogue has made great strides and Jewish-Christian-Muslim trialogue could as well."[13]

2. Islam is the religion of the sword

Although Islam is derived from the same Arabic root as the word for peace, many in the West regard it as anything but the religion of peace. Calling the Quran "a violent and cursed book", the founder of the far-right English Defence League Tommy

Robinson (himself not immune to bouts of uncontrollable violence), claimed that "So long as there is this book, there will be no peace in the world."[14] Of course, Robinson's comments did not come in a vacuum.

Many other leaders and celebrities of the far right, or alt-right, if you prefer, hold precisely the same views about the innate violence of Islam and Muslims. This was demonstrated across the Atlantic, during the Republican primaries, when the candidates not only tried to out-Christian one another, they expressed an alleged dichotomy and incompatibility between their Bible-bound religious beliefs and a benighted Islam. It was in this context that candidate Donald Trump first proposed his idea of banning foreign Muslims from entering the United States, an idea which had been gaining popularity in far-right circles for some years. "There's something [in the Quran] that teaches some very negative vibe," Trump said in a 2011 interview, betraying his trademark eloquence and intellectual clarity. "I mean things are happening, when you look at people blowing up all over the streets."[15]

Ann Coulter, the queen of rightwing punditry, has been peddling the violent Islam trademark for years and is fond of saying: "Not all Muslims may be terrorists, but all terrorists are Muslims,"[16] an assertion that is patently and demonstrably untrue. In Coulter's view, it is not just Islam that is intrinsically and irrationally violent, Muslims are too. "Their immediate response to all bad news is mass violence," she once claimed. "The 'offence to Islam' ruse is merely an excuse for Muslims to revert to their default mode: rioting and setting things on fire."[17]

Funnily enough, like quite a few others who condemn Islam as being a violent religion which was spread by the sword, Ann Coulter has no problem advocating mass murder and even genocide, as she has done repeatedly over the years. "We should invade their countries, kill their leaders and convert them to Christianity," Coulter wrote after 9/11. "We weren't punctilious about locating and punishing only Hitler and his top officers. We carpet-bombed German cities; we killed civilians. That's war. And this is war," she added, apparently unaware of the fact that the mass, indiscriminate slaughter of World War II is the reason we have modern humanitarian laws, to avoid this kind of existential, all-out conflict.[18]

The notion that Islam is some kind of death cult and was spread by a blood-spattered sword has a long history in Christian polemics, which draw a clear distinction between the supposedly peace-loving Jesus and the war-mongering Muhammad. "Show me just what Muhammad brought that was new and there you will find things only evil and inhuman, such as his command to spread by the sword the faith he preached," the Byzantine Emperor Manuel II Palaiologos reportedly said in 1391 (see chapter 7 for a thorough comparison between Jesus and Muhammad).[19]

But is Islam really more violent than Christianity and other religions?

If Trump, Coulter, et al, were actually to delve into the Bible, they may well be surprised by what they find, and even mistake it for the much-maligned Quran. This is exactly what happened in the Netherlands, when a couple of pranksters disguised the Bible as the Quran and read out some shocking passages to unsuspecting passers-by.[20] Even more perplexing would be the computer analysis which revealed the Bible to be statistically more violent than the Quran. While the New Testament was only marginally more violent than the Quran, the Old Testament was a whopping twice as bloody as the Islamic holy book. In it, God regularly destroys and smites unbelievers, and those believers who have wandered off the straight path, and empowers the righteous to commit divinely sanctioned mass murder.[21] Now, you would not use such statistics to suggest that Christianity and Judaism are more violent than Islam, so why do you claim the reverse about Islam without even a factual basis?

Early Christians may have been against war, but for many this was due to their opposition to Rome and rejection of its Imperial Cult than out of any squeamishness about shedding blood.[22] In fact, many were not averse to using religious violence to intimidate and silence 'pagans' and 'heretics'. The desecration and destruction of pagan symbols and temples by Jews and Christians was so common that the early churches considered whether someone who died while destroying a pagan statue could be considered a kind of suicide martyr.[23] Religious violence between various Christian sects and between Jews and Christians was also common.

When Constantine adopted Christianity as the official religion of the Roman empire, what had been arbitrary acts of violence and intimidation against adherents to the various polytheistic religions and cults turned into active and systematic persecution, in which the Christians were no longer the martyrs but the martyr-makers. And the rest is history. As statecraft and Christianity mixed at the top levels, it was used to justify all manner of aggression, violence and war.

None of this is to suggest that Christianity and Judaism are somehow more violent than Islam, or that Islam is solely a religion of peace. Like its Abrahamic predecessors, Islam can be interpreted both as a spiritual vessel for war or a conduit for peace. It was spread both by the sword and the word, not to mention the trade winds. In addition, as I point out earlier in the book, early Muslim rulers were not interested in converting the masses to the new faith, partly for tax reasons and partly out of a sense of Arab elitism, and it took centuries for many of today's Muslim societies to attain a Muslim majority.

Muhammad, like many ancient Biblical prophets, was both a spiritual and a military leader, and the Quran is replete with contradictory passages that call for forgiveness and vengeance, promote violence and non-violence. Islam, like Christianity and Judaism, or any other religious tradition, is what its believers make it to be, and is interpreted differently according to time, place and group.

3. Islam with dhimmitude

Muslims apparently have a serious *dhimmitude* problem. For those unfamiliar with the term, it does not mean attitude or something along those lines. It is a *portmanteau* combing the Arabic word *dhimmi*, a classical Islamic term for non-Muslims in Islamic societies, with 'servitude', to express the alleged Muslim attitude of superiority towards minorities and other non-Muslim groups. To illustrate, ISIS's campaign of persecution and mass killing of non-Muslim minorities, which has been likened to a genocide by some observers,[24] would count as *dhimmitude* on steroids.

But *dhimmitude* is not just an existential threat for minorities living in societies with a Muslim majority, it is a mortal danger everywhere Muslims set foot or lay down roots, according to a theory popular amongst the European and American right. Muslims are not only sneakily and stealthily working to introduce creeping *sharia*, the non-Muslim majority are, inexplicably, aiding and abetting this process by voluntarily bowing down in servitude. In this case, *dhimmitude* is the equivalent of political correctness in the rightwing lexicon. "Dhimmitude is a failure of nerve and loss of pride in one's own life of the mind, religion, society and civilisation," wrote one conservative columnist, who bizarrely criticises Islam for its treatment of non-Muslims yet advocates barring Muslims from and banning Islam in the United States. "Europe is now committing suicide by letting Islam grow inside of it, and what has happened there is happening in the US."[25]

Even though there are some small groups and cells of Muslim extremists in Europe and America who fantasise about subjugating the infidel and bringing the West into Islam's orbit, they are but a small minority of a tiny fringe. Conspiracy theories and attempts to blow the threat out of all out of all proportion can easily pave the way to future persecution, if we are not diligent and attentive. The majority of Muslims in the West do not seek the destruction of western civilisation and its integration into some future caliphate. In truth, despite the all-encompassing label of 'Muslim', the Muslim minorities in the Europe and America are not one homogeneous population. They differ according to their nation of origin, their class, education level, whether they are recent immigrants, or have lived in society for generations. They also differ in their attitudes to Islam. While conservatives get the most media space and air time, the ordinary and the lapsed receive very little attention. For instance, an extensive poll conducted in 2016 found that nearly three-quarters of Muslims in France admire or accept the country's secular laws, including its *burqa* ban, and nearly half defined themselves as secular.[26] "There is no single Muslim community. There are Muslims who are very different and who are increasingly different," said Hakim El Karoui, the author of the report.[27]

Likewise, the attitudes and approaches to non-Muslims vary dramatically in Muslim societies, and differ according to country, group and time. The most restrictive and repressive occurs in ISIS-controlled territory. Each in their own way, Saudi Arabia, Iran, Sudan and Pakistan have serious problems in dealing with minorities, who are not recognised as equals and often actively repressed. But extrapolating the situation of these worst offenders to generalise about Muslim societies everywhere in every age is akin to taking western fascist regimes' treatment of Jews and other minorities as representative of the western treatment of non-Christians. But even in one of the darkest chapters of European history, the hateful Nazi vision was resisted, by a brave minority within Germany and by other European powers, even though discrimination against Jews and overt racism were institutionalised in many countries. The United States, for instance, had segregation and the Jim Crow laws in the south and racism all over the country and, in what would be eerily familiar to us today, a ban was imposed in 1924 on Asian (i.e. non-Christian) immigration and severe restrictions on Eastern European immigration (i.e. Jews and Slavs), which hurt Jews fleeing Russian pogroms and Nazi persecution immensely, costing an untold number their lives.[28]

A comparable situation prevails in the Muslim world today. Not only have ISIS and other jihadist groups elicited widespread disgust and opposition, more established regimes that oppress minorities are facing a groundswell of condemnation and dissent, both internally and externally. This is the case in Pakistan, where liberals voice loud criticism, at potentially great personal risk, against the country's regressive *sharia* laws and condemn the mob violence and intimidation targeted at minorities. "We treat our minorities neither equally nor fairly. Indeed, we don't even pretend to," criticised Irfan Husain in *Dawn*, Pakistan's largest English-language newspaper. "Muslim immigrants in the West don't face a fraction of the injustice and intolerance native non-Muslims have to put up with in

Muslim countries… In the Islamic world, even where anti-discrimination laws exist, they provide scant protection."[29]

Part of the reason that Muslim societies generally treat their minorities worse than western societies is because the majorities are also treated less well than in the West. At a certain level, there is an oft-unspoken pact that compensates disenfranchised citizens by allowing them to let rip their bigotry against the weaker and more vulnerable members of society.

Although 35 Muslim-majority countries restrict religious freedom to some extent, at least a dozen guarantee religious freedom for minorities.[30] This group includes countries like Albania, Kosovo, Senegal, Tunisia and Indonesia. Even in countries which restrict religious freedom, either through government policy or social hostility, indices and statistics only tell a small part of the story. For instance, Pew's religious freedom ranking places Turkey, Egypt and Saudi Arabia in the same category of "very high" restrictions of religious freedom.[31] But the situation in the three countries is not comparable. It is largely driven by religious motivations in the case of Saudi Arabia and largely secular ones in the case of Turkey, when the modern republic's founding father, Mustafa Kemal Atatürk, restricted the role of the *ulema*, or religious scholars, and banned Sufism, both of which were regarded as outdated superstitions[32] (though recently Turkey has also witnessed the rise of muscular political Islam in the form of Recep Tayyip Erdoğan). Saudi Arabia grants nationality only to Muslims and recognises only a very particular version of Sunni Islam as the religion of the state. This means that the estimated 1.2 million Christians, 310,000 Hindus, 90,000 Buddhists and the tens of thousands of foreigners with other or no religious affiliations not only stand no chance of being naturalised, they are not permitted to express their faith publicly.[33]

In contrast, Egypt has the largest Christian minority in the Middle East, of about 5-10%,[34] which means it numbers up to 9 million people, larger than many European countries. Copts and other Christian denominations constitute a vibrant part of Egypt's religious, cultural, social, economic and political topography. Churches dot the landscape, not only in urban areas but also in the deepest countryside. Church and mosque often stand side by side, in an expression of architectural comradeship and brotherhood, one that is not shared by the increasingly radicalised Islamist minority in the country. In addition, the Egyptian constitution states that freedom of belief is absolute but bizarrely limits this 'absolute' freedom to the three Abrahamic faiths (article 64), as well as stating, contradictorily, that "Islam is the religion of the state" (article 2).[35] Despite this official commitment to religious freedom and equality, Christians face formal and informal discrimination on a daily basis, from gaining permits to build or renovate churches, to landing jobs. In addition, Christians have endured a wave of religious violence in recent years that has included mob attacks and terrorists bombings, which have claimed numerous lives. One particularly grotesque example was the mowing down by armed gunmen of pilgrims, including children, on their way to a remote monastery.[36] Much as many Egyptians would like to think otherwise, these attacks do not occur in a vacuum and are not a foreign conspiracy, at least not solely. These violent outbursts are the by-product of years of demonisation and dehumanisation by Islamists, human rights violations by the state, and the government's long insistence, in the name of national unity, that discrimination against Christians did not exist, as well as its occasional attempts to out-Islamise the Islamists.[37]

But dark times not only bring out the worst in people but also the best. The outpouring of solidarity, sympathy and assistance to Egypt's embattled Christian community from decent, open-minded Muslims is uplifting to behold. This has ranged from Muslims protecting churches by forming human shields outside them to activists combating discrimination against Christians. Many point to a time of greater social harmony between Muslims and Christians in Egypt and the pivotal role Christians and other minorities played in Egypt's independence and nationalist movement, its cultural and intellectual life, not to mention the everyday contributions of ordinary Copts in every sector. In Egypt, and across the Arab world, Christians and Jews played a central and pivotal role in the establishment and development of secular Arab nationalism. For instance, the original Ba'ath party, different branches of which ruled Syria and Iraq for decades, was co-founded by a Syrian Christian pan-Arabist and socialist revolutionary, Michel Aflaq, along with Zaki al-Arsuzi (an Alawite) and Salah al-Din al-Bitar (a Sunni).[38]

This secular Arabism was part of a search for an identity that could potentially unify the diverse populations in the Arabic-speaking regions along linguistic, rather than religious lines, that stretches back to the 19th century when the Ottoman empire was withering and crumbling. The most articulate early proponent of this language-based secular identity was Sati' al-Husri (1880-1968), who ironically started life as a loyal servant of the Ottoman empire. "Every person who speaks Arabic is an Arab," he once asserted in no uncertain terms. "Everyone who is affiliated with these people is an Arab."[39] This simplistic formulation that Arabic speakers were naturally of "one heart and one spirit", in al-Husri's words, was to dog pan-Arabism for decades,[40] because it glossed over not only the linguistic differences within the Arab world but more importantly the cultural diversity of the region, which had the ultimate result of transforming the notion of Arab unity into a linguistic slogan rather than a pragmatic political programme.

Pan-Arabism was one of the many political responses (others included local nationalisms, Mediterraneanism and Pharaonism) formulated to the marginalisation of the Arabic-speaking regions of the Ottoman state and the rise of virulent Turkish nationalism as a reaction to the disintegration of the empire. This brutal nationalism, which culminated in the genocidal campaign against Armenians, Assyrians and Greeks in World War I,[41] was a far cry from the heyday of the Ottoman empire, when the state tolerated and thrived on a diverse spectrum of religious, ethnic and linguistic groups. This highlights just how much the classical *dhimmi* system is misunderstood and twisted by modern far-right critics. While it certainly did not grant the kind of full equality to minorities that we aspire to, and some societies have more or less achieved, in the contemporary world, at its best it was one of the nearest examples in the pre-modern world. At a time when Europe defined Jews as 'Christ killers' and indigenous, pre-Christian, European faiths as 'pagan', numerous Muslim empires offered protected minority status (*dhimmi*) to the "people of the book", which traditionally meant Jews, Sabaeans and Christians but was often extended to include Zoroastrians, Buddhists, Hindus and other religious groups.[42] This does not mean that persecution did not occur (it did, periodically), but it made it less likely than in Christendom.

The classical *dhimmi* system and the modern liberal secular system also raise some fundamental questions about how to define freedom and equality. Are they individual or collective rights, and where do we draw the line between the personal and the group? While the *dhimmi* system deprived minorities of some rights provided by liberal secularism, it granted them others which would be anathema to modern secularism, particularly of the French republican model. For instance, the Turkish *millet* (community/nation) system supplied the religious communities with so much autonomy that they often effectively functioned as states within a state.[43] This is something that no modern western nation state could countenance. Imagine if the fictional *sharia* courts which supposedly operate in some European countries were actually a fact. This is how the Ottoman state dealt with its minorities: it allowed them to set their own laws, to run their own courts and even to collect their own taxes. This system had its own shortcomings and challenges. It forced individual citizens to belong to a defined and recognised religious community, even if they did not agree with it, or rejected some or all of its beliefs, or did not accept its leadership's authority. In short, it favoured the collective community over the individual. In addition, while it worked in a vast and diverse empire confident in its variety, it resulted, especially once decline set in and European powers began interfering in Ottoman affairs, in enormous social and cultural fragmentation. This fragmentation haunts us to the modern day, as numerous Muslim societies grapple with the contradictory demands of geographically bound modern nationalism and the remains of the *millet* system, manifest in the confessional courts which continue to regulate personal and family affairs in many former Ottoman lands.

Ironically, and as a manifestation of the law of unintended consequences, the *millet* system – along with ethnic and religious nationalism, state failure and collapse – has contributed, in my analysis, to the religious and sectarian strife we are currently witnessing in the Middle East. On the one hand, the *millet* system helped preserve and create the immensely rich cultural tapestry upon which bloody-minded and blood-soaked bigots are now preying. On the other hand, the *millet* system has perpetuated narrow group identities and mentalities. This is because defining a person's religion and sect from birth, and providing them with differential treatment because of it, leads to social rigidity and identity politics, and makes it difficult and makes it difficult to form hybrid identities.

The modern manifestation of the *millet* system also encourages institutionalised discrimination against minorities, by blocking minorities from the upper echelons of politics in many countries and enabling unscrupulous civil servants and security officials to mistreat those who are different. In extreme cases, it even facilitates persecution. For example, the religion field on Iraqi identity cards has been misused by ISIS and other militias to target citizens who belong to other religions and sects.[44]

One can only hope that the current devastation in the Middle East will lead current reformers and future generations to dispense with officially recognised confessional systems, to put in place mechanisms which guarantee equality in both words and deeds, and to integrate the region into a stable and diverse politico-economic superstructure.

4. Islam's cultural nihilism

The destruction of irreplaceable cultural and historical archaeological sites and monuments by ISIS in Iraq and Syria has shocked the world. Numerous conservative and right-wing western pundits have seen this as an inherently and uniquely Muslim evil which is hardwired into the very DNA of Islam. "The ISIS record fits into an old and common pattern of destruction of historical artefacts by Muslims," asserts Daniel

Pipes. "Destruction of infidel remains confirms the superior power of Muslims and, by implication, the truth of Islam."[45]

This is certainly true for ISIS and some other Muslim rulers throughout history. However, what Pipes disingenuously ignores is that this is by far not a uniquely Islamic trait. In fact, it has been a sadly common and devastating component of conquest and resistance to it, even in polytheistic belief systems. For instance, Rome's imperial age kicked off in earnest following the sack and obliteration of the by-then defenceless Carthage, the wealthiest city in the Mediterranean, costing not only the lives of most of the city's inhabitants but also erasing Phoenician Carthage off the face of the earth – a crime which may count as the first recorded genocide, according to some scholars.[46] A similar fate would befall Jerusalem and its occupants, in 70AD, during the city's siege and destruction, which was later followed by the construction of a Roman town, Aelia Capitolina, atop the ruins.

When Christianity became the official religion of the Roman empire in the fourth century, the once-persecuted became persecutors, and Christian fanatics were able to act on their contempt and rejection of paganism, destroying temples, statues, monuments, as well as persecuting and killing pagans, casting into eternal darkness those who refused to see the same everlasting light of Jesus which they saw. This is what happened to Hypatia, the Alexandrian philosopher and astronomer, who headed the neo-Platonic school in Alexandria. Although Hypatia had many Christian students,[47] some members of the Christian clergy and rabble-rousers did not look kindly upon her teaching of the pagan sciences, with some accusing her of practising "magic, astrolabes and instruments of music" with which "she beguiled many people through her Satanic wiles".[48] The quite literal demonisation of this prominent and popular woman of learning in multicultural Alexandria led to her being set upon by an enraged Christian mob who took her to a church, where they stripped her, beat her to death, skinned her (by some accounts), and later burnt her mangled corpse.[49]

Although Constantine I's Christianisation of the Roman empire led to the systematic annihilation of polytheism, a grassroots war against paganism predated his ascension to the throne by centuries. For example, in the so-called Kitos wars, Jews destroyed pagan shrines and temples, murdering many Roman and Greek worshippers in the process.[50]

Even Santa Claus, that cuddly favourite gift giver of modern Christian children, was not above doing his not so cuddly bit, as a devout Christian, to stamp out paganism, not to mention Christian "heresies". According to legend, Saint Nicholas of Myra (270-343) destroyed all the pagan holy sites in his province. The saint harboured particular fury towards Artemis (Diana, in the Roman pantheon), who was the patron goddess of Myra, where he was bishop, and whose temple was the most magnificent structure around, until the saint reportedly razed it.[51] To add insult to the injury of losing her grand temple, Artemis saw her role as the protector of seafarers usurped by St Nicholas, who became the patron saint of sailors.

By the time Islam had conquered much of the lands ruled by the Christianised Byzantine empire, paganism, i.e. pre-Christian polytheistic religions, had been almost entirely killed off, with many of their rituals and beliefs integrated or appropriated by the church, their monuments destroyed, left in ruin or converted into churches. Even after the fall of Roman rule in Europe, the Christianisation of the continent continued apace, with Christianised tribes going to war against polytheistic tribes, until paganism was stamped out and its holy sites destroyed or converted. Lithuania, the last pagan nation in Europe, adopted Christianity as its official religion in 1387.[52] For Europe's rulers, Christianity would become such a defining and central aspect of their identity that when Islam was driven out of Iberia, its centuries-old heritage was destroyed or converted, including the mosque of Cordoba, which became a cathedral, as were its Muslim and Jewish communities, who were expelled or forcibly converted. In the so-called New World, indigenous culture and heritage were destroyed in the name of spreading Christianity and, to a lesser extent, European imperial powers went about Christianising their colonies in the so-called Old World.

Despite this long history of devastation in the name of Christendom, it reveals a shocking level of self-awareness and self-criticism (two attributes western bigots claim Muslims lack) that some Europeans insist that Islam is uniquely sinister in this regard. For instance, Giulio Meotti, a conservative Italian journalist, claims that "Islam has deleted everything else," without even making a single, passing mention to the devastation Christianity has wrought on the world.[53] But as any non-partisan reading of history will show, Islam, Christianity and Judaism all have tolerant, conservationist strands and intolerant, conservative streams – and there has been a constant struggle between them throughout the centuries, right down to the present day. In Islam this conservationist tendency is expressed in such things as the famous story of caliph Umar ibn al-Khattab's refusal to pray in Jerusalem's Holy Sepulchre to circumvent any possible future attempts to convert this holiest of Christian churches into a mosque. It is also expressed in the collection from across the Islamic empires and beyond of pre-Islamic philosophical and scientific works which were deposited into enormous repositories of knowledge, such as Baghdad's Bayt al-Hikma (House of Wisdom) mentioned earlier. Then there were the Muslim adventurers and travellers who spent their lives exploring every corner of the known world and documenting the weird and beautiful diversity of human existence. The most famous of these was Ibn Battuta who lived around the time of Marco Polo but travelled much more extensively, covering much of the then known world, leaving behind a rich account of "almost every conceivable aspect of human life in that age, from the royal ceremonial of the Sultan of Delhi to the sexual conduct of women in the Maldive islands."[54] Although there is a current conception that Arabs discovered their ancient, pre-Islamic heritage only after western historians and archaeologists took an interest in it, this is not entirely accurate. Some Medieval Arab historians took a keen interest in the region's pre-Islamic heritage, including Egypt, Greece, Rome and Persia. The fascination of classical Islamic scholars writing in Arabic with the glories of Ancient Egypt and its pharaohs would be familiar to a modern audience, with historians studying the various dynasties and monarchs, with Cleopatra, like today, of particular romantic interest, and how the Egyptian state was administered by a pharaoh who, in the words of one admiring medieval historian, "filled the land and built it with justice and generosity," perhaps in a veiled message to his contemporary rulers. Egyptian themes were even woven into Arabic epics. Muslim alchemists even attempted to decipher Egyptian hieroglyphs.[55]

Of course, not all cultural destruction is carried out in the name of religion, or at least not overtly. The near wholesale destruction of European civilisation in World War II included the wilful targeting of some of the continent's most unique and beautiful architecture, such as the beautiful Baroque town centre of Dresden, Germany, including the Frauenkirche, with its enormous dome.[56] In addition to the modern compulsion to preserve and conserve, modernism has also had a devastating effect on cultural heritage. For instance, in America, New York and other beautiful towns were pretty much torn down to their foundations and Manhattan, which had some of the oldest buildings in that young country, became a forest of skyscrapers. "Manhattan has promoted and experienced the process of creative destruction like no other city," describes historian Max Page. "In a generation, developers largely wiped away the city of brownstones and church spires and replaced it with the modern, skyscraper metropolis we recognise today."[57] In addition to skyscrapers, this destructive process was employed to give Manhattan its main area of greenery, Central Park, which is built on the ruins of numerous small villages, derided in the press at the time as squatters living in shanties. This, incidentally, wasn't true. The largest and most developed of these was Seneca village, which was inhabited mostly by freed African slaves with a smattering of Irish residents.[58] At the other end of the political spectrum, China also embarked on its own form of supposedly creative destruction. Mao Zedong's so-called Cultural Revolution only resulted in destructive, devastating destruction, which left up to 2 million dead and was eventually conceded as an unmitigated "catastrophe" for China by the Communist party. Mao's campaign of mass destruction was guided by a little red book. "The Cultural Revolution was so great a disaster that it provoked an even more profound cultural revolution, precisely the one that Mao intended to forestall," historians like Tom Philips assert, arguing that Mao's attempts to raise the star of communism actually paved the way to capitalism.[59]

Supposedly guided by a green Quran rather than a red book, ISIS's perceived creative destruction, despite its puritanical, retrograde religious trappings, bears more than a passing resemblance to Mao's efforts at mass creative destruction and other similar efforts, on the far left and far right, in the 20th century – and, as with Mao, it could well result in the unintended consequence of paving the way for an outcome these zealots do not desire; in this case, tolerant secular governance. Although ISIS uses the past as its reference, its conception of the "Islamic state" resembles no caliphate that actually existed in history, as I explain elsewhere in the book. Through its use of nihilistic violence and destruction, ISIS seeks to create this ahistorical utopia (which the vast majority of Muslims and non-Muslims alike find to be dystopian), by reconstructing an imagined past in the future. Paving the way to this Islamic paradise on earth requires bulldozing the present and the inconvenient elements of the past. "I doubt that the primary factor motivating their destruction of ancient Near Eastern monuments is really a religious one," explains Eckart Frahm, professor of Assyriology at Yale University. "ISIS tries to eradicate Assyrian sites because the ancient civilisation they represent was used by previous political leaders in Iraq to build some kind of national identity across religions, sects, and ethnic groups – something to which ISIS is strongly opposed."[60]

In this, ISIS differs from the general approach pursued by Islamic societies throughout the centuries. Although there have been episodes and periods of destruction and desecration of the holy sites of other faiths, Muslim societies have more often than not taken seriously their prophet's injunction on respecting and protecting the places of worship of other religions. As for pre-monotheistic architecture and heritage, Muslims have traditionally been either curious or ambivalent about them.

CHAPTER ELEVEN

Epilogue: Reforming Islam or reforming Muslims?

Faced with the grim state of the Middle East and the under-performance of many Muslim-majority countries, in terms of economic, scientific and technological development, Islamophiles and Islamophobes, despite their passionate disagreement on almost everything related to Islam, appear to agree on one thing: Islam requires urgent reform. Even some sceptics who believed that Islam was unreformable have seen the light and jumped on the reform bandwagon.[1] These include Ayaan Hirsi Ali, the Somali-born Dutch-American neo-conservative critic of Islam who used to argue that Islam must be "defeated" and urged the West to "crush your enemy".[2]

What they tend to disagree on is what reform Islam needs exactly and who is to carry out these reforms. Muslim reformers generally believe that this process must be internal and led from within, while many western advocates, especially of the neo-conservative or neo-imperial type, are convinced that the West can light the path out of the darkness for Islam, either by example, from its own history, or by imposition, even militarily.

However, there is a problem with all this talk of reform. Islam has already been 'reformed' – too many times to recount fully here. In the modern era, numerous attempts to reform, and in some cases one could say deform, Islam have been set in motion, both by modernists and by traditionalists, some have been successful, while others have failed. On the modernising end of the spectrum, they include the Islamic modernist movement of the 19th and early 20th centuries, the modernist reinterpretation of Islam by secular pan-Arabism, Islamic feminism, Islamic socialism, Islamic communism and Quranism, which basically seeks to make Islam more suitable for the modern era by starting from scratch and relying solely on the Quran and rationalism while ditching the *hadith*, to name but a few. Even the Muslim Brotherhood, widely regarded as regressive and reactionary, have also sought a way to enter and accommodate the modern age while upholding what they regarded as traditional Islamic values – a circle they have not been able to square.

Looking further back, reform and counter-reform have been the order of the day since the very dawn of Islam. "The fact is that since its inception fourteen centuries ago, Islam has undergone bursts of reformation," observes Max Rodenbeck, the prominent journalist and writer, pointing to such examples as the Sunni-Shi'a split, the rationalist schools of the Mu'tazilites, the classical philosophers of Islam, not to mention the esoteric traditions of Sufism.[3]

Iran's Islamic Republic is also, at many levels, an utterly modern invention, driven by both a revolutionary and reformist mindset, even if one disagrees with the reforms instated. Never in the history of Islam had clerics ruled an Islamic society directly, until 1979. Traditionally, they were at the service and mercy of secular leaders, not the inverse. The turning point came with Ayatollah Khomeini's controversial idea of *Velayat-e Faqih* (Guardianship or Governance of the Jurist). Khomeini claimed that the guardianship of the *faqih* had "little need of demonstration, for anyone who has some general awareness of the beliefs and ordinances of Islam," and he blamed the ignorance of this allegedly self-evident truth amongst his lay compatriots on, unsurprisingly, Jewish and western imperialist propaganda.[4] He did not explain how it was that his fellow jurists over the previous 14 centuries were also unaware of this self-evident concept and had never once governed, or why it was that his contemporary ayatollahs rejected his entire theory.[5] Khomeini also kept this plan for theocratic rule from those involved in the Iranian revolution, most of whom rejected the concept of clerical rule, and imposing it required the elimination and purging of thousands of secular revolutionaries.[6] Of course, Islam was not as politically complete as Khomeini had promised and his Islamic Republic borrowed many ideas from the infidel West, including the incorporation of a number of leftist and democratic principles, such as the overthrow of the monarchy, not to mention the ballot box, parliament and the office of president.

An Islamic Reformation

In recent years, many voices in the West have urged a European-style reformation of Islam. One mass-circulation proponent is Thomas Friedman, the self-appointed sage of the *New York Times,* who described the pro-democracy movement in Iran as being "a combination of Martin Luther and Tiananmen Square".[7]

A number of Muslim intellectuals also think that not only does Islam need a Reformation, but that this process is already

339

in full swing, both in the intellectual capitals of the Muslim world and among the Muslim intelligentsia of the West. "Like the reformations of the past, this will be a terrifying event, one that has already begun to engulf the world," Reza Aslan, the Iranian-American academic and best-selling author. "However, out of the ashes of cataclysm, a new chapter in the story of Islam will emerge" and it will do so "after centuries of stony sleep".[8]

As shown earlier in this chapter and throughout this book, Islam has experienced anything but 'stony sleep' throughout its long history, but especially in the modern era. "We shouldn't export terminology. Islam doesn't need a reformation," posits Tariq Ramadan, the modernist but conservative Swiss-Egyptian scholar of Islam, who also happens to be the grandson of Hassan al-Banna, the founding father of the Muslim Brotherhood, "but Muslims need to reform their minds, their interpretations of Islam."[9]

However, this is precisely what has been happening. Reformations and counter-reformations, and counter-counter-reformations have occurred non-stop for the past two centuries, with many taking place simultaneously and in open rivalry with one another. But still the Muslim world generally lags behind most of the West.

In addition to the fact that there has been no shortage of modern reform movements within Islam, using the terminology of the European Reformation involves numerous difficulties, from the distortion and embellishment of history to the misdiagnosis of the causes of success and failure. Such analogies are "lazy and historically illiterate" because they involve "a misreading of how Christianity relates to modernity," argues Theo Hobson, a British theologian and author. "Creating a more liberal political order was not on [Martin]

Luther's agenda, nor on anyone's at that time... The Protestant Reformation was not a matter of Christianity accepting the truth of something else, something beyond itself," he adds.[10]

The spiritual father of the Protestant Reformation, Martin Luther's famous doctrine of the two governments, or two kingdoms, may have been a first and revolutionary step towards the separation of church and state, following the material excesses of the Renaissance,[11] but it did not correspond to our present-day understanding of secularism, such as France's modern conception of *laïcité*, which seeks not just to separate church from state, but also to remove religion from the public sphere. In contrast, though Luther's rebellion was specifically aimed at the Roman Catholic Church's *operandi*, he did not want the clergy to play at worldly politics princes, nor princes to interfere in the beliefs of their subjects as though they priests; instead he believed he believed and insisted that Christianity must take centre stage in governing society. Only true Christians belonged to both the heavenly and worldly kingdoms, while "those who do not have faith are not Christians and do not belong to Christ's kingdom, but to the kingdom of the world, to be coerced and ruled by the Sword and by external government." And the princes bearing the sword of secular rule did so, Luther believed, despite his conviction that princes were neither prudent nor just, as agents of God, not as secular rulers in our modern sense of the term – he even offered these blue-blooded scoundrels tips on how to become truly 'Christian princes'.[12] On the radical fringes of the Reformation, the pacifistic group the Anabaptists, persecuted by Catholicism and Protestantism alike, took Luther's ideas to their extreme and argued for the divorce, not the separation, of the two kingdoms: true Christians should not be involved in politics in any way and that the role of the separation of church and state was to protect the believers' church from the state, not vice-versa, as modern secularists believe.[13]

Luther's belief in the divine right of princes and kings was reflected in his attitude towards the poor and hungry peasantry. When, inspired by Luther's message, German peasants rose up against their masters, he called these impoverished farmers "mad dogs" and "insane" and was outraged that they should rise above their station and revolt. "I think there is not a devil left in hell; they have all gone into the peasants. Their raving has gone beyond all measure," he condemned.[14] While Luther believed that the insurgent peasants should be crushed by any means possible, and that "anyone who is killed fighting on the side of the rulers may be a true martyr in the eyes of God,"[15] bizarrely, he was initially against resisting the Ottomans, who had swept across many parts of eastern and central Europe and besieged Vienna, though he eventually supported a secular defensive war. This was because he saw the victories of the Ottomans, who were the devil incarnate, as divine punishment for errant Christendom, especially the Roman Catholic Church, which he regarded as the Antichrist, and that "to fight against the Turks is to oppose God's visitation on our iniquities." Interestingly, just as many Islamic fundamentalists today hold up the West as an example of how the 'infidel' is more moral than Muslims, Luther was convinced that the Turks were superior in morality and ceremony than his Christian contemporaries.[16]

But this did not mean that Luther's belief in freedom of religion or conscience extended beyond Christians. Four centuries before Hitler penned *Mein Kampf*, Martin Luther wrote a virulently anti-Semitic treatise which accused Jews of murdering Christians and enslaving them with their own money. It incited Christian princes, kings and preachers to burn Jewish homes, synagogues and schools, to destroy their books, to ban their rabbis and stop them from worshipping in public, to confiscate their property, to strip them of all legal protection, and to expel them or force them into hard labour.[17] In his view of Jews, Martin Luther's attitudes are closer to Abu Bakr al-Baghdadi and ISIS's treatment of minorities than they are to a modern liberal's view of equality, regardless of religion or race.

In his passion to return to the supposedly unspoiled essence and fundamental tenets of his religion, essence and fundamental tenets of his religion than later figures of the European Enlightenment. In fact, Martin Luther did not see his mission as paving the way to modern times, but, like today's jihadists, he wished to prepare the faithful for the end time,[18] the apocalypse which was apparently unfolding before his eyes because "all those things which are now going on among us most exactly and fully exhibit Antichrist."[19]

The 18th-century puritanical Islamic scholar Muhammad Ibn Abdul Wahhab (1703-1792) also advocated a puritanical form of Islam stripped off centuries of tradition and intolerant towards people of other faiths. "And [Ibn Abdul Wahhab] didn't produce a tolerant, pluralistic, multifaith utopia, a Scandinavia-on-the-Euphrates. Instead, [he] produced … the kingdom of Saudi Arabia," asserts Mehdi Hasan, the journalist and TV presenter.[20]

So how is it that Abdul Wahhab's fundamentalist reformation resulted in theocratic Saudi Arabia, while Luther's fundamentalist reformation paved the way to secular, liberal Europe?

Well, Luther's revolution almost did not. In fact, it set in motion a long series of religious conflicts and wars, such as the devastating Thirty Years War, which was the deadliest ostensibly religious war in European history, though much of the fighting was over the very worldly issue of territory.[21] The Reformation and Counter-reformation also led to long periods of persecution of Protestants by Catholics and of Catholics by Protestants, and of other spin-offs and derivatives by both, not to mention enormous cultural destruction, such as occurred during the Iconoclastic Fury (*Beeldenstorm* in Dutch or *Bildersturm* in German).[22]

These devastating upheavals took a heavy toll on intellectuals of conscience who came up with ideas that would provide a tolerant, humanist bridge between the Reformation and the later Enlightenment, in words and ideas, if not immediately in deeds. These bridging figures included Baruch Spinoza (1632-1677), born Benedito de Espinosa to a Portuguese-Jewish family in the Netherlands, who developed ideas of staunch rationalism founded on the notion that God was not the interventionist deity of scripture but a kind of passive intellect which encompassed all of creation – a notion which bears remarkable parallels to that of the 11th-century Muslim philosopher Ibn Sina, or Avicenna (see chapter 8 on atheism), whose ideas may have reached Spinoza indirectly through his familiarity with medieval Jewish Sephardic philosophy.[23]

Ironically, Avicenna, Ibn Rushd (Averroes) and other rationalist Islamic philosophers ultimately had a greater impact on the European Renaissance and Enlightenment than they did in Muslim societies. For instance, the English liberal philosopher John Locke (1632-1704), when formulating his theory that humans were born as a 'blank slate' or *tabula rasa* leaned heavily on the empiricism of Ibn Sina. How did these ideas travel across time and place to reach Locke, half a millennium and half a world away? British historians and scholars have long puzzled over Locke's sudden interest in the nature of the mind and knowledge, which had no apparent precursor in his writings and interests. Recent scholarship reveals that this new intellectual direction coincided with (though this was no coincidence) the publication of the publication of the 1671 Latin translation *Philosophus Autodidactus* (*The Self-taught Philosopher*) of the first Arabic-language novel, Ḥayy ibn Yaqẓān (starring a character of the same name whose name translates as *Alive, Son of Awake*), which had been written by Ibn Tufail, the 12ᵗʰ-century Andalusian philosopher and scientist. Building on Avicenna's notion of *tabula rasa*, the story, or thought experiment, plots the fictional experience of a baby who is abandoned on a deserted island and raised by a gazelle, yet still manages to educate himself through observation, experience and experimentation.[24] If this plot line sounds hauntingly familiar to the modern reader, it was because *Philosophus Autodidactus* became a bestseller in England and was translated into numerous European languages, not only helping launch the 'scientific revolution', but also profoundly affecting European literature, including Daniel Defoe's *Robinson Crusoe* trilogy, the first part of which is widely regarded as the first English novel.[25]

Locke also penned a letter in 1689 urging religious tolerance, in which he argued that persuasion, not coercion, was the only acceptable way to impose religious ideas and, contrary to the persuasions of the time, that religious diversity actually caused stability while attempts to impose religious uniformity resulted in conflict. However, Locke's tolerance had limits and did not extend to the Catholic church (though it did to Catholic beliefs), nor to atheists because, rather insultingly, he was convinced that, "Promises, covenants, and oaths, which are the bonds of human society, can have no hold upon an atheist."[26] Although largely unheeded for a long time (even by Locke himself, who was an investor in the slave trade and helped establish a feudal system in the Crown colony of Carolina and developed theories on the disenfranchisement of slaves and native Americans because they possessed supposedly primitive notions of nation and property),[27] Locke's ideas on tolerance and his theory of the social contract were to profoundly affect modern secularism, especially the founding ideologies of the American republic and, indirectly, the French revolution.[28]

Socio-economic chickens and theological eggs

This raises the question of why and how the Reformation led Europe to the Enlightenment and to pioneer modern secularism, while, drawing on a similar philosophical and theological tradition, enlightened Islamic reformations led many modern Muslim societies into something of a modern cul-de-sac, trailing their western counterparts.

Part of the reason is the overemphasis on religion. The entity we now call the West did not reach its current situation through religion and religious reform alone. In fact, there is something of a chicken-and-egg situation: do religious reforms lead to shifts in socio-economic and political reality, or vice-versa? While the relationship is almost certainly bidirectional, I would hazard to say that the far stronger directional flow is from shifting socio-economic and political realities which precipitate changes in religion, which then fuel further changes in society. In short, though religion shapes society, society moulds religion to a far greater extent.

The Renaissance was financed and facilitated by the economic boom starting in the late medieval period experienced by Florence and other Italian city states,[29] which was temporarily interrupted by the Black Death, and trade with the Middle East brought Italy into contact with the 'lost knowledge' of the ancient Greeks and the newer Islamic sciences and philosophies, not to mention the Islamic model of global capitalism,[30] unchristian practices the Italians were able to acquire while the Papacy was temporarily rehoused to Avignon, France.[31]

It is perhaps no coincidence that Martin Luther's famous *Ninety-Five Theses* focused on the sale of indulgences, which outraged Luther because it involved the monetisation of spirituality and represented the church's worldly corruption, but it also spoke of a broader socio-economic reality. The Catholic church was able to maintain its spiritual-economic monopoly in conjunction with the landed aristocracy under the rigid, monopolistic hierarchy of the feudal system. However, many parts of Europe were breaking free of feudalism at the time of the Reformation, building up entrepreneurial and middle classes and more fluid flows of wealth, as well as conceptions of equality and meritocracy. In such dynamic areas, the Reformation was far more likely to take root, while in more traditional territories, the Catholic church tended to defeat it or regain power, according to recent academic research.[32]

In addition, there is a common conviction that the Reformation had a huge impact on economic growth, as reflected in the rise of England and the Netherlands as global economic powers and the relative decline of Spain. Many attribute this to the individual responsibility Protestantism promoted and the so-called Protestant work ethic. However, when put to the test and when comparing like with like, this theory does not stand up to scrutiny. One study of centuries of economic growth in the German-speaking cities of the Holy Roman Empire found no differences in the long-term performance of Protestant and Catholic regions.[33] However (and this will shock today's Christian right in America, which believes in 'limiting' the size of the state and leaving public services in private hands), those

Protestant cities in which the state invested heavily in public goods, such as the provision of mass education, experienced higher levels of sustained growth than their neighbours.[34] This correlation between education and development, rather than religion and development, can be seen to this day, with the most successful societies usually those who invest the heaviest in education and educate effectively the largest proportion of their populations. This has serious long-term implications for places like America, which has been pricing large swathes of their citizens out of the higher education sector and whose state-provided free education is creaking and crumbling, resulting in a huge wealth-based innovation gap, rather than the meritocracy to which it aspires.[35] The Protestant work ethic will not save America from the ravages of educational exclusion and exclusive education.

Closely related to education is technology. The Protestant Reformation would probably have been considerably less successful had Johannes Gutenberg not developed his movable-type printing press a few decades prior. Luther's nailing of his 95 theses to the a church door was great for dramatic effect, but the authorities could simply have ignored them and they would have been quickly forgotten had Luther not taken the precaution of printing many copies of his famous pamphlet. More than religion even, Luther revolutionised how information is produced and distributed. Still in its infancy, Gutenberg's printing press was originally used by the elite for the elite to produce low-circulation texts in Latin. By publishing pulp theology in the German vernacular, Luther became the world's first best-selling author, granting him and his message, for better and for worse, considerable sway.[36]

Technology, science and knowledge played the visible, edifying role in creating the groundwork for the Enlightenment

348

and the subsequent industrial revolution. But a less recognised but pivotal factor, the ugly underbelly, was the massive influx of resources from the European colonies, especially the British and the Dutch ones, the profits from the slave trade, as well as the captive colonial markets and the banning of advanced manufacturing there, such as was the case in Britain's American colonies.[37] This had the dual effect of accelerating development in the mother country, while derailing or delaying it in other parts of the empire. By far the most extreme example of this was India, the 'Jewel in the Crown' of the British empire. Not only did Britain extract enormous amounts of resources from its possessions in the subcontinent, it treated India as a captive market for its goods, and even more insidiously, it destroyed Indian industries in the sectors where India had once enjoyed high competitiveness and global leadership. "The connection between the beginning of the drain of Indian wealth to England and the swift uprising of British industries was not casual: it was causal," writes Sumit K Majumdar, an Indian economist and expert on industrial development. By 1800, it is estimated that 3% of Britain's GDP was coming from its Asian colonies. From Asia and the West Indies, Britain was gathering about half the funds it was investing.[38] When added to the vast coal deposits at Britain's disposal at home, this mammoth flow of wealth reveals that the Industrial Revolution was not born of ideas and inventiveness alone.

This is not to belittle the enormous social, scientific and cultural advances set in motion by the Enlightenment, and the emancipatory struggles triggered by rapid industrialisation. A clear difference can be seen between how Britain and the Netherlands were able to use their colonies to spark development at home, while mercantile Spain floundered. It demonstrates that modernity and our contemporary ideas of progress require enormous amounts of surplus resources to see the light of day, and are not solely the mysterious, even mystical, products of human enlightenment. This continues to be the case, perhaps even more so. While the age of direct rule is over, the major industrial powers of the West rely heavily on the resources extracted from an informal form of neo-imperialism and, as in the early colonial era, corporatism to feed the voracious need for resources required by modern industry and technological innovation.

The economics of decline

The so-called 'golden age' of Islam – which encompassed many of the features we associate with the Enlightenment, such as free-thinking, secularism, scientific inquiry, technological development, an attachment, relative to its time, to rationalism, cultural diversity, with an interplay between many different religious traditions, and intellectual productivity – was founded on similar grounds to its western equivalent. In fact, the history of Islam reveals that globalisation is far from a new phenomenon; what is new is the sheer scale of it, facilitated by mechanisation, automation, and modern transportation and communications technologies.

The vast, largely contiguous lands ruled over by the various Islamic empires and states led to a medieval proto-globalisation, "the most far-reaching and dynamic commercial empire that the world to date had known,"[39] with goods and raw materials travelling great distances from east to west, south to north, and vice-versa. To facilitate this movement, medieval Muslims created international currencies, exchange rates, early banks, commodity exchanges, methods for transferring money quickly across the world, bills of exchange, and entrepreneurs who specialised solely in financial transactions.[40] The complexities involved in managing such gigantic trade flows spurred developments in technology and science, including what some academics have termed the 'Arab Agricultural Revolution'.[41] For example, Muḥammad ibn Musa al-Khwarizmi (780-850) admitted that he had developed his theories, at the request of the caliph, for solving polynomial equations (which became known as 'algebra' based on the title of his treatise), to help tackle all sorts of practical issues by employing "what is easiest and most useful in arithmetic." These included "inheritance, legacies, partition, law suits, and trade," not to mention, "the measuring of lands, the digging of canals [and] geometrical computations".[42] The Industrial Revolution was steam powered. An earlier mini industrial revolution in the Muslim world was powered by water (and to a lesser extent, wind), as engineers perfected ways to exploit the flow of water, including the sea's tidal movements, to power all variety of mills in almost every Muslim region. In addition, as time was increasingly becoming money, Muslims developed a number of ingenious water clocks and even mechanical clocks before they appeared in Europe.[43] With the inevitable inequalities created by free-wheeling capitalism, there were some efforts to introduce some limited tax-based welfare programmes and private trusts, such as Islamic *waqfs*, also funded such activities.

This boom in commerce and knowledge, like its later European counterpart, also had its ugly underbelly. Slavery was a central feature of Islamic societies, as it was in ancient societies generally, though slaves were employed in a far wider range of activities than in the Americas, and some rose to positions of huge influence and prominence. Although Islam was novel in introducing a partial abolition of slavery into the medieval world and granting slaves certain limited rights, this had a

351

huge impact outside the sphere of Islam. The prohibition on enslaving Muslims led Islamic slave traders to send expeditions to kidnap and seize slaves from outside the domains of Islam, which had a devastating impact on Sub-Saharan Africa and on some parts of Europe.[44]

A few scholars posit that the rapid spread of Islam and its conquest of Byzantine territory was a major factor in plunging Europe into its medieval Dark Ages. The most prominent advocate of this theory was the Belgian historian Henri Pirenne who argued that, cut off from the former Roman Empire's Mediterranean heartland, Europe withered on the vine, and entered a period we would today call de-development following the spread of Islam.[45] Most scholars disagree with Pirenne, and identify Rome's decline and collapse to two or three centuries before the appearance of Islam. Factors include plague, famine, internecine conflict with neighbours, over-taxation to finance the overstretched war machine, increasing violence to extract taxes and extensive tax evasion by the aristocracy, a series of incompetent emperors, not to mention Constantine's decision to move the capital and split the empire in two, as well as the rise of the church's political role in Europe.[46]

Islam did not create Europe's Dark Ages but, in my analysis, it likely played a role in perpetuating these centuries of decline, and ensured that Christianity would never again become the dominant faith in the Middle East. The Muslim powers' domination of and hegemony over the medieval world's global economy did not provide Europe with enough breathing space to create the surpluses of wealth that would stimulate development. In addition, direct conflict with and fear of the Muslim enemy, among other factors, enabled and empowered the medieval church to appropriate an outsized role for itself and, in collaboration with the landed elites, managed and perpetuated a repressive feudal system.

In addition to this stifling role, Islam also aided Europe's eventual emergence from the so-called Dark Ages, oft unwittingly, such as by providing Europeans with a common enemy around which to rally. Crusaders brought back many ideas and technologies from their more advanced neighbours. The boom witnessed by the Italian city states which paved the way to the Renaissance, as mentioned above, was facilitated not only by trade with the Muslim powers but also by the wide borrowing and adaptation of Islamic commercial practices and ideas. In fact, some recent scholarship has concluded that the roots of modern western capitalism lie in the domain of medieval Islam.[47] This helped parts of Europe to close the economic gap with there Muslim neighbours.

Meanwhile, the Muslim world entered a period of long relative decline. While some westerners attribute this wholly to some sort of intrinsic inability of Islam to adapt or to Islam's essential incompatibility with modernity, the actual causes are complex, diverse, interwoven and difficult to disentangle. They include both internal and external factors, some were manmade and others were natural, while some were accidents of history and yet others were by design. Domestic factors included growing socio-economic inequality, centuries of domination by imported elite warrior (slave) castes, internal divisions and factionalism when they became the defining feature of the Islamic domains, as well as unstable methods of power transfer. Natural factors included the regularity with which the 'Black Death' (which appears to have originated in Muslim territory) laid waste to many of the main urban and trading centres of Islam in the 14th century. The Muslim world became a victim of the success with which it had integrated economically, providing the deadly bacteria with a ready network by which to conquer vast territory. While the bubonic plague was also deadly in Europe, the integrated economic space of the Muslim world meant that fresh outbreaks occurred regularly, depopulating many urban areas and, crucially, the countryside on several occasions. It also devastated the complex, irrigation-based agricultural system that many parts of the Muslim world, such as Egypt, relied on to produce their once-massive food surpluses, triggering outbreaks of famine. The relatively underdeveloped nature of Europe, as well as more effective quarantine measures, may have helped reduce the future prevalence of the plague.[48] If the plague played a role in Islam's decline, it would provide a kind of poetic mirror of its rise, as some historians attribute the original wildfire spread of Islam partly to an outbreak of plague which had devastated large tracts of the Byzantine and the Sassanid Persian empires in the sixth century.[49]

Equally devastating in their human toll were the series of conquests spearheaded by the Mongols a century earlier, regarded as some of the deadliest in human history, which destroyed many of the main economic and intellectual hubs of the Muslim world, including Baghdad. By arresting the Mongol advance, the Mamluks of Egypt inadvertently spared Western Europe similar devastation at the hands of these ruthless conquerors.[50] The Mamluks also expelled the Crusaders, bringing to an end the two centuries of crusades, which had also caused damage to Islamic territory, but which were minor and manageable compared with the Mongol threat.[51] For a while, the major Islamic powers held their own, namely through the Turkic Ottomans and the Turco-Mongol Mughals.

However, Europe was already in the ascendancy. The point of no return was reached, in my view, around the time Christian Europe had, under the Spanish flag, discovered the so-called 'New World', in a bid to break the Islamic monopoly on global trade by sailing west to reach India, and, for similar motives, Portuguese sailors successfully circumnavigated Africa to reach the fabled East. As the European powers built up their global empires, this had the dual effect of providing them with previously undreamed of levels of wealth and resources, while gradually depriving the Islamic world of the global economic network upon which its former prosperity has been founded. "Assaulted from all quarters, the Muslim world turned in on itself," reflects Amin Maalouf, the Lebanese-French intellectual and author. "It became over-sensitive, defensive, intolerant, sterile."[52]

Reviving Muslim societies

At a certain level, Maalouf's verdict is rather unfair. Over the past couple of centuries, the Muslim world has opened up enormously to the rest of humanity and to outside influences. There was a time not so long ago when certain Muslim countries which are currently considered basketcases or in the grips of enormous turmoil led the march towards progress of the developing world in the 20th century. My native Egypt, for instance, was considerably more developed than what is today South Korea in the 19th century due to an aggressive modernisation drive set in motion by the dynasty of Muhammad Ali, even though the two · countries were of comparable size, agricultural wealth and lack of natural resources.[53] By the 1960s, both countries were about neck-and-neck but, despite also being a military dictatorship at the time,

South Korea managed to achieve the breakthrough to developed country status, while Egypt has been struggling with economic stagnation and gigantic population growth. This is partly due to differences in education levels, which caused skill shortages in Egypt, exacerbated by the huge outflow of Egyptian talent to the better-paying Gulf and West.[54] It is also part of a wider regional malaise. The success of rapid economic and social development in the 20th century, with the attendant population explosion and youth bulge, coupled with the disproportionate ravages of global warming that have afflicted the Middle East, making it the world's most water-stressed region, have acted as a natural break on development – and in some cases have triggered de-development. A prime example of this is Yemen, one of the poorest most water-stressed countries in the Middle East. Climate change, poor water resource management, lack of funds to invest in durable solutions, a shift away from traditional rain harvesting, and rapid population growth all contributed to the water crisis, which in turn helped fuel the country's descent into civil conflict.[55] The ongoing Saudi-led bombing and blockade of Yemen, aimed ostensibly at fighting Iran-backed Houthi rebels, has transformed a crisis into a catastrophe, with millions of Yemenis facing acute water stress, by destroying vital infrastructure, disrupting fuel supplies and delaying the possibility of investing in Yemen's water sector.[56]

For the Arab world, another factor has been the enormous mismatch in resources in this fragmented region. The Middle East's oil wealth generally lies in what were the least-developed areas of the region, with the exception of Iraq and Iran, while the more developed areas, with the human capital and industrial capacity, were generally resource poor. While some of the oil wealth has been shared and invested within the region, far more petrodollars have found their way to investments in

America and Europe, which means the West benefits many times over from the Middle East's petroleum: it dominates the extraction industry, it uses the fossil fuels to run its economies and also receives much of the surplus to enrich its financial and corporate sectors. This has involved enormous and lavish waste in the Gulf, though part of the reason for this is that the states there started from a very low development point. Consider how Norway has used its hydrocarbon wealth and contrast it with Middle Eastern oil producers. That said, efforts to gain a fairer share of the oil wealth to use domestically or in the region often led to conflict with the West, (such as occurred with Iran, and the coup engineered by the CIA and MI6 against reformist prime minister Mohammad Mosaddegh in the early 1950s)[57] or to a Western policy of supporting pliant vassal rulers in the Arab Gulf states.

In contrast, India, despite the huge legacy of poverty left behind by the British era, has, in recent years, managed to embark on the path to rapid development and technological progress. Part of the reason for this is, as with China, economies of scale made possible by a population three to four times that of the Arab world. Nevertheless, in the 1960s, Pakistan was more developed than India, now famed for its innovation and silicon valleys, and won the praise of many Americans, including Samuel P Huntington, of later 'clash of civilisations' fame, and numerous countries sought to emulate its model of rapid development.[58] But instead of building a prosperous country, the Pakistani army ultimately ended up devastating it.

In recent generations, life has changed beyond recognition for most inhabitants of the Muslim world. Most have gained independence, at least formally, and a few have lost it again. Most Muslim-majority countries have modernised their governments, education systems and economies, embarking on a process of rapid industrialisation and urbanisation – but without the wealth and opportunity of the West, this has caused frustration among the population and terror among leaders, especially those of the Middle East's failing or failed states. In some ways, the most dramatic examples of this rapid development are the Gulf states. They went from barely being the backwaters of the Muslim world, with their towns hardly qualifying as villages, to become mini-Americas in the desert, with foreigners significantly outnumbering natives in the smaller princedoms, such as the UAE and Qatar.

While millions live under the yoke of dictators and despots, millions live in some form of democracy or other. Indonesia, the world's largest Muslim-majority country, has evolved into a decentralised, multi-ethnic, multi-religious democracy, the world's third largest, despite the devastating decades of the US-backed Suharto regime. This stands in stark contrast to its authoritarian neighbours in Southeast Asia.[59] Despite his decision to destroy Iraq in order to supposedly liberate it, or to uncover weapons of mass destruction, or to do both, or neither, or simply to secure future Middle Eastern oil supplies, George W Bush, unlike Donald Trump, got one thing right. In 2003, he rightly dismissed as "cultural condescension" the sceptical assertion that "the traditions of Islam are inhospitable to the representative government" and maintained that "Islam – the faith of one-fifth of humanity – is consistent with democratic rule," adding that "more than half of all Muslims in the world live in freedom under democratically constituted governments."[60]

Recent years have shown this to be the case. Despite the efforts of religious conservatives to discredit the notions of democracy as nothing more than fig leaves for western hegemony and meddling, a wave of revolutions has swept many parts of the Muslim world. In 2009, millions of reformist Iranians took to the streets, in the largest demonstrations since the 1979 revolution, to protest the questionable re-election of Mahmoud Ahmadinejad and to demand more than a procedural democracy.[61] A couple of years later, a revolutionary earthquake hit the Arab world, in Yemen, Tunisia, Egypt, Syria and Libya directly, and the rest of the region indirectly. While three of the countries are embroiled in (civil) war, and have become battlegrounds for militias, regional, and international powers, the ideas, hopes and aspirations unleashed by the so-called Arab Spring were powerful, which goes some way to explaining why counter-revolutionary forces have been so vicious in their reactions. Nevertheless, these ideals will remain potent for generations to come.

The main political success story so far has been Tunisia, which went from being one of the most repressive Arab dictatorships which tolerated no dissent, to become a vibrant democracy based on consensus-building and compromise, which earned the Tunisian National Dialogue Quartet the Nobel peace prize.[62] I am constantly impressed by the high level of political debate and the huge respect for freedom of expression and differences of opinion there. However, Tunisia's economy has stalled and is unable to create jobs for the estimated 15% without them, which rises to an unsustainable 32% for the under 25s.[63] This has caused many Tunisians, so soon after changing history, to feel disappointed, bitter and suspicious of the revolution they set in motion. I have met Tunisians from many diverse backgrounds who express nostalgia for the Ben Ali years and a troubling mythology has already evolved among some that those were the 'good old days'. There have been sustained waves of protests and clashes, as well as the blockading of oil, gas and other installations in impoverished regions such as

Tataouine, which led the government to the troubling decision of deploying Tunisia's apolitical army to secure these facilities.[64] It is not that Tunisia's economy has been crashing and burning. It has actually been growing since the revolution, sometimes by as much as 4% per year, but has hovered at around 2%, which is not enough; due to the entrenched economic elite and the nature of contemporary economics, the fruits of growth are not trickling down sufficiently. The Economist Intelligence Unit estimates that Tunisia requires a sustained annual growth rate of 5-6% to make a significant dent in unemployment and to raise living standards.[65]

This provides some insight into the scale of the task at hand. In order to catch up with the West's moving target, most Muslim societies require this high level of economic growth, some for decades, if not generations. Some are making rapid progress down this road. Take Malaysia. At independence, it was impoverished and underdeveloped. Today, it is one of the few countries which has managed to register economic growth of over 7% per year for a quarter of a century, putting it on the cusp of becoming a high-income nation. The World Bank has applauded Malaysia's shift from developing country to 'development partner', i.e. a country that invests in and supports the development of other states.[66]

However, extending the Malayan experience to the entire Muslim world would stretch the world's already stretched natural and food resources to the limit or beyond. With the unprecedented destruction of ecosystems and habitats, and the environmental degradation wrought by pollutions and climate changes pollution and climate change ravaging the Middle East and other Muslim-majority countries in Africa and Asia, it is unlikely that this can be accomplished. This helps explain why and how the West is fond of placing the responsibility for the Muslim world's challenges primarily on religion and culture, because it deflects scrutiny from the fact that we do not just need an Islamic reformation but a global economic reformation to bridge the gaping and widening chasm between the haves and have-nots, not only within individual societies but between them.

That is not to say that Muslims do not need to reform their minds, societies and cultures, and many have done so. However, this is what one might term 'the software of development'. And software is useless without the appropriate hardware. What use is having the operating system for a supercomputer when you only possess a punch-card mainframe to run it on? Whereas in pre-modern times, when Christendom was pirating the latest software from Islamic culture, the hardware requirements, in terms of resources and infrastructure, were relatively modest. Today that is no longer the case. Whereas the Renaissance and Enlightenment could depend on their Universal Men, like the polymaths of Islam, to advance the sum of human knowledge and technological progress, nowadays knowledge acquisition does not just require brains and resourcefulness, it requires huge amounts of resources. As a small illustration, the OECD group of industrialised states spent, in 2009, $874 billion on research and development.[67] To put that in context, the gross domestic product of Egypt, the most populous Arab country, was $336 billion in 2016.[68] And that is just annual spending on R&D. That does not include the huge amounts the West and other industrialised economies invest in education, not to mention the generations-long construction of intellectual and technological capital, in the form of universities, libraries, research labs, patents, legacy technologies, etc.

Pursuing this level of economic and technological development will require access to an unprecedented level of resources for Muslim societies. This can potentially be achieved, at least in part, by keeping a larger share of the natural wealth in resource-rich Muslim countries at home and through the pooling of the capacities of resource-rich countries with those rich in human capacity. Accomplishing such a radical change will require not only enlightened policies on the part of Muslim governments but also on the part of the West and other highly industrialised societies, who tend to do all within their power to keep potential rivals from developing, including meddling in internal affairs, propping up dictators and, in extreme cases, declaring war. In the absence of enlightened national, regional and global mechanisms for wealth and knowledge sharing and redistribution, we are likely to see the burgeoning of conflicts that may make the current upheavals seem minor in comparison. The planet's carrying capacity cannot endure a future population of 9 billion living at current Western standards, let alone projected future ones, especially with the gaping inequalities that have accompanied neo-liberal globalisation and the break-neck automation that is replacing human labour at a terrifying rate.

Of course, development is not just about wealth and technological advancement. While it is difficult to reach western standards of technological progress, at least not for generations to come, it is possible for Muslim societies to set their sights on human development, in terms of socio-economic and political egalitarianism and through respect for the dignity and rights of the individual and through solidarity with the weak and vulnerable. Although this is a possible and desirable outcome, in times of stagnation and/ or decline, local elites tend to do their utmost to hold on to their privileges and brutally repress the masses, who either find comfort and succour in religion and other opiates, or rise up against injustice, or do both. In addition, given that so much of the energy resources that drive the global economy is buried under Muslim lands and seas, as well as other important resources, the great industrial powers, both established and new, are unlikely to sit by and allow for such a radical redefinition of what constitutes development.

But this must be resisted. Most Muslim societies urgently need to reform how they approach wealth and poverty, and socio-economic and political inequality. And it is through such change that a true reformation and enlightenment will take place in Islam and endure, as a by-product of development, not as a pre-requisite for it. Moreover, there is no one-size-fits-all solution, as the notion of an Islamic Reformation implies. While there may be some commonalities, each Muslim country faces its own unique set of challenges and must find its own unique path to tackling them.

ENDNOTES

Foreword

1 'Trump: Kerry probably hasn't read the Bible', Jesse Byrnes, *The Hill*, 24 February 2016. Link: http://thehill.com/blogs/blog-briefing-room/news/270610-trump-kerry-probably-hasnt-read-the-bible

2 'Citing 'Two Corinthians,' Trump struggles To make the sale To evangelicals', Jessica Taylor, *NPR*, 18 January 2016. Link: http://www.npr.org/2016/01/18/463528847/citing-two-corinthians-trump-struggles-to-make-the-sale-to-evangelicals

3 '"Nobody reads the Bible more than me': Trump's claim is a laughing stock', Kenya Sinclair, *Catholic Online*, 25 February 2016. Link: http://www.catholic.org/news/hf/faith/story.php?id=67567

4 'Is Donald Trump 'the Last Trump' Before Jesus Christ's Return?', Stoyan Zaimov, *Christian Post*, 30 January 2017. Link: http://www.christianpost.com/news/is-donald-trump-the-last-trump-before-jesus-christs-return-173779/#QPD6raavJgb8fqvV.99

5 'Trump calls for 'total and complete shutdown of Muslims entering the United States', Jenna Johnson, *Washington Post*, 7 December 2015. Link: https://www.washingtonpost.com/news/post-politics/wp/2015/12/07/donald-trump-calls-for-total-and-complete-shutdown-of-muslims-entering-the-united-states/?utm_term=.1f3bbcd0079b

6 Donald J Trump tweet dated 4 June 2017. Link: https://twitter.com/realdonaldtrump/status/871325606901895168

7 'Transcript of Trump's speech in Saudi Arabia', *CNN*, 21 May 2017. Link: http://edition.cnn.com/2017/05/21/politics/trump-saudi-speech-transcript/index.html

8 'Trump: Clinton won't use the term 'radical Islamic terrorists', Amy Sherman, *PolitiFact*, 9 October 2016. Link: http://www.politifact.com/truth-o-meter/statements/2016/oct/09/donald-trump/trump-clinton-wont-use-term-radical-islamist-terro/

Chapter 1

1 'اللاهوت العربي وأصول العنف الديني', سوسي زيديان, دار الشروق للنشر والتوزيع, 2007, صفحة 142.

2 'Kellyanne Conway defends White House's falsehoods as 'alternative facts', Mahita Gajanan, *Time*, 22 January 2017. Link: http://time.com/4642689/kellyanne-conway-sean-spicer-donald-trump-alternative-facts/

3 'Sean Spicer defends inauguration claim: 'Sometimes we can disagree with facts', David Smith, *The Guardian*, 23 January 2017. Link: https://www.theguardian.com/us-news/2017/jan/23/sean-spicer-white-house-press-briefing-inauguration-alternative-facts

4 Sahih Muslim: Book 50, Hadith 57

5 'What Do Jehovah's Witnesses Believe?', *Jehovah's Witnesses – JW.org*. Link: https://www.jw.org/en/jehovahs-witnesses/faq/jehovah-witness-beliefs/

6 Muhammad is reported to have said: "Whoever frees a Muslim slave, Allah will save all the parts of his body from the (Hell) Fire as he has freed the body-parts of the slave." Source: *Sahih Bukhari*, Volume 3, Book 46, Hadith Number 693.

7 Surat al-Hashr, Chapter 59, Verse 7.

8 *Sahih Muslim*, Book 42, Hadith number 7147

9 *The Alexander Romance in Persia and the East*, edited by Richard Stoneman, David Zuwiyya, Parkhuis, 2012, p205-18, 416 pages.

10 Surat al-Kahf, Chapter 18, Verse 86.

11 Surat al-Mulk, Chapter 67, Verse 5.

12 Surat al-Baqara, Chapter 2, Verse 29.

13 Surat al-Anbya', Chapter 21, Verse 104.

14 Surat al-Saba', Chapter 34, Verse 9.

15 Surat al-Hijr, Chapter 15, Verse 26.

16 Surat Al 'Imran, Chapter 3, Verse 59.

17 'How does an Islamic astronaut face Mecca in orbit?', Bettina Gartner, *Christian Science Monitor*, 10 October 2007. Link: http://www.csmonitor.com/2007/1010/p16s02-stss.html

Chapter 2

1 'Muslim, immigrant woman: I voted Trump', CNN, 11 November 2016. Link: http://edition.cnn.com/videos/politics/2016/11/11/muslim-immigrant-woman-votes-donald-trump-nr.cnn

2 'How moderate are moderate Muslims?', Rod Liddle, *The Spectator*, 23 April 2016. Link: http://www.spectator.co.uk/2016/04/how-moderate-are-moderate-muslims/

3 For a full transcript of Trump's June 2016 speech, see: http://www.vox.com/2016/6/13/11925122/trump-orlando-foreign-policy-transcript

4 'Donald Trump gets small', Harry Hurt III, Esquire, Maw 1991, p24.

5 'Donald Trump in 1994: 'Putting a wife to work Is a very dangerous thing', Jordyn Phelps, ABC News, 1 June 2016. Link: http://abcnews.go.com/Politics/donald-trump-1994-putting-wife-work-dangerous-thing/story?id=39537935

6 'Trump's thunderbolts', Maureen Dowd, *New York Times*, 29 July 2016. Link: http://www.nytimes.com/2016/07/30/opinion/trumps-thunderbolts.html?_r=0

7 'Donald Trump to father of fallen soldier: 'I've made a lot of sacrifices'', Steve Turnham, *ABC News*, 30 July 2016. Link: http://abcnews.go.com/Politics/donald-trump-father-fallen-soldier-ive-made-lot/story?id=41015051

8 'Ghazala Khan: Trump criticized my silence. He knows nothing about true sacrifice', Ghazala Khan, *Washington Post*, 31 July 2016. Link: https://www.washingtonpost.com/opinions/ghazala-khan-donald-trump-criticized-my-silence-he-knows-nothing-about-true-sacrifice/2016/07/31/c46e52ec-571c-11e6-831d-0324760ca856_story.html

9 Post, dated 22 September 2015, on Ben Carson's official Facebook page. Link: https://www.facebook.com/realbencarson/posts/532081783624959

10 '5 Egyptian women breaking into male-dominated industries', *CairoScene*, 8 March 2017. Link: http://www.cairoscene.com/Business/5-Egyptian-Women-Breaking-Into-Male-Dominated-Industries

11 'David Cameron: More Muslim women should 'learn English' to help tackle extremism', Laura Hughes, *The Telegraph*, 17 January 2016. Link: http://www.telegraph.co.uk/news/uknews/terrorism-in-the-uk/12104556/David-Cameron-More-Muslim-women-should-learn-English-to-help-tackle-extremism.html

12 This observation was made in a letter to Louise Colet, dated 27 March 1853. *The Letters of Gustave Flaubert: 1830-1857*, Gustave Flaubert, Harvard University Press, p181, 250 pages.

13 'Gunman kills Dutch film director', *BBC*, 2 November 2004. Link: http://news.bbc.co.uk/2/hi/europe/3974179.stm

14 Surat an-Nisa (Chapter 4, verse 11)

15 Surat an-Nisa (Chapter 4, verse 34)

16 'Outrage as Obedient Wives Club spreads across south-east Asia', Kate Hodal, *The Guardian*, 6 July 2011. Link: https://www.theguardian.com/world/2011/jul/06/outrage-at-obedient-wives-club-singapore

17 'Malaysia bans Obedient Wives Club sex manual', Sam Jones, *The Guardian*, 3 November 2011. Link: https://www.theguardian.com/world/2011/nov/03/malaysia-obedient-wives-sex-manual

18 'Bargaining with patriarchy', Deniz Kandiyoti, *Gender and Society*, Vol 2, No 3, September 1988, p280.

19 'Egypt's parliament under fire for controversial child custody bill', Amira Sayed Ahmed, *Al* Monitor, 15 December 2016. Link: http://www.al-monitor.com/pulse/originals/2016/12/egypt-child-custody-bill-controversy-parliament.html#ixzz4TTrtd7i5

20 For illustrative case studies, see: *The Hidden Face of Eve*, Nawal El Saadawi, Zed Books, 2007 (first published in 1974), p50-65, 325 pages.

21 *Sex and the Citadel*, Shereen El Feki, Chatto & Windus, p104, 345 pages.

22 *The Hidden Face of Eve*, Nawal El Saadawi, Zed Books, 2007 (first published in 1974), p14, 325 pages.

23 See for example: 'Sexual function in women with female genital mutilation', S Sibiani and AA Rouzi, *Fertility and Sterility*, September 2008, Volume 90, Supplement, Page S92

24 'The real roots of sexism in the Middle East', Max Fisher, *The Atlantic*, 25 April 2012. Link: http://www.theatlantic.com/international/archive/2012/04/the-real-roots-of-sexism-in-the-middle-east-its-not-islam-race-or-hate/256362/

25 'Sexual Assault and Rape in Tahrir Square and its Vicinity: A Compendium of Sources 2011-2013', *El-Nadeem Centre*, February 2013, 61 pages. Link: http://nazra.org/sites/nazra/files/attachments/compilation-_of_sexual-violence_-testimonies_between_20111_2013_en.pdf

26 'Why Saudi husbands marry housemaids', Abeer Mishkhas, *Arab News*, 11 May 2001. Link: http://www.arabnews.com/node/211723

27 'Erdoğan: You cannot make men and women equal', *Today's Zaman*, 24 November 2014.

28 'Recep Tayyip Erdoğan: 'A woman is above all else a mother'', *AFP*, 8 March 2016. Link: https://www.theguardian.com/world/2016/mar/08/recep-tayyip-erdogan-a-woman-is-above-all-else-a-mother-turkish-president

29 Genesis 2:22

Endnotes

30 'Saudi Arabia launches girls' council – without any girls', *BBC News*, 14 March 2017. Link: http://www.bbc.com/news/world-middle-east-39264349

31 This is drawn from passage four of the Declaration of Independence, penned by Thomas Jefferson.

32 'Revealed: 100 Most Powerful Arabs Under 40 – Afrah Nasser', *ArabianBusiness.com*, 19 April 2015. Link: http://www.arabianbusiness.com/100-most-powerful-arabs-under-40-589646.html?itemid=589254

33 'Egyptian woman who has lived as man for 40 years voted 'best mum'', Patrick Kingsley, *The Guardian*, 22 March 2015. Link: https://www.theguardian.com/world/2015/mar/22/egyptian-woman-award-lived-as-man

34 *Offside*, directed by Jafar Panahi, 2006.

35 *Historical Dictionary of Women in the Middle East and North Africa*, Ghada Hashem Talhami, Rowman & Littlefield, p337-9, 407 pages.

36 *The Histories of Herodotus*, Herodotus, Book 2, Section 35.

37 *An Account of the Manners and Customs of the Modern Egyptians*, Edward William Lane, J Murray, 1860, p178-82, 619 pages.

38 'The four pillars Of mut'a', Al Islam.org. Link: https://www.al-islam.org/muta-temporary-marriage-in-islamic-law-sachiko-murata/four-pillars-muta

39 'Gulf women could claim an equal share of region's wealth', Zahir Bitar, *Gulf News*, 2 February 2013. Link: http://gulfnews.com/business/sectors/general/gulf-women-could-claim-an-equal-share-of-region-s-wealth-1.1141002

40 *Napoleon's Egypt: Invading the Middle East*, Juan Cole, Palgrave Macmillan, 2007, p80, 304 pages.

41 *Women, Islam, and Abbasid Identity*, Nadia Maria El Cheikh, Harvard University Press, 2015, p70-3, 172 pages.

42 For more information on the Sultanate of Women, see: *The Imperial Harem: Women and Sovereignty in the Ottoman Empire*, Leslie P Peirce, OUP, 1993, 374 pages.

43 'Turkish first lady praises harem as 'school for women'', *AFP*, 9 March 2016.

44 *The Hidden Face of Eve*, Nawal El Saadawi, Zed Books, 2007, pXVII, 325 pages.

45 'National co-chair of march: 'Unapologetically Muslim-American'', *Washington Post*, 21 January 2017. Link: https://www.washingtonpost.com/video/politics/national-co-chair-of-march-unapologetically-muslim-american/2017/01/21/11db04aa-e00a-11e6-8902-610fe486791c_video.html

46 'Believe me when I tell you I am a feminist', Linda Sarsour's blog, 18 July 2011. Link: http://lindasarsour.blogspot.co.il/2011/07/believe-me-when-i-tell-you-i-am.html

47 'Organizer for DC Women's March, Linda Sarsour is pro Sharia law with ties to Hamas', Cristina Laila, *Gateway Pundit*, 21 January 2017. Link: http://www.thegatewaypundit.com/2017/01/figrues-organizer-dc-womens-march-linda-sarsour-pro-sharia-law-ties-hamas/

48 See: https://twitter.com/almostjingo/status/822411501247938560?lang=en

49 For example, Palestinian-Chilean commentator Lalo Dagach collated a number of Sarsour's tweets defending Saudi's record on women's rights. See: https://twitter.com/LaloDagach/status/822858838042955776

50 'An appaling magic', Jonathan Freedland, *The Guardian*, 17 May 2003. Link: https://www.theguardian.com/media/2003/may/17/pressandpublishing.usnews

51 'Coulter on feminism: 'All pretty girls are right-wingers'', Caroline May, *The Daily Caller*, 2 October 2010. http://dailycaller.com/2012/02/10/coulter-on-feminism-all-pretty-girls-are-right-wingers/#ixzz4VXgWAYUu

52 'An Underground Railroad for a Muslim Girl', Jamie Glazov, *FrontPage*, 27 August 2009. Link: http://archive.frontpagemag.com/readArticle.aspx?ARTID=36079

53 'Islam v feminism', Muhammad Legenhausen, Imam Khomeini Education and Research Institute. Link: https://www.al-islam.org/contemporary-topics-islamic-thought-muhammad-legenhausen/islam-vs-feminism

54 'Islamic feminism: Stockholm syndrome', Joumana Haddad, *Now.*, 27 December 2012. Link: https://now.mmedia.me/lb/en/commentaryanalysis/islamic_feminism_stockholm_syndrome

55 *I Have Been Young*, Helena Maria Swanwick, V Gollancz, 1935, p187, 512 pages.

56 For example, Muhammad's favourite wife, Aisha, was asked after his death what the prophet did at home. "The Prophet would do chores for his family and he would go out when it was time for prayer," she responded. *Bukhari 644*.

57 *Higher Education in the Middle East and North Africa: Exploring Regional and Country Specific Potentials*, Yew Meng Lai, Abdul Razak Ahmad and Chang Da Wan, Springer, 2016, pVII, 161 pages.

58 *Táhirih in History: Perspectives on Qurratu'l-'Ayn from East and West*, edited by Jan T Jasion, Shoghi Effendi, Kalimat Press, 2004, p12-22, 292 pages.

59 *Literature, Gender, and Nation-Building in Nineteenth-Century Egypt*, Mervat Hatem, Springer 2011, p4, 234 pages.

60 Ibid, p198.

61 Ibid, p114.

62 If you can read Arabic, you can peruse the electronic archive of al-Fatat on the Women and Memory website: http://www.wmf.org.eg/books%20Flip%20PDF/5260/index.html#p=1

63 Article 31 of the 1956 constitution states that: "All Egyptians are equal under the law in public rights and duties, without discrimination due to sex, origin, language, religion, or belief".

64 'Plan Wilders voor belasting op hoofddoek weggehoond', Trouw, 17 September 2009. Link: http://www.trouw.nl/tr/nl/4324/Nieuws/article/detail/1606766/2009/09/17/Plan-Wilders-voor-belasting-op-hoofddoek-weggehoond.dhtml

65 'Speech by Geert Wilders on the first day of the General Debate in the Dutch parliament', Geert Wilders, official site, 18 September 2009. Link: https://web.archive.org/web/20110717055410/http://www.geertwilders.nl/index2.php?option=com_content&do_pdf=1&id=1595

66 'Marine Le Pen : "Je mets à la porte tous les intégristes étrangers"' *Le Monde*, Link: 21 September 2012. http://www.lemonde.fr/politique/article/2012/09/21/marine-le-pen-je-mets-a-la-porte-tous-les-integristes-etrangers_1763542_823448.html#mUdryySpIgBcGjjz.99

67 'Macron decisively defeats Le Pen in French presidential race', Alissa J Rubin, *New York Times*, 7 May 2017. Link: https://www.nytimes.com/2017/05/07/world/europe/emmanuel-macron-france-election-marine-le-pen.html?mcubz=0

68 'Le Pen vows to ban kippas, all 'religious symbols,' in public if elected', *Times of Israel* and *AP*, 16 October 2016. Link: http://www.timesofisrael.com/le-pen-vows-to-ban-kippas-all-religious-symbols-in-public-if-elected/

69 'France to ban all Christian symbols in latest attempt to 'fight the advance of political Islam'', Kenya Sinclair, *Catholic Online*, 18 October 2016. Link: http://www.catholic.org/news/international/europe/story.php?id=71455

70 'Marine Le Pen proposes banning wearing all public 'conspicuous' religious items in France', JS Herzog, *Ynet*, 17 October 2016. Link: http://www.ynetnews.com/articles/0,7340,L-4867192,00.html

71 *Hijab and the Republic*, Bronwyn Winter, Syracuse University Press, 2009, p347, 418 pages.

72 'Feminists are failing Muslim women by supporting racist French laws', Christine Delphy, *The Guardian*, 20 July 2015. Link: https://www.theguardian.com/lifeandstyle/womens-blog/2015/jul/20/france-feminism-hijab-ban-muslim-women

73 *Public Papers of the Presidents of the United States, George W. Bush, 2004*, Office of the Federal Register, 2007, p375, 1,278 pages.

74 *What Kind of Liberation?: Women and the Occupation of Iraq*, Nadje Sadig Al-Ali, Nicola Christine Pratt, University of California Press, 2009, p80, 221 pages.

75 *The Hidden Face of Eve*, Nawal El Saadawi, Zed Books, 2007, p261, 325 pages.

76 'Bargaining with patriarchy', Deniz Kandiyoti, *Gender and Society*, Vol 2, No 3, September 1988, p283.

77 'The hijab has liberated me from society's expectations of women', Nadiya Takolia, *The Guardian*, 28 May 2012. Link: https://www.theguardian.com/commentisfree/2012/may/28/hijab-society-women-religious-political?fb=native&CMP=FBCNETTXT9038

78 'Piagra: The new pill to preserve Muslim male piety', Adham Sahloul, *Medium*, 1 June 2015. Link: https://medium.com/@AdhamSahloul/piagra-the-new-pill-to-preserve-male-muslim-piety-ad810ee0de56#.oenwiplcw

79

80 For more on the issue of harassment, see: http://chronikler.com/middle-east/womens-issues/sexual-harassment/

81 A video of Amin's comments is available here: https://www.youtube.com/watch?v=0p6Xb88BN_k

82 'ست الحسن - وقائع تحرش شرجي داخل مرح جامعة القاهرة', ON ENT, 17 March 2014. Link: https://www.youtube.com/watch?v=aICv7-UZEO4

83 For more information, check out HARASSmap's Facebook page: https://www.facebook.com/HarassMapEgypt

84 'Women reclaim the streets of Cairo through stunning ballet photos', Priscilla Frank, *Huffington Post*, 16 January 2017. Link: http://www.huffingtonpost.com/entry/ballerinas-of-cairo_us_587ccb36e4b09281d0eb9792

85 'Nude art', Aliaa ElMahdy, A Rebel's Diary, 23 October 2011. Link: http://arebelsdiary.blogspot.co.il/2011/10/nude-art_2515.html

86 Some samples of the death threats ElMahdy received can be found here: http://arebelsdiary.blogspot.co.il/2011/12/death-and-rape-threats-sexism-and.html

87 'Saudi woman pictured not wearing hijab faces calls for her execution', Tom Embury-Dennis, *The Independent*, 1 December 2016. Link:http://www.independent.co.uk/news/world/middle-east/saudi-arabia-woman-no-hijab-execution-abaya-muslim-a7450096.html

88 'Practicing Islam in short shorts', Thanaa El-Naggar, Gawker, 23 February 2015. Link: http://truestories.gawker.com/practicing-islam-in-short-shorts-1683991294

89 The excerpt of the speech can be found here. https://www.youtube.com/ watch?v=TX4RK8bj2W0

90 *The Middle East: A Guide to Politics, Economics, Society and Culture*, Barry Rubin, Routledge, 2015 p583, 700 pages.

91 'Tunisia attacked over headscarves', Magdi Abdelhadi, *BBC*, 26 September 2006. Link: http://news.bbc.co.uk/2/hi/africa/5382946.stm

92 'Turkey lifts decades-old ban on headscarves', *Al Jazeera*, 8 October 2013. Link: http://www.aljazeera.com/news/europe/2013/10/turkey-lifts-decades-old-ban-headscarves-20131081417794370 4.html

93 In Egypt, state TV lifted its ban on hijabbed female newsreaders in 2012. See: http://www.aljazeera.com/news/middleeast/2012/09/201292141141604598.html

94 *The Islamic Veil: A Beginner's Guide*, Elizabeth Bucar, OneWorld Publications, 2012, p108-9, 192 pages.

95 *Rethinking Muslim Women and the Veil*, Katherine Bullock, IIIT, 2002, 97 pages, 275 pages.

96 'Secularism in a veil', Khaled Diab, *The Guardian*, 16 April 2009. Link: https://www.theguardian.com/commentisfree/2009/apr/16/secular-veil-islam-egypt

97 'Arab girls outperforming boys in school but access and gender discrimination remain critical', UNICEF, 18 April 2005. Link: https://www.unicef.org/media/media_26050.html

98 See: https://twitter.com/DiabolicalIdea/status/762704282168729602

99 'Nike hijab faces backlash on social media', Avery Matera, *Teen Vogue*, 13 March 2017. Link: http://www.teenvogue.com/story/nike-hijab-backlash

100 The photo was posted by Ahmed ElGohary at https://www.facebook.com/photo.php?fbid=10151429894938231&set=a.10151035748418231.432064.669983230&type=1&theater

101 'Egyptian women's hijab dilemma: To wear or not to wear', Heather Murdock, *Voice of America*, 5 August 2016. Link: http://www.voanews.com/a/egypt-women-hijab/3451554.html

102 See https://www.facebook.com/StealthyFreedom/

103 See https://www.facebook.com/StealthyFreedom/photos/a.859102224103873.107374 1828.858832800797482/1400360959977994/?type=3&theater

104 'Men in hijab: Two men explain why they are covering their heads to support their wives and family in Iran', Heather Saul, *The Independent*, 31 July 2016. Link: http://www.independent.co.uk/news/people/men-in-hijab-iran-solidarity-wives-family-veil-islam-muslim-womens-rights-a7164876.html

105 'Tunisia tops Arab women's representation in parliament', Iman Zayat, *The Arab Weekly*, 25 September2016. Link: http://www.thearabweekly.com/Special-Focus/6478/Tunisia-tops-Arab-women%E2%80%80%99s-representation-in-parliament

106 'The US made zero progress in adding women to Congress', Laura Cohn, *Fortune*, 10 November 2016. Link: http://fortune.com/2016/11/10/election-results-women-in-congress/

107 'Egypt shuts El Nadeem Centre for torture victims', *Al Jazeera*, 9 February 2017. Link: http://www.aljazeera.com/news/2017/02/egypt-shuts-el-nadeem-centre-torture-victims-170209143119775.html

108 'One woman stands against the Iranian government', Golnaz Esfandiari, *Foreign Policy*, 16 June 2015. Link: http://foreignpolicy.com/2015/06/16/one-womans-stand-against-the-state-in-tehran-iran-nasrin-sotoudeh/

109 'Marriage and Divorce in Egypt: Financial Costs and Political Struggles', Diane Singerman, *Les Cahiers de l'Ifpo*, IFPO Press, 2008, p75-96.
110 The video is available here: https://www.youtube.com/watch?v=1rUn2j1hLOo
111 "God, rid us of men!' The feminist song scandalising Saudi Arabia', *France 24*, 2 January 2017. Link: http://observers.france24.com/en/20170102-god-rid-us-men-feminist-song-shocking-saudi-arabia

Chapter 3

1 'Bill Maher: "If Muslim men could get laid more," there would be no suicide bombers', Glenn Davis, *Mediaite*, 15 April 2011. Link: http://www.mediaite.com/tv/bill-maher-muslim-men-get-laid-suicide-bombers/
2 Reel bad Arabs: How Hollywood vilifies a people, Jack Shaheen, Interlink Publishing, 2012, 617 pages.
3 I wrote an obituary of Omar Sharif in which I showed how he shattered and transcended stereotypes. 'Omar Sharif: Actor without borders', Khaled Diab, *Al Jazeera* English, 11 July 2015. Link: http://www.aljazeera.com/indepth/opinion/2015/07/omar-sharif-actor-borders-150711055745054.html
4 *Reel bad Arabs: How Hollywood vilifies a people,* Jack Shaheen, Interlink Publishing, 2012, p3, 617 pages.
5 Ibid, p530-5
6
7 'I'm an Arab actor who's been asked to audition for the role of terrorist more than 30 times', Amrou Al-Kadhi, *The Independent*, 23 February 2017. Link: http://www.independent.co.uk/voices/oscars-la-la-land-moonlight-arab-muslim-actor-audition-terrorist-i-am-done-a7595261.html
8 'Middle Eastern Acting School', Maz Jobrani, *Dean of Comedy*, 28 April 2013. Link: https://www.youtube.com/watch?v=2mapDelnxXw
9 'Trump fans urge Oscars boycott: 'Put the lying, socialist perverts out of business', Daniel Nussbaum, *Breitbart News*, 26 February 2017. Link: http://www.breitbart.com/big-hollywood/2017/02/26/trump-fans-urge-oscars-boycott/
10 'See the entire history of the Oscars diversity problem in one chart', Eliza Berman and David Johnson, *Time Labs*, 20 January 2016. Link: http://labs.time.com/story/oscars-diversity/
11 'Moonlight is a remarkable achievement in filmmaking', Alissa Wilkinson, *Vox*, 27 February 2017. Link: http://www.vox.com/culture/2017/2/27/14748332/moonlight-best-picture-why-it-won
12 'Fox News' Tucker Carlson is already blaming political correctness for 'Moonlight' Oscar', Zak Cheney Rice, *Mic*, 27 February 2017. Link: https://mic.com/articles/169726/fox-news-tucker-carlson-is-already-blaming-political-correctness-for-moonlight-oscar#.X2z45pZQr
13 '9/11, Stealth Jihad and Obama', Rohini Desilva, Xlibris Corporation, 2012, p91, 440 pages.
14 'Europe's rape epidemic: Western women will be sacrificed at the altar of mass migration', Anne-Marie Waters, *Breitbart News*, 6 October 2015. Link: http://www.breitbart.com/london/2015/10/06/europes-rape-epidemic-western-women-will-be-sacrificed-at-the-alter-of-mass-migration/

15 'The case for banning white male Americans from America', Ben Mathis-Lilley, *Slate*, 6 March 2017. Link: http://www.slate.com/blogs/the_slatest/2017/03/06/white_u_s_men_should_be_banned_by_trump_administration_logic.html

16 'Sexual harassment 'at epidemic levels' in UK universities', David Batty, Sally Weale and Caroline Bannock, *The Guardian*, 5 March 2017. Link: https://www.theguardian.com/education/2017/mar/05/students-staff-uk-universities-sexual-harassment-epidemic

17 'Why do they hate us?', Mona Eltahawy, *Foreign Policy*, 23 April 2012. Link: http://foreignpolicy.com/2012/04/23/why-do-they-hate-us/

18 Official website for season nine: https://www.lbcgroup.tv/watch/34035/%D8%A7%D9%84%D8%AD%D9%84%D9%82%D8%A9-24/ar

19 'Syrian soap opera captivates Arab world,' Dalia Nammari, Associated Press, 12 October 2007. Link: http://www.washingtonpost.com/wp-dyn/content/article/2007/10/12/AR2007101200238.html

20 'Desirable masculinity/femininity and nostalgia of the "Anti-Modern": Bab el-Hara television series as a site of production', Zeina Zaatari, *Sexuality and Culture*, Volume 19, Issue 1, March 2015, p16-36.

21 *The English: A Portrait of a People*, Jeremy Paxman, Overlook Press, 2001, p147, 309 pages.

22 'The girl who ran away to fight ISIS', Lara Whyte, *Broadly*, 25 May 2016. Link: https://broadly.vice.com/en_us/article/joanna-palani-syria-iraq-ran-away-fight-isis

23 'Many Kurdish women join Peshmerga forces to escape abusive marriages or other forms of repression', *Ekurd Daily*, 13 March 2015. Link: http://ekurd.net/many-kurdish-women-join-peshmerga-forces-to-escape-abusive-marriages-2015-03-13

24 'Self-immolations on the rise among Iraqi Kurdish women', Laurene Daycard, *Al Monitor*, 15 March 2017. Link: http://www.al-monitor.com/pulse/originals/2017/03/immolations-iraq-kurdistan-women-violence.html#ixzz4kb3ZHffp

25 'مسلسل «يتربى في عزو» يحيى الفخراني والطاهر جمدى وأبو عمير قرة امرداما التي تصنعها جاذبية «النجم» جهاد الحواد، جريدة المستقبل، 23 سبتمبر 2007. http://www.almustaqbal.com/v4/Article.aspx?Type=np&Articleid=252991

26 'بعدما أصاب بامجموعة هموم الدهشة. يحيى الفخراني لم يشخ دور الرجل مغر خوجة على المألوف، اكتوبر2007 24 الحالية، الحميع، عبد السميع دبع محمود محم

27 'قيادى فلسفى: مسلسل «يومياتى وانيس» محمد صالح، في الأخبار، 22 أبريل 2013 بامتياز»،

28 *Youmiyat Wanis* ran for eight seasons, between 1994 and 2013.

29 'Soap opera upends traditional Arab gender roles', Charlene Gubash, NBC News, 31 July 2008. Link: http://worldblog.nbcnews.com/_news/2008/07/31/4376465-soap-opera-upends-traditional-arab-gender-roles

30 'Dr George Habash address to PFLP Sixth Convention – June 2000', PFLP official site, 20 June 2000. See: http://pflp.ps/english/2000/06/dr-george-habash-address-to-pflp-sixth-convention-june-2000/

31 Traditionally, Arabs call themselves and are called by others 'Abu' or 'Umm' their eldest son, even if he is not the eldest child. A daughter's name is normally only used when there are no male offspring. In that regard, Amiry's father was exceptional. He had a son, but used his oldest daughter's name.

32 'Hero Ibrahim Ahmad: The original female Peshmerga', Tanya Goudsouzian, *Al Jazeera*, 29 October 2015. Link: http://www.aljazeera.com/programmes/women-make-change/2015/10/hero-ibrahim-ahmad-original-female-peshmerga-151027111035570.html

33 'Epidemiology of female sexual castration in Cairo, Egypt', Mohamed Badawi, First International Symposium on Circumcision, 1-2 March 1989.

34 Esam wrote about the dispute, in Arabic, here: http://shababeknaaa.blogspot. com/2013/05/blog-post_5635.html

35 'Male feminist pigs?', Khaled Diab, *The Guardian*, 29 April 2008. Link: https://www. theguardian.com/commentisfree/2008/apr/29/malefeministpigs

36 For an example see: http://blog.iblamethepatriarchy.com/2008/04/30/obnoxious-feminst-korner/

37 'Arab men for equal rights and modernity', KVINFO, 28 September 2015. Link: http:// kvinfo.org/web-magazine/arab-men-fight-equal-rights-and-modernity

38 *Averroes on Plato's 'Republic'*, English translation by Ralph Lerner, Cornell University Press, 1974, first treatise, p59, 176 pages.

39 *Ibid, p58*

40 'Ibn Rushd's (Averroes)' views on women', Nadia Harhash, *Ibn Rushd Magazine*, Issue 16, winter 2014/5. Link: http://www.ibn-rushd.org/typo3/cms/magazine/16th-issue-winter-20142015/nadia-harbash/

41 'Arab men for equal rights and modernity', KVINFO, 28 September 2015. Link: http:// kvinfo.org/web-magazine/arab-men-fight-equal-rights-and-modernity

42 For more on the guardianship system, see: *Boxed In*, Human Rights Watch, July 2016, 102 pages.

43 'Saudi Arabia: Where fathers rule and courts oblige', Human Rights Watch, 18 October 2010. Link: https://www.hrw.org/news/2010/10/18/saudi-arabia-where-fathers-rule-and-courts-oblige

44 'Waleed Abu al-Khair, imprisoned in Saudi Arabia for defending human rights', Amnesty Internation, 9 June 2016. Link: https://www.amnesty.org.uk/saudi-arabia-free-human-rights-lawyer-waleed-abulkhair-abu-al-khair

45 'Unveiling Arab men', Ahmed Qadri, *Le Monde Diplomatique*, 19 December 2013. Link: http://mondediplo.com/outsidein/unveiling-arab-men

46 *The New Arab Man: Emergent Masculinities, Technologies, and Islam in the Middle East*, Marcia Claire Inhorn, Princeton University Press, 2012, p2, 404 pages.

47 'CEO of trillion-dollar company resigned after his daughter told him how much he has missed', Laura Stampler, *Time*, 26 September 2014. Link: http://time.com/3432717/ ceo-of-trillion-dollar-company-resigned-after-his-daughter-told-him-how-much-he-has-missed/

Chapter 4

1 'Sex torment drove him nuts', Leonard Greene, *New York Post*, 30 December 2009. Link: http://nypost.com/2009/12/30/sex-torment-drove-him-nuts/

2 'Ann Coulter: Mid East migrants 'terrifying,' can't 'stop themselves from raping masses of women'', Justin Haskins, *TheBlaze*, 18 March 2017. Link: http://www.theblaze. com/news/2017/03/18/ann-coulter-mid-east-migrants-terrifying-cant-stop-themselves-from-raping-masses-of-women/

3 'Ann Coulter: Women who say they are raped are just "girls trying to get attention"', Joanna Rothkopf, *Salon*, 18 December 2014. Link: http://www.salon.com/2014/12/18/ ann_coulter_women_who_say_they_are_raped_are_just_girls_trying_to_get_ attention/

4   *United in Hate: The Left's Romance with Tyranny and Terror*, Jamie Glazov, WND Books, 2009, p113, 264 pages.
5   *United in Hate: The Left's Romance with Tyranny and Terror*, Jamie Glazov, WND Books, 2009, p120, 264 pages.
6   *The Poison Tree – Planted and Grown in Egypt*, Marwa Rakha, Malamih Publishing House, 2008, 184 pages.
7   The song is available on YouTube at https://www.youtube.com/watch?v=8JSnFy82lgE
8   The full text of the English translation of this classic can be found at: *The Story of Layla and Majnun*, translated by Dr R Gelpke, Bruno Cassirer Ltd, 1966, 221 pages. Link: https://archive.org/stream/TheStoryOfLaylaAndMajnun/Leyla%20and%20Majnun_djvu.txt
9   'Inside the strange saga of a Cairo novelist imprisoned for obscenity', Jonathan Guyer, *Rolling Stone*, 24 February 2017. Link: http://www.rollingstone.com/culture/features/cairo-novelist-imprisoned-for-obscenity-in-egypt-tells-story-w468084
10 '#BBCtrending: The dress that shocked the Arab world', *BBC Trending*, 19 November 2014. Link: http://www.bbc.com/news/blogs-trending-30104554
11 'Haifa Wehbe to the savage critics of her "Breathing You In" music vid: "You're #Vulgar"!', *AlBawaba*, 19 April 2015. Link: http://www.albawaba.com/entertainment/haifa-wehbe-savage-critics-her-breathing-you-music-vid-youre-vulgar-683830
12 'Homage to a Belly-Dancer', Edward Said, *The London Review of Books*, 13 September 1990. Link: https://www.lrb.co.uk/v12/n17/edward-said/homage-to-a-belly-dancer
13 *All the Pasha's Men*, Khaled Fahmy, American University in Cairo Press, 2002, p228-30, 334 pages.
14 *The Cairo Trilogy*, Naguib Mahfouz, translated by William H Maynard, Penguin Random House, 2001, originally published 1956-7, 1,368 pages.
15 *The Hidden Face of Eve: Women in the Arab World*, Nawal El Saadawi, translated by Sherif Hetata, Zed Books, 2007, first published in Arabic in 1977, p202, 325 pages.
16 'First kiss', Tatia Pilieva, 10 March 2014. Link: https://www.youtube.com/watch?v=IpbDHxCV29A
17 'First kiss parody (the Egyptian way)', Handmade Studios, 26 March 2014. Link: https://www.youtube.com/watch?v=sZRj43yBusg
18 For example, here is a list of 10 Egyptian films which deal with sexual frustration. '10 Egyptian films that are actually about sexual frustration', Mona Daoud, *Cairo Scene*, 15 August 2015. Link: http://www.cairoscene.com/ArtsAndCulture/10-egyptian-films-on-sexual-frustration
19 For a summary of the film, see: 'Egypt's cinematic gems: 'Film Thakafy'', Jahd Khalil, *MadaMasr*, 15 March 2014.
20 *Sexual Ethics and Islam: Feminist Reflections on Qur'an, Hadith and Jurisprudence*, Kecia Ali, OneWorld Publications, 2015, p77-8, 320 pages.
21 *Sex and the Citadel*, Shereen El Feki, Chatto & Windus, p111, 345 pages.
22 *Vierges? La nouvelle sexualité des Tunisiennes*, Nédra Ben Smail, Céres édition, 2012, p13-40, 187 pages.
23 *Ibid*, p76.
24 'To look or not to look', Najla Moussa, *Daily News Egypt*, 31 January 2006. Link: http://www.dailynewsegypt.com/2006/01/31/to-look-or-not-to-look/
25 'Donald Trump: 'I think Islam hates us'', Theodore Schleifer, *CNN*, 10 March 2016. Link: http://edition.cnn.com/2016/03/09/politics/donald-trump-islam-hates-us/

26 'Sex, masturbation and the myths within my Islamic family', Shahamat Hussain, *Youth Ki Awaaz*, 9 February 2017. Link: https://www.youthkiawaaz.com/2017/02/sex-masturbation-and-myths-i-grew-up-within-my-islamic-family/

27 'You NEED to talk about sex and it should not be the great Indian taboo word', Rajkanya Mahapatra, *Youth Ki Awaaz*, 20 October 2013. Link: https://www.youthkiawaaz.com/2013/10/need-talk-sex-great-indian-taboo-word-reminding-yet/

28 'Why (Muslim) sex ed can't wait until marriage', Zoha Qamar, *Huffington Post*, 20 May 2016. Link: http://www.huffingtonpost.com/zoha-qamar/why-muslim-sex-ed-cant-wa_b_10065254.html

29 *One Thousand and One Nights*, Hanan Al-Shaykh, A&C Black, 2011, 288 pages.

30 'The humanist message hidden amid the violence of One Thousand and One Nights', Joe Fassler, *The Atlantic*, 25 June 2013. Link: https://www.theatlantic.com/entertainment/archive/2013/06/the-humanist-message-hidden-amid-the-violence-of-i-one-thousand-and-one-nights-i/277210/

31 *A Daughter of Isis: The Early Life of Nawal El Saadawi*, Nawal El Saadawi, translated by Sherif Hetata, Zed Books, 2013, 368 pages.

32 *The Hidden Face of Eve: Women in the Arab World*, Nawal El Saadawi, translated by Sherif Hetata, Zed Books, 2007, first published in Arabic in 1977, p43, 325 pages.

33 'Sex and the ayatollahs', M Cist, *The Guardian*, 10 June 2008. Link: https://www.theguardian.com/commentisfree/2008/jun/10/iran.middleeast

34 'Without sex ed, young Tunisians have to get by on their own', Rihab Boukhayatia, *Huffington Post Maghreb*, 31 August 2015. Link: http://www.huffingtonpost.com/2015/08/31/sex-ed-tunisia_n_8066834.html

35 'Like a virgin (mother): analysis of data from a longitudinal, US population representative sample survey', Amy H Herring et al, *British Medical Journal*, Christmas 2013. Link: http://www.bmj.com/content/347/bmj.f7102

36 'First night sex كيف تستعدان للليلة الزفاف؟', Alyaa Gad, Love Matters, YouTube, 9 December 2013. Link: https://www.youtube.com/watch?v=wNhFbvvAvek

37 'Meet the Egyptian YouTube star who talks about sex', *France 24*, 12 April 2015. Link: http://observers.france24.com/en/20151204-egyptian-youtube-star-sex-education-videos

38 'Fatwa – oral sex', Mufti Shafiq Jakhura, *Darul Ihsan Islamic Centre*. Link: http://www.darulihsan.com/index.php/q-a/fatwa-q-a/nikah-marriage/item/3386-fatwa-oral-sex

39 عن الكدتورة هبه قطب بطب', Heba Kotb's official website, Link: http://www.hebakotb.net/About.aspx

40 'المصريون لايت. شاهد..أغرب 10 نصائح جنسية لـ»قطب بطب«', Link: https://almesryoon.com/story/801422/%D8%B4%D8%A7%D9%87%D8%AF-%D8%A3%D8%BA%D8%B1%D8%A8-10-%D9%86%D8%B5%D8%A7%D8%A6%D8%AD-%D8%AC%D9%86%D8%B3%D9%8A%D8%A9-%D9%84%D9%80-%D9%87%D8%A8%D8%A9-%D9%82%D8%B7%D8%A8

41 'Sex and the married Muslim', Tracy Clark-Flory, *Salon*, 6 June 2007. Link: http://www.salon.com/2007/06/06/kotb/

42 'Can psychiatrists really "cure" homosexuality?', *Scientific American*, Thomas Maier, 22 April 2009. Link: https://www.scientificamerican.com/article/homosexuality-cure-masters-johnson/

43 'Muslim sexologist spices up Arab television', *Fox News*, 28 January 2007. Link: http://www.foxnews.com/story/2007/01/28/muslim-sexologist-spices-up-arab-television.html

44 *Between Yesterday and Today*, Hassan al-Banna, Prelude, first published in 1936, p7, 14 pages.

45 Ghazali's *Incoherence of the Philosophers* played a central role in diminishing the sway of Neoplatonic philosophers. A century later, Ibn Rushd (Averroes) penned the *Incoherence of the Incoherence* to ridicule Ghazali's central tenets, including Ghazali fanciful idea there were no causal effects and that what appeared to be natural laws were the result of God intervening directly in each and every action.

46 *Marriage and Sexuality in Islam*, original title 'Adab an-Nikah', Imam al-Ghazali, translated by Madelain Farah, Islamic Book Trust, 2012, p126, 177 pages.

47 'Let's talk about sex, Ali', Lukas Wiesenhutter, *Qantara*, 12 April 2016. Link: https://en.qantara.de/content/islam-and-eroticism-lets-talk-about-sex-ali

48 *Sex und Erotik bei den muslimischen Gelehrten*, Ali Ghandour, Editio Gryphus, 2015, 104 pages.

49 *A Taste of Honey: Sexuality and Erotology in Islam*, Habeeb Akande, Rabaah Publishers, 2015, p26, 352 pages.

50 *Sex and the Citadel*, Shereen El Feki, Chatto & Windus, p53-5, 345 pages.

51 *The Arabian Nights Encyclopedia, Volume 1*, Ulrich Marzolph, Richard van Leeuwen, Hassan Wassouf, ABC-CLIO, 2004, p699-701, 921 pages.

52 *Eros and Sexuality in Islamic Art*, edited by Francesca Leoni and Mika Natif, Ashgate Publishing, 2013, p4-6, 244 pages.

53 *Ibid*, Amy S Landau, p99-100.

54 *Ibid*, Sussan Babaie, p131-3.

55 *Story-Telling Techniques in the Arabian Nights*, David Pinault, Brill, 1992, p141-2, 262 pages.

56 *Encyclopedia of Arabic Literature, Volume 1*

57 *Unspeakable Love: Gay and Lesbian Life in the Middle East*, Brian Whitaker, Saqi, 2011, p30-31, 282 pages.

58 *Encyclopedia of Lesbian Histories and Cultures*, edited by Bonnie Zimmerman, Francesca Canadé Sautman, p51-3, 920 pages.

59 *Abu Nuwas: A Genius of Poetry*, Philip Kennedy, OneWorld Publications, 2012, p28-9, 160 pages.

60 *Ibid*, p27-8.

61 "Being gay in the Islamic State': Men reveal chilling truth about homosexuality under ISIS', Michael Segalov, *The Independent*, 25 August 2015. Link: http://www.independent.co.uk/news/world/middle-east/being-gay-in-the-islamic-state-men-reveal-chilling-truth-about-homosexuality-under-isis-10470894.html

62 'Half of the countries were same-sex acts are prohibited are Islamic; death penalty in 13', Patrick Goodenough, 14 June 2016. Link: http://www.cnsnews.com/news/article/patrick-goodenough/half-countries-where-same-sex-acts-are-prohibited-are-islamic-death

63 *Sexual Ethics and Islam*, Kecia Ali, Oneworld Publications, 2006, p75-85, 217 pages.

64 'This alien legacy – the origins of "sodomy" laws in British colonialism', *Human Rights Watch*, December 2008, 66 pages. Link: https://www.hrw.org/report/2008/12/17/alien-legacy/origins-sodomy-laws-british-colonialism

65 "Sodomy' laws show survival of colonial injustice', *Human Rights Watch*, 17 December 2008. Link: https://www.hrw.org/news/2008/12/17/sodomy-laws-show-survival-colonial-injustice

66 *A Brief History of the Late Ottoman Empire*, M Şükrü Hanioğlu, Princeton University Press, 2010, 264 pages.

67 'Ahmadinejad: No gays, no oppression of women in Iran', Russell Goldman, *ABC News*, 24 September 2007. Link: http://abcnews.go.com/US/story?id=3642673

68 It is not clear what the difference is between "homosexual" and "gay and lesbian", as the latter are subsets of the former.

69 *Desiring Arabs*, Joseph A Massad, University of Chicago Press, 2008, p162-3, 472 pages.

70 *Unspeakable Love: Gay and Lesbian Life in the Middle East*, Brian Whitaker, Saqi Books, 2011, p104-107, 282 pages.

71 *Orientalism*, Edward W Said, Penguin Books edition, 2006, first published in 1978, p109, 416 pages.

72 'Sexual orientation, controversy, and science', J Michael Bailey, Paul L Vasey, Lisa M Diamond, S Marc Breedlove, Eric Vilain, Marc Epprecht, *Psychological Science in the Public Interest*, Association for Psychological Science, vol 17(2) 2016, p45-101.

73 'Do animals exhibit homosexuality?' Arash Fereydooni, *Yale Scientific*, 14 March 2012. Link: http://www.yalescientific.org/2012/03/do-animals-exhibit-homosexuality/

74 *Handbook of Sexuality-Related Measures*, Clive M Davis, William L Yarber, Robert Bauserman, Sage, 1998, 608 pages.

75 *Abu Nuwas: A Genius of Poetry*, Philip Kennedy, OneWorld Publications, 2012, p22-3, 160 pages.

76 'Book review – Desiring Arabs', Stephanie Tara Schwartz, *Arab Media & Society*, issue 7, winter 2009. Link: http://www.arabmediasociety.com/?article=708

77 'Testimony of Oscar Wilde', Famous Trials by Professor Douglas O Linder. Link: http://www.famous-trials.com/wilde/342-wildetestimony

78 'The Law in England, 1290-1885', Fordham University. Link: http://sourcebooks.fordham.edu/halsall/pwh/englaw.asp

79 , Human Rights *In a time of torture: The assault on justice in Egypt's crackdown on homosexual conduct* Watch, 2004, p22-41, 144 pages.

80 'Outcry over Queen boat trial', Rana Allam, *Al Ahram Weekly*, 23-29 August 2001. Link: http://weekly.ahram.org.eg/Archive/2001/548/eg6.htm

81 'Egypt steps up anti-gay campaign', Bonnie Eslinger and Hossam Bahgat, *San Francisco Chronicle*, 18 July 2001. Link: http://www.sfgate.com/news/article/Egypt-steps-up-anti-gay-campaign-52-men-face-2898806.php

82 'Explaining Egypt's targeting of gays', Hossam Bahgat, Middle East Research and Information Project (MERIP), 23 July 2001. Link: http://www.merip.org/mero/mero072301

83 Official site: www.eipr.org

84 For more on the founder of *Al Ahram Weekly*, see: 'Remembering Hosny Guindy', *Al Ahram Weekly*, 15-21 August 2013. Link: http://weekly.ahram.org.eg/News/3667.aspx

85 'Convicted before the fact', *Al Ahram Weekly*, 20-26 March 2003. Link: http://weekly.ahram.org.eg/archive/2003/630/eg9.htm

86 'Cultures of denial', Khaled Diab, *Al Ahram Weekly*, 4-10 May 2006. Link: http://weekly.ahram.org.eg/Archive/2006/793/cu5.htm

87 'ﺱﻄﻠﻗ ﺖﻔﻌﻴﺸ ﻟﺎﻀﻣﺍﺭﻯ', ﺩﺍﺐﻋ ﺩﺍﻴﻟﺍ ﺪﻴﻤﺤﻟﺍ, MadaMasr, ١٧ ﻡﺎﻳﻭ ٢٠١٥. http://www.
madamasr.com/ar/2015/05/17/opinion/%D9%85%D8%AC%D8%AA%D9%85%D
8%B9/%D8%B3%D9%8F%D9%84%D8%B7%D8%A9-%D8%AA%D9%81%D8
%AA%D9%8A%D8%B4%D9%90-%D8%A7%D9%84%D8%B6%D9%85%D8%
A7%D8%A6%D8%B1/
88 'Homosexuality is not a crime', Dalia Abd El-Hameed, EIPR, May 2015. Link: http://
www.madamasr.com/en/2016/05/17/opinion/society/homosexuality-is-not-a-crime/
89 'Defendants acquitted in 'Ramses bathhouse' case', *MadaMasr*, 12 January 2015. Link:
http://www.madamasr.com/en/2015/01/12/news/u/defendants-acquitted-in-ramses-
bathhouse-case/
90 'Mona Iraqi acquitted in Ramses bath house trial', Shaimaa Raafat, *Daily News Egypt*,
19 January 2016. Link: http://www.dailynewsegypt.com/2016/01/19/mona-iraqi-
acquitted-in-ramses-bath-house-trial/
91 'Turkey police fire rubber bullets at banned Gay Pride parade', *AFP*, 27 June 2016.
Link: http://www.telegraph.co.uk/news/2016/06/27/turkey-police-fire-rubber-bullets-
at-banned-gay-pride-parade/
92 'Albania 'to approve gay marriage'', Mark Lowen, *BBC News*, 30 July 2009. Link: http://
news.bbc.co.uk/2/hi/8177544.stm
93 'Gay marriage threat worries Albanian conservatives', Fatjona Mejdini, *Balkan Insight*,
11 July 2016.
Link: http://www.balkaninsight.com/en/article/albanian-conservatives-see-a-gay-hoax-
in-the-judicial-reform-07-08-2016#sthash.czuXm35t.dpuf
94 'Laws, Tunisia – Homosexuality, sodomy', GayLawNet. Link: http://www.gaylawnet.
com/laws/tn.htm#sodomy
95 'Tunisia: Men prosecuted for homosexuality', *Human Rights Watch*, 29 March 2016.
Link: https://www.hrw.org/news/2016/03/29/tunisia-men-prosecuted-homosexuality
96 'Is homophobia at all-time high in Tunisia?', Conor McCormick-Cavanagh, *Al Monitor*,
4 May 2016.
97 'Tunisia medical council bans forced anal tests for homosexuality after nearly decade of
abuse', Will Worley, *The Independent*, 12 April 2017. Link: http://www.independent.
co.uk/news/world/africa/tunisia-medical-council-anal-tests-homosexuality-abuse-gay-
rights-men-lgbt-document-lgbt-a7680631.html
98 'Dirigente islamista dice no castigarán alcohol, ateísmo ni homosexualidad', *EFE*,
22 October 2011. Link: http://www.elespectador.com/noticias/economia/dirigente-
islamista-dice-no-castigaran-alcohol-ateismo-articulo-307038
99 'Moroccans stage 'kiss-in' in support of arrested teens', *France 24*, 13 October 2013.
Link: http://www.france24.com/en/20131013-morocco-protest-stage-kiss-in-support-
arrested-teens-picture-facebook-kissing-islam
100 'Urfi marriage, an Egyptian version of cohabitation?', Ikran Eum, *Al-Raida*, Vol XXI-
XXII, Summer/Fall 2004-5, p64-9.
101 'Landmark paternity case highlights dangers of urfi marriage', *IRIN*, 5 June 2006. Link:
http://www.irinnews.org/report/26954/egypt-landmark-paternity-case-highlights-
dangers-urfi-marriage
102 'Temporary marriage' on the rise in post-revolutionary Tunisia', Imed Bensaied, *France
24*, 2 February 2012. Link: http://www.france24.com/en/20120131-urfi-marriage-
trend-seen-among-tunisian-university-students

103 'Pakistani model Qandeel Baloch killed by brother after friends' taunts – mother', *AFP*, 28 July 2016. Link: https://www.theguardian.com/world/2016/jul/28/pakistani-model-qandeel-baloch-killed-by-brother-after-friends-taunts-mother

104 *Murder in the Name of Honour,* Rana Husseini, Oneworld Publications, 2009, 264 pages. I reviewed it for *The Guardian* here: https://www.theguardian.com/commentisfree/2009/may/03/honour-killing

105 'Losing my virginity in Egypt: 6 women who broke the taboo', Mariam Raymone, *Cairo Scene,* 9 February 2016. Link: http://www.cairoscene.com/Interviews/Losing-My-Virginity-in-Egypt-6-Women-Who-Broke-The-Taboo

Chapter 5

1 *Khamr* is the generic Arabic word for an intoxicating beverage, although in the language of the Quran it refers specifically to grape or date wine.

2 'Tunisia – Alcohol consumption: levels and patters', *World Health Organisation*, 2014. Link: http://www.who.int/substance_abuse/publications/global_alcohol_report/profiles/tun.pdf

3 '50 percent of Tunisian students have consumed alcohol and marijuana, new study reports', Emna Guizani, *Tunisia Live*, 7 May 2015. Link: http://www.tunisia-live.net/2015/05/07/50-percent-of-tunisian-students-have-consumed-alcohol-and-marijuana-new-study-reports/

4 'Alcohol consumption high in Tunisia, despite prices', Nadya B'chir, *Al Monitor*, 26 April 2013. Link: http://www.al-monitor.com/pulse/culture/2013/04/alcohol-consumption-increases-tunisia-islamists.html

5 Quran, Surat Muhammad, Chapter 47, Verse 15.

6 'Widespread Calamities Upon Muslims: Causes & Cures', Muhammad Faruq Meeruti, Ilmgate. Link: http://www.ilmgate.org/calamities-upon-muslims-causes-cures/

7 'Science and technology in Islam: Technology and applied sciences', Ahmed Y Al-Hassan, UNESCO, 2001, p65-9, 726 pages.

8 *Between Yesterday and Today*, Hassan al-Banna, 1936, featured in *Critical Perspectives on Islam and the Western World*, Jonathan Johansen, Rosen Publishing Group, 2006, p19-24, 182 pages.

9 *Social Justice in Islam*, Sayyid Qutb, translated by John Hardie and Hamid Algar, first published in 1949, Islamic Publications International, 2000, p194, 352 pages.

10 'Westoxification' was a term coined by the Iranian intellectual Jalal al-e Ahmad. See: http://www.oxfordislamicstudies.com/article/opr/t125/e2501

11 *Abbasid Belles Lettres,* edited by Julia Ashtiany, Cambridge University Press, 1990, p219-26, 517 pages.

12 *Abu Nuwas: A Genius of Poetry*, Philip Kennedy, OneWorld Publications, 2012, p50-3, 160 pages.

13 Surat al-Shur'ara, Chapter 26, verses 224-5.

14 *The First Dynasty of Islam: The Umayyad Caliphate AD 661-750,* GR Hawting, Routledge, 2002, p90-94, 176 pages.

15 *Abu Nuwas: A Genius of Poetry*, Philip Kennedy, OneWorld Publications, 2012, p53, 160 pages.

16 *Abbasid Belles Lettres*, edited by Julia Ashtiany, Cambridge University Press, 1990, p227-35, 517 pages.

17 *Rumi - Past and Present, East and West*, Franklin D Lewis, Oneworld Publication, 2014, p247-8, 712 pages.

18 *Haschish Versus Medieval Muslim Society*, Franz Rosenthal, Brill Archive, 1971, p149, 218 pages.

19 'Day of commemoration of Hafez', *IRIB World Service*, 12 October 2015. Link: http://english.irib.ir/radioculture/iran/history/item/217054-day-of-commemoration-of-hafez

20 *The Sacred Books and Early Literature of the East, Vol VIII: Medieval Persia*, Charles F Horne, Poem translated by William Jones, Parke, Austin, & Lipscomb, 1917, p335-6, 434 pages.

21 'Hafez – an overview', Ehsan Yarshater, *Encyclopaedia Iranica*, Vol XI, Fasc 5, 2002, p 461-5.

22 'France, Iran and the affair of the lunch wine', Adam Gopnik, *The New Yorker*, 29 January 2016. Link: http://www.newyorker.com/news/daily-comment/france-iran-and-the-affair-of-the-lunch-wine

23 *A History of Beer and Brewing*, Ian Spencer Hornsey, Royal Society of Chemistry, 2003, p32-6, 742 pages.

24 *Ancient Wine: The Search for the Origins of Viniculture*, Patrick E McGovern, Princeton University Press, 2003, p14-5, 365 pages.

25 *The History of Ancient and Modern Wines*, Alexander Henderson, Baldwin, Cradock, and Joy, 1824, p262-3, 408 pages.

26 'Global status report on alcohol and health 2014', World Health Organisation, 2014, p98, p297, p338, 376 pages.

27 *Cairo, the City Victorious*, Max Rodenbeck, Pan Macmillan, 1998, 395 pages.

28 *Avicenna*, LE Goodman, Routledge, 2013, p14, 255 pages.

29 *Avicenna's Medicine: A New Translation of the 11th-Century Canon with Practical Applications for Integrative Health Care*, Ibn Sina, translated by Mones Abu-Asab, Hakima Amri, Marc S Micozzi, Bear & Co, p264-66, 480 pages.

30 'Liquid fire', *The Economist*, 18 December 2003. Link: http://www.economist.com/node/2281757

31 'Seven die in Iran after drinking homemade alcohol', Thomas Erdbrink, *New York Times*, 3 June 2013. Link: http://www.nytimes.com/2013/06/03/world/middleeast/seven-die-in-iran-after-drinking-homemade-alcohol.html

32 'Sudan's date-gin brewers thrive despite Sharia', Lucy Fleming, *BBC News*, 29 April 2010. Link: http://news.bbc.co.uk/2/hi/africa/8638670.stm

33 'Whip awaiting alcohol drinkers and dealers, Sudan president warns', *Sudan Tribune*, 26 March 2010. Link: http://www.sudantribune.com/spip.php?article34548

34 *Medieval Islamic Civilisation: An Encyclopedia*, edited by Josef W Meri, Gerald R Hawting, Routledge, 2005, p847-848, 1,088 pages.

35 *The Islamic World*, edited by Andrew Rippin, Elton L Daniel, Routledge, 2013, p73-4, 704 pages.

36 *Coptic Identity and Ayyubid Politics in Egypt, 1218-1250*, Kurt J Werthmuller, American University in Cairo Press, 2010, p75-77, 190 pages.

37 *Charlemagne, Muhammad, and the Arab Roots of Capitalism*, Gene W Heck, Walter de Gruyter, 2006, p169-72, 381 pages.

38 Surat al-Nahl. Chapter 16, verse 67.

39 Surat al-Nisa'. Chapter 4, verse 43.

40 Surat al-Baqarah. Chapter 2, verse 219.

41 Surat al-Maidah. Chapter 5, verse 90.

42 *Doubt in Islamic Law*, Intisar A Rabb, Cambridge University Press, 2014, p144-8, 432 pages.

43 'Drinking liquor without getting drunk not sinful: Islamic scholar', *Egyptian Streets*, 13 February 2017. Link: https://egyptianstreets.com/2017/02/13/drinking-liquor-without-getting-drunk-not-sinful-islamic-scholar/

44 'Why alcohol is prohibited in Islam', Azizas Khan, *The Review of Religions*, April 2016. Link: http://www.reviewofreligions.org/12519/why-alcohol-is-prohibited-in-islam/

45 'Possible health benefits of alcohol', Harvard TH Chan School of Public Health. Link: https://www.hsph.harvard.edu/nutritionsource/alcohol-full-story/#possible_health_benefits

46 'To your health!: Re-examining the health benefits of moderate alcohol use', Bisma Ali Sayed and Michael T French, *Social Science and Medicine*, Vol 167, Elsevier, October 2016, p20-28.

47 'Key findings on alcohol cConsumption and a variety of health outcomes from the Nurses' Health Study', Elizabeth Mostofsky *et al*, *The American Journal of Public Health*, Vol 106, No 9, September 2016. Link: http://ajph.aphapublications.org/doi/pdf/10.2105/AJPH.2016.303336

48 *Getting High: Marijuana through the Ages*, John Charles Chasteen, Rowman and Littlefield, 2016, p77-102, 168 pages.

49 *Haschish Versus Medieval Muslim Society*, Franz Rosenthal, Brill Archive, 1971, p163, 218 pages.

50 'Marijuana', National Institute on Drug Abuse, February 2017. Link: https://www.drugabuse.gov/publications/drugfacts/marijuana

51 'Health effects of cigarette smoking', Centres for Disease Control and Prevention. Link: https://www.cdc.gov/tobacco/data_statistics/fact_sheets/health_effects/effects_cig_smoking/

52 'Khat drug profile', European Monitoring Centre for Drugs and Drug Addiction, Link: http://www.emcdda.europa.eu/publications/drug-profiles/khat

53 'Khat cultivation fuels food crisis in Yemen', Adel Aldaghbashy, *SciDevNet*, 3 January 2017. Link: http://www.scidev.net/global/farming/news/khat-cultivation-food-crisis-yemen.html

54 *Food and Foodways of Medieval Cairenes*, BRILL, 2011, p491-2, 626 pages.

55 *Ibn Taymiyya and his Times*, edited by Yossef Rapoport and Shahab Ahmed, Caterina Bori, Oxford University Press, 2010, p23-52, 400 pages.

56 *Food and Foodways of Medieval Cairenes*, BRILL, 2011, p515-518, 626 pages.

57 'WikiLeaks cables: Saudi princes throw parties boasting drink, drugs and sex', Heather Brooke, *The Guardian*, 7 December 2010. Link: https://www.theguardian.com/world/2010/dec/07/wikileaks-cables-saudi-princes-parties

58 'مغر التحريم ومايير صناعة الخمور في تزايد بالممالك العربية السعودية, ز ع, ٢٠١٣. https://www.radiosawa.com/a/ksa-alcohol-industry/220634.html مارس,٢٢ اوس ويدار, فداهلا نيدلا

59 *An Account of the Manners and Customs of the Modern Egyptians*, Edward William Lane, J Murray, 1860, p94, 619 pages.

60 *Ibid*, p149-50.

61 *Food and Foodways of Medieval Cairenes*, BRILL, 2011, p499, 626 pages.
62 *Food and Foodways of Medieval Cairenes*, BRILL, 2011, p455-550, 626 pages.
63 'Egypt's beer industry toasts long history', Omar Foda, *Al Monitor*, 3 November 2014. Link: http://www.al-monitor.com/pulse/originals/2014/10/beer-egypt-stella-heineken-pyramids.html
64 'Stella's Grandpa 1897-1947', Samir Raafat, *Egyptian Mail*, 14 June 1997.

Chapter 6

1 *Merriam-Webster's Encyclopedia of World Religions*, edited by Wendy Doniger, Merriam-Webster, 1999, p406, 1,181 pages.
2 For a brief biography of William Miller, see: https://www.britannica.com/biography/William-Miller
3 For the Adventists' own view of the Great Disappointment, see: 'Great Disappointment remembered 170 years on', Andrew McChesney, *Adventist Review*, 22 October 201. Link: http://www.adventistreview.org/church-news/great-disappointment-remembered-170-years-on
4 'End times pastor Tom Horn: Donald Trump could be the messiah or his forerunner', Brian Tashman, 15 December 2016. Link: http://www.salon.com/2016/12/15/end-times-pastor-tom-horn-donald-trump-could-be-the-messiah-or-his-forerunner_partner/
5 Matthew 19:23-26
6 *The Life of Muhammad*, Muhammad Husayn Haykal, first published 1933, American Trust Publications, 1976, p27-8, 716 pages.
7 Surat Hud, Chapter 11 of the Quran
8 *The A to Z of Prophets in Islam and Judaism*, Scott B. Noegel and Brannon M Wheeler, Scarecrow Press, 2010, p182-3, 550 pages.
9 Surat Hud, Chapter 11 of the Quran
10 *The Prophet Muhammad: A Biography*, Barnaby Rogerson, Paulist Press, 2003, p75-8, 240 pages.
11 *Encyclopedia of Islamic Civilization and Religion*, Edited by Ian Richard Netton, Routledge, 2013, p680-1, 872 pages
12 *Divine Word and Prophetic Word in Early Islam*, William Albert Graham, Walter de Gruyter, 1977, p164-5, 266 pages.
13 *Bandits, Prophets, and Messiahs: Popular Movements at the Time of Jesus*, Richard A Horsley, A&C Black, 1999, p135, 271 pages.
14 *Ibid*, p153.
15 *The Wars of the Jews*, Flavius Josephus, 2.259
16 *Bandits, Prophets, and Messiahs: Popular Movements at the Time of Jesus*, Richard A Horsley, A&C Black, 1999, p171, 271 pages.
17 *Ibid*, p135-89.
18 *The Wars of the Jews*, Flavius Josephus, 2.57-59.
19 *Ibid*, 2.433.
20 *Ibid*, 2.433-450.
21 'British grandfather Mohammad Asghar awaits execution for blasphemy in Pakistan', *Amnesty International UK*, 2 December 2014. Link: https://www.amnesty.org.uk/mohammad-asghar-pakistan-blasphemy-death-row

22 'Family of Mohammad Asghar: 'We just want our father home'', Homa Khaleeli, *The Guardian*, 4 October 2014. Link: https://www.theguardian.com/world/2014/oct/04/family-mohammad-asghar-pakistan-blasphemy-laws

23 'Blasphemy laws are deadly serious – we must stand up for Mohammed Asghar', Frankie Boyle, *The Guardian*, 29 September 2014. Link: https://www.theguardian.com/commentisfree/2014/sep/29/stand-up-for-blasphemers-like-mohammed-asghar-frankie-boyle

24 This was the situation as of March 2016, according to reports in the Scottish media.

25 'Pakistani Muslim man accused of blasphemy killed after release from jail', *The Associated Press*, 8 January 2015.

26 For a short biography, see: 'Al-Mahdi', Richard Leslie Hill, *Encyclopaedia Britannica*. Link: https://www.britannica.com/biography/al-Mahdi-Sudanese-religious-leader

27 For a short biography, see: 'Mīrzā Ghulām Aḥmad', *Encyclopaedia Britannica*. https://www.britannica.com/biography/Mirza-Ghulam-Ahmad

28 'Constitution (Second Amendment) Act, 1974', *Gazette of Pakistan*, Extraordinary, Part I, 21 September 1974.

29 'Ordinance No. XX of 1984', *Gazette of Pakistan*, 26 April 1984.

30 For a detailed account of the Ahmadi post-crucifixion story of Jesus, see: *Jesus in India*, By Mirza Ghulam Ahmad, first edition 1908, republished by Islam International Publications Ltd, 2003, 160 pages.

31 The Ahmadiyyah position on apostasy is outlined here: http://www.wikiahmadiyya.org/beliefs/apostasy-in-islam

32 The Ahmadiyyah position on blasphemy is outlined here: http://www.wikiahmadiyya.org/beliefs/blasphemy-in-islam

33 *Encyclopedia of Islam*, Juan Eduardo Campo, Infobase Publishing, 2009, p264, 750 pages.

34 'Muslim movements and schisms. A study of the Ahmadiyya movement.', anonymous and undated. Link: http://www.answering-islam.org/Gilchrist/Vol1/9c.html

35 'Do Christians and Muslims Worship the Same God?', Albert Mohler, Decision Magazine, 1 December 2013. Link: http://billygraham.org/decision-magazine/december-2013/do-christians-and-muslims-worship-the-same-god/

36 The Alexandria-based priest Arius (256–336) believed that Jesus was the Son of God but differed from the proto-Orthodox view in that he and his followers did not believe in the Trinity and held that Christ was created, or begotten, by God and was not an equal or eternal manifestation of the Lord. For his blasphemy, Arius was exiled, then allowed to return, whereupon he suffered, the "divine retribution" of excreting his innards until he died, according to the gory story related by his enemy Socrates Scholasticus in his *The Ecclesiastical Histories of Socrates Scholasticus*.

37 *The Muslim Jesus: Sayings and stories in Islamic literature*, Tarif Khalidi, Harvard University Press, 2001, p12, 245 pages.

38 Surat al-Ma'idah (Chapter 5, Verse 116).

39 *Following Muhammad: Rethinking Islam in the Contemporary World*, Carl W Ernst, University of North Carolina Press, 2003, p15, 244 pages.

40 Surat Maryam (Chapter 19, Verse 19).

41 This appears more than once in the Quran, including in Surat al-Nisa (Chapter 4, Verse 171).

42 Surat al-Tahrim (Chapter 66, Verse 12).

43 Surat al-Nisa (Chapter 4, Verse 157) posits that those who believed they had executed Jesus "did not kill him, nor did they crucify him; but so it was made to appear to them." This verse has been interpreted to mean that either the Romans were deceived into thinking they crucified Jesus or they crucified someone else instead, either a common criminal or even Judas.

44 *Following Muhammad: Rethinking Islam in the Contemporary World*, Carl W Ernst, University of North Carolina Press, 2003, p14-16, 244 pages.

45 Franklin Graham, Facebook post dated 5 February 2015. See: https://www.facebook.com/FranklinGraham/posts/859293290793520

46 At the National Prayer Breakfast on 5 February 2015, Obama said: "And lest we get on our high horse and think this is unique to some other place, remember that during the Crusades and the Inquisition, people committed terrible deeds in the name of Christ. In our home country, slavery and Jim Crow all too often was justified in the name of Christ."

47 'Graham: 'Assume' Obama is Christian', Tim Mak, *Politico*, 21 February 2012. See: http://www.politico.com/story/2012/02/graham-assume-obama-is-christian-073110

48 'Jesus in Baghdad', Steven Waldman, *Slate*, 11 April 2003. See: http://www.slate.com/articles/news_and_politics/politics/2003/04/jesus_in_baghdad.html

49 These two injunctions appeared in Christ's famous Sermon on the Mount. Matthew 5-7

50 Matthew 10:34.

51 'How a war became a crusade', Jackson Lears, *The New York Times*, 11 March 2003. See: http://www.nytimes.com/2003/03/11/opinion/how-a-war-became-a-crusade.html

52 *Doctrina Jacobi nuper baptizati* was a polemical tract about a Jew newly converted to Christianity which depicts him and other Jews as treacherous and untrustworthy. Although it does not expressly name Muhammad, it was written between 634 and 640 AD, around the time of the Islamic prophet's death.

53 In Numbers 31, God commands Moses to "take vengeance on the Midianites" and not being one to disobey his Lord, Moses assembles an army of 12,000 who "killed ever man… [and] burned all the towns where the Midianites had settled".

54 In Exodus 17, Moses commands Joshua to defeat the Amalekites, which Joshua does with the help of Moses' Staff of God. In Joshua 6, Joshua causes the walks of Jericho to crumble armed with trumpet power. This is known in numerous hymns. Less well known is what came after. Joshua's army destroyed every living thing in Jericho – "men and women, young and old, cattle, sheep and donkeys" – except for one prostitute and her family who had sheltered Israelite spies.

55 Describing Muhammad as the "antichrist" was common throughout the medieval period. Advocates of this view included John of Damascus, and the Christian martyr Álvaro of Córdoba, who saw him as the antichrist's precursor.

56 *The Divine Comedy, Inferno*, Canto 28, Dante Alighieri, The Harvard Classics translation, 1909.

57 *Orientalism*, Edward Said, Penguin edition (2001), first published by Routledge in 1978, p72, 396 pages.

58 For instance, despite the growing mainstreaming of Islamophobic rhetoric in the United States, American attitudes to Muslims and Islam are actually becoming more favourable. See: http://www.politico.com/magazine/story/2016/07/measuring-the-backlash-against-the-muslim-backlash-214034

59 'Megachurch Pastor Robert Jeffress: Satan 'Delivered' Islam to Muhammad, Following Islam Will 'Lead You to Hell'', Samuel Smith, *The Christian Post*,

12 May 2015. Link: http://www.christianpost.com/news/megachurch-pastor-robert-jeffress-satan-delivered-islam-to-muhammad-following-islam-will-lead-you-to-hell-139026/#d2oSEuJctrQt6YBT.99

60 *Symbolic Life: Miscellaneous Writings (Volume 18 of The Collected Works of C. G. Jung)*, Carl Gustav Jung, Routledge, 1977, p 639, 904 pages.

61 *Fundamentals of Rumi's thought: A Mevlevi Sufi perspective,* Şefik Can and Zeki Saritoprak, Tughra Books, 2004, p162, 317 pages.

62 *The Prophet Muhammad: A biography,* Barnaby Rogerson, Hachette UK, 2010, p72, 272 pages.

63 Surat al-Isra (Chapter 17, Verse 93).

64 Surat al-Kahf (Chapter 18, Verse 110).

65 In Exodus 20:4-6, God commands: "Thou shalt not make unto thee any graven image, or any likeness [of anything] that [is] in heaven above, or that [is] in the earth beneath, or that [is] in the water under the earth. Thou shalt not bow down thyself to them, nor serve them: for I the LORD thy God [am] a jealous God, visiting the iniquity of the fathers upon the children unto the third and fourth [generation] of them that hate me; And shewing mercy unto thousands of them that love me, and keep my commandments."

66 'Film Review: 'Muhammad: The Messenger of God'', Alissa Simon, *Variety*, 2 September 2015. Link: http://variety.com/2015/film/festivals/muhammad-the-messenger-of-god-review-1201583569/

67 *Early Christian Art,* Eduard Syndicus, Burns and Oates, 1962, p92, 188 pages.

68 *The mask of Socrates – The image of the intellectual in antiquity,* Paul Zanker, University of California Press, 1995, p297-300, 426 pages.

69 In his 1529 pamphlet 'On War against the Turk', Martin Luther praises the Ottomans because "they tolerate no images or pictures and are even holier than our destroyers of images". Ironically, during the 16th century, the Ottomans produced their greatest number of graphical illustrations of Muhammad.

70 *The Dutch Revolt and Catholic Exile in Reformation Europe,* Geert H Janssen, Cambridge University Press, 2014, p23-31, 217 pages.

71 For more information, see: http://www.discoverislamicart.org/database_item.php?id=obj ect;ISL;tr;Mus01;30;en Some of the images can be found at https://commons.wikimedia.org/wiki/Category:Siyer-i_Nebi

72 'The Koran does not forbid images of the prophet', Christiane Gruber, *Newsweek*, 1 September 2015. Link: http://europe.newsweek.com/koran-does-not-forbid-images-prophet-298298?rm=eu

73 'How to become a real Muslim', Kenan Malik, *Göteborg-Posten*, 18 April 2010. Link: http://www.kenanmalik.com/essays/gp_cartoons.html

74 *Freethinkers of Medieval Islam,* Sarah Stroumsa, Brill, 1999, p37-86, 261 pages.

75 Surat al-Kafirun, Chapter 109, Verse 6.

Chapter 7

1 'This is how Steve Bannon sees the entire world', J Lester Feder, *Buzzfeed*, 16 November 2016. Link: https://www.buzzfeed.com/lesterfeder/this-is-how-steve-bannon-sees-the-entire-world?utm_term=.qfA32Yp73D#.qtnQVpwvQP

2 'The loneliness of the long-distance libertarian', Amit Varma, *India Uncut*, 17 November 2016. Link: http://indiauncut.com/iublog/article/the-loneliness-of-the-long-distance-libertarian/

3 'Steve Bannon, dharma warrior', Akhilesh Pillalamarri, *The Diplomat*, 3 February 2017. Link: http://thediplomat.com/2017/02/steve-bannon-dharma-warrior-hindu-scriptures-and-the-worldview-of-trumps-chief-ideologue/

4 'Jihadist threat not as big as you think', Peter Bergen and Emily Schneider, *CNN*, 29 September 2014. Link: http://edition.cnn.com/2014/09/26/opinion/bergen-schneider-how-many-jihadists/

5 'Can Donald Trump unify a Republican Party he fractured?', *Fox News*, 13 March 2016. Link: http://www.foxnews.com/transcript/2016/03/13/can-donald-trump-unify-republican-party-fractured/

6 'Trump's false Muslim claim', Robert Farley, *FactCheck.org*, 16 March 2016. Link: http://www.factcheck.org/2016/03/trumps-false-muslim-claim/

7 'Donald Trump: 'I think Islam hates us'', Theodore Schleifer, *CNN*, 10 March 2016. Link: http://edition.cnn.com/2016/03/09/politics/donald-trump-islam-hates-us/

8 'Donald Trump's history of suggesting Obama is a Muslim', Chris Moody and Kristen Holmes, *CNN*, 19 September 2015. Link: http://edition.cnn.com/2015/09/18/politics/trump-obama-muslim-birther/

9 'IS tries to lure Washington into confrontation', Abdallah Suleiman Ali, *Al Safir* (translated by *Al Monitor*), 17 November 2014. Link: http://www.al-monitor.com/pulse/politics/2014/11/syria-islamic-state-executions-kassig.html

10 According to Jihad Watch, *taqiyya* is "systematic lying to the infidel [which] must be considered part and parcel of Islamic tactics." See: 'Islam 101', Gregory M Davis, *Jihad Watch*. Link: https://www.jihadwatch.org/islam-101

11 'Jihadists say Trump victory a rallying call for new recruits', Ahmad Sultan and Omar Fahmy, *Reuters*, 14 November 2016. Link: http://www.reuters.com/article/us-usa-trump-jihadists-idUSKBN1390FO

12 'Is Trump's travel ban really a 'blessed ban' for ISIS?', David Iaconangelo, *Christian Science Monitor*, 9 February 2017. Link: http://www.csmonitor.com/World/Middle-East/2017/0209/Is-Trump-s-travel-ban-really-a-blessed-ban-for-ISIS

13 'With his visit to Saudi, Trump attracts the ire of Alt-Right', Kabir Upmanyu, *The Quint*, 22 May 2017. Link: https://www.thequint.com/world/2017/05/22/saudi-visit-trump-again-attracts-ire-alt-right

14 For example: 'Trump in Saudi for... Whatever', Andrew Anglin, *Daily Stormer*, 20 May 2017. Link: https://www.dailystormer.com/trump-in-saudi-for-whatever/

15 Paul Joseph Watson, Twitter, tweet dated 7 April 2017. Link: https://twitter.com/PrisonPlanet/status/850171163527581697

16 'The David Duke Show: The Zio-Orchestrated Donald Trump surrender to radical Islamic terrorism in Saudi Arabia', David Duke, *The Daily Stormer*, 23 May 2017. Link: https://www.dailystormer.com/the-david-duke-show-the-zio-orchestrated-donald-trump-surrender-to-radical-islamic-terrorism-in-saudi-arabia/

17 'Rubio: Paris attacks wake-up call to 'clash of civilizations'', *Bloomberg*, 14 November 2015. Link: https://www.bloomberg.com/politics/trackers/2015-11-14/rubio-paris-attacks-wake-up-call-to-clash-of-civilizations-

18 'Transcript of Bin Laden's October interview', CNN, 5 February 2002. Link: http://edition.cnn.com/2002/WORLD/asiapcf/south/02/05/binladen.transcript/

19 'The clash of civilisations?', Samuel P Huntington, *Foreign Affairs*, summer 1993 issue. Link: https://www.foreignaffairs.com/articles/united-states/1993-06-01/clash-civilizations

20 *The Clash of Civilizations and the Remaking of World Order*, Samuel P Huntington, Simon & Schuster, 1996, 368 pages.

21 *Ibid*, p31-2.

22 *Ibid*, p35.

23 'The roots of Muslim rage', Bernard Lewis, *The Atlantic*, September 1990. Link: https://www.theatlantic.com/magazine/archive/1990/09/the-roots-of-muslim-rage/304643/

24 *East Rome, Sasanian Persia and the End of Antiquity*, JD Howard-Johnston, Ashgate Publishing, 2006, p XV, 318 pages.

25 *Speeches in World History*, Suzanne McIntire and William E Burns, Infobase publishing, 2010, p85, 673 pages.

26 *Urban II (1088-1099): Speech at Council of Clermont, 1095*, Fulcher of Chartres version, Medieval Sourcebook, Fordham University. Link: https://sourcebooks.fordham.edu/source/urban2-5vers.html#Fulcher

27 'Remarks by the president upon arrival', George W Bush, White House press office, 16 September 2001. Link: https://georgewbush-whitehouse.archives.gov/news/releases/2001/09/20010916-2.html

28 'George Bush: 'God told me to end the tyranny in Iraq'', Ewen MacAskill, *The Guardian*, 7 October 2005. Link: https://www.theguardian.com/world/2005/oct/07/iraq.usa

29 'Transcript of Bin Laden's October interview', CNN, 5 February 2002. Link: http://edition.cnn.com/2002/WORLD/asiapcf/south/02/05/binladen.transcript/

30 *Speeches in World History*, Suzanne McIntire and William E Burns, Infobase publishing, 2010, p85, 673 pages.

31 'The campaign of hatred against us', Noam Chomsky, interviewed by Ticky Fullerton, *Four Corners*, 26 January 2002. Link: https://chomsky.info/20020126/

32 '11 September 2001 hijackers', *CIA*, 18 June 2002. Link: https://www.cia.gov/news-information/speeches-testimony/2002/DCI_18_June_testimony_new.pdf

33 'What we know about Saudi Arabia's role in 9/11', Simon Henderson, *Foreign Policy*, 18 July 2016. Link: http://foreignpolicy.com/2016/07/18/what-we-know-about-saudi-arabias-role-in-911/

34 'IS claims Paris attack, warns operation is "first of the storm"', *Site Intelligence Group Enterprise*, 14 November 2015. Link: https://ent.siteintelgroup.com/Statements/is-claims-paris-attacks-warns-operation-is-first-of-the-storm.html

35 *A History of Islamic Spain*, W Montgomery Watt and Pierre Cachia, Transaction Publishers, 1977, p8-9,183 pages.

36 *Mohammed, Charlemagne & the Origins of Europe*, Richard Hodges and David Whitehouse, Cornell University Press, 1983, p120-121, 181 pages.

37 *Charlemagne, Muhammad, and the Arab Roots of Capitalism*, Gene W Heck, Walter de Gruyter, 2006, p169-70, 381 pages.

38 *Ibid*, p181-2.

39 *God's Crucible: Islam and the Making of Europe, 570-1215*, David Levering Lewis, WW Norton, 2009, p244-267, 384 pages.

40 *The Establishment of the Ottoman-Dutch Economic Relations*, Mehmet Bulut, Uitgeverij Verloren, 2001, p111-2, 240 pages.

41 'Déclaration du général Bonaparte au peuple égyptien', Napoléon Bonaparte, 1798.

42 *Napoleon's Egypt: Invading the Middle East,* Juan Cole, Palgrave Macmillan, 2007, 304 pages.

43 'Germany to investigate claims of 'intolerable' spying by Turkey', *AFP*, 28 March 2017. Link: https://www.theguardian.com/world/2017/mar/28/germany-accuses-turkey-of-intolerable-spying-on-gulen-supporters

44 'Christianity bedevils talks on EU treaty', Ian Black, *The Guardian*, 25 May 2004. Link: https://www.theguardian.com/world/2004/may/25/eu.religion

45 'Turkey entry 'would destroy EU'', *BBC*, 8 November 2002. Link: http://news.bbc.co.uk/2/hi/europe/2420697.stm

46 'Too big for Europe?', *The Economist*, 14 November 2002. Link: http://www.economist.com/node/1442045

47 *Pan-Islam: History and Politics,* Jacob M Landau, Routledge, 2015, p94-121, 448 pages.

48 *The Fall of the Ottomans: The Great War in the Middle East,* Eugene Rogan, Penguin Books, 2015, 512 pages.

49 'A war to end jihad', Eugene Rogers, *New York Times*, 1 May 2015. Link: https://www.nytimes.com/2015/05/02/opinion/a-war-to-end-jihad.html?mcubz=0

50 'The Middle Eastern century that wasn't', Khaled Diab, *Al Jazeera*, 3 September 2015. Link: http://www.aljazeera.com/indepth/opinion/2015/09/middle-eastern-century-wasn-150902083410504.html

51 'The origins of British-Saudi relations: The 1915 Anglo-Saudi Treaty revisited', Jacob Goldberg, *The Historical Journal,* vol 28, September 1985, p693-703.

52 'Saudi prince sees Trump as 'true friend' to Muslims (full text)', *Bloomberg News,* 15 March 2017. Link: https://www.bloomberg.com/news/articles/2017-03-15/saudi-prince-sees-trump-as-true-friend-to-muslims-full-text

53 'The clash of ignorances', Edward Said, *The Nation*, 22 October 2001. Link: https://www.thenation.com/article/clash-ignorance/

54 *Emperor of the World: Charlemagne and the Construction of Imperial Authority,* Anne A Latowsky, Cornell University Press, 2013, p20, 304 pages.

55 'The Fourth Crusade and the Latin Empire of Constantinople', Gary Dickson, Thomas F Madden, Marshall W Baldwin, *Encyclopaedia Britannica*, 9 August 2016. Link: https://www.britannica.com/event/Crusades

56 'Address of John Paul II to his beatitude Christodoulos, Archbishop of Athens and Primate of Greece', *EWTN – Global Catholic* Network, 4 May 2001. Link: http://www.ewtn.com/footsteps/words/CHRISTODOULOS_5_4.htm

57 *The Crusades through Arab Eyes,* Amin Maalouf, Al Saqi Books, 1984, p184-5, 293 pages.

58 *A History of Medieval Spain,* Joseph F O'Callaghan, Cornell University Press, 1983, p96-7, 728 pages.

59 *The Cambridge Illustrated Atlas of Warfare: The Middle Ages, 768-1487,* Nicholas Hooper and Matthew Bennett, Cambridge University Press, 1996, p84-5, 192 pages.

60 *The Quest for El Cid*, Richard A Fletcher, Oxford University Press, 1989, 217 pages.

61 *Cairo*, André Raymond, Harvard University Press, 2000, p9-11, 436 pages.

62 *The Chronicle of John, Bishop of Nikiu,* Text and translation society, 1916, Chapter CXXI, 216 pages.

63 *An Economy for the 99%,* Deborah Hardoon, *Oxfam,* 2017, 48 pages. Link: http://policy-practice.oxfam.org.uk/publications/an-economy-for-the-99-its-time-to-build-a-human-economy-that-benefits-everyone-620170

64 *The Global Risks Report 2017,* World Economic Forum, 2017, p6, 70 pages.

65 'Noble winning economist says Trump's plans aggravate income inequality', *Reuters*, 13 May 2017. Link: http://www.newsweek.com/donald-trump-economy-trump-budget-trump-tax-plan-nobel-winner-angus-deaton-608807

66 *Living Standards 2017*, Adam Corlett and Stephen Clarke, Resolution Foundation, February 2017, p10, 93 pages. Link: http://www.resolutionfoundation.org/app/uploads/2017/01/Audit-2017.pdf

67 For more on this, see my article: 'The West's hidden tribalism', Khaled Diab, *Al Jazeera English*, 14 September 2015.

68 'Theresa May's conference speech in full', *Daily Telegraph*, 5 October 2016. Link: http://www.telegraph.co.uk/news/2016/10/05/theresa-mays-conference-speech-in-full/

69 *ISIS: Inside the Army of Terror*, Michael Weiss and Hassan Hassan, Regan Arts, 2015, p11-12, 270 pages.

70 'Iraq: ISIS abducting, killing, expelling minorities', *Human Rights Watch*, 19 July 2014. Link: https://www.hrw.org/news/2014/07/19/iraq-isis-abducting-killing-expelling-minorities

71 'IS threatens Iraq's minority Shabak community', Ali Mamour, *Al Monitor*, 22 August 2014. Link: http://www.al-monitor.com/pulse/originals/2014/08/iraq-minorities-shabak-extinction-islamic-state.html

72 'Turkmen caught between ISIS, Assad and Russia', Umar Farooq, *Syria Deeply*, 26 November 2015. Link: https://www.newsdeeply.com/syria/articles/2015/11/26/turkmen-caught-between-isis-assad-and-russia

73 'ISIS hunts followers of sufi and sentences them to death', Raqqa News, 29 April 2015. Link: http://www.raqqa-sl.com/en/?p=1083

74 '2011 report on terrorism', National Counterterrorism Centre, 2012, p14, 28 pages.

75 *Milestones*, Sayyid Qutb, first published 1964, English translation by Kalamullah, p9-10, 104 pages.

76 For a brief biography, see: 'Ibn Taymiyyah', Henri Laoust, *Encyclopaedia Britannica*, 2014. Link: https://www.britannica.com/biography/Ibn-Taymiyyah

77 'ISIS vs Al Qaeda: Jihadism's global civil war', Daniel L Byman and Jennifer R Williams, *Brookings*, 24 February 2015. Link: https://www.brookings.edu/articles/isis-vs-al-qaeda-jihadisms-global-civil-war/

78 'ISIS-linked Syrian commander killed by rival faction', AFP, 16 November 2015. Link: http://english.alarabiya.net/en/News/middle-east/2015/11/16/ISIS-linked-Syrian-commander-killed-by-rival-faction.html

79 'جبهة النصرة تعلن رسميا مقتل قائد دئاق أول شهداء عملية قاسيون ،(المهروك)، الدرر الشامية، 15 نوفمبر 2015. http://eldorar.com/node/90945

80 *The Legacy of Muslim Spain*, Robert Hillenbrand, edited by Salma Khadra Jayyusi and Manuela Marín, Brill, 1992, p117, 784 pages.

81 *Vibrant Andalusia: The Spice of Life in Southern Spain*, Ana Ruiz, Algora Publishing, 2007, p53-4, 201 pages.

82 Andalucia: A Cultural History, John Gill, Oxford University Press, 2008, p81-2, 272 pages.

83 *Uncommon Grounds: The History of Coffee and How It Transformed Our World*, Mark Pendergrast, Basic Books, 2010, p9, 480 pages.

84 *Uncommon Grounds: The History of Coffee and How It Transformed Our World*, Mark Pendergrast, Basic Books, 2010, p13-14, 480 pages.

85 *Ibid,* p8-9.

86 *The World of Caffeine: The Science and Culture of the World's Most Popular Drug,* Bennett Alan Weinberg and Bonnie K Bealer, Psychology Press, 2001, p77, 394 pages.

87 *Ibid,* pXIV-XV and p71.

88 *Charlemagne, Muhammad, and the Arab Roots of Capitalism,* Gene W Heck, Walter de Gruyter, 2006, p169-72, 381 pages.

89 'Why Iceland banned beer', *BBC Magazine,* 1 March 2015. Link: http://www.bbc.com/news/magazine-31622038

90 *The Jamestown Project,* Karen Ordahl Kupperman, Harvard University Press, 2009, p39-42, 390 pages.

91 *The Ottoman State and Its Place in World History: Introduction,* Halil Inchalik, edited by Kemal H Karpat, p53, 129 pages.

92 *The Ottoman Empire and Early Modern Europe,* Daniel Goffman, Cambridge University Press, 2002, p111-2, 273 pages.

93 *History of the Ottoman Empire and Modern Turkey: Volume 2,* Stanford J Shaw and Ezel Kural Shaw, Cambridge University Press, 1977, p55-171, 548 pages.

94 *An Imam in Paris: Account of a Stay in France by an Egyptian Cleric (1826-1831),* Daniel L Newman, Saqi Books, 2012, 300 pages.

95 *The Princeton Encyclopedia of Islamic Political Thought,* Georges Tamer, edited by Gerhard Böwering, Patricia Crone and Mahan Mirza, 2013, p236-7, 656 pages.

96 *The Muqaddimah: An Introduction to History,* Ibn Khaldun, Translated by Franz Rosenthal, Princeton University Press, 1969, p156, 465 pages.

97 *Habib Bourguiba of Tunisia: The Tragedy of Longevity,* Derek Hopwood and Sue Mi Terry, Springer, 2016, p1-28, 170 pages.

98 *Bourguiba: Un si long règne (1957-1989),* Sophie Bessis and Souhayr Belhassen, Groupe Jeune Afrique, 1989, p55-70, 239 pages.

99 'How Tunisia's Islamists embraced democracy', Karina Piser, *Foreign Policy,* 31 March 2016. Link: http://foreignpolicy.com/2016/03/31/how-tunisias-islamists-embraced-democracy-ennahda/

100 'New Tunisian constitution 'turning point' for Islamist movements', Bissan al-Sheikh, translated by Rani Geha, *Al Monitor,* 14 January 2014. Link: http://www.al-monitor.com/pulse/politics/2014/01/tunisia-new-constitution-ennahda-turning-point-islamists.html#ixzz4chupQBot

Chapter 8

1 'Saudi Arabia: New terrorism regulations assault rights', Human Rights Watch, 20 March 2014. Link: https://www.hrw.org/news/2014/03/20/saudi-arabia-new-terrorism-regulations-assault-rights

2 *Upfront,* Mehdi Hassan, *Al Jazeera,* 13 April 2016. Link: https://www.facebook.com/AJUpFront/videos/1520502238258441/

3 'Arabs can't even do atheism right', Mohammad Al-Buraidi, Saudi Gazette, 11 July 2015. Link: http://saudigazette.com.sa/opinion/local-viewpoint/arabs-cant-even-do-atheism-right/

4 'Survey claims 866 atheists in Egypt, highest in Arab World', *Mada Masr,* 10 December 2014. Link: http://www.madamasr.com/en/2014/12/10/news/u/survey-claims-866-atheists-in-egypt-highest-in-arab-world/

5 'Authorities raid, close 'atheists' cafe' in downtown Cairo', *Mada Masr,* 14 December 2014. Link: http://www.madamasr.com/en/2014/12/14/news/u/authorities-raid-close-atheists-cafe-in-downtown-cairo/

6 "مقلم 'التعليم حصن الطبال من اللليبرابية والعلمانية», ظافر الشعنان, "ألكتوبر 28 ,«المركمة 2016. http://makkahnewspaper.com/article/471320/%D8% A7%D9%84%D8%A8%D9%84%D8%AF/%D8%A7%D9%84%D8%AA%D 8%B9%D9%84%D9%8A%D9%85-%D8%AA%D8%AD%D8%B5%D9%86- %D8%B7%D9%84%D8%A7%D8%A8%D9%87%D8%A7-%D9%85%D9%86- %D8%A7%D9%84%D9%84%D9%8A%D8%A8%D8%B1%D8%A7%D9%84% D9%8A%D8%A9-%D9%88%D8%A7%D9%84%D8%B9%D9%84%D9%85%D 8%A7%D9%86%D9%8A%D8%A9

7 'Man 'sentenced to death for atheism' in Saudi Arabia', Bethan McKernan, *The Independent,* 26 April 2017. Link: http://www.independent.co.uk/news/world/middle-east/saudi-arabia-man-sentenced-death-atheism-ahmad-al-shamri-hafar-al-batin-appeal-denied-a7703161.html

8 'Saudi Arabia sentences a man to 10 years in prison and 2,000 lashes for expressing his atheism on Twitter', Ashley Cowburn, *The Independent,* 27 February 2016. Link: http://www.independent.co.uk/news/world/middle-east/saudi-arabia-sentence-man-to-10-years-in-prison-and-2000-lashes-for-expressing-his-atheism-on-a6900056.html

9 'Saudi blogger receives first 50 lashes of sentence for 'insulting Islam'', *Associated Press,* 10 January 2015. Link: https://www.theguardian.com/world/2015/jan/09/saudi-blogger-first-lashes-raif-badawi

10 'A look at the writings of Saudi blogger Raif Badawi – sentenced to 1,000 lashes', Ian Black and Mona Mahmoud, *The Guardian,* 14 January 2015. Link: https://www.theguardian.com/world/2015/jan/14/-sp-saudi-blogger-extracts-raif-badawi

11 'My family's torture – dealing with Raif Badawi's flogging', Ensaf Haidar, *Global Voices,* Amnesty International, 19 June 2015. Link: https://www.amnesty.org.uk/blogs/global-voices/ensaf-raif-badawi-wife-flogged-blogger-saudi-arabia

12 'Saudi Arabia uses capital offence of 'apostasy' to stifle debate', *Amnesty International,* 24 December 2012. Link: https://www.amnesty.org/en/latest/news/2012/12/saudi-arabia-uses-capital-offence-apostasy-stifle-debate/

13 'Palestinian poet Ashraf Fayadh's death sentence quashed by Saudi court', David Batty and Mona Mahmood, *The Guardian,* 2 February 2016. Link: https://www.theguardian.com/world/2016/feb/02/palestinian-poet-ashraf-fayadhs-death-sentence-overturned-by-saudi-court

14 'Saudi writer Hamza Kashgari faces charge of blasphemy after tweets about Muhammad', David Keyes, *The Washington Post,* 9 February 2012. Link: https://www.washingtonpost.com/opinions/saudi-writer-detained-after-tweets-about-muhammad/2012/02/09/gIQApsgW2Q_story.html?utm_term=.3f18eda3b140

15 'Saudi 'blasphemy' prisoner Hamza Kashgari tweets for first time after release', Ellen Knickmeyer, *Zawya Dow Jones,* 29 October 2013. Link: http://gulfnews.com/news/gulf/saudi-arabia/saudi-blasphemy-prisoner-hamza-kashgari-tweets-for-first-time-after-release-1.1248548

16 *Arabs Without a God,* second edition, Brian Whitaker, Amazon, p68-9, 250 pages.

17 'Freedom in the world 2016 – Saudi Arabia', Freedom House. Link: https://freedomhouse.org/report/freedom-world/2016/saudi-arabia

18 *Global Index of Religiosity and Atheism*, WIN-Gallup International, 2012, p11, 25 pages.

19 'Interview with a Saudi atheist', William Bauer, *Your Middle East*, 30 April 2013. Link: http://www.yourmiddleeast.com/columns/article/interview-with-a-saudi-atheist_11146

20 'In Islam, there's more than one way to be an 'atheist'', Nesrine Malik, *The Guardian*, 5 May 2014. Link: https://www.theguardian.com/commentisfree/2014/may/05/islam-atheist-saudi-arabia-terrorists-faith-muslim-world

21 *Epic of Gilgamesh*, translated by William Muss-Arnolt, 1901, Tablet XI.

22 *Kierkegaard's Thought*, Gregor Malantschuk, Princeton University Press, 2015, p93-5, 402 pages.

23 'Cardinal: UK a land of spiritual homelessness', Martin Beckford, *The Telegraph*, 8 May 2008.

24 '50% of British atheists – struggling with spiritual vacuum', *Hizb ut-Tahrir*, 14 May 2017. Link: http://www.hizb.org.uk/news-comment/50-of-britain-atheist-struggling-with-spiritual-vacuum/

25 'Ethical dilemma: I was a Muslim. Now I'm an atheist. But I crave religion', Joan Reisman-Brill, *TheHumanist.com*, 12 June 2015. Link: https://thehumanist.com/voices/the_ethical_dilemma/ethical-dilemma-i-was-a-muslim-now-im-an-atheist-but-i-crave-religion

26 'New gene therapy treatment boosts quest for vision loss cures', *Press Association*, 28 April 2016. Link: https://www.theguardian.com/society/2016/apr/28/blindness-gene-therapy-treatment-oxford-university

27 'The origins of religion: evolved adaptation or by-product?', Ilkka Pyysiäinen and Marc Hauser, *Trends in Cognitive Sciences*, vol 14, issue 3, March 2010, p104-9.

28 'Professor rethinks origins of religion', Adam T Horn, *The Harvard Crimson*, 10 February 2010. Link: http://www.thecrimson.com/article/2010/2/10/religion-hauser-moral-cognitive/

29 'Blogger Kareem Amer finally released', *Reporters Without Borders*, 17 November 2010. Link: https://rsf.org/en/news/blogger-kareem-amer-finally-released

30 'Jailhouse blog', Khaled Diab, *The Guardian*, 8 November 2007. Link: https://www.theguardian.com/commentisfree/2007/nov/08/jailhouseblog1

31 'About this campaign', *FreeKareem*. Link: http://www.freekareem.org/about/

32 'Innocence of Muslims: a dark demonstration of the power of film', Peter Bradshaw, *The Guardian*, 17 September 2012. Link: https://www.theguardian.com/film/filmblog/2012/sep/17/innocence-of-muslims-demonstration-film

33 'Egypt court jails blogger Alber Saber for blasphemy', *BBC*, 12 December 2012. Link: http://www.BBC.com/news/world-middle-east-20695992

34 'Egypt's National Plan to Fight Atheism', Ishak Ibrahim, The Tahrir Institute for Middle East Policy, 8 August 204. Link: https://timep.org/commentary/egypts-national-plan-fight-atheism/

35 'Constitution of The Arab Republic of Egypt 2014', official translation, 67 pages.

36 'Egypt: 3-year sentence for atheist', *Human Rights Watch*, 13 January 2015. Link: https://www.hrw.org/news/2015/01/13/egypt-3-year-sentence-atheist

37 'Penetrating the secret world of atheists in Egypt', *90 Minutes*, Mehwar channel, first broadcast 10 November 2013.

38 'Ismail Mohamed', YouTube. Link: https://www.youtube.com/user/fiberoty/videos

39 *Cairo Today*, Al Youm Channel, 29 May 2013.

Endnotes

40 '"No God" film angers Tunisian Islamists', Andrew Hammond, *Reuters*, 6 July 2011. Link: http://www.reuters.com/article/us-tunisia-islamists-tension-idUSTRE7652VZ20110706

41 "Islam is the solution" and the "Quran is our constitution" are among the popular slogans used by the Muslim Brotherhood.

42 'Father Egyptian Atheist and the sheikhdom of atheism', Andeel, *Mada Masr*, 25 October 2015. Link: https://www.madamasr.com/en/2015/10/25/opinion/culture/father-egyptian-atheist-and-the-sheikhdom-of-atheism/

43 'Salafi woman turned atheist recounts her journey', Mounir Adib, *Egypt Independent*, 21 October 2013. Link: http://www.egyptindependent.com/salafi-woman-turned-atheist-recounts-her-journey

44 'Sabaya El-Kheir', Al Nahar TV, first aired on 13 May 2014.

45 'خيرات الإلحاد في الإسلام', عبد الرحمن بدوي, مكتبة النهضة المصرية, 1945, ص صفحة 241, اي-ب

46 *Freethinkers of Medieval Islam*, Sarah Stroumsa, BRILL, 1999, p37-86, 261 pages.

47 *Freethinkers of Medieval Islam*, Sarah Stroumsa, BRILL, 1999, p37-86, 261 pages.

48 'Ibn Sina's Metaphysics – Causality and Cosmology', *Stanford Encyclopaedia of Philosophy*, 2 December 2015. Link: https://plato.stanford.edu/entries/ibn-sina-metaphysics/#EmaCelIntSouBod

49 'Avicenna (Ibn Sina) (c. 980-1037) – 6. Epistemology', Sajjad H. Rizvi *Internet Encyclopaedia of Philosophy*. Link: http://www.iep.utm.edu/avicenna/#H6

50 'Ibn Sina [Avicenna]', *Stanford Encyclopaedia of Philosophy*, 15 September 2016. Link: https://plato.stanford.edu/entries/ibn-sina/#Conc

51 *The Incoherence of the Philosophers*, al-Ghazali, translated by Sabih Ahmad Kamali, Pakistan Philosophical Congress, 1963, 267 pages.

52 *Avicenna*, LE Goodman, Routledge, 2013, p38-9, 255 pages.

53 *The Incoherence of the Incoherence*, Ibn Rushd, translated by Simon Van Den Bergh, Luzac, 1954, 215 pages.

54 'Richard Dawkins: 'I am a secular Christian'', Sarah Knapton, *The Guardian*, 24 May 2014. Link: http://www.telegraph.co.uk/culture/hay-festival/10853648/Richard-Dawkins-I-am-a-secular-Christian.html

55 'Dawkins: Islam is 'one of the great evils in the world'', *Freethought Nation*, 9 February 2011. Link: http://freethoughtnation.com/richard-dawkins-islam-is-one-of-the-great-evils-of-the-world/

56 'Graham stands by statement calling Islam 'wicked, violent'', Todd Starnes, *Baptist Press*, 19 November 2001. Link: http://www.bpnews.net/12201/graham-stands-by-statement-calling-islam-wicked-violent

57 'Three in four in US still see the Bible as word of God', Lydia Saad, *Gallup*, 4 June 2014. Link: http://www.gallup.com/poll/170834/three-four-bible-word-god.aspx

58 'What do Americans think of Islam', Barna Group, 3 June 2013. Link: https://www.barna.com/research/what-do-americans-think-about-islam/

59 'How Americans feel about religious groups', *Pew Research Centre*, 16 July 2014. Link: http://www.pewforum.org/2014/07/16/how-americans-feel-about-religious-groups/

60 'Al-Ma'arrī', *Encylopaedia Brittanica*. Link: https://www.britannica.com/biography/al-Maarri

61 *The Epistle of Forgiveness,* نارفغلا ةلاسر, Abu l-Ala al-Maarri, edited and translated by Geert Jan van Gelder and Gregor Schoeler, New York University Press, 2013, pXV-XX, 464 pages.

62 *The Diwan of Abu'l-Ala,* Abu al-Ala al-Ma'ari, adapted into English by Henry Baerlein, John Murrat, 1909, verse XXXVI, 66 pages.

63 *Ibid,* verse LXXXI.

64 'Jihadists behead statue of Syrian poet Abul Ala al-Maari', *France 24,* 14 February 2013. Link: http://observers.france24.com/en/20130214-jihadists-behead-statue-syrian-poet-abul-ala-al-maari

65 *The Epistle of Forgiveness,* نارفغلا ةلاسر, Abu l-Ala al-Maarri, edited and translated by Geert Jan van Gelder and Gregor Schoeler, New York University Press, 2013, p185, 464 pages.

66 *Ibid,* p193.

67 *Ibid,* pXX-XXVIII.

68 'Al-Zahawi's Revolt in Hell', Firas Massouh, *Jadaliyya,* 9 January 2012. Link: http://www.jadaliyya.com/pages/index/3876/al-zahawis-revolt-in-hell-(part-i)

69 *Biographical Dictionary of Modern Egypt,* Arthur Goldschmidt, Lynne Rienner Publishers, 2000, p81-2, 299 pages.

70 *Taha Husain's Education: From Al Azhar to the Sorbonne,* Abdelrashid Mahmoudi, Routledge, 2014, p199-202, 268 pages.

71 *The Middle East in Modern World History,* Ernest Tucker, Routledge, 2016, p176, 432 pages.

72 *Studies in Arabic and Islam,* edited by Stefan Leder, FM Corrao, Peeters Publishing, 2002, p175-84, 541 pages.

73 'Adonis', Elias N Azar, *Ancient History Encyclopaedia,* 21 February 2016. Link:http://www.ancient.eu/Adonis/

74 '"Now the writing starts": An interview with Adonis', Jonathan Guyer, *New York Review of Books,* 16 April 2016. Link: http://www.nybooks.com/daily/2016/04/16/syria-now-writing-starts-interview-adonis/

75 'Adonis: Poetry is only written by atheists', Marcia Lynx Qualey, *Arabic Literature,* 8 November 2010. Link: https://arablit.org/2010/11/08/adonis-poetry-is-only-written-by-atheists/

76 '25 Street artists from around the world who are shaking up public art', Katherine Brooks, *Huffington Post,* 5 July 2014.

77 The image can be viewed here: http://68.media.tumblr.com/afb526ce1bed63f5cdbcdc1cdaa10445/tumblr_inline_ogujnqFaLf1u3g17m_540.jpg

78 'Gulf atheism in the age of social media', Sultan Sooud Al Qassemi, *Al Monitor,* 3 March 2014. Link: http://www.al-monitor.com/pulse/originals/2014/03/gulf-atheism-uae-islam-religion.html

79 https://.دئاوفلا ديص, ‹دحلم ةياكحو داحلإ ةصق ... يميصقلا هللادبع‹ ,صالخلا ةرخص رخص, saaid.net/arabic/ar74.htm

80 أهيا العقل من لقأ ,كأر‹ ,هللادبع يميصقلا ,مؤسس الانتشار العلار ب

81 *Islam in Russia: The Politics of Identity and Security,* Shireen Hunter, Jeffrey L Thomas, Alexander Melikishvili, ME Sharpe, 2004, p28-37, 592 pages.

82 'Mapped: The world's most (and least) religious countries', Oliver Smith, *Daily Telegraph,* 16 April 2017. Link: http://www.telegraph.co.uk/travel/maps-and-graphics/most-religious-countries-in-the-world/

Endnotes

83 'The world's Muslims: Unity and diversity', *Pew Research Centre,* 9 August 2012. Link: http://www.pewforum.org/2012/08/09/the-worlds-muslims-unity-and-diversity-executive-summary/

84 *Albanian Identities: Myth and History,* edited by Stephanie Schwandner-Sievers and Bernd Jürgen Fischer, Ger Duijzings, p60-69, Indiana University Press, 2002, 238 pages.

85 *Albania: From Anarchy to a Balkan Identity,* Miranda Vickers and James Pettifer, C Hurst & Co, 1997, p96-117, 324 pages.

86 *Arabs Without a God,* second edition, Brian Whitaker, Amazon, p34-5, 250 pages.

87 'تلك صورتها اذهو انتحار العاشق), محمود درويش, محمود درويش تراتخم شعرية ونثرية
(مع ملح القصائد الغنائ), Al Manhal, 2011ص122-141, 399 صفحة.

88 'محمود درويش أشعار بين الطنية والكفار, ماه غزع, شبكة فلسطين للحوار,
ربمتبس 42009. https://www.paldf.net/forum/showthread.php?t=296917

89 *Imagining Home: Class, Culture, and Nationalism in the African Diaspora,* edited by Sidney J Lemelle and Robin DG Kelley, Barbara Harlow, Verso, 1994, p181, 373 pages.

90 '"Empire of the Machine": The Arabic oil novel', Ellen McLarney, *Boundary 2,* Duke University, June 2009, p177-98.

91 *Men in the Sun,* Ghassan Kanafani, first published in 1962, Three Continents Press, 1983, p52, 90 pages.

92 *Islam and the Politics of Meaning in Palestinian Nationalism,* Nels Johnson, Routledge, 2013, p62, 128 pages.

93 'Naguib Mahfouz, The Art of Fiction No 129', Charlotte El Shabrawy, *Paris Review,* Issue 123, summer 1992. Link: https://www.theparisreview.org/interviews/2062/naguib-mahfouz-the-art-of-fiction-no-129-naguib-mahfouz

94 'The novelist and the sheikh', Mary Anne Weaver, *The New Yorker,* 30 January 1995. Link: http://www.newyorker.com/magazine/1995/01/30/the-novelist-and-the-sheikh

95 'Naguib Mahfouz, The Art of Fiction No 129', Charlotte El Shabrawy, *Paris Review,* Issue 123, summer 1992. Link: https://www.theparisreview.org/interviews/2062/naguib-mahfouz-the-art-of-fiction-no-129-naguib-mahfouz

96 *Text and Trauma: An East-West Primer,* Ian Richard Netton, Routledge, 2012, p22, 176 pages.

97 'Salman Rushdie', Ameena Meer, *BOMB – Artist in Conversation,* Issue 27, Spring 1989. Link: http://bombmagazine.org/article/1199/

98 'Bill Moyer on faith and reason', Bill Moyer and Salman Rushdie, *PBS,* 23 June 2006. Link: http://www.pbs.org/moyers/faithandreason/print/faithandreason101_print.html

99 *Self-Criticism After the Defeat,* Sadiq al-Azm, Saqi Books, first published in 1968, 2012, p54-5, 176 pages.

100 *Critique of Religious Thought,* Sadiq al-Azmn, Gerlach Press, first published in 1969, 2014, 229 pages.

101 *Contemporary Arab Thought: Cultural Critique in Comparative Perspective,* Elizabeth Suzanne Kassab, Columbia University Press, 2010, p78-81, 496 pages.

102 'The Importance of Being Earnest about Salman Rushdie', Sadiq al-Azm, *Die Welt des Islams,* Issue XXXI, 1991, p1-49.

103 *The Truth about the Alleged Punishment for Apostasy in Islam,* Mirza Tahir Ahmad, Islam International, 2005, p139-40, 175 pages.

104 *Arabs Without a God,* second edition, Brian Whitaker, Amazon, p165-8, 250 pages.

105 *The Early Islamic Conquests,* Fred M Donner, Princeton University Press, 2014, p82-90, 512 pages.

106 The Middle East, Bernard Lewis, Simon and Schuster, 2009, p237-40, 448 pages.

107 Medieval Heresies, Christine Caldwell Ames, Cambridge University Press, 2015, p88-93, 368 pages.

108 The House of Wisdom: How the Arabs Transformed Western Civilisation, Jonathan Lyon, Bloomsbury Publishing USA, 2010, p67-77, 272 pages.

109 Surat al-Baqara, Chapter 2, Verse 256.

110 Surat al-Kafirun, Chapter 109.

111 See, for example, Surat al-Imran, Chapter 3, Verse 90.

Chapter 9

[1] As you may be aware, 'jihad' in Arabic can refer to 'holy war' but can also simply mean 'struggle', rather like the word 'crusade'. Many Muslims, particularly Sufis and the secular, believe that the greater jihad is the jihad of the self, i.e. the struggle to live a virtuous life. However, the hadith upon which this is based is generally considered weak by Islamic scholars.

[2] 'Jihad selfies: These British extremists in Syria love social media', Aris Roussinos, *Vice,* 5 December 2013. Link: http://www.vice.com/read/syrian-jihadist-selfies-tell-us-a-lot-about-their-war

[3] 'ISIS posts Nutella selfies to Twitter, and yeah, it's weird', Chris Tognotti, Bustle, 26 August 2014. Link: http://www.bustle.com/articles/37250-isis-posts-nutella-selfies-to-twitter-and-yeah-its-weird

[4] 'Cat got your gun? Iraq, Syria jihadist pictures go viral', Al Arabiya News, 22 June 2014. Link: http://english.alarabiya.net/en/variety/2014/06/22/ISIS-fighters-big-on-cats.html

[5] 'Two British men admit to linking up with extremist group in Syria', Vikram Dodd, *The Guardian,* 8 July 2014. Link: https://www.theguardian.com/world/2014/jul/08/two-british-men-admit-linking-extremist-group-syria

[6] 'What the jihadists who bought 'Islam For Dummies' on Amazon tell us about radicalisation', Mehdi Hasan, *Huffington Post,* 21 August 2014. Link: http://www.huffingtonpost.co.uk/mehdi-hasan/jihadist-radicalisation-islam-for-dummies_b_5697160.html

7 *ISIS: Inside the Army of Terror,* Hassan Hassan and Michael Weiss, Simon and Schuster, updated edition 2016, p204, 448 pages.

8 *Through our enemies' eyes,* Michael Scheuer, Potomac Books, 2002, p68, 394 pages.

9 'The solid base [al-Qaeda]', Abdullah Azzam, *al-Jihad no 41,* April 1988.

10 *The Father of Jihad: 'Abd Allāh 'Azzām's jihad ideas and implications to national security,* Muhammad Haniff Hassan, World Scientific, 2014, p139-141, 368 pages.

[11] 'From `Abdullah `Azzam to Djamel Zitouni', Shane Drennan, Combating Terrorism Centre, 15 June 2008. Link: https://www.ctc.usma.edu/posts/constructing-takfir-from-abdullah-azzam-to-djamel-zitouni

[12] 'The believer', William McCants, *The Brookings Essay,* 1 September 2015. Link: http://www.brookings.edu/research/essays/2015/thebeliever.html%7Cwork=

[13] A short bio of Ibn Taymiyyah can be found at: https://www.britannica.com/biography/Ibn-Taymiyyah

[14] For brief overviews on Ibn Taymiyyah's influence on ISIS, see: *ISIS: Race to Armageddon,* Adil Rasheed, Vij Book India, 2015, p29-33, 184 pages. *ISIS: Inside the Army of Terror,* Hassan Hassan and Michael Weiss, Simon and Schuster, updated edition 2016, p62-62, 448 pages.

15 'The Terror Strategist: Secret Files Reveal the Structure of Islamic State', Christoph Reuter, *Der Spiegel*, 18 April 2015. Link: http://www.spiegel.de/international/world/islamic-state-files-show-structure-of-islamist-terror-group-a-1029274.html

16 'Who are the new jihadis?', Olivier Roy, *The Guardian*, 13 April 2017. Link: https://www.theguardian.com/news/2017/apr/13/who-are-the-new-jihadis

17 'British Jihadists Fighting In Syria 'Regret Their Decision To Leave UK And Want To Come Home', The *Huffington Post*, 5 September 2014. Link: http://www.huffingtonpost.co.uk/2014/09/05/british-jihadists-islamic-state-syria_n_5770400.html

18

19 *Victims, perpetrators, assets: The narratives of Islamic State defectors*, Peter Neumann, ICSR, 2015, 16 pages. Link: http://icsr.info/wp-content/uploads/2015/09/ICSR-Report-Victims-Perpertrators-Assets-The-Narratives-of-Islamic-State-Defectors.pdf

20 'Would-be jihadists' letters home reveal unhappy, mundane life in ISIS', Lucy Draper, *Newsweek*, 1 December 2014. Link: http://europe.newsweek.com/would-be-jihadists-letters-home-reveal-unhappy-mundane-life-isis-288556?rm=eu

21 'Austrian teens latest victims of rape by IS 'husbands' now want to come home as Raqqa sex slave camp run by Brit jihadists may have pushed them over the edge', Martin Jay, *An-Nahar*, 12 October 2014. Link: http://en.annahar.com/article/179305-austrian-teens-latest-victims-of-rape-by-by-is-husbands-now-want-to-come-home-as

22 "Recruiter' of UK jihadis: I regret opening the way to ISIS', Tracy McVeigh, *The Guardian*, 13 June 2015. Link: https://www.theguardian.com/world/2015/jun/13/godfather-of-british-jihadists-admits-we-opened-to-way-to-join-isis

23 'Radical Muslim dubbed 'founding father of western jihad' reveals how he now regrets opening the door to ISIS', Tim Macfarlan, *Daily Mail*, 14 June 2015. Link: http://www.dailymail.co.uk/news/article-3123373/Founding-father-western-jihad-Abu-Muntasir-regrets-opening-door-ISIS.html

24 'Most young Arabs reject Isis and think 'caliphate' will fail, poll finds', Ian Black, *The Guardian*, 12 April 2016. Link: https://www.theguardian.com/world/2016/apr/12/vast-majority-young-arabs-isis-shunning-poll

25 *The House of Wisdom: How the Arabs Transformed Western Civilisation*, Jonathan Lyon, Bloomsbury Publishing USA, 2010, 272 pages.

26 'Education in Mosul under the Islamic State (ISIS)', Iraqi Institute for Development, 2016. Link: http://www.campaignforeducation.org/docs/reports/ISIS%20in%20Iraq_2015%20-%202016%20Education%20in%20Mosul_English_FINAL.pdf

27 'Europe cringes at Bush 'crusade' against terrorists', Peter Ford, *The Christian Science Monitor*, 19 September 2001. Link: http://www.csmonitor.com/2001/0919/p12s2-woeu.html

28 'George Bush: 'God told me to end the tyranny in Iraq', Ewan MacAskill, *The Guardian*, 7 October 2005. Link: https://www.theguardian.com/world/2005/oct/07/iraq.usa

29 'Bin Laden rails against Crusaders and UN', *BBC*, 3 November 2001. Link: http://news.BBC.co.uk/2/hi/world/monitoring/media_reports/1636782.stm

30 'Backgrounder: The president's quotes on Islam', The White House. Link: https://georgewbush-whitehouse.archives.gov/infocus/ramadan/islam.html

31 *Milestones*, Sayyid Qutb, Mother Mosque Foundation, 1981 (original edition, 1964), p159, 160 pages.

32 'Islamist cleric Anwar al-Awlaki killed in Yemen', *BBC*, 30 September 2011. Link: http://www.BBC.com/news/world-middle-east-15121879

33 'Message to the American people', Anwar Al-Awlaki, *Archive.org,* 2010. Text and audio available at: https://archive.org/details/AwlakiToUsa

34 'Isis hails Donald Trump's Muslim immigration restrictions as a 'blessed ban'', Bethan McKernan, *The Independent,* 30 January 2017. Link: http://www.independent.co.uk/news/world/middle-east/isis-donald-trump-muslim-ban-immigration-iraq-iran-restrictions-travel-islamic-state-us-visa-a7552856.html

35 'Message to the American people', Anwar Al-Awlaki, Archive.org, 2010. Text and audio available at: https://archive.org/details/AwlakiToUsa

36 For a good historical and theological overview, see: 'Caliphate, a disputed concept, no longer has a hold over all Muslims', Recep Dogan, *The Conversation,* 2 July 2015. Link: http://theconversation.com/caliphate-a-disputed-concept-no-longer-has-a-hold-over-all-muslims-41521

37 *The Muslim World: a Historical Survey – Part 1 the Age of the Caliphs,* Bertold Spuler, Brill, 1960, p48-100, 129 pages.

38 *Black Banners from the East: The Establishment of the 'Abbāsid State: Incubation of a Revolt, Volume 1,* Moshe Sharon, JSAI, 1983, p18-28, 265 pages.

39 *Conflict and Conquest in the Islamic World: A Historical Encyclopedia,* Alexander Mikaberidze, ABC CLIO, p174-6, 1,042 pages.

40 *From Slave to Sultan: The Career of Al-Manṣūr Qalāwūn and the Consolidation of Mamluk Rule in Egypt and Syria,* Linda Northrup, Franz Steiner Verlag, 1998, p164-6, 349 pages.

41 *The Cambridge History of Islam: A. The central Islamic lands from pre-Islamic times to the First World War,* Ann Katherine Swynford Lambton and Bernard Lewis, Cambridge University Press, 1977, 318-23, 527 pages.

42 For instance, the Egyptian Islamic scholar Ali Abdel-Raziq (1888-1966) maintained that the caliphate had no scriptural basis in Islam, and that Islam and Muhammad demand no particular form of government or specific political institutions. Ref: *The Islamic World: Past and Present,* John L Esposito, OUP, 2004, p171, 744 pages.

43 Various translations of the charter can be found here: https://en.wikisource.org/wiki/Medina_Charter

44 For a legal analysis of the charter, see: 'A short note on the Medina charter', Kassim Ahmed, *The Constitution Society.* Link: http://www.constitution.org/cons/medina/kassim2.htm

Chapter 10

1 'Do Christians and Muslims worship the same God?', Albert Mohler, *Billy Graham Evangelistic Association,* 1 December 2013. Link: https://billygraham.org/decision-magazine/december-2013/do-christians-and-muslims-worship-the-same-god/

2 'The 'same God' belief: a fatal heresy and a theological Trojan horse', Zosimas, *Facing Islam Blog,* 10 August 2016. Link: https://facingislam.blogspot.com/2016/08/the-same-god-belief-fatal-heresy-and.html

3 A thorough, sourced refutation is available here: http://www.loonwatch.com/2011/08/the-allah-is-the-moon-god-nonsense-could-be-the-stupidest-anti-muslim-conspiracy-theory-yet-page-i/

4 *The Islamic Invasion,* Robert A Morey, originally published 1992, Xulon Press, 2011, p49-60, 340 pages.

5 'Political correctness', Robert Morey, *Faith Defenders,* 11 November 2014. Link:http://www.faithdefenders.com/from-the-desk/Political_Correctness.html

6 'Malaysia's highest court backs a ban on Allah in Christian bibles', *AFP*, 23 June 2014. Link: https://www.theguardian.com/world/2014/jun/23/malaysia-highest-court-allah-bible-ban

7 'Malaysia would be misguided to ban Arabic word for God', Khaled Diab, *The National,* 3 October 2013. Link: http://www.thenational.ae/thenationalconversation/comment/malaysia-would-be-misguided-to-ban-arabic-word-for-god

8 *The Qur'an: An Encyclopedia*, Oliver Leaman, Taylor and Francis, 2006, p34, 771 pages.

9 *The Cambridge History of Islam: A. The central Islamic lands from pre-Islamic times to the First World War*, Ann Katherine Swynford Lambton and Bernard Lewis, Cambridge University Press, 1977, p24, 527 pages.

10 *Dictionary of Deities and Demons in the Bible*, Karel van der Toorn, Bob Becking, Pieter Willem van der Horst, Wm. B. Eerdmans Publishing, 1999, p910-17, 960 pages.

11 'Playing God', chapters 1, 2 and 3, Anatoly Liberman, *OUPblog*, 5 August 2015. Link: https://blog.oup.com/2015/08/god-word-origin-etymology-part-1/

12 'Do Muslims and Christians worship the same God?', Mark Galli, *Christianity Today*, 15 April 2015. Link: http://www.christianitytoday.com/ct/2011/april/muslimchristianssamegod.html

13 'Is Allah God?', Daniel Pipes, *FrontPage*, 28 June 2005. Link: http://archive.frontpagemag.com/readArticle.aspx?ARTID=8128

14 'Piers confronts Tommy Robinson over controversial Muslim comments', *Good Morning Britain*, 20 June 2017. Link: https://www.youtube.com/watch?v=4hwkhM041ig

15 'Brody File exclusive: Donald Trump says something in Koran teaches a 'very negative vibe'', David Brody, *CBN News*, 4 December 2011. Link: http://www1.cbn.com/thebrodyfile/archive/2011/04/12/brody-file-exclusive-donald-trump-says-something-in-koran-teaches

16 'Future widows of America: Write your congressman', Ann Coulter, *Jewish World Review*, 28 September 2001. Link: http://www.jewishworldreview.com/cols/coulter092801.asp

17 'Muslim bites dog', Ann Coulter, official site, 15 February 2016. Link: http://www.anncoulter.com/columns/2006-02-15.html

18 'This is war', Ann Coulter, *Townhall*, 14 September 2001. Link: https://townhall.com/columnists/anncoulter/2001/09/14/this-is-war-n865496

19 *The most pious Emperor, friend of Christ, MANUEL PALEOLOGUS, to his most dear brother, the most fortunate born-in-the-purple despot, Theodore Paleologus*, Dialogue 7, 1399. English translation: http://www.ccel.org/ccel/pearse/morefathers/files/manuel_paleologus_dialogue7_trans.htm

20 'Pranksters film people's shocked reactions at reading violent passages from the Bible - after being told they are from the Koran', Siofra Brennan, *Daily Mail*, 7 December 2015. Link: http://www.dailymail.co.uk/femail/article-3349272/Pranksters-film-people-s-shocked-reactions-reading-violent-passages-Bible-told-Koran.html Read more: http://www.dailymail.co.uk/femail/article-3349272/Pranksters-film-people-s-shocked-reactions-reading-violent-passages-Bible-told-Koran.html#ixzz4IUiFRJHz Follow us: @MailOnline on Twitter | DailyMail on Facebook

21 "Violence more common' in Bible than Quran, text analysis reveals', Samuel Osborne, *The Independent*, 9 February 2016. Link: http://www.independent.co.uk/arts-entertainment/books/violence-more-common-in-bible-than-quran-text-analysis-reveals-a6863381.html

22 *Christians and the Roman Army from Marcus Aurelius to Constantine*, John Helgeland, Walter De Gruyter, 1979, 111 pages.

23 *Violence in Ancient Christianity: Victims and Perpetrators,* edited by Albert Geljon and Riemer Roukema, Danny Praet, BRILL, 2014, p31-55, 260 pages.

24 'ISIS atrocities against religious minorities are genocide, says US House', Amanda Holpuch, *The Guardian,* 15 March 2016. Link: https://www.theguardian.com/world/2016/mar/15/isis-genocide-of-religious-minorities-us-house-statement

25 'Dhimmitude and Trump', Sha'i ben-Tekoa, *The American Thinker,* 13 December 2015. Link: http://www.americanthinker.com/articles/2015/12/dhimmitude_and_trump.html

26 'Religion, famille, société : qui sont vraiment les musulmans de France', *Le Journal du Dimanche,* 18 September 2016. Link: http://www.lejdd.fr/Societe/Religion/Religion-famille-societe-qui-sont-vraiment-les-musulmans-de-France-810217

27 'Survey shows Muslims integrated, but a minority at odds with secular France', Lisa Bryant, *Voice of America,* 18 September 2016/ Link: https://www.voanews.com/a/survey-french-muslims-integration/3514264.html

28 'The Immigration Act of 1924 (The Johnson-Reed Act)', Office of the Historian, US State Department. Link: https://history.state.gov/milestones/1921-1936/immigration-act

29 'Muslims and minorities', Irfan Husain, *Dawn,* 28 January 2012. Link: https://www.dawn.com/news/691264

30 'Are Muslim countries really unreceptive to religious freedom?', Daniel Philpott, *The Washington Post,* 10 July 2015. Link: https://www.washingtonpost.com/news/monkey-cage/wp/2015/07/10/are-muslim-countries-really-unreceptive-to-religious-freedom/?utm_term=.e74b57551db0

31 *Latest Trends in Religious Restrictions and Hostilities,* Pew Research Centre, 2015, 85 pages.

32 *Ataturk: An Intellectual Biography,* Şükrü Hanioğlu, Princeton University Press, 2011, p129-59, 296 pages.

33 'Saudi Arabia 2015 – international religious freedom report', US Department of State, 2015, 18 pages.

34 *Global Christianity,* Pew Research Centre, 2011, p65, 130 pages.

35 'Constitution of The Arab Republic of Egypt 2014', official translation, 67 pages.

36 'Coptic Christians killed in Minya bus attack', *Al Jazeera,* 26 May 2017. Link: http://www.aljazeera.com/news/2017/05/egypt-gunmen-attack-bus-carrying-coptic-christians-170526100440001.html

37 'Egypt's Christians in the crosshairs', Khaled Diab, *Al Jazeera,* 14 December 2016. Link: http://www.aljazeera.com/indepth/opinion/2016/12/egypt-christians-cross-hairs-161213143256890.html

38 *Arab Socialism. [al-Ishtirakīyah Al-'Arabīyah]: A Documentary Survey,* edited by Sami Ayad Hanna and George H Gardner, BRILL, 1969, p297-8, 418 pages.

39 *The Making of an Arab Nationalist: Ottomanism and Arabism in the Life and Thought of Sati' Al-Husri,* William L Cleveland, Princeton University Press, 1971, p83-127, 228 pages.

40 'The language of the Arabs has more often divided than united', Khaled Diab, The National, 20 December 2014. Link: https://www.thenational.ae/opinion/comment/the-language-of-the-arabs-has-more-often-divided-than-united

41 *Genocide in the Ottoman Empire: Armenians, Assyrians, and Greeks, 1913-1923,* George N Shirinian, Berghahn Books, 2017, 444 pages.

Endnotes

42 'Minorities in Muslim societies', *The Oxford Encyclopedia of the Islamic World*. Link: http://www.oxfordislamicstudies.com/article/opr/t236/e0536#

43 'Millet', *The Oxford Encyclopedia of the Islamic World*. Link: http://www.oxfordislamicstudies.com/article/opr/t236/e0533

44 'Human Rights Watch researcher reports ISIS abuses in Iraq', *NPR*, 24 July 2014. Link: http://www.npr.org/2014/07/24/334942455/human-rights-watch-researcher-reports-isis-abuses-in-iraq

45 'Islam bulldozes the past', Daniel Pipes, *The Washington Times*, 20 March 2015. Link: http://www.washingtontimes.com/news/2015/mar/20/daniel-pipes-islam-bulldozes-past/

46 'The first genocide: Carthage, 146 BC', Ben Kiernan, *Diogenes*, vol 51, issue 3, August 2004.

47 *City and School in Late Antique Athens and Alexandria*, Edward Jay Watts, University of California Press, 2006, p195-6, 288 pages.

48 *The Chronicle of John, Bishop of Nikiu*, John, Bishop of Nikiu, Arx Publishing, Chronicle 84, p100-1, 216 pages.

49 *Ecclesiastical history, comprising a history of the Church, in seven books, from the accession of Constantine, A.D. 305, to the 38th year of Theodosius II*, Socrates Scholasticus (379-440), London HG Bohn, 1853, p348-9, 488 pages.

50 *Violence in Ancient Christianity: Victims and Perpetrators*, edited by Albert Geljon and Riemer Roukema, Danny Praet, BRILL, 2014, p31-55, 260 pages.

51 *From Temple to Church: Destruction and Renewal of Local Cultic Topography in Late Antiquity*, edited by Johannes Hahn, Stephen Emmel and Ulrich Gotter, Helen Saradi, BRILL, 2008, p130-1, 378 pages.

52 'The conversion of Lithuania 1387', William Urban, *Lituanus*, Vol 33, No 4, 1987. Link: http://www.lituanus.org/1987/87_4_03.htm

53 'Where Islam treads, it leaves a desert', Giulio Meotti, 29 September 2014. Link: http://www.israelnationalnews.com/Articles/Article.aspx/15723

54 *The Adventures of Ibn Battuta: A Muslim Traveler of the Fourteenth Century*, Ross E Dunn, University of California Press, 2012, p5, 384 pages.

55 *Egyptology: The Missing Millennium – Ancient Egypt in Medieval Arabic Writings,* Okasha El Daly, Cavendish Publishing, 2005, 239 pages.

56 'Beautiful landmarks destroyed by Second World War bombs – and resurrected', *The Telegraph*, 13 February 2015. Link: http://www.telegraph.co.uk/travel/galleries/Beautiful-landmarks-destroyed-by-Second-World-War-bombs-and-resurrected/

57 *The Creative Destruction of Manhattan, 1900-1940*, Max Page, University of Chicago Press, 2001, p5, 317 pages.

58 'A village dies, a park is born', Douglas Martin, *New York Times*, 31 January 1997. Link: http://www.nytimes.com/1997/01/31/arts/a-village-dies-a-park-is-born.html?mcubz=0

59 'The Cultural Revolution: all you need to know about China's political convulsion', Tom Phillips, *The Guardian*, 11 May 2016. Link: https://www.theguardian.com/world/2016/may/11/the-cultural-revolution-50-years-on-all-you-need-to-know-about-chinas-political-convulsion

60 'ISIS' destruction of cultural antiquities: Q&A with Eckart Frahm', Susan Gonzalez, YaleNews, 16 March 2015. Link: http://news.yale.edu/2015/03/16/isis-destruction-cultural-antiquities-qa-eckart-frahm

Chapter 11

1 *Heretic: Why Islam Needs a Reformation Now*, Ayaan Hirsi Ali, Harper Collins, 2015, 320 pages.

2 'The trouble is the West', Rogier van Bakel, *Reason*, November 2007. Link: http://reason.com/archives/2007/10/10/the-trouble-is-the-west

3 'Islam confronts its demons', Max Rodenbeck, *The New York Review of Books*, 29 Apirl 2004. Link: http://www.nybooks.com/articles/2004/04/29/islam-confronts-its-demons/

4 *Islamic Government: Governance of the Jurist*, Ruhollah Khomeini, first published 1970, Alhoda UK, 2002, p1-2, 139 pages.

5 *Khomeini: Life of the Ayatollah*, Baqer Moin, IB Tauris,1999, p158-9, 352 pages.

6 *Democracy in Iran*, Misagh Parsa, Harvard University Press, 2016, p61-98, 406 pages.

7 'An Islamic Reformation', Thomas L Friedman, *The New York Times*, 4 December 2002. Link: http://www.nytimes.com/2002/12/04/opinion/an-islamic-reformation.html

8 *No God But God*, Reza Aslan, Arrow Books, 2006, p254, 310 pages.

9 'Tariq Ramadan: 'Muslims need to reform their minds'', David Shariatmadari, *The Guardian*, 28 February 2017. Link: https://www.theguardian.com/world/2017/feb/28/tariq-ramadan-muslims-need-to-reform-their-minds

10 'Why calling for an 'Islamic Reformation' is lazy and historically illiterate', Theo Hobson, *The Spectator*, 7 February 2015. Link: https://www.spectator.co.uk/2015/02/why-calling-for-an-islamic-reformation-is-lazy-and-historically-illiterate/#

11 'Reformation and Counter-reformation', *Encyclopaedia Britannica*. Link: https://www.britannica.com/topic/history-of-Europe/Reformation-and-Counter-Reformation

12 *Luther and Calvin on Secular Authority*, edited by Harro Höpfl, Martin Luther, Cambridge University Press, 1991, p3-46, 95 pages.

13 *The Anabaptists and Contemporary Baptists: Restoring New Testament*, edited by Malcolm B Yarnell, Thomas White, B&H Publishing Group, 2013, p65-82, 306 pages.

14 *Against the Robbing and Murdering Hordes of Peasants*, Martin Luther, circa 1525. https://www.scrollpublishing.com/store/Luther-Peasants.html

15 *Ibid.*

16 *Luther's Last Battles: Politics and Polemics 1531-46*, Mark U Edwards, Fortress Press, 2004, p98-100, 272 pages.

17 *The Jews and Their Lies*, Martin Luther, 1543, English translation by the Christian Nationalist Crusade, 1948, 64 pages.

18 *Luther's Last Battles: Politics and Polemics 1531-46*, Mark U Edwards, Fortress Press, 2004, p97-114, 272 pages.

19 *Select Works of Martin Luther: An Offering to the Church of God in "the Last Days"*, Martin Luther, translated by Henry Cole, Lutheran Church, 1826, p540-1, 588 pages.

20 'Why Islam doesn't need a reformation', Mehdi Hasan, *The Guardian*, 17 May 2015. Link: https://www.theguardian.com/commentisfree/2015/may/17/islam-reformation-extremism-muslim-martin-luther-europe

21 'The Thirty Years' War', *Encyclopaedia Britannica*. Link: https://www.britannica.com/topic/history-of-Europe/The-Thirty-Years-War#toc58351

22 *The Political Thought of the Dutch Revolt 1555-1590*, Martin van Gelderen, Cambridge University Press, 2002, p82-90, 348 pages.

Endnotes

23 *Spinoza and Medieval Jewish Philosophy*, edited by Steven M Nadler, Charles H Manekin, p36-58, Cambridge University Press, 2014, 239 pages.

24 *The 'Arabick' Interest of the Natural Philosophers in Seventeenth-Century England*, GA Russel, BRILL, 1994, p224-65, 320 pages.

25 'Hayy was here, Robinson Crusoe', Tom Verde, *Aramco World*, May/June 2014. Link: http://archive.aramcoworld.com/issue/201403/hayy.was.here.robinson. crusoe.htm

26 'A Letter Concerning Toleration', John Locke, translated by William Popple, 1689. Link: http://www.constitution.org/jl/tolerati.htm

27 *An Approach to Political Philosophy: Locke in Contexts*, James Tully, Cambridge University Press, 1993, p137-76, 333 pages.

28 *Encyclopedia of the Age of Political Revolutions and New Ideologies, 1760-1815: A-L*, edited by Gregory Fremont-Barnes, John Waskey, Greenwood Publishing Group, 2007, p419-22, 867 pages.

29 *A Short History of the Italian Renaissance*, Kenneth R Bartlett, University of Toronto Press, 2013, p138-164, 402 pages.

30 *Charlemagne, Muhammad, and the Arab Roots of Capitalism*, Gene W Heck, Walter de Gruyter, 2006, p6, 381 pages.

31 *The Cambridge World History: Volume V: Expanding Webs of Exchange and Conflict, 500 CE-1500 CE*, edited by Merry E Wiesner-Hanks and Benjamin Z Kedar, Michel Balard, Cambridge University Press, 2015, p257-86, 748 pages.

32 'An economic analysis of the Protestant Reformation', Robert B Ekelund et al, *Journal of Political Economy*, 110, no 3, June 2002, p646-671.

33 'The economic effects of the Protestant Reformation: Testing the Weber hypothesis in the German Lands', Davide Cantoni, *Journal of the European Economic Association*, vol 13, issue 4, August 2015, p561-98.

34 'Origins of growth: How state institutions forged during the Protestant Reformation drove development', Jeremiah Dittmar and Ralf R Meisenzahl, 26 April 2016, *Centre for Economic Policy Research*. Link: http://voxeu.org/article/protestant-reformation-economic-institutions-and-development

35 'The great invention gap between rich and poor kids – and why it matters', Dylan Matthews, *Vox*, 16 March 2015. Link: https://www.vox.com/2015/3/16/8225165/patents-innovation-social-mobility

36 'The power of Luther's printing press', Colin Woodard, *The Washington Post*, 18 December 2015. Link: https://www.washingtonpost.com/opinions/the-power-of-luthers-printing-press/2015/12/18/a74da424-743c-11e5-8d93-0af317ed58c9_story.html?utm_term=.fd2f62823d57

37 *The Enlightenment*, Dorinda Outram, Cambridge University Press, 2013, 48-50, 173 pages.

38 *India's Late, Late Industrial Revolution: Democratizing Entrepreneurship*, Sumit K Majumdar, Cambridge University Press, 2012, p87-90, 26 pages.

39 *Charlemagne, Muhammad, and the Arab Roots of Capitalism*, Gene W Heck, Walter de Gruyter, 2006, p41-80, 381 pages.

40 'Capitalism in Medieval Islam', Subhi Y Labib, *The Journal of Economic History*, vol 29, issue 1, March 1969, p79-96.

41 'The Arab Agricultural Revolution and Its Diffusion, 700–1100', Andrew M Watson, *The Journal of Economic History*, vol 34, issue 1, March 1974, p8-35.

42 *The Algebra of Mohammed ben Musa*, Muḥammad ibn Mūsā al-Khwārizmī, Oriental Translation Fund, originally published circa 820, 1831, p3-4, 208 pages.

43 *Science and Technology in Islam: Technology and Applied Sciences*, edited by A Y Al-Hassan, Donald R Hill, *UNESCO*, 2001, p165-92, 726 pages.

44 *The Historical Encyclopedia of World Slavery*, Junius P Rodriguez, ABC-CLIO, 1997, page xvii-xviii and 534-6, 805 pages.

45 *Mohammed and Charlemagne*, Henri Pirenne, first published 1939, Routledge, 2008, 296 pages.

46 *Charlemagne, Muhammad, and the Arab Roots of Capitalism*, Gene W Heck, Walter de Gruyter, 2006, p13-40, 381 pages.

47 *Ibid*, p211-58.

48 *Encyclopedia of the Black Death*, Joseph P Byrne, ABC-CLIO, 2012, p106-9, 429 pages.

49 *Ibid*, p198-99.

50 *Islam: History, Religion, and Politics*, Tamara Sonn, John Wiley & Sons, 2015, p71- 81,224 pages.

51 *The Crusades Through Arab Eyes*, Amin Maalouf, Saqi, 2012, p159-76, 296 pages.

52 *The Crusades Through Arab Eyes*, Amin Maalouf, Saqi, 2012, p179, 296 pages.

53 'Comparative analysis of economic development in colonial and post-colonial Egypt and Korea', Khairy Tourk, *Seoul Journal of Economics*, vol 27, no 3, autumn 2014, p223-55.

54 'A slow learning curve', *The Economist*, 15 July 2010. Link: http://www.economist.com/node/16564142

55 'Water scarcity in Yemen: the country's forgotten conflict', Frederika Whitehead, *The Guardian*, 2 April 2015. Link: https://www.theguardian.com/global-development-professionals-network/2015/apr/02/water-scarcity-yemen-conflict

56 'Yemen is on the verge of running out of water', Michael Cruickshank, *ThinkProgress*, 13 March 2017. Link: https://thinkprogress.org/yemen-humanitarian-crisis-water-54a9c0b52831

57 'CIA admits role in 1953 Iranian coup', Saeed Kamali Dehghan and Richard Norton-Taylor, *The Guardian*, 19 August 2013. Link: https://www.theguardian.com/world/2013/aug/19/cia-admits-role-1953-iranian-coup

58 *The Idea of Pakistan*, Stephen P Cohen, Brookings Institution Press, 2004, p64-7, 367 pages.

59 'Democracy in Indonesia: A cause for celebration', Max Walden, Lowy Institute, 20 February 2017. Link: https://www.lowyinstitute.org/the-interpreter/democracy-indonesia-cause-celebration

60 'Remarks by President George W Bush at the 20th anniversary of the National Endowment for Democracy', George W Bush, *White House*, 6 November 2003. Link: http://www.presidency.ucsb.edu/ws/?pid=844

61 'Iran uprising turns bloody', Ian Black and Saeed Kamali Dehghan, *The Guardian*, 16 June 2009. Link: https://www.theguardian.com/world/2009/jun/15/iran-elections-protests-mousavi-attacks

62 'Tunisian national dialogue quartet wins 2015 Nobel peace prize', Julian Borger, Angelique Chrisafis and Chris Stephen, *The Guardian*, 9 October 2015. Link: https://www.theguardian.com/world/2015/oct/09/tunisian-national-dialogue-quartet-wins-2015-nobel-peace-prize

63 'Tunisia: After the revolution', Heba Saleh, *Financial Times*, 10 March 2016. Link: https://www.ft.com/content/4f215d9c-d402-11e5-829b-8564e7528e54

64 'Tunisia army deployed to protect oil and gas fields against economic protests', 10 May 2017. Link: http://www.dw.com/en/tunisia-army-deployed-to-protect-oil-and-gas-fields-against-economic-protests/a-38791870

65 'Tunisia's economic challenges', *The Economist Intelligence Unit*, 14 January 2015. Link: http://country.eiu.com/article.aspx?articleid=1342653318&Country=Tunisia&topic=Economy

66 'Malaysia: From Developing Nation to Development Partner', Axel Van Trotsenburg, World Bank, 28 January 2015. Link: http://blogs.worldbank.org/eastasiapacific/malaysia-developing-nation-development-partner

67 'Science and technology – research and development', OECD, 2012. Link: http://www.oecd.org/std/08_Science_and_technology.pdf

68 'Egypt, Arab Rep', World Bank data. Link: http://data.worldbank.org/country/egypt-arab-rep

GLOSSARY

ABC of Islam

Abu/Umm X: In numerous Arab societies, the name of a couple's first-born son is adopted by the parents as an honorific, both for Muslims and non-Muslims. For instance, if the eldest son is called Hassan, his father becomes Abu Hassan while his mother is Umm Hassan, even if Hassan has an older sister. Couples who have no son, take on the name of their eldest daughter. On rare occasions, parents who believe in gender equality will adopt the name of their eldest child, even if she is a girl. Childless people sometimes also adopt this honorific. This is common among Palestinian political groups, where this naming convention is used as a *nom de guerre*. Yasser Arafat, for instance, took on the name 'Abu Ammar'. Foreigners not familiar with Arabic sometimes think this is a *first name/surname* naming convention and, hilariously, refer to interlocutors as just *Abu* or *Umm*.

Allah: In Arabic, 'Allah' simply means 'God'. Throughout this book, I have used God instead of Allah, and this should, in my view, always be the case (see chapter 10 for more explanation). It only makes sense to refer to God as Allah for Arabic speakers or in Arabic texts. In other languages, the local word for God should be used.

Allahu Akbar: To westerners unfamiliar with Islam, the words '*Allahu Akbar*' are terrifying to hear because of their association with terrorist attacks, when fanatics often yell out this two-word phrase. Translated literally, the term means God is Greater or the Greatest, and is known as '*takbir*'. In day-to-day language, it is used to express a wide range of sentiments, including joy, pride, defiance, admiration and amazement gratitude and grief. At concerts and weddings, audiences often chant *Allahu Akbar*, not because they intend to mount a terrorist attack but because they are impressed by the skill of the singer. It should be noted that contemporary Arabic employs more religiously derived stock phrases than contemporary English, partly due to the secularisation of English that has occurred with the drift away from religion in Western Europe.

Arab or Arabic: These two words are often confused or used interchangeably. Arabic refers to the Semitic language which was originally spoken in parts of Arabia until Islam spread it across the Middle East and beyond. While educated Arabic speakers generally understand and can use classical or standard Arabic, known as *fus'ha*, there are numerous national and local dialects of Arabic, some of which are mutually unintelligible. Arab is an ethnicity. Once, it referred to the inhabitants of Arabia. In its modern sense, 'Arab' has become more ambiguous and often refers to all Arabic speakers, though what is meant by this is open to wide interpretation.

Atheism, theism, deism and agnosticism: Theism is the belief that a single, monotheistic god or a pantheon of polytheists gods exist, while atheism is the rejection of the existence of any gods of any sort. Deism is a kind of middle ground between the two, and tends to describe belief in some kind of supreme being, while rejecting the concept of revealed religions. Agnosticism proposes that the existence or absence of a god or gods is ultimately unknowable or unprovable. Some of these terms can be combined. For example, agnostic atheism is the conviction that a god as described in scripture does not exist but do not exclude the possibility that some kind of non-interventionist deity may exist.

Baladi: Derived from *balad*, the Arabic for country or land, *baladi* is an adjective used in some dialects, especially Egyptian, to refer to something that is native or indigenous to the local culture or part of traditional, often working class lifestyles. In some senses of the word, it is similar to the English word 'folk'. It can be used to refer to dancing, music and food. A related term is *ibn* or *bint balad*, a quintessential representation of the virtuous, gritty, upright, poor but proud local.

Caliph(ate): In Arabic, *khalaf* means to succeed or follow, and that is at the heart of what the caliphate is and is about. When Muhammad died, he had appointed no successor, or *caliph*, nor had he outlined how the nascent Muslim community should be governed. Without a blueprint, it was left up to the early Muslims to (s)elect a leader to succeed their prophet. Early Muslims had different ideas about how and whether Muhammad should be succeeded. At times, they managed to resolve their differences peacefully and find a consensus candidate. At other times, it led to splits, schisms and warfare, such as the Ridda or Apostasy Wars immediately following Muhammad's death or the First Fitna, a civil war during which two caliphs, Uthman and Ali, were assassinated. The first caliphate was known as the Rashidun (Rightly Guided). This was followed by the Umayyads, who were eventually overthrown by the Abbasids. Other Muslim leaders have also claimed the title of 'caliph', including the Ottoman sultans, until Mustafa Kemal Atatürk abolished the caliphate in 1924. Some modern Islamist groups have sought to restore the caliphate, with ISIS claiming to have done just that.

Hadith: Meaning 'report' or 'account', a *hadith* is an action, habit or saying of Muhammad as reported by those around him or those who came into contact with him. Originally transmitted orally, there were millions of them in circulation. Many generations after Muhammad's death, scholars began to gather these *hadiths* into presumably authoritative collections in which the reliability of each individual *hadith* was decided by its chain of transmission back to the prophet, though how ultimately reliable this methodology is remains open to question. For most schools of Islamic jurisprudence, *hadith* is a secondary source of Islamic practice and law, with the Quran generally regarded as the only primary source.

Halal/Haram: For many non-Muslims, *halal* is generally associated with food, and specifically meat. While *halal* does refer to Islamic dietary restrictions and regulations, its meaning is much wider. *Halal* refers to everything which is 'permissible', while its antonym, *haram*, refers to things that are forbidden. Beyond the *halal-haram* poles, there is a spectrum of actions which are more or less permissible, including recommended or preferred (*mustahab*), neutral (*mubah*) and reprehensible (*maqrouh*).

Hijab: In the Quran, *hijab* refers to a curtain or screen and is used in both the metaphorical and literal sense. Nowhere does the Quran specifically refer to women having to cover up or dress in a *hijab*, but it does specify the need to screen off the visitor's area of Muhammad's house from that of his wives. Many Muslims use this passage, along with certain *hadith*, to argue that Muslim women must cover their hair. There are numerous types of head covering for women in Islam. *Hijabs* cover the hair and neck but tend to fit tightly. *Khimars* cover the hair and neck and drape over the chest to obscure the shape of the breasts. *Niqabs* include a veil for the face which usually leaves the eyes visible. A *burka* is a loose-fitting, all-body garment which covers the eyes too with a net. A *chador* is a piece of fabric which is worn in Iran and some other countries as an outer garment and is loosely wrapped around the body. In Egypt and some other Arabic-speaking countries, it is known as a *melaya laf.*

Houris: The Quran promises the believer that the mysterious *houris* await him (and perhaps even her) in paradise. However, who or what *houris* are, what they look like, how many each believer will receive and their gender(s) are open to interpretation. Although the etymology of the word is disputed, *houri* appears to describe the largeness and beauty of their eyes, with their sharply contrasting black and white. The Quran does not generally specify the gender of the *houris*, but grammatical and contextual analysis suggest that both men and women will be entitled to these forever-youthful companions, implying they are of both genders. However, there are times when they are described as untouched by man or *jinn*, implying they are female virgins. Although no number is specified, there is a *hadith* attributed to Muhammad which claims that the martyr will receive six rewards in heaven, including 72 *houris*, though some scholars claim that the chain of transmission is weak.

Islam: Islam is the monotheistic religion established by Muhammad. It is derived from the same root as the Arabic word for peace and 'to make peace with [God]' (i.e. to submit or to surrender to). In a broader sense, the religion claims the previous Abrahamic prophets as being its own, and that Abraham was the first 'Muslim'. This implies that anyone who believes in the one God is a kind of Muslim.

Islamic or Islamist: Islamic is an adjective and is used to refer to things relating to the religion of Islam, such as Islamic art, civilisation, culture, law, etc. Islamist is an adjective which refers to Islamism, or political Islam, i.e. the idea that Islam should play a central role in the political and public life of Muslim societies. Islamist can also be a noun and refers to someone who believes in or advocates for political Islam. Islamism is not a single, homogeneous ideology but a broad range of movements and philosophies, from the secular-leaning, non-violent al-Nahda party in Tunisia to jihadist groups fighting to build theocracies in Syria and Iraq.

Jahiliyya: Muslims traditionally refer to the period of pre-Islamic history in Arabia *jahiliyya*. Derived from the Arabic word of ignorance, it is no neutral term and depicts Arabia before the advent of Islam as being plunged in its own dark ages. However, it is unclear how much of the history of the *'jahiliyya'* period depicts actual realities and how much of it is later pro-Islamic propaganda. Numerous modern historians have questioned the accuracy and validity of some of the accounts of and assumptions about the so-called *jahiliyya*. In addition, pre-Islamic Arabia was not just home to nomadic and semi-nomadic tribes but also some extremely advanced ancient civilisations, such as the Nabateans and the Sabaeans, who gave us the Biblical Queen of Sheba. Despite our contemporary impressions, monotheism also played a prominent role during the pre-Islamic era in Arabia. Some modern-day salafists believe that Muslim societies are living through a second *Jahiliyya*, with serious consequences (see *takfirism*).

Jihad: Derived from the Arabic word for to 'struggle', jihad means, in the Islamic context, to strive in the path of God. 'Striving' can be a metaphysical or physical endeavour. At the metaphysical level, this can involve the spiritual struggle of overcoming one's selfish and material desires in order to get closer to God or to serve fellow believers. Some Muslims believe this spiritual battle to be the 'greater jihad', while the 'lesser jihad' is that of the battlefield. In the West, the military component of 'jihad' is the one most commonly associated with the term. Originally, jihad was an expansionist military ideology, but one governed by an elaborate set of rules, including non-harm to civilians. With time, military jihad evolved into a predominantly defensive ideology. Today, jihad has become largely obsolete for Muslim states but non-state actors have revived it as an offensive military ideology, though one not governed by the stringent ethical codes of traditional jurisprudence.

Kafir: Derived from the Arabic for to 'cover' or 'conceal', *kafir*, in the religious context, means 'infidel' or 'unbeliever'. It is usually used as a derogatory term. Who counts as a *kafir* and what counts as unbelief (*kufr*) has been a subject of heated debate for centuries. The plural of *kafir* is *kuffar*.

Munafiq (Hypocrite): At its core, the Arabic for hypocrite (*munafiq*) and hypocrisy (*nifaq*) mean essentially the same thing as their English equivalent. However, in the Islamic context, *munafiq* has a very specific meaning and context, referring to individuals who outwardly profess to be Muslims but secretly hold on to their old beliefs, or actively seek to undermine or oppose the community and the religion, like a "sheep confused between two herds", in the words of Muhammad. Although hypocrisy is despised just about everywhere, the Quran and the Islamic prophet take a particularly dim view of *munafiqun* (plural). In addition to the universal contempt towards liars and cheats, an additional factor for this hostility may have been the vulnerability of the early Muslim community, which was not only tiny but was also under attack from multiple fronts, making loyalty and trustworthiness vital.

Muslim: Muslim is an adherent or follower of the religion of Islam. Today, the overwhelming majority of people defined as 'Muslim' are born into the faith, with conversions constituting only a tiny fraction of the global community. In the early history of Islam, the situation was the reverse. The fact that the label 'Muslim' is imposed by society rather than chosen by the individual, this means that the term covers an enormously broad range of actual beliefs and practices, including ultra-conservative, mainstream or moderate, liberal, progressive, lapsed, non-practising and even outright atheists. Muslim is far more common in modern usage. In the Quran and medieval Islam, Muslims tended to be referred to simply as 'believers'.

Muslim Brotherhood: *Jamāʿat al-Ikhwan al-Muslimeen,* the Society of Muslim Brothers, or Muslim Brotherhood, for short, is one of the world's oldest extant Islamist groups and one of its most successful. Established in 1928 by Hassan al-Banna, an Egyptian scholar of Islam school teacher, the movement started off as a social reform, political activism and charity

413

group, rapidly spreading across the country. From there, it inspired other groups to establish their own national chapters in numerous Arab and Muslim countries, though these chapters are autonomous of one another and often behave more like foes than allies. As a non-state actor, the Egyptian Muslim Brotherhood often engaged in political violence and terrorism until it officially renounced violence in the 1970s. The Brotherhood eventually entered the mainstream political sphere, with its crowning achievement being Egypt's first president elected following the 2011 revolution, Mohamed Morsi. Since Morsi's ouster by the Egyptian military in 2013, and his replacement by General Abdel-Fattah al-Sisi, the Muslim Brotherhood has been persecuted in the country where it was founded, with most of its leadership behind bars. The Egyptian Muslim Brotherhood is now outlawed and officially designated as a 'terrorist organisation'. Although Muslim Brothers share a general commitment to injecting Islam into politics, there is great divergence in what they believe this means, with the younger generation generally being more secularly inclined than the older. In broad terms, the Muslim Brotherhood seeks to combine modernism with tradition, while Salafism, and specially Wahhabism, is about turning back the clock to a supposedly pristine past.

People of the Book: Islam regards itself as an extension of the monotheistic tradition of Abraham. Other adherents to Abrahamic monotheism are described in the Quran as "People of the Book", a designation which provides them with protection as a recognised religious minority or group. This encompasses Jews, Christians and the mysterious 'Sabians'. Different theories have been proposed over the centuries as to who exactly the Sabians were. Most scholars identify this group as originating in Mesopotamia, and either believed in Mandaeism, a dualist religion which revered John the Baptist. An alternative theory put forward by medieval Islamic scholars is that the Sabians believed in a mix of Judaism and Zoroastrianism, a faith that had been established by Jews who remained in Mesopotamia following the Babylonian exile. In practice, the term People of the Book was often as elastic as the frontiers of Islamic territorial control and, at different times and places, it was extended to embrace Zoroastrians, Samaritans, Buddhists and even polytheistic Hindus.

Salafism: Salafism is an umbrella term used to refer to a number of puritanical interpretations of Islam that seek to return to the presumed fundaments of the faith, as supposedly practised by Muhammad and the early Muslim community, i.e. *al-salaf al-saleh* (the 'pious predecessors or ancestors'). Salafist movements tend to reject what they regard as *bid'a* ('innovations') and adopt an emulative, often literal, approach to Islam. Muhammad ibn Abdel-Wahhab founded one of the most puritanical and restrictive schools of salafism. Known to outsiders as Wahhabism, it is the guiding ideology in Saudi Arabia. Confusingly, 19th-century reformers who sought to set in motion an Islamic 'renaissance' or *nahda* also referred to themselves as 'salafis' because they believed that the spirit of modernity was integral to the success of Islam's 'golden age' and reviving Islam required a return to these rationalist roots.

Sufism: Viewing mainstream orthodox Islam as being overly concerned with worldly matters, Sufism developed as a mystical and spiritual manifestation of the religion. The word itself either derives from the Arabic for wool and may have been a reference to the coarse garments worn by early ascetic adherents to Sufism. There is no single Sufism and Sufis belong to a wide range of orders, each of which is known as a *tariqa*, or path, in Arabic. Sufis express their faith and their spiritual elation in numerous devotional practices, including through music, song, poetry, trance-like dances and repetitive chanting through such rituals as *zikr* (remembrance of God). This, along with their reverence towards numerous saints, means that rationalist, modernist and salafist Muslims tend to take a dim view of Sufis. In the popular western imagination, Sufism is often associated with the whirling dervishes and their energetic, dizzying dances.

Sunna or Sunni: Meaning 'habits' or 'customs', *sunna* refers to the Muhammad's way of life in its entirety, which Muslims generally believe should be a model for their own lives and one to which they should aspire. The concept of *sunna* predates Islam and Arab tribes used to derive many of their social customs and norms from the example of elders and ancestors. In early Islam, many Muslims used to also rely heavily on the *sunna* of Muhammad's companions as well. *Sunna* is similar to *hadith* but far broader in scope, as it encompasses every aspect of Muhammad's behaviour, including his silent permissions and prohibitions. Whereas *hadith* is used as a source of Islamic law, *sunna* is generally employed as a source for Islamic customs, and it tends to be of a recommended, rather than a compulsory, nature. *Sunni* refers to the largest branch of Islam and is an abbreviation of *ahl el-sunna weh al-jama'a* ('The People of the Sunna and the Community'). The choice of names is political, as both Sunnis and Shi'a strive to emulate Muhammad. 'Sunni' suggests that adherents to this branch perceive themselves as being closer in spirit to what the prophet intended and that it is his example, not bloodline, which counts.

Sunni or Shi'a: Sunni and Shi'a are the two main branches of Islam, with Sunni being by far the larger of the two numerically. Even today, after centuries of dispute, barely a split hair separates Sunnis from Shi'a doctrinally. Both branches believe in all the same fundamentals of the faith (including Muhammad's status as the final prophet, the unity of God and the five pillars of Islam) and most of the same details too. The schism started as a political one, when the *shi'a* or 'party' of Ali believed that Muhammad's cousin and son-in-law, Ali, should succeed the prophet (i.e. be his caliph) because of the close bloodline they shared. The majority decided that the community should elect or select its caliph. Following the assassination of Ali after he became caliph, the abdication of his son Hassan, and the slaying of his other son, Hussein, at the famous Battle of Karbala. With these disappointments and periodic persecutions, Shi'a ideology generally drifted away from the worldly sphere, which it regarded as a domain of pain and suffering, and pursued redemption in the future return of the 'Hidden Imam' or 'Mahdi'.

Takfir: When a self-proclaimed Muslim is declared a *kafir* or excommunicated, this is known as *takfir*. This practice is and has always been controversial, and Muslims differ on what constitutes unbelief among Muslims and what should be done about it. The most tolerant currents of Islam hold that no Muslim can declare another Muslim to be a *kafir* and that this is the sole prerogative of God. Others maintain that the *umma*, or community, as collectively represented by the state and its *ulema*, can take such a grave decision. Throughout Islamic history, radical splinter groups have conferred on themselves the right to issue *takfir*. In recent times, this fringe idea has gained added potency with the notion proposed by the

Egyptian Sayyid Qutb that the entire modern Muslim world was living in *jahiliyya* (i.e. pre-Islamic ignorace), which paved the way to condemning all Muslims who did not abide to a strict *salafist* interpretation of Islam as 'unbelievers'.

Taqiyya: This is one of those paradoxical phenomena when Islamophobes are more familiar with an Islamic term than the clear majority of Muslims, though their understanding of its vastly different. *Taqiyya*, according to *Jihad Watch*, is the "systematic lying to the infidel" and "disinformation intended to induce the infidel world to let down its guard". However, according to Islamic theology, *taqiyya* is an exceptional measure which permits a Muslim to conceal their faith or lie about it if (s)he is at risk of persecution, serious harm or death. Unsurprisingly, given the repeated persecutions Shi'a Muslims have faced, this concept is more common in Shi'a than in Sunni Islam. Of course, some Islamophobes will regard this entry, and the book as a whole, as a form of *taqiyya*.

Ulema: Derived from the Arabic for knowledge, an 'alem' (singular) and 'ulema' (plural) refers, in the religious context, to scholars of Islam and in the secular context to scientists.

Umma: Derived from the same root as the Arabic word for mother, *umma* means 'nation' or 'community'. In the traditional Islamic context, it is usually used to refer to a cross-border spiritual entity encompassing all the Muslims of the world wherever they may live. However, in Muhammad's time, the *umma* was defined by geography and encompassed everyone who lived within the territory controlled by the early Muslim community, regardless of their religious beliefs. In Muhammad's Constitution of Medina, even pagans were defined as part of the *umma* and were granted equal civil rights.

Wahhabism: See entry for 'salafism'.

Waqf: Rather like a charitable trust in the West, an Islamic *waqf* is a charitable endowment in which some kind of asset is donated in perpetuity to finance a pre-determined charitable or social cause, such as a mosque, school, university or hospital.